T0334068

Classical Economics and Modern Theory

Heinz D. Kurz and **Neri Salvadori** are two well-known economists working in economic theory and the history of economic thought. Their previous collection of essays, *Understanding Classical Economics*, sparked intriguing debates within economics and this new volume shows the development of the authors' thinking since that book appeared.

Areas covered by the book include:

- alternative interpretations of classical economists;
- new growth theory;
- the relationship between Sraffian theory and von Neumann;
- the collaboration between Sraffa and his mathematical friends;
- the treatment of capital in neoclassical long-period theory;
- the analysis of exhaustible resources in a 'classical' framework.

The essays reprinted in the book contain original findings and new vistas on old problems and show the reader how the different parts hang together. As such the book will be of great interest to every scholar working within the field of economic theory and the history of economic thought.

Heinz D. Kurz is Professor of Economics at the University of Graz, Austria.

Neri Salvadori is Professor of Economics at the University of Pisa, Italy.

Routledge studies in the history of economics

Classical Economics and Modern Theory

Studies in long-period analysis

**Heinz D. Kurz and
Neri Salvadori**

Routledge
Taylor & Francis Group

LONDON AND NEW YORK

First published 2003
by Routledge

Published 2017 by Routledge
2 Park Square, Milton Park, Abingdon, Oxon OX14 4RN
711 Third Avenue, New York, NY 10017, USA

*Routledge is an imprint of the Taylor & Francis Group,
an informa business*

Typeset in Times New Roman by
Newgen Imaging Systems (P) Ltd, Chennai, India

British Library Cataloguing in Publication Data
A catalogue record for this book is available
from the British Library

Library of Congress Cataloging in Publication Data
Kurz, Heinz-Deiter.
　　Classical economics and modern theory: studies in long-period
analysis / Heinz D. Kurz and Neri Salvadori.
　　　　p. cm. – (Routledge studies in the history of economics ; 63)
　　Includes bibliographical references and index.
　　　　1. Neoclassical school of economics. 2. Classical school of economics.
　　3. Economic development. I. Salvadori, Neri. II. Title. III. Series.

HB98.2.K87 2003
330.15′3–dc21　　　　　　　　　　　　　　　　　　　2002037167

ISBN13: 978-0-415-36952-7 (hbk)
ISBN13: 978-0-415-40637-6 (pbk)

Contents

Acknowledgements

We are grateful to the following publications for allowing us to reproduce articles which originally appeared in their pages: *Economic Systems Research* for ' "Classical" Roots of Input–Output Analysis: A Short Account of its Long Prehistory'; *The European Journal of the History of Economic Thought* for 'Friedrich Benedikt Wilhelm Hermann on Capital and Profits'; *Economics and Philosophy* for 'Burgstaller on Classical and Neoclassical Theory' (book review); *Contemporary Economic Issues. Proceedings of the Eleventh World Congress of the International Economic Association, Tunis. Volume 4 Economic Behaviour and Design*, Murat R. Sertel (ed.), London: Macmillan, and New York: St Martin's Press, 1999, for 'Theories of "Endogeneous" Growth in Historical Perspective'; *Economic Issues* for 'What Could the "New" Growth Theory Teach Smith or Ricardo?'; *Metroeconomica* for 'A Linear Multisector Model of "Endogenous" Growth and the Problem of Capital'; *Piero Sraffa's Political Economy. A Centenary Estimate*, T. Cozzi and R. Marchionatti (eds), London and New York: Routledge, 2000, for 'Sraffa and the Mathematicians: Frank Ramsey and Alister Watson'; *Review of Political Economy* for 'Sraffa and von Neumann'; *Indian Economic Journal* for 'Production Theory: An Introduction'; *Metroeconomica* for 'Classical Economics and the Problem of Exhaustible Resources'; *Structural Change and Economic Dynamics* for 'Reverse Capital Deepening and the Numeraire: A Note'; *Economics, Welfare Policy and the History of Economic Thought. Essays in Honour of Arnold Heertje*, Martin M. G. Fase, Walter Kanning, and Donal A. Walker (eds), Cheltenham (UK): Edward Elgar, 1999, for 'Reswitching. Simplifying a Famous Example'; *Journal of Economic Behavior and Organization* for 'Franklin Fisher on Aggregation' (book review); *History of Political Economy* for 'Wicksell and the Problem of the "Missing" Equation'. Publication details and dates of all these articles are given in the text.

1 Classical economics and modern theory

An introduction

Heinz D. Kurz and Neri Salvadori

This volume contains a set of chapters written by the two of us, by one of us alone, or by one of us in collaboration with some other co-author, plus a letter to the author by Kenneth Arrow, here published as an appendix to one of the chapters. With the exception of Chapters 2 and 9 all chapters have been previously published. The collection is a follow-up to the 1998 volume with essays from us entitled *Understanding 'Classical' Economics. Studies in Long-period Theory* (Kurz and Salvadori, 1998a). Since the introduction to the latter contains a detailed discussion of what we mean by 'classical' economics and why we think it necessary to resurrect the 'standpoint of the old classical economists from Adam Smith to Ricardo', we can be brief here. The interested reader is asked to kindly consult our previous book.[1] Since several of the chapters reprinted in this volume contain essentially a continuation of arguments developed in chapters published in the previous volume – some directly in response to critics of our work – the reader might find it useful to have also the previous volume at hand when reading this one.

The material is subdivided in five parts.

Part I deals with 'Classical theory and its interpretations' and has five chapters. Chapter 2 is a paper written in response to Mark Blaug's criticism of the 'Sraffian' interpretation of the classical economists published in 1999 in *HOPE* (Blaug, 1999; see also Blaug, 1987). A considerably shortened version of our chapter was published in the same journal entitled 'The surplus interpretation of the classical economists: a reply to Mark Blaug' (Kurz and Salvadori, 2002).[2] In the chapter we show that Blaug's criticism cannot be sustained and that (unwittingly) he has himself adopted a very special variant of Sraffa's surplus-based interpretation of the classical economists' approach to the theory of value and distribution. Chapter 3 presents a short prehistory of input–output analysis. It is argued that the concepts of circular flow and physical real costs can be traced back far in the history of political economy. In addition it is argued that modern input–output analysis has lost sight of important problems raised and solutions provided by classical

---

1 For a still more complete picture of our ideas on the matter, see also Kurz and Salvadori (1995) and our entries in Kurz and Salvadori (1998b).
2 See also the rejoinder by Blaug (2002) and the reply to Blaug by Garegnani (2002).

economics. These concern first and foremost the determination of the system of relative (normal) prices and all shares of income other than wages, starting from the given system of production in use and a given real wage rate. The idea of given value-added coefficients as it is entertained in price models of input–output analysis is rejected on the ground that these coefficients have to (and actually can) be ascertained endogenously. Chapter 4 deals with the contribution of the German economist Friedrich Benedikt Wilhelm Hermann to the theory of capital and income distribution. Hermann was a contemporary of Johann Heinrich von Thünen and was rightly considered one of the most excellent German economic theorists of the nineteenth century. Hermann's writings reflect a period in travail. Theoretically, there are several elements in Hermann's analysis which contribute to the further development of classical theory, but there are also important elements which involve a sharp break with it and point in the direction of marginalism. Chapter 5 is a review of André Burgstaller's book *Property and Prices. Toward a Unified Theory of Value* (Burgstaller, 1994) in which the claim has been put forward that, seen from a higher perspective, classical theory and neoclassical theory are fully compatible with one another. This claim is critically assessed.

Part II is devoted to the problem of 'Growth theory and the classical tradition' and has four chapters, one of which is a newly written post-script to one of the others. Chapter 6 is a paper that was given by us as an invited lecture at the Eleventh World Congress of the International Economic Association in Tunis in 1995. The chapter provides an historical perspective on old and 'new' growth theories. It is argued that Adam Smith, David Ricardo, Robert Torrens, Thomas Robert Malthus and Karl Marx up to John von Neumann regarded the balanced and the actual rates of capital accumulation and thus both the balanced and the actual rates of growth of output as depending on agents' behaviour, that is, as endogenously determined. On the contrary, neoclassical theory, which determines distribution on the basis of the demand and supply of all 'factors of production', is naturally inclined to approach the problem of economic growth from the prespective of exogenous growth. Finally it is shown that the new growth theory revolves essentially around a set of important ideas which have been anticipated by earlier economists, most notably Adam Smith and David Ricardo. Chapter 7 reprints the Economic Issues Lecture given by one of us on the occasion of the 1997 Annual Conference of the Royal Economic Society in Stoke-on-Trent. The argument is developed in terms of a fictitious dialogue between Adam Smith and David Ricardo serving on a research assessment committee asked to evaluate the contribution of the so-called 'new' growth theory. Kenneth Arrow has kindly sent the author a letter with detailed comments on the paper. With his kind permission we publish the letter as an appendix to the chapter. Chapter 8 elaborates a linear multisector model of 'endogenous' growth with heterogeneous capital goods. The purpose of this exercise is to show that this kind of model is exempt from the capital theory critique put forward against the conventional long-period neoclassical growth model *à la* Solow. This confirms previous claims that at least some of the 'new' growth models are somewhat extraneous to neoclassical analysis and actually exhibit the logical structure of classical theory. In addition it is shown that the use of an intertemporal analysis to establish a correct long-period position is not necessary and that the adoption of the long-period method may speed up the elaboration of new scientific results. The model of Chapter 8 was further elaborated by one of us in collaboration with Giuseppe Freni and Fausto Gozzi and also by these two scholars alone or in collaboration with others. Chapter 9 provides some of the results of this further research, which are also partially critical of the presentation of Chapter 8.

The three chapters of Part III have a closer look at 'Sraffa's contribution'. To the reader of the preface of Sraffa's 1960 book it will perhaps come as a surprise that there is no expression of gratitude to any of his fellow economists for comments, suggestions, or assistance during the long period over which the book had been in preparation. The only people Sraffa thanks are three mathematicians: 'My greatest debt is to Professor A. S. Besicovitch for invaluable mathematical help over many years. I am also indebted for similar help at different periods to the late Mr Frank Ramsey and to Mr Alister Watson' (Sraffa, 1960: vi–vii). Chapter 10 is devoted to the discussions Sraffa had with Ramsey from the late 1920s until Ramsey's untimely death from an attack of jaundice on 19 January 1930 and with Watson in the first half of the 1940s and in the second half of the 1950s when Sraffa prepared the manuscript of his book for the publisher. There is no doubt that amongst the three mathematicians Sraffa owed Besicovitch the greatest intellectual debt. Yet a proper treatment of the assistance Sraffa received from Besicovitch is beyond the scope of this chapter and is the object of another work of ours. Chapter 11 compares Sraffa's 1960 analysis with John von Neumann's model (von Neumann, [1937] 1945). It is argued that despite some important analitico-mathematical differences the two share a similar conceptual framework which is 'classical' in substance. The chapter comments also on references to von Neumann's model and Champernowne's commentary published alongside with the English version of it (Champernowne, 1945) in Sraffa's unpublished papers and correspondence. Chapter 12 contains a summary account of important propositions contained in Sraffa's book. The emphasis is on single production in a two-sector framework and the problems of fixed capital and capital utilization in the most simple conceptualizations possible.

Part IV is devoted to 'Exhaustible resources and the long-period method'. In our book *Theory of Production* (Kurz and Salvadori, 1995) we included a chapter entitled 'Limits to the long-period method' in which we discussed several cases the analysis of which, we contended, made it necessary to transcend the received long-period method. One of the cases under consideration was that of exhaustible resources. It is obvious that with the depletion of the stocks of the resources their prices and therefore the real wage rate and/or the 'rate of profits' cannot be assumed to be stationary. A somewhat more correct presentation of our argument was published two years later (Kurz and Salvadori, 1997). Our analysis received some attention and criticism in the literature. The chapters in this part are essentially responses to our critics in which we attempt to clarify more precisely the difficulties at hand and the way we think is appropriate to deal with them. Chapter 13 contains our contribution to a symposium in the journal *Metroeconomica*. We discuss exhaustible resources in terms of a simple model. Chapter 14 contains a dynamic input–output model with exhaustible resources and discusses the development of relative prices, royalties and quantities, given the real wage rate.

Part V has four chapters devoted to a 'Criticism of neoclassical theory'. Chapter 15 discusses the implication of reverse capital deepening for neoclassical theory, placing special emphasis on the role of the numéraire. It is shown that under certain assumptions a supply function of and a demand function for capital can be built up that are independent of each other. The question is whether a change in the numéraire can affect the mathematical properties of the economic system under consideration. We argue that this is not possible. In particular we show that a change of numéraire affects both the supply and the demand functions for 'capital' in marginalist theory but leaves the stability property of equilibrium, if there is one, unaffected. The chapter was inspired by a note by Paola Potestio which was later published (1999; see also our reply, 2001, to her). Chapter 16 is rather technical and simplifies the famous numerical example of reswitching presented in Garegnani (1970). Chapter 17 is a review of the collected papers by Franklin Fisher entitled *Aggregation: Aggregate Production Function and Related Topics* (Fisher, 1994). The chapter illustrates the difficulties involved in aggregating capital as studied by Fisher and remarks that if firms produce different commodities and labour is the only primary factor, then the aggregate production function exists if and only if the labour theory of value holds. This is a result which played some role in the reswitching debate: Garegnani (1970), for instance, proved that the marginalist theory was exempt from criticism only in this case. Nevertheless Fisher mentions the UK Cambridge contributors to the debate only in order to criticize them. Chapter 18 deals with Knut Wicksell's theory of capital and interest and contributes to the recent debate on Wicksell's so-called 'missing equation'. It is argued that there is no equation missing in Wicksell: he took as given the 'quantity of capital' the relative scarcity of which was taken to hold the key to an explanation of the rate of interest. However, Wicksell became increasingly aware of the fact that he could take as given only the *value* of capital, measured in some consumption unit. This destroyed the alleged analogy between the factor of production (heterogeneous) 'capital' and its remuneration, interest or profit, on the one hand, and that of (homogeneous) land and its remuneration, (intensive) rent, on the other.

References

Blaug, Mark (1987). 'Classical economics', in J. Eatwell, M. Milgate and P. Newman (eds), *The New Palgrave: A Dictionary of Economics*. London: Macmillan, vol. 1.

Blaug, Mark (1999). 'Misunderstanding classical economics: the Sraffian interpretation of the surplus approach', *HOPE*, **31**, pp. 213–36.

Blaug, Mark (2002). 'Kurz and Salvadori on the Sraffian interpretation of the surplus approach', *HOPE*, **34**, pp. 237–40.

Burgstaller, André (1994). *Property and Prices. Toward a Unified Theory of Value.* Cambridge: Cambridge University Press.

Champernowne, D. G. (1945). 'A note on J. v. Neumann's article on "A Model of Economic Equilibrium" ', *Review of Economic Studies*, **13**, pp. 10–18.

Fisher, Franklin M. (1994). *Aggregation. Aggregate Production Functions and Related Topics*. Cambridge, MA: The MIT Press.

Garegnani, Pierangelo (1970). 'Heterogeneous capital, the production function and the theory of distribution', *Review of Economic Studies*, **37**, pp. 407–36.

Garegnani, Pierangelo (2002). 'Misunderstanding classical economics? A reply to Blaug', *HOPE*, **34**, pp. 241–54.

Kurz, Heinz D. and Salvadori, Neri (1995). *Theory of Production: A Long-Period Analysis*. Cambridge: Cambridge University Press.

Kurz, Heinz D. and Salvadori, Neri (1997). 'Exhaustible resources in a dynamic input–output model with "Classical Features"', *Economic Systems Research*, **9**, pp. 235–51.

Kurz, Heinz D. and Salvadori, Neri (1998a). *Understanding 'Classical' Economics. Studies in Long-Period Theory*. London and New York: Routledge.

Kurz, Heinz D. and Salvadori, Neri (eds) (1998b). *The Elgar Companion to Classical Economics*. Cheltenham, England: Edward Elgar, 2 vols.

Kurz, Heinz D. and Salvadori, Neri (2001). 'The aggregate neoclassical theory of distribution and the concept of a given value of capital: a reply', *Structural Change and Economic Dynamics*, **12**, pp. 479–85.

Kurz, Heinz D. and Salvadori, Neri (2002). 'Mark Blaug on the "Sraffian interpretation of the surplus approach"', *HOPE*, **34**, pp. 225–36.

Neumann, J. von (1937). 'Über ein ökonomisches Gleichungssystem und eine Verallgemeinerung des Brouwerschen Fixpunktsatzes', *Ergebnisse eines mathematischen Kolloquiums*, **8**, pp. 73–83.

Neumann, J. von (1945). 'A model of general economic equilibrium', *Review of Economic Studies*, **13**, pp. 1–9. English translation of von Neumann (1937).

Potestio, Paola (1999). 'The aggregate neoclassical theory of distribution and the concept of a given value of capital: towards a more general critique', *Structural Change and Economic Dynamics*, **10**, pp. 381–94.

Sraffa, Piero (1960). *Production of Commodities by Means of Commodities*. Cambridge: Cambridge University Press.

Part I

Classical theory and its interpretations

2 Understanding 'classical' economics

A reply to Mark Blaug

Heinz D. Kurz and Neri Salvadori

> Knowing as I do how much we are influenced by taking a particular view of a subject, and how difficult it is to destroy a train of ideas which have long followed each other in the mind, I will not say I am right . . . , and therefore it is possible that five years hence I may think as you do on the subject, but at present I do not see the least probability of such a change for every renewed consideration of the question confirms me in the opinion which I have long held.
>
> Ricardo to Malthus in a letter dated 29 November 1820
> (Ricardo, *Works*, vol. VIII, p. 311)

1. Introduction

In a paper published in *HOPE* Mark Blaug has put forward a critical assessment of Piero Sraffa's interpretation of the classical economists. He entitled his paper 'Misunderstanding classical economics: the Sraffian interpretation of the surplus approach' (Blaug, 1999; in this chapter all isolated pages cited refer to this paper). Blaug's essay is essentially a review article commenting on the literature inspired by Sraffa's contribution, including some of our works (cf. Kurz and Salvadori, 1995, 1998a,b).

Since elements of the uneasiness with the interpretation of 'the old classical economists from Adam Smith to Ricardo' (Sraffa, 1960, p. v) under consideration appear to be shared by several historians of economic thought, Blaug's review article offers a welcome opportunity to discuss the matters in dispute. We engage in this debate in the hope and expectation that the differences of opinion may gradually be narrowed and a better understanding of the specificity and fecundity of the analysis of the classical economists emerges. Since the problems dealt with are both important and complex, it appears to be a prerequisite to a fruitful exchange to supress any inclination to polemics and cheap rhetoric. Setting aside a few instances, we read Blaug's paper as an invitation to discuss the matters in dispute as scholars should discuss them: soberly and with a quest for truth. In this reply we deal only with those objections of Blaug that directly concern our writings or points of view shared by us. The emphasis will be on the classical approach to the theory of income distribution and relative prices.

Blaug's exposition is organized around two methodological issues: the distinction between rational and historical reconstructions, on the one hand, and the 'core-periphery' metaphor, on the other. Sections 2 and 3 of the present paper are devoted to short discussions of these concepts. Section 4 deals with another preliminary question, that is, the role of analytical rigour in the classical economists. In this section we challenge Blaug's first main objection to the interpretation we endorse, namely, that the formalization of the classical approach to the theory of value and distribution and the concern with the consistency of an argument amount to 'sterile formalism'. In the following sections we turn to the substance of his criticism. Section 5 prepares the ground by summarizing what we consider to be the logical structure of the classical approach to the theory of value and distribution. Section 6 addresses Blaug's second main objection which is that the Sraffian interpretation fundamentally distorts the real concerns of the classical economists. In the light of the evidence put forward from the writings of the classical authors it is shown that this criticism cannot be sustained. Section 7 scrutinizes Blaug's alternative characterization of the 'core' of classical economics and, ironically, shows that he arrives at essentially the same view of the logical structure of the classical approach to the theory of value and distribution as Sraffa. Section 8 contains some concluding remarks. In addition there is an appendix in which we point out propositions contained in Blaug's paper which are obviously unwarranted or false.

2. 'Rational' versus 'historical reconstruction'

Blaug defines *rational reconstruction* as 'the tendency to view history as a relentless march of progress from past errors to present truths' (p. 213); and *historical reconstruction* as an attempt 'to recover the ideas of past thinkers in terms that they, and their contemporaries, would have recognized as a more or less faithful description of what they had set out to do' (ibid.).[1] His discussion culminates in the maxim: 'I vote for historical reconstructions as *the only legitimate* occupation of historians of economic thought' (p. 214, emphasis added).

A definition as such cannot be true or false, but it can be useful or not. There are clear indications that Blaug's two definitions are not very useful. As regards the latter, Blaug stresses repeatedly that there is no such thing as a purely historical reconstruction of past thinkers. In one place he writes: 'I admit that faithful historical reconstructions are literally impossible and that, of course, every new departure in modern economics leads to an inevitable tendency to construct a historical pedigree' (p. 232). Therefore he is bound to contradict his above maxim. He states that there is 'a *perfectly legitimate* role for rational reconstructions' (p. 214, emphasis added); he even admits that there are 'rational reconstructions [that] are valid historical reconstructions' (ibid.), although there are only 'very few' of them.

---

1 It is not clear how Blaug thinks it could ever be known what 'past thinkers' would recognize as 'faithful' interpretations of their works?

Clearly, according to his definitions this is impossible: a 'rational reconstruction' cannot at the same time be an 'historical reconstruction'. Blaug does not use his definitions in a consistent manner and quickly distances himself from the maxim he proposes.

Quite different definitions can be obtained by consulting a well known paper by Lakatos (1978b) on the 'History of science and its rational reconstruction'. In this chapter Lakatos first discusses four theories of the rationality of scientific progress and shows how each of them provides a theoretical framework for the rational reconstruction of the history of science. A rational reconstruction makes claims about the history of theories or analytical approaches to certain problems by focusing on how this history *should* have happened if the scientists had been well-informed of the relevant developments, and had been perfectly honest and intellectually acute. It makes *empirical* claims, that is, claims that can (and should) be checked by the actual sequence of events, which is the task of an historical reconstruction. These claims happen to be inspired by a *normative* heuristics. The task of a historical reconstruction therefore involves scrutinizing whether earlier formulations of a theory have indeed been superseded by later ones because of their superiority or because of other reasons (including politico-ideological ones). Paraphrasing the first sentence of Lakatos's essay, which is a paraphrase of a famous dictum by Kant, it could be said that 'Economic theory without history of economic thought is empty; history of economic thought without economic theory is blind'. In Lakatos's words:

> Each rational reconstruction produces some characteristic pattern of rational growth of scientific knowledge. But all of these *normative* reconstructions may have to be supplemented by *empirical* external theories to explain the residual non-rational factors. The history of science is always richer than its rational reconstruction. *But rational reconstruction or internal history is primary, external history only secondary, since the most important problems of external history are defined by internal history.*
>
> (Lakatos 1978b, p. 118, emphases in the original)

Lakatos added: 'Whatever problem the historian of [economic thought] wishes to solve, he has first to reconstruct the relevant section of the growth of objective scientific knowledge, that is, the relevant section of "internal history". As it has been shown, what constitutes for him internal history, depends on his [economic theory], whether he is aware of this fact or not' (ibid., where we replaced 'science' by 'economic thought' and 'philosophy' by 'economic theory'). And later: 'Internal history is not just a *selection* of methodologically interpreted facts: it may be, on occasions, their *radically improved version*' (ibid., p. 119).[2]

---

2 The second part of Lakatos's essay is devoted to showing that as all scientific theories function as historiographical theories, at the same time they can be criticized by criticizing the rational historical reconstructions to which they lead. But this part need not concern us here.

We insist with Blaug that historians of economic thought ought to apply the historical method with rigour. However, that method includes what in the introduction to our book we called 'rational reconstruction' (see Kurz and Salvadori, 1998b, p. 1). We used the concept in a way that was inspired by Lakatos's disquisition.

We should like to add the following observations. First, the ideas put forward by an author are generally neither independent of what earlier and contemporary authors said or wrote nor are they without impact on the ideas of later authors. Ricardo tried to rectify views of Smith he considered erroneous and to solve problems Smith had left unsolved. Ricardo's analysis was the background against which John Stuart Mill and Karl Marx wrote, and so on. The history of economic thought is essentially a history about continuities and discontinuities in economic analysis over time. This requires rational reconstructions of the emergence, development, gradual transformation and occasionally the disappearance of ideas and concepts. It is significant that Blaug's main work on the subject carries the title *Economic Theory in Retrospect* (Blaug, [1962] 1997). The book abounds with rational reconstructions (in the sense of Lakatos), and for good reasons.

Second, the process of the adoption of ideas and concepts of earlier authors is generally selective and there is hardly ever an adoption which does not also involve some adaptation. Therefore, we were puzzled to see Mark Blaug on the one hand enumerate several themes in Smith, Ricardo or Marx which play no role or only a small one in our reconstruction, and on the other hand accuse us of paying more attention to some themes than the authors' mentioned. Analytical progress presupposes selection. We contend that every historian of economic thought, Blaug included, will in his or her interpretation of past authors proceed selectively. It simply does not make much sense to give all the problems an author was concerned with the same weight as he or she did.

Third, all contemporary readers of earlier authors are socialized in terms of some modern theory. This may be an effective hindrance to understanding some earlier authors, especially if the reader cannot refrain from seeing their works too narrowly through the lens of such a theory. The history of economic thought abounds with examples which provide badly distorted pictures of the contributions of earlier authors because of what we may for short call the triumph of modernity over the past. However, this need not be the case. It all depends on how meticulous the interpreter is and on how the modern theory under consideration relates to the earlier conceptualizations. A modern theory which shares a similar outlook on certain phenomena but provides a more correct and sophisticated conceptualization of their interrelation may turn out to be a powerful tool of interpretation, because it allows one to see and understand in some earlier authors what otherwise could not have been seen and understood. We interpret Blaug in this sense when he calls the 'Sraffian' rational reconstruction 'illuminating, . . . capable of affording a springboard for a wholly new style of long-run equilibrium theorizing' (p. 214), 'ingenious' (p. 218), 'ingenious and even striking' (p. 219), and writes that 'the core/periphery distinction is perfectly defensible for a rational reconstruction of classical economics' and 'will stand' as such (p. 232). By comparing the literature before and after 1951 there is no doubt that Sraffa's interpretation has rekindled the profession's interest in the classical authors and has greatly enhanced our understanding of their achievements.

3. The 'core-periphery' metaphor

Blaug appears to have been deceived by the 'core-periphery' metaphor. Garegnani (1984), to whom Blaug refers in this context, did not use the word 'periphery'. He rather distinguished between a 'core' of classical analysis, that is, the theory of value and distribution, which is developed in terms of a variant of data (a)–(d) (see, Section 5), and what is 'outside the core'. His basic idea, which appears to be similar to Ricardo's distinction between two spheres of economic analysis (see Section 4), is the following: 'The multiplicity of these influences [outside the core] and their variability according to circumstances was in fact understood to make it impossible to reconduct them to *necessary* quantitative relations like those, studied in the "core", between distributive variables and relative prices and between outputs or techniques and the dependent distributive variables and prices' (Garegnani, 1984, p. 297, emphasis in the original). Hence, Garegnani's distinction concerns relations that can be formulated in precise, quantitative terms, on the one hand, and those that cannot, on the other. Blaug, on the contrary, interprets the metaphor as involving a totally different distinction, namely, between what is important and what is not. He attacks the concept of the core against the background of his very different distinction and accuses Sraffian authors of regarding as unimportant or less important what in some classical authors was considered important or very important.[3] Obviously, in order for a criticism of Garegnani's idea of the core to be pertinent it would have to be shown that the classical economists held the view that what according to Garegnani belongs outside the core can also be formulated in precise, quantitative terms, or what lies in the core cannot. Alas, Blaug does not even make an attempt in this direction.[4]

4. Different spheres of analysis in classical economics and the role of formalization

Blaug conjectures that the content of the classical theory of value and distribution is unavoidably betrayed by modern formulations of it because of the latter's concern with analytical rigour and mathematical formalization. In one place he objects to

3 Blaug contends that 'To his credit, [Garegnani] alone among all Sraffian interpreters, denies that the core is somehow superior to or more significant than the periphery . . . , but that is merely a fail-safe rhetorical device' (pp. 231–2). Yet he provides no evidence in support of either proposition. We should like to add that we never used the metaphor of the 'core'.

4 Perhaps Blaug's misreading of Garegnani's concept of 'core' is due to him projecting onto it some of the meaning the word 'core' has in Imre Lakatos's philosophy of science. (See Lakatos, 1978a; for Blaug's view on Lakatos, see Blaug, 1980.) Within Lakatos's system, the 'hard core' of a research programme is a set of propositions which are preserved from refutation. These propositions generate various theories.

our efforts in this regard: 'they simply cannot conceive of analytical rigor except in modern terms' (p. 233, fn. 13). As against this it should suffice to recall the untiring efforts of Ricardo and his followers to elaborate a coherent theory of value and distribution. As a contemporary noted, Ricardo 'meets you upon every subject that he has studied *with a mind made up*, and opinions in the nature of mathematical truths' (Ricardo, *Works*, vol. V, p. 152, fn. 2, emphasis in the original). And in a letter to James Mill of 1 January 1821 Ricardo specified his own point of view *vis-à-vis* Malthus's explicitly as follows: 'Political Economy he says is not a strict science like mathematics, and therefore he thinks he may use words in a vague way, sometimes attaching one meaning to them, sometimes another and quite different. *No proposition can surely be more absurd*' (Ricardo, *Works*, vol. VIII, p. 331, emphasis added).

Against this background the mathematical form of an argument in itself can hardly be taken as involving a break with the classical authors and especially Ricardo. Nor does it imply, as Blaug contends, 'read[ing] Smith and Ricardo and Marx through Walrasian-tinted glasses' (p. 229). To classify Sraffa's counting of equations and unknowns as 'pure Walras' (ibid.) mistakes the mathematical form of an argument for its substance. Blaug puts forward the following warning: 'to pursue ruthlessly the goal of a watertight, mathematically consistent theory of price determination is to fall into the type of sterile formalism that has characterized general equilibrium theory in its modern Arrow-Debreu form' (ibid.). *A formalism is a formalism. Its qualification as 'sterile' presupposes forming a judgement on the economic content conveyed by means of the formalism.*

We now come to the crux of the matter. Ricardo, as we have seen, was definitely and positively in favour of analytical rigour and mathematical precision in his 'most favourite subject': political economy. Does this mean that he thought that economic laws could indiscriminately be established like mathematical truths with regard to *all* spheres of socio-economic life? The answer is clearly no. Indirect evidence is provided in the *Principles* where there is a striking contrast, in terms of whether strict, quantitatively knowable relations can be postulated, between the analysis of a *given* economic system and the distributive variables and relative prices pertaining to it (see, in particular, chapter I), on the one hand, and Ricardo's probing into the problem of economic *change* (see, e.g. chapter XXI), on the other. However, there is also some direct evidence available showing that Ricardo distinguished between different spheres of economic analysis and the capability of the theorist to establish economic laws within them. In his letter to Malthus of 9 October 1820 Ricardo took issue with the latter's definition of the subject and wrote:

Political Economy you think is an enquiry into the nature and causes of wealth – I think it should rather be called an enquiry into the laws which determine the division of the produce of industry amongst the classes who concur in its formation. *No law can be laid down respecting quantity, but a tolerably correct one can be laid down respecting proportions.* Every day I am more satisfied that the former enquiry is vain and delusive, and the latter only the true objects of the science.

(*Works*, vol. VIII, pp. 278–9, emphasis added)[5]

No law can be laid down respecting quantity. In Ricardo's writings this is especially reflected by the fact that when discussing the dependence of relative prices on income distribution, Ricardo proceeded in terms of *given output proportions*, setting aside any responses of outputs to changes in relative prices. This does not mean that in Ricardo's view there are no such responses or rather interactions between prices, outputs and income distribution. It only means that there is no reason to presume that the theorist can expect to find general laws expressing their interrelations, as they are postulated, for example, in neoclassical *demand functions*. The economist simply cannot avoid studying the historical particulars of an economic change – whether it is predominantly due to the introduction of a new method of production and whether this affects the system of production as a whole or is confined to a single industry only; or whether it is due to the introduction of an entirely new kind of commodity; or whether it is due to the exhaustion of some natural resources; etc. Increasing returns to scale that turn out to be external to each industry or group of industries, as in Smith's discussion of the division of labour, for example, are a case highlighting Ricardo's 'no law respecting quantities' dictum: how could one ascertain a priori the evolution of quantities and prices? There are simply no demand functions that could be known by the theorist. This is admitted by Blaug, who even contends 'that Ricardo had no theory of how the level of output is determined' (p. 223). Then follows the adjunct: 'But then neither did any other premodern economist' (ibid.). This must not be read as implying that 'modern economists' are possessed of a theory of outputs in conditions of an ever deeper division of labour and the product and process innovations that come with it: neoclassical demand theory presupposes given and unchanging 'preferences' in deriving demand functions; however, preferences will certainly not remain unaffected by these changes. Even 'modern' economics has little to say about *how* this will be the case.

---

5 Malthus replied on 26 October 1820: 'With regard to your new definition of the objects of Political Economy, I own it appears to me very confined.... In the same manner when you reject the consideration of demand and supply in the price of commodities and refer only to the means of supply, you appear to me to look only at half of your subject' (ibid., p. 286). To this Ricardo responded on 24 November: 'I do not dispute ... the influence of demand on the price of corn and on the price of all other things [the reference is obviously to "market prices"], but supply follows close at its heels, and soon takes the power of regulating prices [the reference is obviously to "natural price"] in his own hands, and in regulating it he is determined by cost of production. I acknowledge the intervals on which you so exclusively dwell, but still they are only intervals' (ibid., p. 302).

Things are different as regards *proportions*, Ricardo maintained.[6] Here 'a tolerably correct law' can be laid down and has in fact been laid down by him. An important aspect of this concerns the fact that, given the system of production (or technique) in use, once the real wage (or the share of wages) is known, the rate of profits is determined, with a rise in the former involving a fall in the latter and *vice versa* (see, in particular, Ricardo, *Works*, vol. II, pp. 61–2). This analytical discovery by Ricardo has been acclaimed by virtually all his interpreters; Blaug, ([1962] 1997, p. 96) spoke of Ricardo's 'fundamental theorem of distribution'. Interestingly, in the context of discussing this 'theorem' Blaug showed a pronounced concern with the problem of the internal consistency of Ricardo's argument and explicitly had recourse to a model (by Luigi Pasinetti) in order 'to spell out Ricardo's meaning in mathematical terms' (ibid., p. 97). Incidentally, in that model the rate of profits and the price of corn in terms of gold at any given moment of time are precisely determined on the basis of (a simplified version of) the set of data (a)–(d) discussed in the next section. Hence, there might appear to be a contradiction between Blaug (1999) and Blaug ([1962] 1997). In Section 7 we shall see that any such contradiction is more apparent than real, however, as is Blaug's criticism of our contributions.[7]

5. The 'classical' approach to the theory of value and distribution

The reader will find not one passage in our writings to support Blaug's contention that we interpret the classical authors as holding that what in their approach to the problem of value and distribution are considered independent variables (see data (a)–(d)) are 'determined outside their theoretical system' (p. 228, with reference

---

6 What is meant by 'proportions' in the present context is clarified in a famous passage in the preface of the *Principles*: 'But in different stages of society, the proportions of the whole produce of the earth which will be allotted to each of these classes, under the names of rent, profit, and wages, will be essentially different. . . . To determine the laws which regulate this distribution, is the principal problem in Political Economy' (*Works*, vol. I, p. 5).

7 A misunderstanding of Blaug's needs to be cleared up. He makes a mockery of regarding as 'a sacrosanct first step' in rigorous analysis 'the counting of equations and unknowns to check how many variables we need to take as data'. He adds: 'Marshall knew better, he kept his general equilibrium theory in an appendix and employed the ceteris paribus method of partial equilibrium to practice substantive economics' (p. 230). Marshall, of course, did not know better. When he resorted to his method of partial equilibrium of single markets, he reduced the number of unknowns to two: the quantity and the price of the good under consideration. In order to determine these unknowns he needed two independent equations which he thought he could provide by constructing a 'demand function' and a 'supply function'. The prices and quantities of all other goods he took as given and constant, independently of what happened on the single market under consideration. Therefore, as regards the requirements to be satisfied in order to get a determinate solution there is no difference at all between Marshall's theory and some less partial equilibrium theories. However, as Sraffa (1925, 1926) showed, Marshall's partial equilibrium method cannot be applied other than in exceedingly special cases (see also the next section). What Blaug calls 'substantive economics' may simply be wrong.

to the wage rate). On the contrary, he will encounter passages maintaining the opposite:

> the concern of the classical economists from Adam Smith to David Ricardo was the laws governing the emerging capitalist economy, characterized by wage labour, an increasingly sophisticated division of labour, the co-ordination of economic activity via a system of interdependent markets in which transactions are mediated through money, and rapid technical, organizational and institutional change. In short, they were concerned with an economic system in motion.
>
> (Kurz and Salvadori, 1998b, p. 3)[8]

We added that 'the attention focused on the factors affecting the pace at which capital accumulates and the economy expands and how the growing social product is shared out between the different classes of society: workers, capitalists and landowners' (ibid.).

This concern of the classical economists with an economic system incessantly in movement has never been denied by us or any of the 'Sraffian' authors, let alone Sraffa himself, to whom Blaug refers in his paper. We are also not aware that any of the scholars mentioned, including us, has ever advocated the view that in the classical authors the problem of the dynamism of the modern economy, its growth and structural change, is extraneous to the economic theory they elaborated. Hence the problem is not *whether* these 'dynamic' issues were a part and parcel of classical economic theory – *of course they were* – but rather *how* the classical economists dealt with them. *This* is the crucial question to which we have to turn.

The ingenious device of the classical authors to see through the highly complex system in motion consisted in distinguishing between the 'market' or actual values of the relevant variables, in particular the prices of commodities and the rates of remuneration of primary inputs (labour and land), on the one hand, and 'natural' or normal values on the other. The former were taken to reflect all kinds of influences, many of an accidental or temporary nature, whereas the latter were conceived of as expressing the persistent, non-accidental and non-temporary factors governing the economic system. The 'gravitation' of market values to their natural levels was seen as the result of the self-seeking behaviour of agents and especially of the profit-seeking actions of producers. In conditions of *free competition*, that is,

---

8 See also Kurz and Salvadori (1999), where we deal, *inter alia*, with the theories of accumulation and growth of Smith, Ricardo, Torrens and Marx. There it is stressed *vis-à-vis* the so-called 'new' growth theory that classical growth theory in general and Smith's in particular are theories of *endogenous* growth. In Smith's discussion of the division of labour the evolution of technology and the growth of labour productivity are insolubly intertwined with the accumulation of capital. Therefore it came as a surprise to us that Blaug could write of his reason to deplore an 'utter indifference of Sraffian interpreters to the opening three chapters of the *Wealth of Nations* on the division of labor, a subject they never discuss or even mention' (p. 220). Anyone with access to the books written or edited by us and quoted by Blaug may confirm that this is simply not true.

the absence of significant and lasting barriers to entry and exit from all markets, the case with which the classical authors were primarily concerned, profit seeking necessarily involves cost minimization.[9] Hence their attention focused on what may be called *cost-minimizing systems of production*.

The method of analysis adopted by the classical economists is known as the method of *long-period positions* of the economy. Any such position is the situation towards which the system is taken to gravitate, given the fundamental forces at work in the particular historical situation under consideration. In conditions of free competition the resulting long-period position is characterized by a uniform rate of profits (subject perhaps to persistent inter-industry differentials), uniform rates of remuneration for each particular kind of primary input, and prices that are assumed not to change between the beginning of the uniform period of production (usually a year) and its end.

In his paper Blaug stresses repeatedly that classical economics is characterized by 'a particular theory of value and distribution' (p. 233), which is different from the neoclassical demand and supply theory. In our brief summary of what we consider to be the salient features of this theory we shall pay special attention to the contribution of Ricardo.

According to Ricardo the study of the laws governing the distribution of income involved (i) isolating the factors determining that distribution *in a given place and time* and (ii) investigating the causes of changes in these factors *over time*. Ricardo, we take it, isolated the following factors:

(a) The set of technical alternatives from which cost-minimizing producers can choose.
(b) The size and composition of the social product, reflecting the needs and wants of the members of the different classes of society and the requirements of reproduction and capital accumulation.
(c) The ruling real wage rate(s) (or the share of wages).
(d) The quantities of different qualities of land available and the known stocks of depletable resources, such as mineral deposits.

Nobody familiar with Ricardo's writings can deny that to him the actual state of technical knowledge in a given situation constituted a main factor determining the levels of the rate of profits and the rent rates. For instance, when discussing the tendency of the rate of profits to fall, Ricardo started from the assumption of a given technical knowledge and then added that this tendency 'is happily

---

9 Blaug contends that 'Kurz and Salvadori (1998b, pp. 16, 53) refer to "free or perfect competition" as if it were the same thing' (p. 230). The reader will search in vain for evidence in support of this contention on the pages given. We are aware that the two concepts are radically different, in particular that the classical concept does not define the market form and thus competition in terms of the number of agents operating on each side of the market. See again, for example, the subject index of our 1995 book and especially chapter 1 of it on 'Free competition and long-period positions'. Blaug's claim that 'We read . . . Kurz, Salvadori . . . in vain looking for so much as a reference to the classical conception of competition' (p. 230) is contradicted by the facts.

checked at repeated intervals by the improvements in machinery . . . as well as by discoveries in the science of agriculture' (*Works*, vol. I, p. 120). Nobody familiar with Ricardo's writings can deny that to him essentially the same applied with regard to the levels of total output, because with diminishing returns in agriculture and mining it matters whether little or much corn is to be produced and little or much ore to be extracted, given the information summarized in (d). As Ricardo stressed: 'The exchangeable value of *all* commodities, whether they be manufactured, or the produce of the mines, or the produce of land, is always regulated . . . by the most unfavorable circumstances, the most unfavorable under which *the quantity of produce required*, renders it necessary to carry on the production' (*Works*, vol. I, p. 73; emphases added). Nobody familiar with Ricardo's writings will deny that in his view the rate of profits depends on the level of wages (see, e.g. the evidence provided in Kurz and Salvadori, 1995, pp. 472–3; see also Section 6). And, most important, unlike his contemporary Malthus and the later marginalist authors, Ricardo did *not* conceive of wages (and thus the rate of profits) as determined in terms of demand and supply (see, Section 4).[10]

Ricardo singled out these factors as the dominant ones determining the rate of profits, the rates of rent and 'natural' prices *in a given place and time*. However, at the same time he saw the above independent *variables* as containing the key to the problem of the long-run development of income distribution, that is, which long-run course the rate and share of profits would take, and what would happen to the rates of rent on the different qualities of renewable and depletable natural resources, the overall share of rents and relative prices. In his analysis of capital accumulation and of different forms of technical change Ricardo emphasized the interaction of the independent variables among themselves and of them and the dependent variables. As regards the first kind of interactions, think, for example, of capital accumulation which would entail rising levels of output of many commodities and falling levels of some other commodities due to the gradual exhaustion of certain natural resources, that is, an endogenous change in at least some of the independent variables summarized under (b) and (d). As Ricardo stressed, a swift accumulation of capital might also tend to raise the real wage rate and thus affect (c). A change in wages might then have an impact on the chosen methods of production and the composition of output. Recall, for example, the chapter 'On Machinery', added to the third edition of the *Principles*, in which Ricardo stressed: 'Machinery and labour are in constant competition, and the former can frequently not be employed

10 It is interesting to note that some early marginalist authors apparently had less difficulties than some present-day commentators to see that the classical economists in fact started from the set of data (a)–(d) when determining the rate of profits and relative prices. See, for example, William Stanley Jevons ([1871] 1965, pp. 268–9), Léon Walras ([1874] 1954, part VII, lessons 38–40) and Knut Wicksell ([1893] 1954, pp. 34–40), who provide some indirect evidence in support of the interpretation given here. In particular, these authors were clear that in determining the rate of profits Ricardo took the quantities of output and the real wage rate as given, and criticized him for this, because according to their fundamentally different theory quantities and prices (including the distributive variables) had to be determined simultaneously. See also Kurz and Salvadori (2002).

until labour [i.e. the wage] rises' (*Works*, vol. I, p. 395). As regards the second kind of interactions, Ricardo focused attention on the prime mover of economic growth and structural change: technological progress. Blaug (pp. 219–20) rightly refers to Ricardo's discussion of different forms of agricultural improvements and of machinery (*Works*, vol. I, chapter II, pp. 79–84, and chapter XXXI).[11] Over time the size and composition of output can be expected to change, reflecting a multitude of influences interacting in a complex way. The availability of new methods of production which make possible the reduction of production costs and prices of known commodities and the introduction of entirely new commodities, or of better qualities of known commodities, would interact with the needs and wants of the different classes of society and thus give rise to new patterns of consumption. Hence, what in the determination of the rate of profits and the rates of rent in a given place and time was taken as given under (b) is bound to change over time, reflecting learning processes on the part of producers and consumers and involving changes in income distribution and relative prices. As regards the real wage rate of common labour Ricardo kept stressing: 'It is not to be understood that the natural price of labour, estimated even in food and necessaries, is absolutely fixed and constant. It varies at different times in the same country, and very materially differs in different countries. It essentially depends on the habits and customs of the people. . . . Many of the conveniences now enjoyed in an English cottage, would have been thought luxuries at an earlier period of our history' (*Works*, vol. I, pp. 96–7).

Before we enter into a discussion of Blaug's criticisms, it deserves to be stressed that Ricardo's intuition was correct: on the basis of the above data (a)–(d) one can in fact determine in a coherent way the unknowns or independent variables in a given place and time: the long-period levels of the rate of profits, the rents of land and relative prices. No other information or data are needed. This is an important fact in itself. In addition it is to be emphasized that *any* coherent long-period theory of value and distribution must start from a set of data which either implies the set of data of the classical approach, (a)–(d) above, or is equivalent to it. As we shall see in Section 7, Blaug's alternative conceptualization is no exception to this rule.

6. Independent variables are still *variables*

Economic theory invariably proceeds by cutting slits into the 'seamless absolute whole' (Georgescu-Roegen) of socio-economic phenomena. This involves, among other things, adopting some bold simplifications. This does not mean that anything goes. It only means that there must be a judicious selection of aspects to be dealt with, and how to deal with them, setting aside in a first step of the analysis some other aspects. This selection requires some intimate knowledge of the corresponding phenomenal domain, and it seems that our high esteem for the achievements of the classical economists concerns no less this knowledge of the

11 For a detailed discussion of Ricardo's changing views on machinery, see Jeck and Kurz (1983); for Ricardo's views on technological progress and diminishing returns in agriculture and their respective impacts on the long-term tendency of the rate of profits, see Kurz (1998); for a discussion of Ricardo's views on agricultural improvements, see Gehrke *et al.* (2003).

subject matter than their analytical skills. The classical approach to the theory of value and distribution in terms of the set of independent variables (a)–(d) exemplifies this. Clearly, none of the classical authors would have denied that outputs, techniques, the distribution of the product and relative prices are interdependent and that each of these sets of magnitudes was bound to change over time. However, in determining the rate of profits, the rents of land and relative prices *in a given economy at a given time* Ricardo and the other classical economists started from *given* data (a)–(d), reflecting in particular the achieved state of the accumulation of capital and technical knowledge, the scarcity of the available natural resources and, last but not least, the relative strengths of the parties, 'whose interests are by no means the same', in the 'dispute' over the distribution of income, as Smith (*WN*, I.viii.11) kept stressing.

This should make it abundantly clear that it never occurred to us to interpret the classical economists as assuming that the independent variables or 'data' (a)–(d) above are data characterizing once and forever the economy under consideration, that is, *historical constants*. Nor are we aware that Sraffa or any of the scholars working in his tradition, including us, has ever written anything that could possibly be misunderstood in this way. Yet, surprisingly enough, this is precisely the interpretation Blaug contends we are advocating. Nothing could be farther from the truth.[12]

It hardly needs to be emphasized that independent variables are still *variables*. The magnitudes under consideration are only treated as known or given in one part of classical theory: the determination of the shares of income other than wages, and relative prices, in given conditions of the economy; in other parts of the theory they are themselves treated as dependent variables or unknowns. In other words, *variables (a)–(d), while magnitudes external to the classical approach to the theory of value and distribution in particular, are magnitudes internal to the classical theory as a whole.*

To see better what we mean it is useful to have a closer look at Blaug's criticism. Following his discussion, we shall focus attention on the independent variables (a)–(c), because (d) seems to be uncontroversial.

6.1. Technical alternatives

As regards parameter (a), Blaug maintains that what is meant are the given 'fixed coefficients' posited for the production of different commodities 'that are written down on the first page of Sraffa's book' (p. 219). To this he adds: 'It is perfectly true that the classical economists rarely addressed the problem of the choice of technique, virtually implying that it was usually impossible to choose among a number of technical alternatives' (ibid.). Hence, with regard to an economy at

---

12 If Blaug were to apply the same kind of reasoning he applies to our interpretation of the classical approach to the theory of value and distribution also to Marshall's partial equilibrium method, he would have to interpret Marshall's *ceteris paribus* clause as involving the assertion that what is taken as given will never change.

a given time Blaug interprets the classical authors more narrowly than we do, and indeed too narrowly, because they did not turn a blind eye to the problem of the choice of technique: for example, at the very heart of the theory of rent there is the problem of which qualities of land to cultivate from a set of given qualities (extensive rent) or of which methods of production to employ on a given quality of land (intensive rent), that is, a problem of the choice of technique. (See also again the choice of technique problem discussed by Ricardo in the context of the machinery question referred to in Section 5.)

Interestingly, Blaug explicitly admits what we have stated in terms of the independent variable (a). His references to Ricardo's discussion of 'agricultural improvements' or of machinery (p. 219) are materially of no import, because we have never denied that *over time* technical knowledge will change. Yet, Blaug's references provide a welcome opportunity to illustrate that our interpretation is faithful to Ricardo's approach to the theory of value and distribution. Take, for example, the latter's discussion of what may be called 'land saving improvements' (similarly his discussion of 'capital or labour saving improvements') (see also Gehrke *et al.*, 2003). As Ricardo's numerical illustration makes clear, he took as given the amounts of the different qualities of land available in the economy, the real wage rate, the methods of production employed on the lands actually cultivated prior to the improvement, and the methods of production available after the improvement. He stated: 'These improvements absolutely enable us to obtain *the same produce* from a smaller quantity of labour' (*Works*, vol. I, p. 80, emphasis added). Hence he compared two situations defined in terms of the *same* information concerning data (b)–(d), but different information concerning datum (a). (Ricardo left no doubt that this is only a first step in an analysis of the impact of technical change on income distribution and relative prices.) For a similar procedure, see Ricardo's chapter on machinery.

In his discussion relating to 'datum' (a) Blaug expresses a view that is potentially misleading or difficult to sustain. We were surprised that in the context of a discussion of Marx's analysis of the 'labour process' he could write: 'Far from technology being given to capitalists, the choice of technique is at the very heart of the contested terrain between workers and capitalists' (p. 222). Here it suffices to point out that the problem of the choice of technique forms a centrepiece of Sraffa's analysis (1960, part III) and the literature inspired by it (see, e.g. Kurz and Salvadori, 1995).[13] It should also be recalled that Marx's discussion of the 'labour

---

13 Later in his paper Blaug comments on the fact that Sraffa's equations of production exhibit one degree of freedom which is then removed by taking one of the distributive variables as given: 'the problem of not-enough-equations would not even arise if Sraffa had allowed production coefficients to vary' (p. 229). To be clear, to have a number of methods of production to choose from that is larger than the number of commodities the prices of which are to be ascertained is one thing, to determine which of these methods will actually be chosen by cost-minimizing producers is a totally different thing. The latter decision requires information about the level of wages (or, alternatively, the rate of profits). This will be immediately clear to people familiar with the von Neumann model, in which real wages (paid *ante factum*) are taken as given.

process' assumes special weight in the context of an analysis of what he called the production and appropriation of 'relative surplus value'. He means here the additional surplus value obtained not in terms of a lengthening of the working day, other things being (roughly) equal, but in terms of an increase in labour productivity due to organizational and technological changes. Here specific forms of such *changes* are considered instrumental to the capitalists' interest to alter the balance of power between themselves and the workers in their favour. However, both the classical economists and Marx treated the intensity of work in normal conditions of a particular economy in a particular time as given. Marx, for example, stressed: 'The labour-time socially necessary is that required to produce an article under the *normal conditions of production*, and with the *average degree of skill and intensity prevalent at the time*' (Marx, 1954, p. 47, emphasis added).[14]

6.2. Outputs

The interpretation of the approach of the classical economists to the theory of value and distribution as starting from given levels of output Blaug tries to counter in terms of the remark: 'Come, come: the volume of output, alongside the size of the labor force, is constantly rising in Ricardo' (p. 224). True, output levels (at least of many products) in the year 1817 may be higher than output levels in the year 1776, but in order to ascertain the rate of profits, the rent rates and relative prices in 1776 (or 1817), what matters are output levels (and, of course, techniques and the real wage rate) in 1776 (or 1817).

The same misunderstanding reappears in several forms. For example, Blaug tries to ridicule the assumption of given quantities in order to determine the endogenous variables just mentioned in a given place and time with reference to Marx's 'law of the falling rate of profit'. Marx, he contends, would have been 'surprised . . . to learn that his extended investigation . . . was not proper classical economics because it violated the fundamental postulate of "given quantities" ' (p. 223). Marx was perfectly clear about the fact that any fall (or rise) in the rate of profits between two years, say 1776 and 1817, was due to changes in the fundamental factors at work reflected in particular constellations of data (a)–(d) (see Marx, 1959, part III). Blaug also maintains: 'There is ample evidence in Ricardo's *Principles* that he had in mind a moving equilibrium' (p. 224, see also p. 226). One can only wonder in which terms Ricardo, according to Blaug, characterized that 'equilibrium' at any given moment of time and whether that characterization differs from the one proposed in Section 5. (An answer to this question is given in Section 7.)

At the heart of Blaug's respective criticism appears to be a confusion between attributing a particular analytical method to the classical economists and attributing

---

14 While Blaug is correct in stressing the 'incompleteness' of the labour contract, especially as regards the intensity of work to be performed, this aspect concerns first and foremost the relative strengths of the different parties involved, workers and capitalists, and would be best treated in the context of a discussion of 'datum' (c).

particular propositions about reality to them. Blaug contends: 'Sraffa tells us that there are "no changes in output" in "the old classical economists"' (p. 224). This is, of course, not true: Sraffa never maintained that there are no changes in output contemplated by the classical authors. He rather specified that in his book 'the investigation is concerned exclusively with *such properties of an economic system* as do not depend on changes in the scale of production or in the proportion of "factors"' (1960, p. v, emphasis added). To focus attention on such properties of an economic system does not mean, of course, to maintain that there are no such changes. It only means that these changes are set aside in the respective investigation. What is at stake is a *method* designed to analyse an aspect of the economic system under consideration and not a factual proposition that the system is stationary. This becomes clear in the statement that follows the one just quoted: 'This *standpoint*, which is that of the old classical economists from Adam Smith to Ricardo, has been submerged and forgotten since the advent of the "marginal" *method*' (ibid., emphases added). The latter focuses attention on (marginal) changes in the scale of production and in the proportions of factors. It attempts to determine relative prices and the distributive variables in terms of incremental quantitative changes. This is in stark contrast with the classical method in the theory of value and distribution, which Sraffa was keen to revive: his aim was the determination of the competitive rate of profits and, using the 'classical terms' (ibid., p. 8), the corresponding 'necessary prices' or 'natural prices' or 'prices of production'. In other words, Sraffa's book, following the classical economists, studies the problem of value and distribution in given conditions by taking the levels of outputs as known magnitudes.[15] The book is not about accumulation, growth, technical change, etc. However, as we know from Sraffa's unpublished manuscripts, it was meant to prepare the ground for an analysis of these important features of the modern economy very much in the same way as Ricardo's approach to the theory of value and distribution in chapters I–IV of the *Principles* was meant to prepare the ground for his discussion of these issues.

6.3. Wages

We now come to the independent variable (c). It should be stressed immediately that what the classical economists took as given with regard to a particular economy at a particular time in order to determine the other distributive variables

---

15 To start from given levels of gross outputs, designed to reflect the degree of the division of labour reached by a particular economy at a given stage of its development, is therefore not a 'myth' invented by Sraffa (p. 222), but rather a premise congenial to Smith's important concept (see Kurz and Salvadori, 1998a, vol. I, pp. 325–9). Interestingly, Blaug relates Sraffa's assumption of given quantities explicitly to Smith's analysis. He comments on the former: 'As a description of what the *Wealth of Nations* is all about, even the chapters in book I on the theory of value and distribution, this is simply grotesque' (p. 223). It hardly needs to be stressed that that assumption was not designed by Sraffa for the purpose invoked by Blaug. However, we wonder whether in the light of what has been said above the assumption still looks 'simply grotesque' to him.

and relative prices was the wage rate of 'common labour' and the scale of wage differentials. The latter is considered to be fairly stable over time (see, e.g. Smith, *WN*; I.x.c.63, and Ricardo, *Works*, vol. I: 20–1). Smith mentioned the following factors accounting for wage differentials: (i) differences in the costs of production of different skills; (ii) the scarcity of particular talents; (iii) differences in the degree to which the labourers' capacity to work can be utilized in different employments; (iv) differences in the trust that must be reposed in the workers; and (v) different risks involved in becoming qualified for the employment to which one is educated. Since we have tried to reformulate Smith's ideas within the framework of modern classical theory of value and distribution (see Kurz and Salvadori, 1995; chapter 11), we may immediately turn to the given wage of common labour.

It is difficult to see wherein precisely Blaug disagrees with us. We share Blaug's emphasis on the classical authors' 'attention to the institutional setting' of the problem under consideration (p. 228). There appears to be also no material difference between our view and his that the classical authors 'regarded the minimum-level-of-existence wage rate . . . as something that was determined by slowly changing *historical traditions* [conditions?] and which, therefore, *could be taken as given* in analyzing a practical question, like a tax on wage goods' (p. 227, emphases added). Analyzing a practical question presupposed that the theoretical framework was already in place. And indeed it was and allowed the classical authors to ascertain the non-wage incomes (profits and rents) and relative prices in a given place and time, taking the wage rate as a known magnitude. The impact of a tax on wage goods on profits, rents and relative prices, for example, given the real wage rate, could then be discussed at will. As Blaug indicated in the passage just quoted, in the classical authors even the minimum real wage rate was not an absolutely fixed magnitude. And the market wage rate could rise well above that minimum. Thus, Smith and Ricardo kept stressing that in conditions of rapid accumulation capitalists would start bidding up the real wage rate, which, in conditions of unchanged technical conditions of production, would depress profitability (see, e.g. Ricardo, *Works*, vol. II, pp. 252 and 264–5). Hence, to take actual wages as given in a particular place and time in order to determine the actual rate of profits, rents and relative prices in that place and time does not mean to assume that wages will forever remain at that level (any more than Marshall's use of *ceteris paribus* means that the givens are and will remain constant). These considerations should also suffice to dispel Blaug's following suspicion: 'to say that [in the determination of the rate of profits, rents and relative prices] the classical economists treated the "natural price" of labor as exogenous [means that it is] determined outside their theoretical system' (p. 228). This is a *non sequitur*. To repeat what has already been said in the above: In the classical authors the real wage rate is treated as a known magnitude when it comes to the determination of the other distributive variables and relative prices in a given place and time, but it is of course treated as a magnitude to be determined in their theoretical system as a whole, depending, *inter alia*, on cultural, institutional and historical factors. In order to avoid confusion one ought to distinguish between the different spheres of their analyses.

Blaug's final objection in the present context reads: 'Besides (and now we come to the crux of the matter), the idea that the classical economists must have taken the real wage as a datum because the logical consistency of their theory demanded it is a perfect example of a rational reconstruction of past theories: it reads Smith and Ricardo and Marx through Walrasian-tinted glasses' (p. 229). This is a misrepresentation, because the argument is *not*, as Blaug maintains, that the classical economists *ought* to have taken the real wage rate as a datum when determining the rate of profits, etc., but that they actually *did* take it as such. It would be interesting to see whether Blaug can provide any evidence that in determining the rate of profits, rents and relative prices in a given place and time Smith, Ricardo or Marx did not start from a given real wage rate. In his paper Blaug provides no such evidence and indeed no such evidence can possibly be provided, whereas it is easy to provide evidence to the contrary.[16] In one place Blaug indirectly appears to admit this when he writes: 'Ricardo's question was: how do relative prices change when income distribution varies and, in particular, when technology causes the rate of profit to decline in real time?' (p. 232). Here we have what may be called the purely hypothetical cases of both the 'static' and the 'dynamic' problem of value and distribution: How does the rate of profits and do relative prices change when there is a change in the real wage rate, in conditions in which the technical alternatives of production are for simplicity taken as given? And how does the rate of profits and do relative prices change when capital accumulates, the population grows and less and less fertile lands have to be cultivated or lands of a given fertility have to be cultivated more intensively, in conditions in which the real wage rate is for simplicity taken as given? We called the two cases contemplated by Ricardo (see, especially, his *Notes on Malthus*, *Works*, vol. II) purely hypothetical because Ricardo was, of course, very clear that what is taken as given can be expected also to change because of the interaction of the different variables under consideration.[17] To see that the interpretation of Ricardo and the classical economists we endorse is faithful to their writings, we may draw Blaug's attention again to Ricardo's discussion of 'agricultural improvements', where the real wage rate in terms of corn is taken as given (otherwise Ricardo could not have considered the capitals employed on the different kinds of land as known magnitudes), or to chapter I of the *Principles* in which the dependence of the rate of profits and relative prices on the real wage is discussed in

---

16 See, for example, the title of section III of chapter III, 'Interchange', of James Mill's *Elements*, 'Effect upon Exchangeable Values of a Fluctuation in Wages and Profits' (Mill, [1826] 1844, p. 105), and Marx's discussion in chapter XI of volume III of *Capital* of the 'Effects of General Wage Fluctuations on Prices of Production', 'all else remaining the same' (Marx, 1959, p. 200).

17 The two hypothetical cases are also discussed by Marx in vol. III of *Capital*. It is interesting to note that in his attempt to establish a tendency of the rate of profits to fall, Marx explicitly assumed a given and constant real wage rate: 'Nothing is more absurd . . . than to explain the fall in the rate of profit by a rise in the rate of wages, although this may be the case by way of an exception' (Marx, 1959, p. 240).

detail and what Blaug called Ricardo's 'fundamental theorem of distribution' is established.

To conclude this section, to take wages as given when determining the rate of profits, rents and relative prices is certainly not a consistency requirement imposed by us on the classical authors; the premise under consideration is rather encountered in the classical economists themselves. There is every reason to presume that this is so, because, understandably, *they* were concerned with consistent arguments and despised inconsistent ones.

According to Blaug one must 'aim to make historical reconstructions as descriptively accurate as possible' (p. 232). We agree. He adds: 'This is an aim of which Sraffians have totally lost sight' (ibid.). Blaug's claim just cannot be reconciled with the above cited evidence.

7. Blaug's alternative conceptualization of the 'core'

Blaug concludes his paper by asking: 'So, is there a "core" of classical economics?' (p. 232). His answer is: 'Obviously, yes if by *core* we mean a *central strand* by which we recognize a work as belonging to "classical economics", the strand that unites Smith in 1776, Mill in 1848, and Marx in 1867. It is made up, all commentators agree, of a *particular theory of value and distribution*' (pp. 232–3, emphasis added). This contention is dubious, because what can at most be said is that there is a particular classical *approach* to the theory of value and distribution, whereas the specific variants of that approach put forward by Smith, Ricardo and Marx differ in several respects.[18] Thus, when we talk of the 'classical' theory of value and distribution we can only refer to the *essence* of the theories put forward by authors such as Petty, Cantillon, the Physiocrats, Smith, Ricardo and Marx, that is, in the words of Sraffa, 'not the theory of any one of them, but an extract of what . . . is common to them' (D3/12/4, 12).[19]

So what is common to these authors, especially as opposed to the advocates of neoclassical economics? Blaug insists: 'First, classical value theory focuses on long-period equilibrium prices characterized by a uniform rate of profit on capital, uniform rates of pay for every different type of labor, and uniform rents per acre for every different type of land; in short, what Smith called "natural prices" in contrast to "market prices", subject to the vagaries of demand and supply' (p. 233). Blaug's specification concerns what was called above the *long-period method*. This is indeed a first characteristic feature of the classical approach to the theory of value and distribution. Yet since this method was essentially adopted also by all

---

18 It seems that Blaug was misled by the vague term 'central strand' he uses. Apparently he equivocated between a *substantial theory* and an *analytical approach* to a particular problem. It is the latter that is relevant in the present context.

19 The reference is to Sraffa's unpublished papers which are kept in the Wren Library, Trinity College, Cambridge. The references given follow the catalogue prepared by Jonathan Smith, archivist. We are grateful to Pierangelo Garegnani, literary executor of Sraffa's papers and correspondence, for granting us permission to quote from them.

major marginalist economists until the late 1920s, including Jevons, Walras, Böhm-Bawerk, Marshall, Wicksell and John Bates Clark (see Garegnani, 1976; Kurz and Salvadori, 1995, pp. 427–55), we must turn to the *content* of the different kinds of approaches in order to be able to discriminate between a classical and a marginalist (or neoclassical) approach.

As regards the content of the former, Blaug emphasizes that the 'natural prices were determined... *in the context of a technology of production* characterized in physical terms and expressed for practical purposes in hours of labor' (p. 233, emphasis added). The reader may wonder what is the difference between datum (a), which postulates a given set of technical alternatives from which cost-minimizing producers can choose, and a given 'context of a technology of production'. The latter involves the former (and perhaps something more; see below). And if the 'technology of production' were not taken as *given*, how could natural prices or hours of labour expended in the production of the different commodities ever be determined?

Is the long-period method, together with Blaug's version of datum (a), sufficient to distinguish the classical approach from the neoclassical one? The answer is obviously no. The two elements are also present in all versions of traditional marginalist theory. See, for example, the conventional representation of the available technical alternatives in terms of given production functions for different products in Wicksell or Clark or the specification of given methods of production in terms of 'coefficients de fabrication' in Walras. Hence, more is needed in order to identify the specificity of the classical approach to the theory of value and distribution.

Blaug is aware of this and adds that 'the "core" of classical economics always involved some version of the labor theory of value' (p. 233).[20] Before we continue with the main argument two clarifications are needed. First, the quantities of labour embodied in the different commodities cannot generally be determined independently of the *levels of output*. As is well known, in Ricardo the attention concerning the relevant amount of labour needed in the production of one quarter of

---

20   The reader will recall Blaug's earlier statement that the classical authors 'expressed [the technical conditions of production] *for practical purposes* in hours of labor' (p. 233; emphasis added). From this point of view the labour theory of value can hardly be said to have been an indispensable element of classical analysis. It was simply a useful tool at a certain stage of the development of the analysis that could be dispensed with as soon as the role performed by it could be assumed by a more correct theory. As Wittgenstein put it, a particular theory may be compared to a ladder that is useful to reach a higher standpoint. However, once this standpoint is reached and a fuller view of the landscape is possible, the ladder may turn out to be an instrument that is inferior to some other device to reach that higher standpoint and beyond and will therefore be dispensed with. The same can be said with regard to the labour theory of value: it was an instrument that provided useful services to the classical economists, but once the problem of the relationship between income distribution and relative prices, given the system of production in use, had been fully solved, the labour theory of value had not only become dispensable, but actually had to be dispensed with because it did not provide a fully correct picture of that relationship. The fact that they were not possessed of a correct theory of value and distribution might contribute to explaining why, according to Blaug, 'both Ricardo and Marx were so obsessed with the labor theory of value' (p. 217).

corn focuses on the conditions of production on the marginal land, which, however, cannot be ascertained independently of the total amount of corn to be produced and the quantities of the different qualities of land available in an economy. Blaug is, of course, aware of this (see p. 224).[21] Hence, in order to determine labour values some information of the kind summarized in data (b) and (d) is needed. Since Blaug does not separately specify these data, we have only one option: in order not to level an unjust criticism against his interpretation of the classical authors, we must interpret his above formula 'in the context of a technology of production' as a catch-all phrase involving both independent variables or data (a), (b) and (d). Second, we have already mentioned Blaug's attempt to ridicule the casting of problems in the theory of value and distribution in terms of systems of simultaneous equations (and inequalities) (pp. 229 and 233). However, when production is recognized to be circular (rather than unidirectional), as, for example, in Quesnay's *Tableau Economique*, Torrens's and Marx's schemes of reproduction, or Ricardo's discussion of the productive interrelationship between agriculture and manufactures – how can labour values be determined other than in such terms? The fact that for illustrative purposes Ricardo and other authors frequently used simple numerical examples with unidirectional production (of finite duration) must not be mistaken to imply that they were uninterested in giving, as Blaug puts it, 'due attention to the interdependencies between markets' (p. 229).

We must now come back and ask: Can the classical theory of value be discriminated from other theories of value, especially the traditional marginalist one, in terms of the presence of 'some version of the labor theory of value'? The answer is obviously no. First, none of the authors mentioned by Blaug (Smith, Mill, Marx) was of the opinion that (other than in singularly special cases) relative prices are strictly proportional to the relative quantities of labour embodied in the different commodities, which is the usual meaning of the labour theory of value. Smith restricted the applicability of the quantity of labour rule of exchangeable values explicitly to the 'early and rude state of society'; Mill reiterated Ricardo's view that relative prices are not exclusively regulated by the technical conditions of production reflected in hours of labour needed directly and indirectly in the production of the various commodities; and Marx indicated already in volume I of *Capital*, and expounded in some detail in volume III, that (relative) prices are bound to systematically deviate from (relative) labour values, *namely*, the (in)famous 'transformation problem'. Second, many of the early marginalist authors, despite their completely different approach to the theory of value and distribution, can also be said to have held 'some version of the labor theory of value'. Ironically, some of these authors were stern advocates of the view that with regard to reproducible goods the then novel (marginal) utility theory of value amounted to materially the same thing as the pure labour theory of value. See, for example, William Stanley

---

21 Blaug even admits that Ricardo assumed a given level of corn output that is independent of the price of corn or rather: 'the demand for corn was perfectly inelastic, . . . and that is precisely what Ricardo seems to have assumed' (ibid.).

Jevons ([1871] 1965, pp. 186–9), Philip H. Wicksteed ([1884] 1999, pp. 717–18), Friedrich von Wieser (1884, pp. 159–60) and Eugen von Böhm-Bawerk (1892, pp. 329–30). John Bates Clark insisted: 'In the subjective valuations of society, as an organic whole, the product of two hours' labor is always worth just twice as much as is the product of one. Mere labor time is an accurate gauge of the values of different complements of goods' (Clark 1899, p. 390).

Blaug's above criterion therefore cannot perform the role of a litmus test of what is to be considered as genuinely 'classical' in the theory of value and distribution. Before we continue, we ask a question Blaug could (and indeed should) have raised, but didn't. That question lingers at the back of his rather vague notion of '*some* version of the labor theory of value': Why did none of the classical authors (or J. S. Mill) advocate the pure and simple version of that theory which claims that relative prices are strictly proportional to relative labour quantities (or labour values)? Because at least since Ricardo they knew very well that this would have been strictly correct only in the singularly special case of uniform proportions of direct labour to means of production (or indirect labour) and uniform degrees of durability of fixed capital across all lines of production, or uniform 'organic compositions of capital,' to use Marx's concept. Blaug is aware of this, and he is equally aware of the fact that in the only interesting, because realistic, case of non-uniform proportions, prices depend not only on the technical conditions of production but also on income distribution. This is made abundantly clear, for example, in sections IV and V of chapter I of Ricardo's *Principles* (see *Works*, vol. I, pp. 30–43), and in part II of volume III of Marx's *Capital* (1959). Clearly, data (a), (b) and (d) (which appear to be equivalent to Blaug's assumption of a given 'technology of production') generally do not suffice to determine relative prices and, as the classical authors knew very well, they never suffice to determine the competitive rate of profits. In order to render the theory determinate, something like datum (c) was needed.

We now turn to the way in which Blaug completes his purportedly alternative conceptualization of the characteristic features of the classical theory of value and distribution. He contends that the 'core' of classical economics involved also 'a more or less detailed analysis of the forces making for capital accumulation and, of course, a thin or thick version of the Malthusian theory of population' (p. 233). The interplay between capital accumulation and the Malthusian population mechanism is discussed in chapter V of Ricardo's *Principles*. That interplay is invoked by Ricardo in order to argue that the market wage rate tends to move towards the natural wage rate. This involves a particular view of how the real wage rate is determined. Hence, we could say that in his rational reconstruction Blaug's reference to the Malthusian theory of population provides the missing piece in terms of a very special form of datum (c) that renders the theory determinate. Notwithstanding his frontal assault on the set of independent variables (a)–(d) as a characteristic feature of the classical approach to the theory of value and distribution in the main part of his paper, Blaug in the end endorses a special version of precisely that set.

The Malthusian theory of population, we suggest, does not form a constituent part of the classical approach to the problems of value and distribution. Blaug, who, as we have seen, counts Marx – a fierce critic of Malthus – among the classicists, will have difficulties to discern traces of that theory, whether thick or thin, in the latter's analysis. Smith held essentially a bargaining theory of wages, focusing attention on the relative strengths of the parties, 'workmen' and 'masters', in the conflict over the distribution of the product, with the emphasis placed on cultural, legal and political factors (cf. *WN*, I.viii). In the case of Ricardo things are particularly complex. While there are references to the Malthusian theory of population, Ricardo's works abound with observations questioning its validity. We have already seen that according to Ricardo 'the natural price of labour, estimated even in food and necessaries, . . . essentially depends on the habits and customs of the people' (*Works*, vol. I, pp. 96–7). In an 'improving society' with the 'market' wage rate exceeding the natural rate it is possible that 'custom renders absolute necessaries' what in the past had been considered comforts or luxuries, that is, the natural wage is driven upward by persistently high levels of the actual wage rate. Interestingly, in Ricardo's view 'population may be so little stimulated by ample wages as to increase at the slowest rate – or *it may even go in a retrograde direction*' (*Works*, vol. VIII, p. 169, emphasis added).[22] And in his *Notes on Malthus* he insisted that 'population and necessaries are not necessarily linked together so intimately': 'better education and improved habits' may break the population mechanism (*Works*, vol. II, p. 169). Hence, in Ricardo we encounter propositions that are decidedly anti-Malthusian. Blaug's claim that classical economics 'always involved . . . a thin or thick version of the Malthusian theory of population' (p. 233) cannot be sustained.

We conclude that Blaug's own reconstruction of the 'core' of classical analysis is a variant of the set of data (a)–(d) expounded in Section 5. We have also provided evidence showing that his variant cannot be considered an interpretation that is historically more faithful to what is common to the authors under consideration than the one advocated by Sraffa and economists working in his tradition.

Finally, we should like to stress once again that the classical approach to the theory of value and distribution is alive and thriving. As was stressed above, data (a)–(d) specify its *logical structure* with its *asymmetric* treatment of the distributive variables. An author, or parts of his analysis, may therefore be called 'classical' if we encounter this logical structure in the theory of value and distribution put forward by him or her. The approach could only survive because it does not depend on particular historical conceptualizations of some of its elements; more specifically: it does not stand or fall with the validity of the labour theory of value or of the Malthusian theory of population. The approach is entirely independent of these theories. Therefore, the classical approach to the theory of value and distribution

---

22 We owe this quotation to Pierangelo Garegnani. On a possible reason for Ricardo's inconsistency, see Stirati (1994, pp. 147–57).

should not only be of interest to the historian of economic thought, but also to the modern economic theorist.[23]

8. Conclusion

The paper discusses Mark Blaug's recent criticism of the interpretation of the classical economists inspired by Piero Sraffa's work. It is argued that, contrary to Blaug's claim, we have given a faithful interpretation of the classical authors. In particular, it is shown that the latter treated the technical alternatives of production, the levels of output of the different commodities produced, the real wage rate of common labour (and the quantities of the different qualities of land available) as independent variables, or data, when determining the competitive rate of profits, the rates of rent and relative price in a given place and time. However, while these magnitudes are treated as variables that are external, or exogenous, to the classical approach to the theory of value and distribution, they are internal, or endogenous, to the classical theory as a whole. This draws attention to the fact that the classical authors distinguished between different spheres of economic analysis necessitating the employment of different methods. While one sphere is suited to the application of deductive reasoning – this relates to the investigation of the relations between the distributive variables and relative prices, given the system of production – the other sphere requires more inductive lines of reasoning and research – this relates to an investigation of the sources and consequences of economic change, in particular technological progress, economic growth, changing consumption patterns, the exhaustion of natural resources etc. It was then demonstrated that Blaug's suggested alternative specification of the 'core' of classical economics amounts to a very special version of the Sraffian interpretation.

Appendix: claims and contentions by Mark Blaug that are obviously false

Blaug's paper contains several propositions that are unwarranted or false. In this appendix we shall point out some of them.

Blaug informs the reader that 'everything in this article I have said before (Blaug, 1987) but apparently to no purpose, because Sraffian writers have simply ignored my objections' (p. 216, fn. 2). However, later in his paper, in the context of a discussion of Ricardo's search for an 'invariable measure of value' and its relationship with Sraffa's concept of the 'Standard commodity', he contradicts himself: 'I said exactly that in 1987 (Blaug, 1987, p. 157). . . . Kurz and Salvadori (1998b, pp. 144–5) criticize me, quite rightly, for suggesting that Sraffa's standard commodity makes prices independent of distribution, which is logically impossible

---

23 In some of the papers reprinted in our book (Kurz and Salvadori, 1998b) we have shown that the logical structure of the classical approach to the theory of value and distribution can also be discerned in more recent contributions such as, for example, the von Neumann model, the non-substitution theorem, and in some of the so-called 'new' growth models.

since the standard commodity is only a particular *numéraire*' (p. 227, fn. 11).[24]
Hence, while it is not true that Blaug's objections have been ignored by us, it is
true that we felt no need to answer each and every one of them.

Blaug sees reason to deplore an 'utter indifference of Sraffian interpreters to the
opening three chapters of the *Wealth of Nations* on the division of labor, a subject
they never discuss or even mention' (p. 220). This is a remarkable contention.
Any reader with access to the books written or edited by us and quoted by Blaug
can quickly check whether this is true. A look into the subject indexes or table of
contents of the three works might suffice: 'division of labor, 18, 268, 328n, 330n,
433, 471–2' (Kurz and Salvadori 1995); see, especially, the entries 'Cumulative
Causation', 'Division of Labour' and 'Growth' in Kurz and Salvadori (1998a);
'division of labour 3, 57, 59, 68–9, 73, 86, 192, 242; see also returns, increasing'
(Kurz and Salvadori, 1998b).

Blaug contends that 'Kurz and Salvadori (1998b, pp. 16, 53) refer to "free or
perfect competition" as if it were the same thing' (p. 230). The reader will search
in vain for the expression 'free or perfect competition' on the indicated pages of
our book. As a matter of fact, on those pages the concept of competition, whether
'free' or 'perfect', is never mentioned. Is it possible that Blaug erroneously referred
to our 1998b book where he should instead have referred to our 1995 one?[25] On
p. 53 of the latter there is no reference to the concept of competition; and on p. 16
we refer explicitly only to 'free competition' in the context of a discussion of the
classical approach. (That concept was defined at the very outset of that book in
terms of 'the absence of significant and lasting barriers to entry or exit'; see Kurz
and Salvadori, 1995, p. 1.) While there is no evidence whatsoever in support of
Blaug's accusation, there is, on the contrary, a lot of evidence in support of the
fact that in our view the two concepts are *not* the same thing. We are perfectly
aware of the fact that the two concepts are radically different, in particular that
the classical concept does not define the market form and thus competition in
terms of the number of agents operating on each side of the market. The difference
between the two concepts is reflected in the subject index of our 1995 book, which
has both 'competition, free' and 'competition, perfect', but not 'free or perfect
competition'. Moreover, the title of chapter 1 of the book is 'Free competition and
long-period positions'. One can only wonder how this could have escaped Blaug's
attention. His claim that 'We read ... Kurz, Salvadori ... in vain looking for so

---

24 Incidentally, our criticism of the view Blaug now considers untenable was first put forward in Kurz
and Salvadori (1993), a paper reprinted in Kurz and Salvadori (1998b). See also Salvadori (1977)
and Steedman (1975, 1995) for critical discussions of some of Blaug's views.

25 There are instances in Blaug's paper where it is obvious that he confused our two books. For
example, on p. 215 he cites (not fully accurately) a passage from our 1998b book. Immediately
afterwards he adds: 'However, approximately 200 out of the 600 pages of their book are devoted to
matters of historical exegesis, demonstrating clearly that what may well have started out for the two
authors as a useful rational reconstruction serves them at the same time as a penetrating historical
reconstruction.' Since our 1998 book has only 283 pages, Blaug's reference cannot be to it. It is
more likely that he had in mind our 1995 book, which has 571 pages.

much as a reference to the classical conception of competition' (p. 230) squarely contradicts the facts.[26]

Blaug writes: 'A recent handbook to classical economics, edited by Kurz and Salvadori (1998a), adds *more than one hundred names* to the list of those who endorse the Sraffian "understanding" of classical economics' (p. 218, fn. 4, emphasis added). The reference is to the two volumes of *The Elgar Companion to Classical Economics*. The companion has altogether 129 authors who contributed altogether 187 entries, some written jointly by two authors. When planning the work we were keen to involve all those who we knew were experts of classical economic thought, old and new, or aspects thereof. We sent out the list of entries prepared by us, asking for criticism and suggestions.[27] In the introduction to the companion we stated:

> In selecting entries and authors, we took pains to arrange for a fairly compre-
> hensive treatment of the subject, written by some of the most distinguished
> scholars in the field. It hardly needs to be stressed that our notion of classical
> economics had some impact on the decision as to whom we should invite to
> write on what. However, aware of the fact that other scholars entertain differ-
> ent views on the matter, we were keen to make sure that these views are heard
> in these volumes. This does not mean that the reader should expect a perspec-
> tive on classical economics and its major representatives that is equidistant
> from the different interpretations available. Whilst this Companion has a clear
> orientation, it is not, we hope, one-sided.
>
> (Kurz and Salvadori, 1998a, p. xiv)

We wonder whom of the following randomly selected names of contributors to the *Companion* Mark Blaug regards as scholars who 'endorse the Sraffian "understanding" of classical economics': Stephan Böhm, Mauro Boianovsky, Anthony Brewer, Vivienne Brown, José Luis Cardoso, Carlo Casarosa, Bruce T. Elmslie, Walter Eltis, Gilbert Faccarello, Riccardo Faucci, Heiner Ganssmann, Marco E. L. Guidi, Samuel Hollander, Aiko Ikeo, Bruna Ingrao, Prue Kerr, Mario Morroni, Fred Moseley, Antoin Murphy, Takashi Negishi, Denis P. O'Brien, Ugo Pagano, Morris Perlman, Cosimo Perrotta, Pier Luigi Porta, Heinz Rieter, Paul A. Samuelson, Francis Seton, Andrew Skinner, Philippe Steiner, Richard

---

26 The passage quoted above continues: 'And why this lacuna in such otherwise acute economists? Because there is no competition of any kind in Sraffa, not even of the perfect-competition variety. Competitive prices are just competitive prices in Sraffa, and not a word is wasted on telling us how we got there and how we would get back to them in case of a demand or supply shock' (p. 231). According to Smith, under free competition the market mechanism ensures that market prices constantly tend towards natural prices (see *WN*, I.vii.5). This view is shared by Ricardo. Sraffa (1960, p. 9) emphasizes that his concern is precisely with these kind of prices. Hence it is clear that he presupposes competitive conditions in the classical sense.

27 We invited, among others, also Mark Blaug to contribute. Unfortunately, he declined on the ground of his involvement with the publisher of the *Companion*.

Sturn, Stefano Zamagni. Even if Blaug's classification applied to all those not mentioned (which we do not imply, of course), he would be in need of at least four more names in order to arrive at the minimum of 101 names suggested in the passage quoted above.

Acknowledgements

We are grateful to Christian Bidard, Carlo Casarosa, Giancarlo de Vivo, Gilbert Faccarello, Pierangelo Garegnani, Christian Gehrke, Geoffrey Harcourt, Samuel Hollander, Peter Kalmbach, Philippe Mongin, Gary Mongiovi, Bertram Schefold and Ian Steedman for valuable suggestions and comments on an earlier version of this paper. We also benefitted from reading a comment, by Carlo Panico, on a previous version of Blaug's paper, delivered at a Conference in Rome in memory of Giovanni Caravale. We should also like to thank the participants of a session at the annual conference of the European Society for the History of Economic Thought, Graz, 24–27 February 2000, and of a seminar at the University of Rome III in May 2000 for useful discussions. The responsibility for any remaining errors and the views presented rests entirely with the authors. Neri Salvadori gratefully acknowledges financial supports from MURST and CNR.

References

Blaug, Mark 1980. *The Methodology of Economics: How Economists Explain*, Cambridge: Cambridge University Press.

Blaug, Mark 1987. Classical Economics. In J. Eatwell, M. Milgate and P. Newman eds, *The New Palgrave: A Dictionary of Economics*, London: Macmillan, vol. 1.

Blaug, Mark [1962] 1997. *Economic Theory in Retrospect*, Cambridge: Cambridge University Press, 5th edn.

Blaug, Mark 1999. Misunderstanding Classical Economics: The Sraffian Interpretation of the Surplus Approach. *HOPE*, 31.2: 213–36.

Böhm-Bawerk, Eugen von 1892. Wert, Kosten und Grenznutzen. *Jahrbücher für Nationalökonomie und Statistik* (Third Series), 3: 321–67.

Clark, John Bates 1899. *The Distribution of Wealth. A Theory of Wages, Interest and Profits*, New York: Macmillan. Reprint 1965: New York, Kelley.

Garegnani, Pierangelo 1976. On a Change in the Notion of Equilibrium in Recent Work on Value and Distribution. In M. Brown, K. Sato and P. Zarembka eds, *Essays in Modern Capital Theory*, Amsterdam: North Holland.

Garegnani, Pierangelo 1984. Value and Distribution in the Classical Economists and Marx. *Oxford Economic Papers*, 36.2: 291–325.

Gehrke, Christian, Heinz D. Kurz and Neri Salvadori 2003. Ricardo on Agricultural Improvements: A Note. *Scottish Journal of Political Economy*, 50.

Jeck, Albert and Heinz D. Kurz 1983. David Ricardo: Ansichten zur Maschinerie. In H. Hagemann and P. Kalmbach eds, *Technischer Fortschritt und Beschäftigung*, Frankfurt am Main: Campus, 38–166.

Jevons, William Stanley 1965. *The Theory of Political Economy*, 1st edn 1871. Reprint of the 5th edn 1957 by arrangement with H. Stanley Jevons, New York: Kelley.

Kurz, Heinz D. 1998. Marx on Technological Change: The Ricardian Heritage. In R. Bellofiore ed., *Marxian Economics: A Reappraisal. Essays on Volume III of Capital*, London: Macmillan, 119–38.

Kurz, Heinz D. and Neri Salvadori 1993. The 'Standard commodity' and Ricardo's Search for an 'invariable measure of value'. In M. Baranzini and G. C. Harcourt eds, *The Dynamics of the Wealth of Nations. Growth, Distribution and Structural Change. Essays in Honour of Luigi Pasinetti*, New York: St Martin Press, 95–123.

Kurz, Heinz D. and Neri Salvadori 1995. *Theory of Production: A Long-Period Analysis*, Cambridge: Cambridge University Press.

Kurz, Heinz D. and Neri Salvadori eds 1998a. *The Elgar Companion to Classical Economics*, 2 vols, Cheltenham, UK: Edward Elgar.

Kurz, Heinz D. and Neri Salvadori 1998b. *Understanding 'Classical' Economics: Studies in Long-Period Theory*, London: Routledge.

Kurz, Heinz D. and Neri Salvadori 1999. Theories of 'Endogenous' Growth in Historical Perspective. In M. Bruno ed., *Contemporary Economic Issues. Proceedings of the Eleventh World Congress of the International Economic Association, Tunis*, vol. 4: *Economic Behaviour and Design*, edited by M. Sertel, Houndmills, Basingstoke and London: Macmillan, 225–61.

Kurz, Heinz D. and Neri Salvadori 2002. One Theory or Two? Walras's Critique of Ricardo. *History of Political Economy*, 34: 365–98.

Lakatos, Imre 1978a. *Philosophical Papers*, J. Worrall and G. Currie eds, 2 vols, Cambridge: Cambridge University Press.

Lakatos, Imre 1978b. History of Science and its Rational Reconstructions. In I. Lakatos, *Philosophical Papers*, vol. I: *The Methodology of Scientific Research Programmes*, J. Worrall and G. Currie eds, Cambridge: Cambridge University Press, 102–38.

Marx, Karl 1954. *Capital*, Moscow: Progress Publishers, vol. I. English translation of *Das Kapital*, vol. I (1867), Hamburg: Meissner.

Marx, Karl 1959. *Capital*, Moscow: Progress Publishers, vol. III. English translation of *Das Kapital*, vol. III, F. Engels ed. (1894), Hamburg: Meissner.

Mill, James (1844). *Elements of Political Economy*, 1st edn 1821; 3rd edn 1826, reprint 1844, London: Henry G. Bohn.

Ricardo, David 1951–73. *The Works and Correspondence of David Ricardo*. Edited by Piero Sraffa with the collaboration of M. H. Dobb, 11 vols, Cambridge: Cambridge University Press. In the text referred to as *Works*, volume number.

Salvadori, Neri 1977. Blaug e la critica della teoria neoclassica della distribuzione. In M. Blaug, *La Rivoluzione di Cambridge*, Napoli: Liguori, 1977.

Smith, A. 1976. *An Inquiry into the Nature and Causes of the Wealth of Nations*, 1st edn 1776, vol. II of *The Glasgow Edition of the Works and Correspondence of Adam Smith*, R. H. Campbell, A. S. Skinner and W. B. Todd eds, Oxford: Oxford University Press. In the text quoted as *WN*, book number, chapter number, section number, paragraph number.

Sraffa, Piero 1925. Sulle relazioni fra costo e quantità prodotta. *Annali di Economia*, 2: 277–328. English translation in Luigi L. Pasinetti ed., *Italian Economic Papers*, vol. 3, Bologna: Il Mulino and Oxford: Oxford University Press, 1999.

Sraffa, Piero 1926. The Laws of Returns under Competitive Conditions. *Economic Journal*, 36: 535–50.

Sraffa, Piero 1960. *Production of Commodities by Means of Commodities. Prelude to a Critique of Economic Theory*, Cambridge: Cambridge University Press.

Steedman, Ian 1975. Critique of the Critic. (Review of M. Blaug, *The Cambridge Revolution: Success or Failure?* Hobart Paperback No. 6, The Institute of Economic Affair.) *The Times Higher Education Supplement*, 31 January 1975.

Steedman, Ian 1995. Sraffian Economics and the Capital Controversy. In F. Moseley ed., *Heterodox Economic Theories: True or False?*, Aldershot: Edward Elgar.

Stirati, Antonella 1994. *The Theory of Wages in Classical Economics. A Study of Adam Smith, David Ricardo and their Contemporaries*, Aldershot: Edward Elgar.

Walras, Léon 1954. *Elements of Pure Economics*. London: Allen and Unwin. English translation by W. Jaffé of the definitive edition of *Eléments d'economie politique pure*, first published 1874, Lausanne.

Wicksell, Knut 1954. *Value, Capital and Rent*. Translation of the German original (1893), London: Allen and Unwin.

Wicksteed, Philip Henry 1999. *Das Kapital*: A Criticism. Originally published in *ToDay*, vol. II (New Series), October 1884, 388–409. Reprinted in *Collected Works of Philip Henry Wicksteed*, edited and introduced by Ian Steedman, Thoemmes Press: Bristol, vol. II, 705–33.

Wieser, Friedrich von 1884. *Über den Ursprung und die Hauptgesetze des wirthschaftlichen Werthes*, Wien: Alfred Hölder.

3 'Classical' roots of input–output analysis*

A short account of its long prehistory

Heinz D. Kurz and Neri Salvadori

1. Introduction

According to Wassily Leontief, 'Input–output analysis is a practical extension of
the classical theory of general interdependence which views the whole economy
of a region, a country and even of the entire world as a single system and sets
out to describe and to interpret its operation in terms of directly observable basic
structural relationships' (Leontief, 1987, p. 860).

The key terms in this characterization are 'classical theory', 'general interdependence' and 'directly observable basic structural relationships'. In this overview of
contributions, which can be said to have prepared the ground for input–output analysis proper, 'classical theory' will be interpreted to refer to the contributions of the
early classical economists, from William Petty to David Ricardo; further elaborated
by authors such as Karl Marx, Vladimir K. Dmitriev, Ladislaus von Bortkiewicz
and Georg von Charasoff; and culminating in the works of John von Neumann and
Piero Sraffa. 'General interdependence' will be taken to involve two intimately
intertwined problems, which, in a first step of the analysis, may however be treated
separately. First, there is the problem of *quantity*, for which a structure of the levels
of operation of processes of production is needed, in order to guarantee the reproduction of the means of production that are used up in the course of production
and the satisfaction of some 'final demand'; that is, the needs and wants of the different groups (or 'classes') of society, perhaps making allowance for the growth of
the system. Second, there is the problem of *price*, for which a structure of exchange
values of the different products or commodities is needed in order to guarantee
a distribution of income between the different classes of income recipients that is
consistent with the repetition of the productive process on a given (or increasing)
level. It is a characteristic feature of input–output analysis that both the independent
and the dependent variables are to be 'directly observable', at least in principle.
The practical importance of this requirement is obvious, but there is also a theoretical motivation for it: the good of an economic analysis based on magnitudes
that cannot be observed, counted and measured is necessarily uncertain.

* Reprinted with permission from *Economic Systems Research*, Vol. 12, No. 2, 2000.

In this chapter, an attempt is made to locate input–output analysis within economics and to show which tradition in economic thought it belongs to. This necessitates tracing its roots to earlier economic theory. We shall see that input–output analysis can indeed look back at a formidable history prior to its own proper inception, which is often dated from the early writings of Wassily Leontief. These writings include his 1928 paper 'Die Wirtschaft als Kreislauf' (The economy as a circular flow) (Leontief, 1928) and his 1936 paper on 'Quantitative input–output relations in the economic system of the United States' (Leontief, 1936). Because of its applied character, the latter is occasionally considered 'the beginning of what has become a major branch of quantitative economics' (Rose and Miernyk, 1989, p. 229). The account of the prehistory of input–output analysis may also throw light on wider issues which played an important role in the past, but are commonly set aside in many, but not all, modern contributions to input–output analysis. This concerns, first and foremost, the subject of value and distribution. While in earlier authors, and also in Leontief (1928), that issue figured prominently, in modern contributions it is frequently set aside or dealt with in a cavalier way. This raises a problem, because production, distribution and relative prices are intimately intertwined and cannot, in principle, be tackled independently of one another. Scrutinizing the earlier literature shows why.

The historical point of view provides some new perspectives on the potentialities of input–output analysis. This is the main motivation for writing this chapter. It goes without saying that only a very small selection of the relevant historical material can be reviewed. It is to be hoped, however, that the chapter contains some useful hints of the origins and gradual development of certain concepts used in modern input–output analysis, which allow the reader to locate its place in the history of economics and to see whether and where this history is characterized by continuity, or otherwise. By way of contrast with earlier contributions, the chapter may also contribute to a better understanding of the method, scope and content of contemporary input–output analysis, both its strengths and weaknesses, and its potential for further development. The present chapter leads up to the material covered in the survey articles by Stone (1984) and Rose and Miernyk (1989).[1]

It is perhaps useful to specify more clearly right at the beginning of this chapter what is meant by the *classical* approach to the theory of value and distribution and to contrast it with the alternative marginalist or *neoclassical* approach. In the theory of value and distribution, the elaborated versions of the former typically start from the following set of data:

(i) The set of technical alternatives from which cost-minimizing producers can choose. (In an extreme case, only one technique is taken to be available; i.e., the problem of the choice of technique is set aside.)

---

1 In preparing this chapter we have made extensive use of the material contained in Kurz and Salvadori (1995, 1998). See also the 'Introduction to Part I: Foundations of Input–Output Analysis' in Kurz *et al.* (1998; vol. I, pp. xix–xxxviii).

(ii) The size and composition of the social product, reflecting the needs and wants of the members of the different classes of society and the requirements of reproduction and capital accumulation.

(iii) The ruling real wage rate(s) (or, alternatively, the general rate of profit).

(iv) The quantities of different qualities of land available and the known stocks of depletable resources, such as mineral deposits. (In an extreme case, natural resources are, for simplicity, set aside; i.e. taken to be 'free goods'.)

In the analysis the emphasis is on free competition; that is, the absence of significant barriers to entry in and exit from markets. The treatment of wages (or, alternatively, the rate of profit) as an independent variable, and of the other distributive variables – the rate of profit (the wage rate) and the rents of land – as dependent residuals exhibits a fundamental *asymmetry* in the classical approach. Prices are considered to be the means of distributing the social surplus in the form of profits and rents (and possibly interest). It also deserves to be emphasized that these data, or independent variables, all satisfy Leontief's criterion of observability. Moreover, these data are sufficient to determine the unknowns, or dependent variables: the rate of profit (the wage rate), the rent rates and the set of relative prices supporting the cost-minimizing system of producing the given levels of output. No other data, such as, for example, demand functions for commodities and factors of production are needed. The classical approach allows the consistent determination of the variables under consideration. It does so by separating the determination of income distribution and prices from that of quantities, taken as given in (ii) above. The latter were considered as determined in another part of the theory; that is, the analysis of capital accumulation, structural change and socio-economic development.

In contradistinction, the set of data in terms of which the neoclassical approach attempts to determine normal income distribution and relative prices exhibits some striking differences from the classical approach. First, it introduces independent variables, or explanatory factors, that are not directly observable, such as agents' preferences or utility functions. Second, it takes as given not only the amounts of natural resources available but also the economy's 'initial endowments' of labour and 'capital'. The data from which neoclassical theory typically begins its reasoning are:

(a) The set of technical alternatives from which cost-minimizing producers can choose.

(b) The preferences of consumers.

(c) The initial endowments of the economy with all 'factors of production', including 'capital', and the distribution of property rights among individual agents.

The basic novelty of marginalist theory consists of the following. While the received classical approach conceives of the real wage as determined prior to profits and rents, in the neoclassical approach all kinds of income are explained *symmetrically* in terms of supply and demand with regard to the services of the respective factors of production: labour, 'capital' and land. Supply and demand are conceptualized as functional relationships (or correspondences) between the price of a service (or good) and the quantity supplied or demanded. Here, there is no need to enter into a discussion of the marginalist long-period theory and its difficulties (see for example, Kurz and Salvadori, 1995, ch. 14). Suffice it to say that while Leontief's characterization of input–output analysis, cited above, appears to be fully compatible with the classical approach, it is not obvious that it can be reconciled with the neoclassical one. This chapter provides some evidence indicating why this is so.

The structure of the chapter is the following. Section 2 deals briefly with William Petty and Richard Cantillon, to whom we owe clear statements of the concepts of production as a circular flow, reproduction and surplus product. Section 3 turns to the physiocrats, placing special emphasis on François Quesnay's *Tableau Économique*. Section 4 is devoted to a summary of ideas put forward by Achille-Nicolas Isnard, who was a critic of the narrow concept of productivity entertained by Quesnay and who stressed the role of prices in distributing the social surplus. Section 5 deals with the contribution of Robert Torrens, who anticipated, in embryonic form, the duality relationship between the quantity and the price system. Section 6 summarizes the contribution of Karl Marx, focusing attention on the schemes of reproduction in his theoretical construction. Section 7 has a look at the work of Vladimir K. Dmitriev who formalized Ricardo's approach to the theory of relative prices and income distribution, and the work of Ladislaus von Bortkiewicz who elaborated on Dmitriev's analysis in his criticism of Marx's labour value-based reasoning. Section 8 provides an overview of the contribution of Georg von Charasoff who analysed the duality between quantity and price system and anticipated the Leontief inverse. Section 9 turns to Wassily Leontief's early contributions; the emphasis is on his essay on the economy as a circular flow and his early input–output analysis. It is argued that Leontief's approach is firmly rooted in the classical tradition of economic thought and, setting aside some purely formal similarities, has little in common with Walras's general equilibrium model. Section 10 draws the attention to Robert Remak's contribution to establishing the existence of a unique non-negative solution to the relevant system of linear equations. Section 11 contains some concluding remarks.

2. Contributions prior to the writings of the physiocrats: Petty and Cantillon

The importance of early contributions to the development of classical Political Economy lies first and foremost in the concepts and method put forward. Thus, the concepts of production as a circular flow, of productive interdependences between different sectors of the economy and of social surplus are clearly discernible in earlier authors. Scrutinizing their works, the attentive reader will come across some primitive conceptualizations of input–output systems designed to portray the relationships of production in the economy. These generally form the basis of an inquiry into the laws governing the production and distribution of the wealth of a nation. It is hardly an exaggeration to say that input–output analysis is an offspring of systematic economic analysis whose inception is in the seventeenth and eighteenth centuries. In this section this will be documented in terms of a few authors writing before the physiocrats.

While the notion of productive interdependence between different producers in a system characterized by the division of labour and that of the normal cost of production are already present in embryonic form in the doctrines of *justum pretium* (just price) in scholastic economic thought, an important author in the genealogy of input–output analysis is William Petty (1623–87). He coined the famous dictum: 'Labour is the Father and active principle of Wealth, as Lands are the Mother' (Petty, 1986, p. 68). Marx considered him the founder of classical Political Economy (cf. Marx, 1954, p. 85, fn. 2). As early as the *Treatise of Taxes and Contributions*, his first economic work, published in 1662, Petty put forward a clear concept of *social surplus*. He expressed the agricultural surplus as corn output minus necessary corn input, including the subsistence of labourers measured in terms of corn, and identified it with the *rent* of land (Petty, 1986, p. 43).

Petty pointed out that, given the means of subsistence per person, the surplus can also be expressed in terms of the extra number of people that could be maintained by a certain number of labourers engaged in the production of necessaries, given the socio-technical condition of production. He regarded the cost of production of commodities as the main cause determining their true or 'natural value', which was seen to measure the difficulty of acquiring them. While the 'natural value' expresses the 'permanent Causes' governing the price of things, the 'accidental value' also reflects the 'contingent Causes' ruling in a particular situation (Petty, 1986, pp. 51 and 90). His main concern was, of course, with the 'natural' magnitudes. Hence, Petty saw the aspects of the production, distribution and disposal of the wealth of a nation as intimately intertwined, and the problem of value as reflecting the interrelationship among these aspects. There is no discussion of profits in Petty: since in his time most trades were in the hands of artisans, profits were not clearly distinguishable from wages. It is worth mentioning that Petty already introduced the principle of extensive (differential) rent in its simplest form: rent owing to the different distances of the plots of land on which corn is grown from, for example, the town, where most of the net output of corn is consumed (see Petty, 1986, p. 48). He was clear about the fact that larger amounts of corn may only be provided at rising unit cost.

Richard Cantillon (1697–1734), who was greatly influenced by Petty's work, distinguished between market price and 'intrinsic value' of a commodity. Of the latter he wrote in his *Essai sur la nature du commerce en général*, published posthumously in 1755, that it 'is the measure of the quantity of Land and of Labour entering into its production, having regard to the fertility or produce of the Land and to the quality of Labour' (Cantillon, 1931, p. 29; similarly p. 107). Market prices may deviate from natural prices or 'intrinsic values' due to a mismatch of demand and actual production. This deviation is reflected in differences in entrepreneurial rates of return, which will prompt producers to reallocate their capital. In this way market prices will tend to be equal with 'intrinsic values', which themselves are taken to be invariant or only slowly changing (see Cantillon, 1931, p. 31). This foreshadows Adam Smith's idea of market prices oscillating around and gravitating towards natural prices.

Cantillon saw a tripartite distribution of the (gross) product between the proprietors of land, farmers and undertakers, and assistants and 'mechanicks', and had a very clear concept of *reproduction*. He emphasized that all members of society subsist on the basis of the produce of land. This seems to imply that, in his view, the source of any surplus can only be agriculture. However, there are passages in the *Essai* according to which a surplus can also arise in manufacturing as profits (see, e.g. Cantillon, 1931, p. 203).

3. François Quesnay and the *Tableau Économique*

The view that only agriculture can generate a surplus, a *produit net*, was most clearly expressed by Quesnay (1694–1774) and his followers (INED, 1958). It was around the concept of net product that Quesnay's entire economic analysis and not only the *Tableau Économique* was built: in particular, it was taken to hold the key to an explanation of the distribution of income in contemporary France. The *Tableau* contains a sophisticated two-sector expression of the production of commodities by means of commodities. Marx called the *Tableau* 'an extremely brilliant conception, incontestably the most brilliant for which political economy has up to then been responsible' (Marx, 1956, p. 344), and elaborated his schemes of reproduction taking it as a starting point. Leontief related his 1936 paper explicitly to the work of Quesnay when he wrote: 'The statistical study presented . . . may be best defined as an attempt to construct, on the basis of available statistical materials, a *Tableau Économique* of the United States for 1919 and 1929' (Leontief, 1936, p. 105).

The *Tableau*, the first version of which was published in 1758, was meant to portray the whole process of production, distribution and expenditure as a reproduction process, with the circulation of commodities and money as a part and parcel of this process. An important goal of the analysis was to lay bare the origin of revenue and thus the factors affecting its size – factors that can be manipulated by economic policy aimed at fostering national wealth and power.

According to their economic role in the reproduction process, Quesnay distinguished among the 'productive class' (*classe productive*), the 'sterile class' (*classe stérile*) and the class of proprietors of land and natural resources (*classe propriétaire*). The productive class, that is, those working in primary production, in particular, agriculture, are called 'productive' because the value of the commodities produced by them exceeds the incurred costs of production. The difference between total proceeds and total costs, where the latter include the upkeep of those employed in the primary sector, is distributed as rent to the propertied class. In contradistinction to the productive class, the sterile class, that is, those employed in manufacturing (and commerce), do not generate a revenue, or surplus: the prices of manufactures cover just costs of production, including, of course, the subsistence of artisans, tradesmen, etc. In the two-sector scheme put forward, neither sector can exist on its own. In addition to *intra*sectoral flows of commodities there are *inter*sectoral flows: agriculture receives produced means of production from industry, and industry receives raw materials and means of subsistence from agriculture. Indeed, both (composite) commodities enter directly or indirectly into the production of both commodities. Hence, the system of production underlying the *Tableau* can be represented by a matrix of material inputs (i.e. means of production-cum-means of subsistence) that is indecomposable.

The characteristic features of the *Tableau* can be summarized as follows. First, the *Tableau* starts from the following set of data or independent variables: the system of production in use, defined in terms of (i) the (average) methods of production employed to produce (ii) given levels of (aggregate) output; and (iii) given real rates of remuneration of those employed in the two sectors of the economy; that is, essentially, wages.[2] The reference is to some 'normal' levels of output, defined in terms of some average of the conditions of production over a sequence of years (balancing good and bad harvests). Second, the *Tableau* distinguishes between capital of different durability, where all kinds of capital relate to productive capital only. The *avances annuelles* refer to yearly advances or circulating capital (raw materials, sustenance of workers, etc.); the *avances primitives* to fixed capital (tools, buildings, machines, horses, etc.); and the *avances foncières* to capital incorporated in the land (land melioration of all kinds, etc.). Exclusively those parts of capital that are used up during the process of production and have to be replaced periodically are taken into account in the table. This presupposes that the stocks of durable means of production employed in different branches of the economy, their modes of utilization and thus their patterns of wear and tear (and therefore depreciation) are known. Third, all shares of income other than wages are explained in terms of the surplus product (representing a certain surplus value), or residual, left after the means of subsistence in the support of workers (and masters) and what is necessary for the replacement of the used-up means of production has been deducted from the annual output. Hence, the distributive variables are treated *asymmetrically*: the wage rate is taken to be an *exogenous* variable, whereas the (rate of) rent is an *endogenous* variable. Fourth, and closely related to what has just been said, the physiocrats conceived of any surplus product that may exist as *generated* in the sphere of production and only *realized* in the sphere of circulation. Fifth, the process of circulation is assumed to work out smoothly. This involves, *inter alia*, the existence of a system of *relative* prices which support the process of reproduction, and a system of *absolute* prices compatible with the stock of money available in the economy and the going habits of payment. While in the *Tableau* the problem of accumulation of capital is set aside, it is well known that Quesnay was concerned with the sources of economic growth and stressed the role of accumulation (see Eltis, 1975).

Before we turn to the English classical economists, the work of one man must be mentioned, not least because it is hardly known and yet can be said to have anticipated important findings of the subsequent literature: Achille-Nicolas Isnard.

---

2 Notice the close similarity to the data describing the classical approach in the Introduction.

4. Achille-Nicolas Isnard

Isnard (1749–1803), a French engineer, was a critic of the physiocratic doctrine that only agriculture is productive. In his view, this doctrine was contradicted already by the fact that the *produit net* in the *Tableau Économique* consisted both of agricultural and manufactured products. More important, Isnard argued that whether a sector of the economy generates an income in excess of its costs of production cannot be decided independently of the exchange ratios between commodities, or *relative* prices. The latter do not only reflect the real physical costs of production of the various commodities, but, in addition, the rule according to which the surplus product is distributed between the propertied classes.[3]

In 1781, Isnard published, in two volumes, his *Traité des richesses* (Isnard, 1781); volume I is of particular interest to us. Isnard's analysis revolved around the concepts of production as a circular flow and of surplus, or 'disposable wealth'. He wrote: 'In the whole of the riches, and setting aside values, there are in reality two parts, one required in production, the other destined to enjoyments . . . The latter is the noble part of goods and the part which is nobly enjoyed by the proprietors' (Isnard, 1781, pp. 35–6).[4] Isnard added that they, or a part of them, may also be accumulated in order 'to increase the mass of productive wealth' (Isnard, 1781, p. 36). He emphasized that the magnitude of the surplus depends on the technical conditions of production and the 'exigence of nature' (Isnard, 1781, p. 37).

The impression generated by the physiocrats that only agriculture is productive is closely related to the system of prices underlying their schema. These prices are such that the entire *produit net* is indeed appropriated by the landowners in the form of rent. Other rules of distribution would immediately reveal the peculiarity of the physiocratic doctrine. Isnard stressed: 'The values of the different products determine the portions of total wealth allotted to the various producers; these portions change with the values of the objects which each producer has to acquire for production' (Isnard, 1781, p. xv; similarly p. 37). The first book of the *Traité* was designed to clarify, by way of a mathematical argument, the role of relative prices as the media to realize a given distribution of income.

Isnard started with a system of the division of labour with only two commodities. Each producer produces a certain amount of one commodity, a part of which he uses as a means of production and as a means of subsistence. He swaps the sectoral surplus for the other commodity he is in need of, but does not produce himself. Isnard put forward the following system of simultaneous equations (our notation):

$$(1 - a)p_1 + bp_2 = p_1$$
$$ap_1 + (1 - b)p_2 = p_2$$

where a represents the surplus of the first commodity, b that of the second, and p_1 and p_2 are the unit prices of commodities 1 and 2, respectively. He showed that

---

3 For the following see also Jaffé (1969) and Gilibert (1981).
4 Translations of sources of which no English version was available are ours.

the exchange rate that guarantees the repetition of the process of production and consumption is given by: $p_1/p_2 = b/a$.

He then turned to a system with three commodities and argued that the exchange ratios between the commodities can again be determined, provided we are given (i) the commodity surplus in each line of production and (ii) the way it is distributed between the two remaining sectors. Let a, b and c be the amounts of surplus in the three sectors. Each surplus is then divided in two parts, depending on the sector (or proprietor) they are designated for. Let e be the share of the surplus of commodity 1 earmarked for sector 2; $(1 - e)$ is, accordingly, the share that goes to sector 3. Let f be the share of the surplus of commodity 2 earmarked for sector 3; $(1 - f)$ is, accordingly, the share that goes to sector 1. And let h be the share of the surplus of commodity 3 earmarked for sector 1; $(1 - h)$ is, accordingly, the share that goes to sector 2. Isnard emphasized that a solution to the problem of relative prices can be found 'if there are as many equations as there are commodities' (Isnard, 1781, p. 19). The system of equations he put forward is

$$\left.\begin{array}{r}(1 - a)p_1 + (1 - f)bp_2 + hcp_3 = p_1 \\ eap_1 + (1 - b)p_2 + (1 - h)cp_3 = p_2 \\ (1 - e)ap_1 + fbp_2 + (1 - c)p_3 = p_3\end{array}\right\} \quad\quad (3.1)$$

where p_i is the price of commodity i, $i = 1, 2, 3$. This is a closed system in the sense that the above coefficients reflect both the amounts of the means of production plus the means of subsistence needed in the three sectors (per unit of output), that is, what the classical economists were to call 'productive consumption', and the consumption of the propertied classes, that is, 'unproductive consumption'.

Obviously, the sum of the quantities of any column is equal to the sum of the corresponding row. For example, the sum of the second column is $(1 - f)b + (1 - b) + fb$, which equals 1. This means that only two of the three equations are independent. Taking one of the commodities as a standard of value, or numeraire, as it was to be called later, system (3.1) allows one to determine the remaining two prices. In this view, prices reflect the dominant conditions of production and distribution. The prices of the *Tableau* represent but a special system of prices, which gives rise to the misconception that only agriculture is productive. If the producers in agriculture would have to pay more of their own (composite) product per unit of the manufactured (composite) product, the situation would be different: the surplus of agriculture would be smaller or, in the extreme, nil, whereas the surplus of industry would be positive or, in the extreme, equal to the surplus of the system as a whole.

Isnard (1781, p. 36) even put forward a numerical example of two sectors of production which can be tabulated as follows:

10 qr. wheat + 10 t. iron → 40 qr. wheat

5 qr. wheat + 10 t. iron → 60 t. iron

The figures to the left of each arrow give total inputs in the sector, consisting of means of production and means of subsistence in the support of workers, whereas the figure to the right gives gross output. Accordingly, the system as a whole produces a net product consisting of (40 − 15 =) 25 qr. wheat and (60 − 20 =) 40 t. iron. The distribution of this net product between the two kinds of producers cannot be decided independently of the price of wheat relative to that of iron. It is also clear that if the (physical) net product of one of the commodities were nil, this need not imply that the producers of the respective sector would not get a share of the surplus: it all depends on which price ratio occurs. He concluded: 'When a production does not guarantee a producer a disposable income, one must not infer from this that his activity is not productive, because in reality he produces some of the things which are partly absorbed as costs and partly, via the exchanges, are passed on to the class of disposable riches.... Quesnay and *les économistes* were therefore wrong in asserting that industry is generally not productive' (Isnard, 1781, pp. 38–9).

5. Robert Torrens

The concepts of production as a circular flow and of the surplus product surfaced again in the writings of Adam Smith (1723–90), who also provided an analysis of the interdependence of the different sectors of the economy (Smith, 1976, Book V, Ch. V). The concepts are present in David Ricardo's (1772–1823) *Essay on the Influence of a low Price of Corn on the Profits of Stock* published in 1815 (cf. Ricardo, 1951–73; *Works, IV*), and in his *Principles* (cf. Ricardo, 1951–73; *Works, IV*). However, the author who put these concepts again into sharp relief within an explicit input–output framework was Robert Torrens (1780–1864) in the second edition of his *Essay on the External Corn Trade* (cf. Torrens, 1820). In his formulation, the two problems identified above – that of relative quantities and the rate of growth and that of relative prices and the rate of profit – emerged with great clarity.

Torrens made clear that the concept of surplus provides the key to an explanation of shares of income other than wages and the rate of profit. In the *Essay* he determined the agricultural rate of profit in physical terms as the ratio between the net output of corn and corn input (corn as seed and food for the workers) and took the exchange value of manufactured goods relative to corn to be so adjusted that the same rate of profit obtains in manufacturing. This he called a 'general principle' (Torrens, 1820, p. 361) and acknowledged his indebtedness to Ricardo's 'original and profound inquiry into the laws by which the rate of profits is determined' (Torrens, 1820, p. xix).[5]

It was, of course, clear to the older authors that the capital advanced in a sector is never homogeneous with the sector's product. We encounter a first relaxation of this bold assumption in Torrens's *Essay on the Production of Wealth*, published in 1821. There he put forward an example with two sectors, both of which use

---

5 Torrens's 'general principle' is the same thing as the 'basic principle' referred to by Sraffa in his discussion of Ricardo's early theory of profits (cf. Sraffa, 1951, p. xxxi).

both products in the same proportions as inputs (see Torrens, 1821, pp. 372–3). He concluded that the rate of profit is given in terms of the surplus left after the amounts of the used-up means of production and the means of subsistence in the support of labourers have been deducted from gross output. With the surplus and the social capital consisting of the same commodities in the same proportions, the general rate of profit can be determined without having recourse to the system of relative prices.

However, the physical schema is not only important for the determination of the rate of profit (and relative prices), it also provides the basis for assessing the potential for expansion of the economy. As Torrens stressed, 'this surplus, or profit of ten per cent they (i.e. the cultivators and manufacturers) might employ either in setting additional labourers to work, or in purchasing luxuries for immediate enjoyment' (Torrens, 1821, p. 373). If in each sector the entire surplus were to be used for accumulation purposes in the same sector, then the rates of expansion of the two sectors would be equal to one another and equal to the rate of profit. Champernowne in his commentary on von Neumann's growth model was later to call a constellation of equi-proportionate growth a 'quasi-stationary state' (Champernowne, 1945, p. 10).

The next author we have to turn to is Karl Marx. In his treatment of the aspect of quantities, Marx was concerned with studying under which conditions the system is capable of reproducing itself either on the same or an upward spiralling level, that is, the case of 'simple' and that of 'extended reproduction'.

6. Karl Marx

Marx (1818–83) was an attentive student of the writings of the physiocrats and praised Quesnay and his followers as 'the true fathers of modern political economy' (Marx, 1963, p. 44). We have already heard what he had to say about the *Tableau Économique*. The latter was of crucial importance in shaping his own ideas and constituted, in modified form, the backbone both of his theory of reproduction and his theory of value and distribution.[6]

According to Marx the linchpin of the classical approach to the theory of value and distribution is the concept of 'surplus product' – that is, all shares of income other than wages – and its relationship to the real wage. Taking the methods of production employed and thus the productivity of labour as given, the higher the real wage rate, the smaller is the surplus product, and *vice versa*. This idea also constituted the nucleus of the elaborate form of the classical argument in Ricardo with its emphasis on the inverse relationship between the *rate of profit* on the one hand and the real wage rate, or rather the total amount of labour needed to produce the wage commodities, on the other.

6 See, in particular, Bródy (1970) and Gehrke and Kurz (1995).

6.1. The schemes of reproduction

In Marx's view the *Tableau* had been unduly neglected by the English political economists so that an important achievement of economic analysis had been lost sight of for almost an entire century (cf. Marx, 1963, p. 344). He called the system of the physiocrats 'the first systematic conception of capitalistic production' (Marx, 1956, p. 363). The *Tableau* was the foil against which Marx developed his own *schemes of reproduction* (see Marx, 1956, part III). The schemes are concerned with the distribution of labour among the different sectors of the economy. That distribution was envisaged by Marx to depend on the socially dominant techniques of production, the distribution of income between wages and profits, and the expenditures out of these incomes, especially whether or not parts of profits are accumulated. In principle, the quantity system could be studied without any recourse to the problem of valuation. Marx nevertheless chose to provide both a description of the requirements of reproduction in physical terms (use-values) and in value terms (labour values). Thus, he intended to show that the physical reproduction of capital and its value reproduction are two sides of a single coin.

An early version of the scheme of simple reproduction was elaborated in Marx's letter to Engels of 6 July 1863. Scrutiny shows that Marx's scheme shares all the features of Quesnay's *Tableau* enumerated above (cf. Section 3). Marx divided the economy into two 'classes' or 'categories': class I represents the production of the means of subsistence, class II that of the means of production, that is, commodities 'which enter as raw materials, machinery etc. in the process of production'; the latter commodities 'form the *constant capital*' (MEW 1956 *et seq.*). (In volume II of *Capital* the numbering of departments is reversed.) Marx emphasized that the two classes or departments represent productive *aggregates* in a special sense.[7] This becomes clear with regard to agriculture, in which 'a part of the same products (e.g. corn) forms means of subsistence, whereas another part (e.g. corn) enters again as a raw material in its natural form (e.g. as *seeds*) into the reproduction. This does not change things, since according to one characteristic these branches of production belong in class II and according to the other in class I' (MEW 30, p. 363; emphasis in the original).

Marx's numerical example can be rewritten in a form which became prominent with volume II of *Capital* (Marx, 1956, ch. XX), that is,

$$\text{class I:} \quad 700 = 400_c + 100_v + 200_s$$

$$\text{class II:} \quad 933\tfrac{1}{3} = 533\tfrac{1}{3}_c + 133\tfrac{1}{3}_v + 266\tfrac{1}{3}_s$$

where the subscripts c, v and s stand for 'constant capital', 'variable capital' and 'surplus value', respectively. Simple reproduction requires that the constant

---

7 As in the *Tableau* the concept of an 'industry', 'sector' or 'department' is an analytical one. Yet while in Quesnay the dividing line between the two departments is whether a line of production is 'productive' or not, in Marx the dividing line is whether it produces means of production or means of consumption.

capitals used up in both sectors ($400_c + 533\frac{1}{3}_c$) are equal to the total product of class II ($933\frac{1}{3}$); and that the variable capitals, or wages bills ($100_v + 133\frac{1}{3}_v$), plus the surplus values, or profits ($200_s + 266\frac{2}{3}_s$), of the whole system are equal to the total product of class I (700). Accordingly, simple reproduction involves (using again the notation employed in volume II of *Capital*):

$$I(400_c) = II\left(133\tfrac{1}{3}_v + 266\tfrac{2}{3}_s\right)$$

In contrast to Quesnay's *Tableau*, here the labour performed in both sectors is taken to be productive, that is, generating a surplus value. If a part of the surplus value is saved and invested, the system reproduces itself on an ever larger scale. This is dealt with in Marx's schemes of extended reproduction (cf. Marx, 1956, ch. XXI), which provide a theory of the relationship between quantities, or sectoral proportions, and the rate of growth of the economic system as a whole.

6.2. Prices of production

However, Marx saw that the importance of the *Tableau* was not restricted to the problem of quantities and growth: it also provided a much needed *general* framework to determine the general rate of profit consistently. While Ricardo had a clear view of the inverse relationship between the rate of profit and the real wage rate, in Marx's view he had failed to show how the level of the rate of profit was actually ascertained, given the real wage rate. Marx saw that the data on which Ricardo's argument was based were essentially the same as the data (i)–(iii) underlying the *Tableau* (see Section 3). There was a single important difference between the physiocratic and the classical scheme: the rule according to which the social surplus is distributed – as rent in the case of the physiocrats, and as rent and profits in the case of the classical economists from Smith to Ricardo. It was indeed the determination of the general rate of profit which became a major focus of classical analysis. The implicit question was whether Ricardo's labour-based approach could be integrated with an appropriately modified *Tableau*. This reformulation had to leave the basic structure of the approach defined in terms of the exogenous variables untouched. Marx's theory of the general rate of profit and prices of production in part II of volume III of *Capital* can indeed be interpreted as an amalgamation and elaboration of the insights Marx owed, first and foremost, to the physiocrats and Ricardo. There, the problem of the rent of land is set aside altogether. The entire surplus is assumed to accrue in the form of profits at a uniform rate.

Marx made clear that a determination of the rate of profit and relative prices presupposes taking into account the 'total social capital' and its distribution in the different 'spheres of production' (Marx, 1959, pp. 158 and 163). He proposed a two-step procedure which was aptly dubbed 'successivist', as opposed to 'simultaneous' (see von Bortkiewicz, 1906–07, I, p. 38). In a first step he specified the general rate of profit as the ratio between the (labour) value of the economy's surplus product, or surplus value, and the (labour) value of social capital, consisting of a constant capital (means of production) and a variable capital (wages). In a second step this (value) rate of profit was then used to calculate prices. We may illustrate his procedure as follows. Marx started from a description of the economic system divided into several sectors or spheres of production, each of which is represented by an equation giving the value of the sectoral output (z_i) as the sum of the sectoral constant capital (c_i), its variable capital (v_i) and the surplus value (s_i) generated in the sector (cf. Marx, 1959, ch. IX). This description involved given methods of production and a given real wage rate. Otherwise it would be impossible to derive the labour-value magnitudes. With a given and uniform real wage rate and a given and uniform length of the working day (reflecting free competition in the labour market), the rate of surplus value is uniform across sectors. The larger the real wage rate, the larger is the variable capital and the smaller is the sectoral surplus value. Assuming only two sectors in order to facilitate a comparison with the *Tableau* and setting aside the problem of fixed capital, we have

$$z_I = c_I + v_I + s_I$$
$$z_{II} = c_{II} + v_{II} + s_{II}$$

where sector I is now the sector that produces means of production and sector II means of subsistence. It was Marx's contention that from this system *alone*, reflecting the set of data specified above, both the general rate of profit, ρ, and prices of production can be determined. The former is given by

$$\rho = \frac{s_I + s_{II}}{c_I + v_I + c_{II} + v_{II}} = \frac{\Sigma_i s_i}{\Sigma_i (c_i + v_i)}$$

In Marx's view it is here that the labour theory of value is indispensable, because it allegedly allows the determination of the rate of profit *independently of, and prior to*, the determination of relative prices.

In a second step this 'value' rate of profit, ρ, as we may call it, is then used to discount forward sectoral costs of production, or 'cost prices', measured in terms of labour values (cf. Marx, 1959, p. 164). This is the (in)famous problem of the 'Transformation of Values of Commodities into Prices of Production' (Marx, 1959; part II). With p_i, as the value–price transformation coefficient applied to the product of department i, $i = I, II$, we have, following Marx's procedure,

$$\left. \begin{array}{l} z_I p_I = (1 + \rho)(c_I + v_I) \\ z_I p_{II} = (1 + \rho)(c_{II} + v_{II}) \end{array} \right\} \tag{3.2}$$

Counting the number of equations and that of the unknowns, there are two equations with two unknowns: the value–price transformation coefficients p_I and p_{II}. Hence, the 'prices of production' seem to be fully determined.

Marx's successivist procedure cannot be sustained. A first and obvious error concerns the fact that in the above price equations (3.2) the capitals ought to be expressed in price rather than in value terms. Marx was aware of this slip in his argument (cf. Marx, 1959, pp. 164–5 and 206–7), but apparently thought that it could easily be remedied without further consequences. He was wrong. Once the necessary corrections suggested by Marx himself are carried out, it becomes clear that it cannot generally be presumed that the 'transformation' of values into prices of production is relevant to single commodities only, while it is irrelevant to commodity aggregates, such as the surplus product or the social capital, the ratio of which gives the rate of profit. Since the rate of profit cannot be determined before knowing the prices of commodities, and since the prices cannot be determined before knowing the rate of profit, the rate of profit and prices have to be determined *simultaneously* rather than successively.

Does Marx's blunder also falsify his intuition that, starting from the set of data (i)–(iii), which he had discerned in the *Tableau* and Ricardo, relative prices and the rate of profit can be determined in a logically coherent way? An answer to this question was provided by Vladimir K. Dmitriev and Ladislaus von Bortkiewicz.

7. Vladimir Karpovich Dmitriev and Ladislaus von Bortkiewicz

In 1898, the Russian mathematical economist Dmitriev (1868–1913) published, in Russian, 'An attempt at a rigorous analysis' of Ricardo's theory of value and distribution (Dmitriev, 1974). Dmitriev investigated first what is meant by the total amount of labour expended in the production of a commodity and how this amount can be ascertained. In particular, are we in need of a 'historical regress' in order to determine the indirect labour, that is, the one contained in the capital goods used up and thus transferred to the commodity in the course of its production? Dmitriev disposed of this misconception by showing that it is from a knowledge of the current conditions of production of the different commodities alone that one can determine the quantities of labour embodied (see Dmitriev, 1974, p. 44). Assuming single production, that is, setting aside joint production, and using matrix notation, the problem amounts to solving the following system of simultaneous equations:

$$\mathbf{z}^T = \mathbf{z}^T \mathbf{A} + \mathbf{l}^T$$

where $\mathbf{A}$ is the $n \times n$ matrix of material inputs, $\mathbf{l}$ is the n-vector of direct (homogeneous) labour inputs and $\mathbf{z}$ is the n-vector of quantities of labour embodied in the different commodities, or labour values. (T is the sign for transpose.) Replacing repeatedly the $\mathbf{z}$ on the right-hand side of the equation by the right-hand side gives

$$\mathbf{z}^T = \mathbf{l}^T + \mathbf{l}^T \mathbf{A} + \mathbf{l}^T \mathbf{A}^2 + \mathbf{l}^T \mathbf{A}^3 + \cdots, \tag{3.3}$$

where equation (3.3) is known as the 'reduction to dated quantities of labour'. In the single-products case contemplated by Dmitriev there are as many series of dated quantities of labour as there are products, and thus there are as many equations as unknowns.

Next, Dmitriev turned to an analysis of the rate of profit and 'natural' prices. He praised Ricardo, who had clearly specified the factors determining the general rate of profit, that is, (i) the real wage rate and (ii) the technical conditions of production in the wage goods industries: 'Ricardo's immortal contribution was his brilliant solution this seemingly insoluble problem' (Dmitriev, 1974, p. 58). Prices are explained in terms of a reduction to (a finite stream of) dated wage payments, properly discounted forward. With **p** as the n-vector of prices, w as the nominal wage rate and r as the competitive rate of profit, and taking wages as paid *ante factum*, we get from equation (3.3):

$$\mathbf{p}^T = w[(1+r)\mathbf{l}^T + (1+r)^2\mathbf{l}^T\mathbf{A} + (1+r)^3\mathbf{l}^T\mathbf{A}^2 + \cdots] \tag{3.4}$$

Dmitriev also confirmed Ricardo's finding that relative prices are proportional to relative quantities of labour embodied in two special cases only: (i) when the reduction series are linearly dependent pairwise; and (ii) when the rate of profit is zero.

Ricardo's concept of the inverse relationship between the rate of profit and the real wage rate, given the technical conditions of production, or *wage–profit relationship*, was rendered precise in Dmitriev's flow-input point-output framework. Assume that the commodity content of real wages is proportional to the n-vector **b**, **b** $\geqslant$ **0**. Let ω designate the number of units of the elementary real wage basket. Then we have

$$w = \omega\mathbf{p}^T\mathbf{b} \tag{3.5}$$

With the basket **b** as the standard of value,

$$\mathbf{p}^T\mathbf{b} = 1 \tag{3.6}$$

and inserting equation (3.5) in (3.4), multiplying both sides by **b**, and taking into account (3.6), we get

$$1 = \omega[(1+r)\mathbf{l}^T + (1+r)^2\mathbf{l}^T\mathbf{A} + (1+r)^3\mathbf{l}^T\mathbf{A}^2 + \cdots]\mathbf{b} \tag{3.7}$$

which, for a given ω, is one equation to determine the only unknown: r. With a ω that is low enough, equation (3.7) has a unique positive solution.[8] Equation (3.7) also demonstrates the correctness of Ricardo's dictum that the rate of profit depends exclusively on the conditions of production in the industries that produce wage goods and in those industries that directly or indirectly provide the former with means of production.[9]

---

8 It is necessary and sufficient that

$$\omega < 1/(\mathbf{l}^T + \mathbf{l}^T\mathbf{A} + \mathbf{l}^T\mathbf{A}^2 + \cdots)\mathbf{b}$$

9 Dmitriev deserves the credit for having demonstrated that starting from the data of Ricardo's approach, relative prices and the rate of profit can be determined simultaneously. The system is complete and not underdetermined, as Walras (1954, Lesson 40) had objected. Walras's further criticism that Ricardo's 'cost of production explanation of prices' is circular, 'defining prices from prices', while based on a correct observation, is beside the point: prices and the rate of profit are fully determined in terms of the given technical conditions of production and the given real wage rate.

The concept of production as a circular flow and that of the surplus product was further developed by Ladislaus von Bortkiewicz (1868–1931), who was born in St Petersburg into a family of Polish descent. From 1901 he taught economics and statistics at the University of Berlin, the same university which, in the late 1920s, also had Leontief, von Neumann and Robert Remak among its members. In 1906, Bortkiewicz published the first part of his three-part treatise 'Wertrechnung und Preisrechnung im Marxschen System'; the remaining two parts followed in the subsequent year (von Bortkiewicz, 1906–07; I, II and III). (Parts II and III were translated into English as 'Value and price in the Marxian system'; see von Bortkiewicz, 1952.) In 1907 there followed his paper 'Zur Berichtigung der grundlegenden theoretischen Konstruktion von Marx im dritten Band des "Kapital" ' (von Bortkiewicz, 1907) ('On the correction of Marx's fundamental theoretical construction in the third volume of "Capital" '; see von Bortkiewicz, 1952). A major source of inspiration for von Bortkiewicz was Dmitriev's treatment of Ricardo's theory of distribution and 'natural' prices.

The main objects of von Bortkiewicz's contributions can be summarized as follows. First, he wanted to demonstrate that Marx's construction of necessity failed. Second, he was concerned with showing that value analysis is not an indispensable step on the way to a consistent theory of the rate of profit and prices of production. Third, and notwithstanding what has just been said, he wanted to show that prices and the profit rate can be related to value and surplus value magnitudes in a logically consistent way. Fourth, this made him reject the then dominant critique of Marx which erroneously took the value-based reasoning in itself, rather than Marx's mistaken use of it, as the source of various misconceptions. Finally, and perhaps most importantly, von Bortkiewicz attempted to show that Ricardo's doctrine is superior to Marx's in almost every respect. His treatise is indeed as much about Ricardo as it is about Marx. He accused Marx of retrogressing in various ways to opinions that had already been shown to be defective by Ricardo.

Von Bortkiewicz pointed out that the *data* from which the classical approach to the theory of value and distribution starts are sufficient to determine the rate of profit and relative prices; no additional data are needed to determine these variables. He developed his argument both in terms of an approach in which it is assumed that commodities are obtained by a finite stream of labour inputs, that is, production is 'linear' (von Bortkiewicz, 1906–07), and one in which production is 'circular' (von Bortkiewicz, 1907). Following Dmitriev, von Bortkiewicz cast his argument in algebraic form. Considering the set of price equations associated with a given system of production with n commodities, it is recognized that the number of unknowns exceeds the number of equations by two: there are $n + 2$ unknowns (n prices, the nominal wage rate and the rate of profit) and n equations. With the real wage rate given from outside the system and fixing a standard of value or numeraire, one gets two additional equations (and no extra unknown) and the system can be solved for the rate of profit and prices in terms of the numeraire. Von Bortkiewicz, among other things, generalized the approach to cover fixed capital.

As we have seen, von Bortkiewicz was predominantly concerned with the price and distribution aspect, while the quantity and growth aspect was given little attention by him. It was Georg von Charasoff (1877–?) who pointed out a fundamental *duality* between the two.

8. Georg von Charasoff

Von Charasoff was born in Tiflis. He wrote his PhD thesis in mathematics at the University of Heidelberg. He published two books in 1909 and 1910, respectively, both in German, the second of which, *Das System des Marxismus. Darstellung und Kritik*, is of particular interest to us (see von Charasoff, 1910). In it, von Charasoff anticipated several results of modern reformulations of the classical approach and of input–output analysis. Because of his highly condensed and abstract argument, which is mathematical without making use of formal language, his contribution was largely ignored at the time of its publication and has only recently been rediscovered (see Egidi and Gilibert, 1984).

Von Charasoff developed his argument within the framework of an interdependent model of (single) production, which exhibits all the properties of the later input–output model. The central concept of his analysis is that of a 'series of production': it consists of a sequence, starting with any (semipositive) net output vector (where net output is defined exclusive of wage goods), followed by the vector of the means of production and means of subsistence in the support of workers needed to produce this net output vector, then the vector of the means of production and means of subsistence needed to produce the previous vector of inputs, and so on. He called the first input vector 'capital of the first degree', the second input vector 'capital of the second degree', etc. This series 'has the remarkable property that each element of it is both the product of the following and the capital of the preceding element; its investigation is indispensable to the study of all the theoretical questions in political economy' (von Charasoff, 1910, p. 120).

The series under consideration is closely related to the expanded Leontief inverse. Let $\mathbf{y}$ denote the n-dimensional vector of net outputs and $\mathbf{A}$ the $n \times n$-matrix of 'augmented' input coefficients; each coefficient represents the sum of the respective material and wage-good input per unit of output, since von Charasoff, like the classical economists and Marx, reckoned wage payments among capital advances.[10] Then the series is given by

$$\mathbf{y}, \mathbf{A}\mathbf{y}, \mathbf{A}^2\mathbf{y}, \ldots, \mathbf{A}^k\mathbf{y}, \ldots$$

With circular production this series is infinite. Tracing it backwards: first, all commodities that are 'luxury goods' disappear from the picture; next, all commodities that are specific means of production needed to produce the luxury goods disappear; then the specific means of production needed in the production of these

---

10 If a technique is defined in terms of the material input matrix $\mathbf{A}^*$ and the vector of direct labour inputs $\mathbf{l}$, and if $\omega\mathbf{b}$ is the vector of commodities consumed per unit of labour employed, then $\mathbf{A} = \mathbf{A}^* + \omega\mathbf{b}\mathbf{l}^\mathrm{T}$.

means of production disappear, etc. On the assumption that none of the commodities mentioned so far enters in its own production, 'it is clear that from a certain finite point onwards no further exclusions have to be made, and all the remaining elements of the series of production will always be made up of the selfsame means of production, which in the final instance are indispensable in the production of all the different products and which therefore will be called *basic products*'. He stressed: 'The whole problem of price boils down . . . to the determination of the prices of these basic products' (von Charasoff, 1910, p. 120–1).

A further property of the series of production deserves to be stressed: the capital of the second degree (A^2y) is obtained by multiplying the capital of the first degree (Ay) by A. 'Yet since the physical composition of a sum of capitals is obviously always a medium between the physical composition of the summands, it follows that capitals of the second degree deviate from one another to a smaller extent than is the case with capitals of the first degree' (von Charasoff, 1910, p. 123). The farther one goes back, the more equal the compositions of the capitals become; that is, capitals of a sufficiently high degree 'may practically be seen as different quantities of one and the same capital: the *original* or *prime capital*'. This finding is of the utmost importance for determining the rate of profit and the maximum rate of growth of the system. For it turns out that 'this original type, to which all capitals of lower degree converge, possesses the property of growing in the course of the process of production without any qualitative change, and that the rate of its growth gives the general rate of profit' (von Charasoff, 1910, p. 124).

The rate of profit can thus be ascertained in terms of a comparison of two quantities of the same composite commodity: the 'original capital'. Let u designate the n-dimensional vector of an elementary unit of the original capital, $u \geqslant 0$, then Au is the (original) capital corresponding to u, and we have

$$u = (1 + r)Au$$

with r as the general rate of profit. Von Charasoff emphasized: 'The original capital expresses the idea of a surplus-value yielding, growing capital in its purest form, and the rate of its growth appears in fact as the general capitalist profit rate' (von Charasoff, 1910, p. 112). And: 'The original capital is nothing else than the basic production, whose branches are taken in particular dimensions. As regards these dimensions the requirement is decisive that gross profits of the basic production . . . are of the same type as its total capital' (von Charasoff, 1910, p. 126). This finding can be said to generalize Torrens's 'general principle' referred to above: it relies neither on the existence of a single sector whose capital is physically homogeneous with its product and whose product is used by all sectors as an input nor on the special case in which all sectors exhibit the same input proportions.[11]

---

11 Von Charasoff's construction also bears a close resemblance to Sraffa's device of the Standard system in which the rate of profit 'appears as a ratio between quantities of commodities irrespective of their prices' (Sraffa, 1960, p. 22).

These considerations provide the key to a solution of the problem of price. For, if the various capitals can be conceived of 'as different amounts of the selfsame capital . . . , then prices must be proportional to the dimensions of these, and the problem of price thus finds its solution in this relationship based on law' (von Charasoff, 1910, p. 123). Let **p** designate the n-dimensional vector of prices, **p** $\geqslant$ **0**, then we have the following price system

$$\mathbf{p}^T = (1 + r)\mathbf{p}^T\mathbf{A}$$

Thus, while **u** equals the right-hand eigenvector of **A**, **p** equals the left-hand eigenvector; $1/(1 + r)$ equals the dominant eigenvalue of matrix **A**. The solution to the price problem can therefore be cast in a form in which 'the concept of labour is almost entirely bypassed' (von Charasoff, 1910, p. 112). Implicit in this reasoning is the abandonment of the labour theory of value as a basis for the theory of relative prices and the rate of profit.

With von Neumann (1937) von Charasoff shared a concern with the possibility of equi-proportionate growth. In the hypothetical case in which all profits are accumulated, the proportions of the different sectors equal the proportions of the original capital. In this case the actual rate of growth equals the rate of profit: the system expands along a von Neumann ray. Von Charasoff was perhaps the first author to note clearly what von Neumann more than two decades later was to call 'the remarkable duality (symmetry) of the monetary variables (prices p_j, interest factor β) and the technical variables (intensities of production, q_i, coefficient of expansion of the economy α)' (von Neumann, 1945, p. 1).

9. Wassily Leontief

Leontief (1905–99) was born in St Petersburg. After his studies at the university of his home town, then Leningrad, he went to Berlin to work on his doctorate under the supervision of von Bortkiewicz. In 1928 he published a part of his thesis entitled 'Die Wirtschaft als Kreislauf'.[12] In it Leontief put forward a two-sectoral input–output system that was designed to describe the production, distribution and consumption aspects of an economy as a single process. In 1932 he joined the faculty at Harvard University and began the construction of the first input–output tables of the American economy. These tables, together with the corresponding mathematical model, were published in 1936 and 1937 (see Leontief, 1941; see also Leontief, 1987). In this section we shall first deal with Leontief's 1928 article and then provide a summary statement of the closed and open input–output model. We shall see that Leontief's 1928 approach bears a close resemblance to Isnard's, dealt with in Section 4.

---

12 An English translation entitled 'The economy as a circular flow' which, unfortunately, omits certain passages, was published in 1991; see Leontief (1991). In what follows, the English version will be used whenever this is possible. Page numbers in square brackets refer to the latter.

9.1. The economy as a circular flow

In his thesis, Leontief advocated the view that economics should start from 'the ground of what is objectively given' (Leontief, 1928, p. 583); economic concepts are meaningless and potentially misleading unless they can be observed and measured. He adopted a 'naturalistic' perspective (Leontief, 1928, p. 622; the English translation [p. 211] speaks of a 'material' perspective). The starting point of the marginalist approach, the *homo oeconomicus*, is considered inappropriate because it gives too much room to imagination and too little to facts (Leontief, 1928, pp. 619–20). Economic analysis should rather focus on the concept of circular flow, which expresses one of the fundamental 'objective' features of economic life. A careful investigation of its 'technological' aspects is said to be an indispensable prerequisite to any economic reasoning.

Leontief distinguished between 'cost goods' and 'revenue goods', that is, inputs and goods satisfying final demand. Throughout his investigation he assumed single production and constant returns to scale; scarce natural resources are mentioned only in passing. The argument is developed within the confines of what was to become known as the *Non-substitution Theorem* (see Koopmans, 1951; Samuelson, 1951). In much of the analysis it is also assumed that the system of production (and consumption) is indecomposable. Leontief suggested (1928, p. 585) that the process of production should be described in terms of three sets of 'technical coefficients': (i) 'cost coefficients'; that is, the proportion in which two cost goods h and k participate in the production of good j (in familiar notation: a_{hj}/a_{kj}); (ii) 'productivity coefficients'; that is, the total quantity produced of good j in relation to the total quantity used up of the ith input (in familiar notation: $1/a_{ij}$); (iii) 'distribution coefficients'; that is, the proportion of the total output of a certain good allotted to a particular point (or pole) in the scheme of circular flow; as is explained later in the chapter, such a point may represent a particular group of property income receivers. A major concern of Leontief's was with a stationary system characterized by constant technical coefficients; in addition he discussed cases in which one or several coefficients change, thereby necessitating adjustments of the system as a whole. Here we shall set aside the second problem.

Starting from a physically specified system of production-cum-distribution, Leontief is to be credited with having provided a clear idea of the concept of *vertical integration* (Leontief, 1928, p. 589). As regards the reduction to dated quantities of labour (Leontief, 1928, pp. 596 and 621–2), he pointed out that because of the circular character of production 'a complete elimination of a factor of production from the given system is in principle impossible. Of course, the size of the "capital factor" can be reduced to any chosen level by referring back to even earlier periods of production' (Leontief, 1928, p. 622 [p. 211]). This reduction has nothing to do with an historical regress (Leontief, 1928, p. 596, fn. 6 [p. 192 fn]).

Next, Leontief addressed exchange relationships. The emphasis is on 'the general conditions which must be fulfilled within the framework of a circular flow' (Leontief, 1928, p. 598 [p. 193]). The concept of 'value' adopted is explicitly qualified as one that has nothing to do with any intrinsic property of goods, such as utility; it rather refers to the 'exchange relation deduced from all the relationships . . . analysed so far' (Leontief, 1928, p. 598 [p. 193]). In the case of a model with two goods, the 'relations of reproduction' are expressed as follows:

$$\left.\begin{array}{l} aA + bB \to A \\ (1-a)A + (1-b)B \to B \end{array}\right\} \tag{3.8}$$

where A and B give the total quantities produced of two, possibly composite, commodities, and a and b [$(1-a)$ and $(1-b)$] give the shares of those commodities used up as means of production and means of subsistence in the first (second) sector. It should be stressed that the system, albeit stationary, generates a surplus.

Leontief, in fact, assumed that a part of the product of each sector is appropriated by a so-called ownership group: 'In the general circular flow scheme, income from ownership is of course considered alongside other cost items without the slightest direct reference to how it originates (the phenomenon of ownership). It is the task of the theory of interest [profit] to investigate these fundamental relationships' (Leontief, 1928, p. 600 [p. 196]). His argument resulted in setting up price equations which reflect the going rule that fixes the distribution of income. Counting unknowns and equations, Leontief found that the number of variables exceeds the number of equations by one. He concluded: 'No clear resolution of this problem is possible. One may vary at will the exchange proportions and consequently the distribution relationships of the goods without affecting the circular flow of the economy in any way' (Leontief, 1928, pp. 598–9 [p. 194]). In other words, the same quantity system is assumed to be compatible with different price systems reflecting different distributions of income. He added: 'The sense of the surplus theory is represented by the classical school (e.g. even by Ricardo) and . . . is best understood if one enquires into the use of this "free" income. The answer is: it either accumulates or is used up unproductively' (Leontief, 1928, p. 619 [p. 209]). Hence, the exchange ratios of goods reflect not only 'natural', that is, essentially technological, factors, but also 'social causes'. Given the rate of profit together with the system of production, relative prices can be determined. 'But this is the "law of value" of the so-called objective value theory' (Leontief, 1928, p. 601 [p. 196]), Leontief concluded. The reader will notice a striking similarity between Leontief's considerations and those of Isnard.

Before we turn briefly to Leontief's contributions to input–output analysis, more narrowly defined, it should be recalled that in the late 1920s he was a member of a research group at the University of Kiel, Germany. The group was led by Adolf Löwe (later Adolph Lowe) (1893–1995), and included Fritz (later Fred) Burchardt (1902–58) and Alfred Kähler (1900–81), among others. One of the main issues tackled by this group was the displacement of workers by technical progress and their absorption, or lack thereof, through capital accumulation. To enable them to take into account both the direct and indirect effects of technical progress, they developed multisectoral analyses. In two instalments in the *Weltwirtschaftliches Archiv*, Burchardt in 1931 and 1932 published an essay in which he attempted to cross-breed Marx's scheme of reproduction and Eugen von Böhm-Bawerk's temporal view of production (Burchardt, 1931–32). Alfred Kähler in his PhD thesis of 1933 entitled *Die Theorie der Arbeiterfreisetzung durch die Maschine* (The theory of labour displacement by machinery) put forward a sophisticated argument which entailed a static input–output model and the way different forms of technical progress affect the coefficients of production of the different sectors and how these effects yield secondary effects etc. (Kähler, 1933; see also the paper by Gehrke, 2000). He also tried to calculate the change in the price system made necessary by technical change, assuming that any improvement is eventually passed on to workers in the form of a higher wage rate.

9.2. Input–output analysis

While Leontief conceived of his early contribution as firmly rooted in the classical tradition, he called his input–output method developed in the 1930s and 1940s 'an adaptation of the neo-classical theory of general equilibrium to the empirical study of the quantitative interdependence between interrelated economic activities' (Leontief, 1966, p. 134). Scrutiny shows, however, that in his input–output analysis he preserved the concept of circular flow and did not, as is maintained by some interpreters, adopt the Walras–Cassel view of production.[13] In the second edition of *The Structure of American Economy*, published in 1951, he even explicitly rejected the view of production as a one-way avenue that leads from the services of the 'original' factors of production: land, labour and capital – the 'venerable trinity' – to final goods (Leontief *et al.*, 1951, p. 112). Unlike the theories of Walras and Cassel, in Leontief there are no given initial endowments of these factors. We shall refrain from speculating about the reasons for the change in Leontief's characterization of his own approach, which seems to have occurred after his move from Europe to the United States.[14]

Input–output analysis is meant to provide a detailed (that is, disaggregated) quantitative description of the structural characteristics of all component parts of a given economic system. The interdependence among the different sectors of a given system is described by a set of linear equations; the numerical magnitudes of the coefficients of these equations reflect the system's structural properties. The values of the coefficients are ascertained empirically; they are commonly derived from statistical input–output tables, which describe the flow of goods and services between the different sectors of a national economy over a given period of time, usually a year. In static input–output analysis the input coefficients are generally assumed to be constant, that is, independent of the overall level and composition of final demand. The problem of the choice of technique, which plays an important role in classical and neoclassical analysis, is often given only slight attention.

---

13 For a characterization of the Walras–Cassel point of view, see, for example, Kurz and Salvadori
    (1995; chapter 13, subsection 7.1).
14 See also Gilibert (1981, 1991).

(i) *The closed Leontief model.* When all sales and purchases are taken to be endogenous, the input–output system is called 'closed'. In this case, final demand is treated as if it were an ordinary industry: the row associated with it represents the 'inputs' it receives from the various industries, and the corresponding column giving the value added in the various industries is assumed to represent its 'output' allocated to these industries. With **A** as the non-negative 'structural matrix' of an economy giving both material input requirements and final demand, and **x** as the *n*-vector of gross outputs, the closed input–output model is given by the linear homogeneous system:

$$\mathbf{x} = \mathbf{A}\mathbf{x}$$

that is,

$$(\mathbf{I} - \mathbf{A})\mathbf{x} = \mathbf{0}$$

This model was discussed in Leontief (1941). In order for the system of equations to have non-negative solutions, the largest real eigenvalue of matrix **A** must be unity.[15] The price system which is dual to the above quantity system is

$$\mathbf{p}^{\mathrm{T}} = \mathbf{p}^{\mathrm{T}}\mathbf{A}$$

that is,

$$\mathbf{p}^{\mathrm{T}}(\mathbf{I} - \mathbf{A}) = \mathbf{0}^{\mathrm{T}} \tag{3.9}$$

The problem of the existence of a (non-negative) solution of system (3.9) was first investigated by Remak (1929) (see Section 10).

(ii) *The open Leontief model.* In the second edition of Leontief (1941), which was published a decade later, Leontief elaborated the 'open' input–output model which treats the technological and the final demand aspects separately. Now **A** represents exclusively the matrix of interindustry coefficients and **y** the vector of final demand, which is given from outside the system. The matrix of input coefficients is then used to determine the sectoral gross outputs as well as the necessary intersectoral transactions that enable the system to meet final demand and reproduce all used up means of production. The equation describing the relationship

---

15 This does not mean that the economy is unable to produce a surplus. In fact, if $(\mathbf{A}^*, \mathbf{l})$ is a technique, where $\mathbf{A}^*$ gives the material input matrix and $\mathbf{l}$ the vector of direct labour inputs per unit of output in the different sectors of the economy, then

$$\mathbf{A} = \begin{bmatrix} \mathbf{A}^* & \mathbf{v} \\ \mathbf{l}^{\mathrm{T}} & h \end{bmatrix}$$

where **v** is the vector of values added per unit of output, and h is the input of labour in households per unit of labour employed. Therefore, if the largest eigenvalue of matrix $\mathbf{A}^*$ is not larger than unity, then the definitions of **v** and h imply that the largest eigenvalue of matrix **A** equals unity.

between **x** and **y** is

$$\mathbf{Ax} + \mathbf{y} = \mathbf{x}$$

that is,

$$(\mathbf{I} - \mathbf{A})\mathbf{x} = \mathbf{y}$$

On the assumption that the inverse of matrix $(\mathbf{I} - \mathbf{A})$ exists, we get as the general solution of the open input–output model:

$$\mathbf{x} = (\mathbf{I} - \mathbf{A})^{-1}\mathbf{y}$$

The 'Leontief inverse matrix' $(\mathbf{I} - \mathbf{A})^{-1}$ is semipositive if the largest real eigenvalue of matrix $\mathbf{A}$ is smaller than unity (cf. Hawkins and Simon, 1949).

As to the determination of prices in the open input–output model, Leontief proposed a set of 'value-added price equations'. The price each productive sector is assumed to receive per unit of output equals the total outlays incurred in the course of its production. These outlays comprise the payments for material inputs purchased from the same or another productive sectors plus the *given* 'value added'. Assuming a closed economy without a government, the latter represents payments to the owners of productive factors: wages, rents, interest and profits. The price system, which is dual to the above quantity system, is given by

$$\mathbf{p}^{\mathrm{T}}(\mathbf{I} - \mathbf{A}) = \mathbf{v}^{\mathrm{T}}$$

where **p** is the n-vector of prices and **v** is the n-vector of values added per unit of output. Solving for **p** gives

$$\mathbf{p}^{\mathrm{T}} = \mathbf{v}^{\mathrm{T}}(\mathbf{I} - \mathbf{A})^{-1}$$

The main problem with this approach is that the magnitudes of value added per unit of output in the different sectors cannot generally be determined prior to, and independently of, the system of prices. Another way of putting it is that in this formulation two things are lost from sight: the constraint binding changes in the distributive variables, and the dependence of relative prices on income distribution – facts rightly stressed by Leontief in his 1928 paper.

9.3. Input–output analysis and Walrasian general equilibrium theory

In the literature on input–output analysis, one frequently encounters the view that the Leontief-system is an offspring of the general equilibrium model put forward by Léon Walras (1834–1910) in his *Eléments d'économie politique pure* (Walras, 1874). Leontief at times has himself expressed the opinion that his analysis and that of Walras are compatible with one another. Here we shall, on the contrary, draw the reader's attention to some aspects of the two approaches that appear to be difficult to reconcile.

First, there is the problem of method. Leontief opted for a 'naturalistic' or 'material' point of view. He insisted that the investigation should focus on 'directly observable basic structural relationships' (Leontief, 1987, p. 860) and not, like Walras's general equilibrium theory, on utility, demand functions etc., that is, things that are not directly observable. Second, there is the content of the theory. Some observers may be inclined to base the hypothesis of close similarity between the analyses of Leontief and Walras on the observation that the systems of price equations elaborated by Leontief in his 1928 paper, starting from schema (3.8), and those of Walras in his models of pure exchange in parts II and III of the *Eléments* are formally similar. Essentially the same formal similarity appears to have prompted some interpreters to consider that the analyses of Walras and Isnard belong to the same tradition in the theory of value and distribution.[16] However, it has to be pointed out that Isnard's argument, as well as Leontief's, does not refer to a pure exchange economy, but to an economy in which both capital and consumption goods are produced and reproduced.[17] Additionally, in Isnard as well as in Leontief, the parameters that determine relative prices are technological and institutional data, whereas in Walras's case of the pure exchange economy the 'effective demands' are ultimately rooted in the agent's utility maximizing disposition. There is a real and close similarity between the contributions of Leontief and Isnard, whereas there is only a questionable one between those of Leontief and Walras. Finally, as regards systems with production, in Isnard and Leontief the problem of distribution is not approached in terms of relative 'scarcities' of the respective factors of production, that is, in terms of the set of data (a)–(c) of Section 1 of this chapter. In Leontief, the rate of interest is not conceived of as a scarcity index of a given endowment of capital. Walras's theory on the other hand starts from a given vector of capital goods and attempts to determine the 'rate of net income' (rate of profit) in terms of the demand for and the supply of capital (see Kurz and Salvadori, 1995, pp. 22–6). We may conclude that, setting aside purely formal similarities, the analyses of Leontief and Walras have little in common.

10. Robert Remak

We now turn to the contribution of Robert Remak (1888–1942). He studied mathematics and, in 1929, acquired the *venia legendi* at the University of Berlin and was a *Privatdozent* there until 1933. According to the information gathered by

16 Thus, Schumpeter contended: 'The first to attempt a (primitive) mathematical definition of equilibrium and a (also primitive) mathematical proof of that proposition was Isnard, who has as yet to conquer the position in the history of economic theory that is due him as a precursor of Léon Walras' (Schumpeter, 1954, p. 217). And: 'In his not otherwise remarkable book there is an elementary system of equations that . . . describes the interdependence within the universe of prices in a way suggestive of Walras' (Schumpeter, 1954, p. 307; see also p. 242).

17 Hence, the appropriate point of reference would be Walras's developed theory including the production of consumption goods and the reproduction of capital goods proper. For a comparison of that theory with the 'classical' theory, see Kurz and Salvadori (1995, pp. 23–6).

Wittmann, from some of Remak's former friends and colleagues, Remak was in all probability stimulated by a group of economists around Bortkiewicz to study the problem of the conditions under which positive solutions of systems of linear equations obtain (cf. Wittmann, 1967, p. 401). As we have seen, Leontief's 1928 analysis was, for the most part, limited to the two-commodity case. One year later, Remak published a paper entitled 'Kann die Volkswirtschaftslehre eine exakte Wissenschaft werden?' (Can economics become an exact science?), generalizing the system to the n-commodity case, $n \geqslant 2$ (Remak, 1929).

Remak's paper begins with a definition of what is meant by an exact science, which bears a striking resemblance to Leontief's point of view: an exact science regards as 'exactly correct' only what can be ascertained by physical observation, counting or calculation (Remak, 1929, p. 703). Conventional economics, which Remak tended to equate with Marshallian demand and supply analysis, is said not to allow 'quantitative calculations that can also be carried out practically' (Remak, 1929, p. 712). The alternative are 'superposed' or 'reasonable' prices: 'A superposed price system has nothing to do with values. It only satisfies the condition that each price covers the costs of the things required in production, and the consumption of the producer on the assumption that it is both just and feasible' (Remak, 1929, p. 712). Its calculation requires a detailed knowledge of the socio-technical relations of production, that is, the methods of production in use and the needs and wants of producers (Remak, 1929, pp. 712–13).

Remak then constructs 'superposed prices' for an economic system in stationary conditions in which there are as many single-product processes of production as there are products, and each process or product is represented by a different 'person' or rather activity or industry.[18] The amounts of the different commodities acquired by a person over a certain period of time in exchange for his or her own product are of course the amounts needed as means of production to produce this product and the amounts of consumption goods in support of the person (and his or her family), given the levels of sustenance. With an appropriate choice of units, the resulting system of 'superposed prices' can be written as

$$\mathbf{p}^{\mathrm{T}} = \mathbf{p}^{\mathrm{T}}\mathbf{C} \tag{3.10}$$

where $\mathbf{C}$ is the augmented matrix of inputs per unit of output, and $\mathbf{p}$ is the vector of exchange ratios. Discussing system (3.10) Remak arrived at the conclusion that there is a solution to it, which is semipositive and unique except for a scale factor. The system refers to a kind of ideal economy with independent producers, no wage labour and hence no profits. However, in Remak's view it can also be interpreted as a socialist economic system.

---

18 The somewhat unfortunate phrasing of the problem by Remak may have been the source of the misconception that his concern was with a pure exchange economy; for this interpretation, see Gale (1960, p. 290).

11. Concluding remarks

This chapter contains a short account of some of the most important contributions to the long prehistory of input–output analysis. It has been shown that the latter is an offspring of classical economics with its emphasis on production as a circular flow and the capacity of the economy to create a surplus over and above the physical real costs of production, including the necessary means of subsistence in the support of workers. The physical scheme of production was considered as crucial for an understanding both of the problem of growth and that of the distribution of income and relative prices.

The theoretical efforts just surveyed bore two major fruits. On the one hand they laid the foundation to Leontief's empirical work, his input–output analysis, which turned out to be an indispensable tool in applied economics. On the other hand they stimulated further developments in the theory of value, distribution and growth. Two contributions are of particular importance in this regard: John von Neumann's famous growth model[19] and Piero Sraffa's 1960 book, which was explicitly designed to resurrect the 'classical' approach. A discussion of these contributions is, however, beyond the scope of this chapter.

References

Bortkiewicz, L. von (1906–07) Wertrechnung und Preisrechnung im Marxschen System, *Archiv für Sozialwissenschaft und Sozialpolitik*, 23 (1906), pp. 1–50; 25 (1907), pp. 10–51 and 445–88; in the text referred to as essays I, II and III.

Bortkiewicz, L. von (1907) Zur Berichtigung der grundlegenden theoretischen Konstruktion von Marx im 3. Band des 'Kapital', *Jahrbücher für Nationalökonomie und Statistik*, 34, pp. 319–35.

Bortkiewicz, L. von (1952) Value and price in the Marxian system, *International Economic Papers*, 2, pp. 5–60. English translation of von Bortkiewicz (1906–7 II and III).

Bródy, A. (1970) *Proportions, Prices and Planning* (Amsterdam, North-Holland).

Burchardt, F. (1931–32) Die Schemata des stationären Kreislaufs bei Böhm-Bawerk und Marx, *Weltwirtschaftliches Archiv*, 34 (1931), pp. 525–64; 35 (1932), pp. 116–76.

Cantillon, R. (1931) *Essai sur la nature du commerce en Général*, edited with an English translation by H. Higgs (London, Macmillan, 1931).

Champernowne, D. G. (1945) A note on J. v. Neumann's article on 'A model of economic equilibrium', *Review of Economic Studies*, 13, pp. 10–18.

Charasoff, G. von (1910) *Das System des Marxismus: Darstellung und Kritik* (Berlin, H. Bondy).

Dmitriev, V. K. (1974) *Economic Essays on Value, Competition and Utility*, edited with an introduction by D. M. Nuti (Cambridge, Cambridge University Press).

---

19 We have argued elsewhere (see Kurz and Salvadori, 1993) that John von Neumann's paper on equi-proportionate growth (Neumann, 1937) can be interpreted as containing an implicit comment on Remak. In his paper, von Neumann put forward a general linear analysis of production, distribution and economic expansion, allowing for joint production, fixed capital and a choice of technique.

Egidi, M. and Gilibert, G. (1984) La teoria oggettiva dei prezzi, *Economia Politica*, 1, pp. 43–61. An English translation of the paper entitled 'The objective theory of prices' was published in *Political Economy. Studies in the Surplus Approach*, 5 (1989), pp. 59–74.

Eltis, W. (1975) François Quesnay: a reinterpretation. 2: The theory of economic growth, *Oxford Economic Papers*, 27, pp. 327–51.

Gale, D. (1960) *The Theory of Linear Economic Models* (New York, McGraw-Hill).

Gehrke, C. (2000) Alfred Kähler's *Die Theorie der Arbeiterfreisetzung durch die Maschine*: an Early Contribution to the Analysis of the Impact of Automation on Workers, *Economic Systems Research*, 12, pp. 199–214.

Gehrke, Ch. and Kurz, H. D. (1995) Karl Marx on physiocracy, *The European Journal of the History of Economic Thought*, 2, pp. 53–90.

Gilibert, G. (1981) Isnard, Cournot, Walras, Leontief. Evoluzione di un modello, *Annali della Fondazione Luigi Einaudi*, 15, pp. 129–53.

Gilibert, G. (1991) La scuola russo-tedesca di economia matematica e la dottrina del flusso circolare, in G. Beccatini (ed.), *Le scuole economiche*, (Turin, Utet), pp. 387–402.

Hawkins, D. and Simon, H. A. (1949) Note: Some conditions of macroeconomic stability, *Econometrica*, 17, pp. 245–8.

INED (1958) *François Quesnay et la physiocratie*, two vols (Paris, Institut Nationale d'Etudes Démographiques).

Isnard, A.-N. (1781) *Traité des richesses*, two vols (London and Lausanne, F. Grasset).

Jaffé, W. (1969) A. N. Isnard, progenitor of the Walrasian general equilibrium model, *History of Political Economy*, 1, pp. 19–43.

Kähler, A. (1933) *Die Theorie der Arbeiterfreisetzung durch die Maschine*, (Greifswald).

Koopmans, T. C. (1951) Alternative proof of the substitution theorem for Leontief models in the case of three industries, in Koopmans, T. C. (ed) (1951) *Activity Analysis of Production and Allocation*, (New York, John Wiley and Sons).

Kurz, H. D. and Salvadori, N. (1993) von Neumann's growth model and the 'classical' tradition, *The European Journal of the History of Economic Thought*, 1, pp. 129–60.

Kurz, H. D. and Salvadori, N. (1995) *Theory of Production. A Long-period Analysis*, (Cambridge, Cambridge University Press).

Kurz, H. D. and Salvadori, N. (eds) (1998) *The Elgar Companion to Classical Economics*, two vols (Cheltenham, Edward Elgar).

Kurz, H. D., Dietzenbacher, E. and Lager, Ch. (eds) (1998) *Input–Output Analysis*, three vols (Cheltenham, Edward Elgar).

Leontief, W. (1928) Die Wirtschaft als Kreislauf, *Archiv für Sozialwissenschaft und Sozialpolitik*, 60, pp. 577–623.

Leontief, W. (1936) Quantitative input–output relations in the economic system of the United States, *Review of Economic [s and] Statistics*, 18, pp. 105–25.

Leontief, W. (1941) *The Structure of American Economy, 1919–1939: An Empirical Application of Equilibrium Analysis*, 2nd enlarged edition (White Plains, N. Y., International Arts and Sciences Press, 1951).

Leontief, W. (1966) *Input–Output Economics* (New York, Oxford University Press).

Leontief, W. (1987) Input–output analysis, in: J. Eatwell, M. Milgate and P. Newman (eds), *The New Palgrave. A Dictionary of Economics*, vol. 2, pp. 860–4.

Leontief, W. (1991) The economy as a circular flow, *Structural Change and Economic Dynamics*, 2, 1991, pp. 177–212. English translation of parts of Leontief (1928) with an introduction by P. A. Samuelson.

Leontief, W. *et al.* (1951) *Studies in the Structure of the American Economy: Theoretical and Empirical Explorations in Input–Output Analysis* (White Plains, N. Y., International Arts and Sciences Press).

Marx, K. (1954) *Capital*, vol. I (Moscow, Progress Publishers). English translation of *Das Kapital*, vol. I (Hamburg, Meissner, 1867).

Marx, K. (1956) *Capital*, vol. II (Moscow, Progress Publishers). English translation of *Das Kapital*, vol. II, edited by F. Engels (Hamburg, Meissner, 1885).

Marx, K. (1959) *Capital*, vol. III (Moscow, Progress Publishers). English translation of *Das Kapital*, vol. III, edited by F. Engels (Hamburg, Meissner, 1894).

Marx, K. (1963) *Theories of Surplus Value*, part I (Moscow, Progress Publishers). English translation of *Theorien über den Mehrwert*, part 1 (Berlin, Dietz, 1956).

MEW (1956 et seq.) *Marx-Engels-Werke* (Berlin, Dietz).

Morishima, M. (1964) *Equilibrium, Stability and Growth* (Oxford, Clarendon Press).

Neumann, J. v. (1937) Über ein ökonomisches Gleichungssystem und eine Verallgemeinerung des Brouwerschen Fixpunktsatzes, *Ergebnisse eines mathematischen Kolloquiums*, 8, pp. 73–83.

Neumann, J. v. (1945) A model of general economic equilibrium. English translation of von Neumann (1937), *Review of Economic Studies*, 13, pp. 1–9.

Petty, W. (1986) *A Treatise of Taxes and Contributions*. Reprinted in *The Economic Writings of Sir William Petty*, edited by C. H. Hull, two vols (originally published in 1899, Cambridge, Cambridge University Press). Reprinted in one volume (New York, Kelley, 1986).

Remak, R. (1929) Kann die Volkswirtschaftslehre eine exakte Wissenschaft werden?, *Jahrbücher für Nationalökonomie und Statistik*, 131, pp. 703–35.

Ricardo, D. (1951–73) *The Works and Correspondence of David Ricardo*, edited by Piero Sraffa with the collaboration of Maurice H. Dobb (Cambridge, Cambridge University Press), 11 vols.

Rose, A. and Miernyk, W. (1989) Input–output analysis: the first fifty years, *Economic Systems Research*, 1, pp. 229–71.

Samuelson, P. A. (1951) Abstract of a theorem concerning substitutability in open Leontief models, In: Koopmans, T. C. (ed) *Activity Analysis of Production and Allocation* (New York, John Wiley and Sons).

Schumpeter, J. A. (1954) *History of Economic Analysis* (New York, Oxford University Press).

Smith, A. (1976) *An Inquiry into the Nature and Causes of the Wealth of Nations*, first published in 1776, *The Glasgow Edition of the Works and Correspondence of Adam Smith*, vol. I (Oxford, Oxford University Press).

Sraffa, P. (1951) Introduction, in Ricardo (1951–73), *Works* I, pp. xiii–lxii.

Sraffa, P. (1960) *Production of Commodities by Means of Commodities* (Cambridge, Cambridge University Press).

Stone, R. (1984) Where are we now? A short account of input–output studies and their present trends. In: *Proceedings of the Seventh International Conference on Input–Output Techniques* (New York, United Nations).

Torrens, R. (1820) *An Essay on the Influence of the External Corn Trade upon the Production and Distribution of National Wealth*, 2nd edn (London, Hatchard).

Torrens, R. (1821) *An Essay on the Production of Wealth*, London, Longman, Hurst, Rees, Orme and Brown. Reprint edited by J. Dorfman (New York, Augustus M. Kelley, 1965).

Walras, L. (1874) *Eléments d'économie politique pure*, Paris, Guillaumin & Cie. Definitive edition (5th edn) (Paris, F. Richon, 1926). English translation by W. Jaffé of the definitive edition as *Elements of Pure Economics* (London, George Allen & Unwin, 1954).

Wittmann, W. (1967) Die extremale Wirtschaft. Robert Remak – ein Vorläufer der Aktivitätsanalyse, *Jahrbücher für Nationalökonomie und Statistik*, 180, pp. 397–409.

4 Friedrich Benedikt Wilhelm Hermann on capital and profits*

Heinz D. Kurz

1. Introduction

In the second part of *Der isolierte Staat* Johann Heinrich von Thünen called our author's treatment of profits 'the most profound and valuable disquisition on the issue I ever encountered' (Thünen, [1850] 1990, p. 334 n).[1] Julius Kautz, who in 1860 published one of the first histories of German economic thought, saw in him 'one of the greatest and most important thinkers' whose work started 'the *golden age* of German economic literature'; Kautz added that 'among all the continental experts he comes closest to the great authorities of the *new-English school*' and praised his 'mathematical sharpness and the decidedness of his method which is informed by the natural sciences' (Kautz, 1860, pp. 633–4, 637–8). Albert Schäffle considered him 'the sharpest of the German economists, their first mathematical thinker' (Schäffle, 1870, p. 122; similarly Helferich, 1878, pp. 640–1). Carl Menger credited him with avoiding 'the most frequent mistake that is made not only in the classification but also in the definition of capital', which is said to consist 'in the stress laid on the *technical* instead of the *economic* standpoint' (Menger, [1871] 1981, p. 303). In Wilhelm Roscher's view our author was 'doubtless one of the most excellent economists of the 19th century' (Roscher, 1874, p. 861). John Kells Ingram spoke of his 'rare technological knowledge', which 'gave him a great advantage in dealing with some economic questions', and pointed out that for his 'keen analytical power' his fellow countrymen compared him with Ricardo; our economist is, however, said to avoid 'several one-sided views of the English economist' (Ingram, [1888] 1967, pp. 181–2). Alfred Marshall saw his 'brilliant genius' to have led German economists to develop 'careful and profound analyses which add much to our knowledge' and which have 'greatly extended the boundaries of economic theory' (Marshall, [1890] 1977, p. 634). James W. Crook in 1898 wrote that his work 'marks a great advance on previous theoretical economic studies, and even to-day exercises considerable influence on economic thought' (Crook, 1898, p. 22). According to Joseph A. Schumpeter our author was 'miles above'

---

* Reprinted with permission from *The European Journal of the History of Economic Thought*, 5:1, 1998.

1 Translations from German sources are mine. Unless otherwise stated, all emphases in quotations are in the original.

his contemporaries in Germany in terms of 'the sharpness of his eye, analytical talent and originality' (Schumpeter, 1914, p. 56): his work is said to represent 'the culminating point of the highroad of German economists of his time' (1914, p. 55). In a later work Schumpeter expressed the fear that 'we might feel inclined to discount the reputation' of our author 'on the ground that he stands out for lack of competition' (Schumpeter, 1954, p. 503).

Ironically, the author on whom so much praise has been showered has almost totally fallen into oblivion. His name is not only absent from general contributions to economics but also from many studies devoted to the history of economic thought. He is neither mentioned in the first three editions of Blaug (1962)[2] nor in Spiegel (1971), Routh (1975), Brems (1986), Niehans (1990) and Rima (1991). He is mentioned only once in Ekelund and Hébert (1983) and twice in Pribram (1983). The situation is somewhat more favourable in books devoted to the history of economic thought written in his mother tongue, German: see especially Stavenhagen (1957), Schneider (1962) and more recently Brandt (1992) and Baloglou (1995). However, the impression remains that for the community of historians of economic thought taken as a whole the economist under consideration barely existed. To be praised may be the first step to being lost sight of.

The author under consideration is Johann Benedikt Wilhelm Hermann.[3] He was born in 1795 in the free town of Dinkelsbühl, which later fell to the kingdom of Bavaria. After his studies (1813–17) at the Alexander Universität Erlangen and the Julius Universität Würzburg he, together with a friend, founded a private school for boys in Nürnberg. When in 1821 he left the school he became a teacher of mathematics, first in Erlangen and then in Nürnberg. In 1826 and 1828 he published a textbook on algebra and arithmetic and two volumes on polytechnic institutes. In 1827 he assumed the position of an *Extraordinarius* of technology, political arithmetic and political economy at the Ludwig-Maximilians-Universität München; in 1832 he was promoted to a full professorship. 1832 saw the publication of his *magnum opus*, the *Staatswirthschaftliche Untersuchungen* (Hermann, 1832). In 1839 King Ludwig I appointed Hermann to the position of the Director of the newly founded Bavarian Statistical Bureau which Hermann held during the rest of his life; the establishment of the Bureau was mainly his work. In addition, one year later he assumed a position in the Ministry of the Interior and in 1845 was promoted to the rank of a Councillor to the Ministry. In the late 1830s he had already become the main advisor on economic and social questions to Maximilian II of Bavaria. In 1848–9 he was a member of the German National Assembly in Frankfurt am Main. He sided with the liberals and advocated, among other things, a federalist structure of the emerging German nation state; the inclusion of Austria, that is, a 'great German solution' (*großdeutsche Lösung*); the abolition of nobility by birth; and the recognition of the sovereignty of the people. This did not pass unnoticed in Munich and after his return from the Frankfurt Paulskirche he had to leave the Ministry for a lack of adequate missions. From 1849 to 1855 he was a member of the Bavarian parliament. 1850 saw his reappointment to the Bavarian

2 He is mentioned once in the two subsequent editions (cf., e.g. Blaug, 1997).
3 On Hermann's life and work, see Weinberger (1925) and Pix (1995).

civil service: the king thought that Bavaria was badly advised to dispense with the services of a man possessed of as many talents and qualities as Hermann. He served in the Ministry of Finance; chaired, in 1852, the newly founded Commission on Science and Technology of the Bavarian Academy of Sciences; and was appointed, in 1855, to the positions of a Councillor to the Bavarian Government and the Director of the Administration of Bavarian Mines and Saltworks. Hermann died in 1868 from pneumonia. His students included Lujo Brentano, Adolf Held, Alfons R. von Helferich, the successor to his chair at the University of Munich, Georg Friedrich Knapp and Georg Mayr. A second edition of the *Untersuchungen* was published two years after Hermann's death by Helferich and Mayr (Hermann, 1870); 1874 saw a reprint of the book.

Hermann's knowledge of contemporary English and continental economic literature was remarkable. One might be inclined to think that this reflects the impact of his teachers in Erlangen, in particular Karl Heinrich Rau. However, Hermann attended only Rau's lecture on agriculture and forestry, Johann Paul Harl's lecture on political economy and public finance and Michael Alexander Lips's lecture entitled 'Encyclopedia of Cameralism'. None of these lectures seems to have been very fertile in the sense of exposing the student to different traditions of economic thought. Apparently, Hermann was essentially self-taught: he read the English and continental authors in their mother languages (English, French, Italian) and thus did not see them through the lenses of received German interpretations. In his curriculum vitae he writes that he had 'studied cameralism and Say'. Belonging to a minority of Protestants in an environment dominated by Roman Catholics, Hermann appears to have followed the Protestant *Bildungsideal* as best he could. In 1817 he got his doctoral degree without presenting an inaugural dissertation. When in 1823 he applied for a *Habilitation*, a fight broke out in the Philosophical Faculty about the procedure. Eventually, Hermann presented two dissertations, one in mathematics, the other in cameralism. Only the latter had to be printed and, curiously, Hermann was forced to defend it twice. The work is written in Latin and deals with economic concepts and analyses in early Roman authors (cf. Hermann, 1823). Interestingly, the dissertation foreshadows several of the concerns and ideas of the *Untersuchungen*.

This chapter attempts to recall some of the achievements of this remarkable German economist, paying special attention to his contribution to the theory of capital and profits. The emphasis will be on the first edition of the *Untersuchungen*, which contains Hermann's original contributions.[4] Given his multifarious interests and activities, he was left little time to publish in the field of political economy.

---

4 This view is also expressed by Roscher (1874, pp. 862–3) who writes that while the first edition witnesses Hermann's 'early achieved maturity', the 'substantially expanded' second edition documents his 'long preserved freshness'. Roscher adds that it is 'remarkable that in such a long time span of a healthy and active life the man has not intellectually grown more.' See also Streissler (1994). It comes as no surprise that in 1924 Karl Diehl edited a reprint of the first and not the second edition. Recently Horst Claus Recktenwald published a facsimile edition of the first edition, accompanied by a commentary (Recktenwald, 1987). Alas, Recktenwald's assessment of Hermann's work is in some instances grossly misleading.

Apart from his *magnum opus* there are only a few articles mainly on statistical matters and several book reviews or review articles. In what follows I shall occasionally refer to the latter.[5]

The structure of the chapter is as follows. Section 2 deals with the aim and composition of the *Staatswirthschaftliche Untersuchungen*. Section 3 introduces some basic concepts of Hermann's analysis. Section 4 summarizes his criticism of the then conventional distinction between 'productive' and 'unproductive' labour. Section 5 is dedicated to Hermann's notion of 'capital'. Section 6 addresses his theory of price which was meant to rectify and generalize the classical doctrine. Section 7 enters into a discussion of what he and many of his interpreters considered his main contribution: his theory of profits. It will be argued that Hermann was one of the first authors who attempted to generalize the classical principle of diminishing returns and the related concept of the scarcity of a factor of production from the explanation of the rent of land to the explanation of all distributive variables, including wages and profits. Section 8 continues this discussion in terms of a summary statement of Hermann's criticism of Senior's 'abstinence' theory of profits. Section 9 scrutinizes Hermann's analysis of innovations and technological change. Section 10 contains some concluding remarks.

2. The aim and structure of *Staatswirthschaftliche Untersuchungen*

Hermann makes it clear right at the beginning of the *Untersuchungen* that the book is not a compendium. It rather seeks to address only those issues with regard to which its author finds the state of the art unsatisfactory. In the preface he writes: 'To many people contemporary political economy [*National-Oekonomie*] appears to be so complete, its doctrines so immune from attacks, that they believe there is little else to be done than to order its principles in a way that is most convenient for teaching and to foster its dissemination to the reading audience by means of popular presentations' (Hermann, 1832: III). However, according to him political economy is far from complete. There are particularly the following problems which, in his opinion, have not been dealt with satisfactorily: the relationship between selfishness (*Eigennutz*) and public spirit (*Gemeinsinn*); the notions of 'economic good' and 'economic production'; and the difference between 'productive' and 'unproductive' labour. Yet there is one area in which the state of the art is said to be especially disappointing: the theory of capital, which has negative implications for the theory of profits. In Hermann's view this is partly to be explained by the difficulty of the subject:

> The most intricate problem in political economy is presumably the question what determines the level of profits and how profits and wages act upon each other. The first more exact investigation of this problem has been undertaken

5 For summary accounts of Hermann's reviews of books and the handwritten records by students of his lectures on political economy and public finance in Munich (the so-called 'Collegienhefte'), see Kurz (1998, sections 3 and 4).

by Ricardo; however, since he does not proceed in a sufficiently general way, his results are often only valid under restrictions, which deprive them of almost any truth value.

(Hermann, 1832, p. V)

Hermann stresses that an investigation of the 'laws of profit' necessitates the development of a theory of prices, since the problems of distribution and value are intimately intertwined (ibid.: VI).

The *Untersuchungen* is thus first and foremost a contribution to the theory of capital and distribution. Out of the eight chapters four are devoted exclusively to this problem: chapter 3, 'Of capital. First treatise. The notion of capital'; chapter 4, 'Of price'; chapter 5, 'Of profits'; and chapter 6, 'Of capital. Second treatise. Effects, estimation, and origin of capital'. These four chapters account for more than two thirds of the 374 pages of the book, the chapter on profits being the longest (121 pages). The remaining chapters either prepare the ground for the main discussion or draw some conclusions for other parts of economic analysis: chapter 1 deals with 'Basic concepts and principles of political economy' such as 'want', 'good' and 'economy', while chapter 2 is 'On the productivity of labour'; chapter 7 is entitled 'Of income' and chapter 8 'Of the consumption of goods'.

Hermann generally proceeds in three steps. He first summarizes the received views on a particular problem. Characteristically, he groups them according to the language or nationality of their advocates. The group of British authors includes Sir James Steuart, Adam Smith, David Ricardo, Robert Torrens, John Ramsay McCulloch, James Mill, Thomas Robert Malthus and Samuel Read; his favourite economist is Smith.[6] The group of French and French-speaking authors encompasses the Physiocrats, Jean Baptiste Say, Louis Say, Charles Ganilh and Simonde de Sismondi. Among the German authors attention focuses on the contributions of Rau, Gottlieb Hufeland, Ludwig Heinrich von Jakob, Heinrich Storch and Johann Friedrich Eusebius Lotz.[7] In a second step he puts forward his objections to the doctrines just summarized. The third step consists of an elaboration of his own view on the matter under discussion.[8]

---

6 In a book review published in 1836 Hermann writes: 'Who ever knows something of political economy [*Staatswirthschaft*] in regard to the main principles of this science cannot but consider himself a student of Adam Smith' (Hermann 1836b: 418).

7 Hermann is one of the first to acknowledge and propagate the achievements of Johann Heinrich von Thünen, an outsider to the profession who never held an academic position. He also draws attention to Daniel Bernoulli's treatment of the so-called 'St Petersburg problem' and makes use of it in his theory of demand. Gilbert Faccarello reminded me of the fact that prior to Hermann Condorcet had made use of Bernoulli's finding in the context of a discussion of the optimal level of taxation and public expenditure; see Faccarello (1990).

8 Roscher (1874, p. 860) aptly remarked that Hermann does not belong to the 'vain' people who 'try to provide a foil, which is effective only with nonexperts, for their own originality by suppressing or belittling their precursors'.

3. Basic concepts of Hermann's analysis

In his 'masterly analysis of wealth' (Marshall, [1890] 1977, p. 46, fn.), Hermann defines a 'good' as anything 'that satisfies some want of man' (Hermann, 1832, p. 1). He sees each good as specified in terms of three aspects:

(1) its physical characteristics,
(2) the location and
(3) the date of its availability (ibid., pp. 22–3 and 27).

Hermann thus anticipates the modern definition as it is to be found, for example, in Böhm-Bawerk ([1884] 1921, p. 203) and, more recently, in Debreu (1959, pp. 29–30). In his lectures in Munich and then in the second edition of the *Untersuchungen* Hermann provides a definition of 'want' (*Bedürfniß*) which was to become famous: 'the feeling of a need [*Mangel*] and the desire to overcome it' (Hermann, 1870, p. 5).

Hermann is occasionally credited with an achievement which does not belong to him: the distinction between 'economic' and 'free' goods (see, e.g. Menger, [1871] 1981, p. 290). Economic goods have both use value and exchange value, whereas free goods lack exchange value (Hermann, 1832, pp. 3–4).[9] Hermann was, however, anticipated by several authors, including Adam Smith and Ricardo. To be clear about the issue one ought to distinguish between two kinds of 'free' goods: the services of factors of production, in particular different qualities of land and different types of capital goods, on the one hand, and produced commodities, on the other. The notion that the services of certain factors, such as some qualities of land, which are in excess supply assume a zero price, was a standard element in classical rent theory.[10] It was also admitted that in the short run some extant capital goods may be superfluous. It is this notion of 'free' good we encounter also in Hermann. As regards produced goods, with single production no good can be a free good other than in the ultra-short period. It is only with joint production that the proportions in which the products can be produced need not coincide with those in which they are wanted. While Hermann mentions cases of multiple-product processes of production in passing, he does not envisage the possibility of some

9 Menger did not agree with Hermann's notion of 'economic good' as something that can be obtained 'only for a definite sacrifice in the form of labour or monetary consideration' (Hermann, 1832, p. 3), since 'it makes the economic character of goods depend on labor or on trade between men' (Menger, [1871] 1981, p. 290). The fruits gathered by an isolated individual from trees are also said to be economic goods, provided 'they are available to him in smaller quantities than his requirements for them' ([1871] 1981, p. 290). Hermann may have countered this objection by pointing out that the process of gathering fruits does require labour.

10 See, for example, the following statement by Ricardo in which reference is to land available in abundant quantity: 'no rent could be paid for such land, for the reason stated why nothing is given for the use of air and water, or for any of the gifts of nature which exist in boundless quantity' (Ricardo *Works* I, p. 69). In the section on the rent of land in chapter 5 of his book, Hermann explicitly calls the marginal land a 'free good' (cf. Hermann, 1832, p. 168). The main authors he refers to in rent theory are Ricardo and von Thünen.

products being persistently overproduced and thus fetching a zero price. This was noticed, however, by Smith who introduced in economics some kind of 'Rule of Free Goods': joint products that are provided in excess supply will be 'thrown away as things of no value' (see Smith, *WN*: I.xi.c.4; see also Kurz, 1986).

Yet we do owe Hermann the distinction between goods that are 'internal' and those that are 'external' to man (cf. also Marshall, [1890] 1977, p. 46, fn.). The former man 'finds in himself given to him by nature or which he educates in himself by his own free action, such as muscular strength, health, mental attainments. Everything that the outer world offers for the satisfaction of his wants is an external good to him' (Hermann, 1832, p. 1). External goods comprise 'social relationships' (ibid., p. 4). The idea to reckon rights or the legal system as goods goes back to Sir James Steuart and is also to be found in Jean Baptiste Say. Hermann goes a step further and includes a large number of relationships on the grounds that they facilitate the functioning of the economy. He mentions formal as well as informal relationships, the goodwill of firms, cultural and religious traditions, etc. Unfortunately, Hermann fails to translate these relationships, their emergence and economic role, in analytical terms.[11]

Hermann emphasizes the distinction between the technical and the economic aspect of production. A production can be called 'economic' if and only if the value of the goods produced is at least as large as that of the goods used up (including the means of subsistence of the labourer) (ibid., p. 27). Economic production is a prerequisite for the preservation or increase of the wealth of an individual or the economy as a whole. In competitive conditions producers will be forced to minimize costs: 'The battle of producers and consumers, both among themselves and between them, implies that in the long run products will be brought to the market at lowest cost' (ibid., p. 36). He adds:

> In each case the judgement about the usefulness or reasonableness of the price and thus the productivity of a service may easily be left to the parties, whose thousandfold interwoven interest will bring each good to that person that pays most for it and therefore will render the largest value to all the goods brought to the market.
>
> (Hermann, 1832, p. 37)

Hermann's notion of income is inspired by Storch (cf. Roscher, 1874, p. 811) and based on the principle of the conservation of wealth. He defines the income of a single person as well as that of the economy as a whole as that which can be consumed during a period 'without reducing the stock of wealth [*Stammvermögen*]' (Herman, 1832, p. 299).

11 It appears to be clear, however, that in Hermann's view it is a characteristic feature of the 'relationships' under consideration that they are the source of positive economic externalities. Streissler (1994, p. 11) interprets them as property rights in a wider sense, the saving of transaction costs and information networks.

The object of political economy, Hermann surmises, are the laws governing the production, distribution and use of national wealth (ibid., pp. 10–11). He rejects the doctrine, which he wrongly ascribes to Smith, that nothing more than selfishness is necessary for society to achieve desirable social outcomes. For a good society to obtain, a 'public' or 'communal spirit' ought to be developed and selfish behaviour retrenched.[12] Despite this credo, most of the first edition of his *magnum opus* proceeds on the premiss that agents are self-seeking. The substantially enlarged second edition, which deals also with public finance, enters into a more detailed discussion of the public as opposed to the private sphere and revolves around the concepts, in modern parlance, of social welfare and public goods. Owing to a lack of space we have to set aside this aspect of Hermann's work.

Chapter 8, 'Of the consumption of goods', is mainly interesting because of the 'schemes' of reproduction and consumption put forward. As regards consumer theory it offers next to nothing. While Hermann's entire argument is cast in terms of supply and demand, and stresses over and over again the subjective aspect of valuation, he has little to say that is new. Schumpeter was basically right when he wrote:

As in France, perhaps in part under French influence, a utility-theory tradition had developed in Germany. But it was equally inoperative: it stopped at recognitions of the utility element that are difficult to distinguish from the Ricardian way of assigning to utility the role of a condition of value. Hermann went further than others but he also confined himself substantially to working with supply and demand.

(Schumpeter, 1954, p. 600)

Indeed, as regards the analysis of use value, Hermann did not really go beyond his contemporaries, in particular Rau.[13] It deserves to be stressed that in Hermann we do not encounter the concept of marginal utility. Even in the second edition of his *magnum opus* there is still no trace of the concept. In a book review published in 1836, we can see the reason why. After having defined the economic principle as 'trying to get as much from the smallest exertion of force [*Kraft*] and as satisfying one's wants as best as one can with as small a sacrifice as possible', Hermann stresses:

This necessitates a comparison of goods, which, however, can only be precise if it is founded on quantitative estimations of them. Yet, seen in isolation,

---

12 In this context it deserves to be mentioned that the private school Hermann and his friend founded in Nürnberg was based on pedagogical principles in the tradition of Pestalozzi, Basedow, Falk and others. A major concern was with educating the young to become valuable members of the commonwealth of human beings, possessed of a clear understanding of social needs and wants.

13 Hermann himself did not claim priority in this regard. In a book review published in 1837 he stressed that 'since Hufeland's new *Grundlegung der Staatswirthschaftskunst*, 1807, the German authors are clear about the issue' (Hermann, 1837b; column 42).

each person has only his relation to the want or the *usefulness* as auxiliary means [*Hilfsmittel*] to estimate the goods, both of which are too dissimilar and uncertain to allow one to exactly compare different goods by means of them.

(Hermann, 1836c; columns 102–3)

Here Hermann opposes strongly what later utility theory was to postulate, namely, the ability of agents to compare different goods or bundles of goods, and rank them, independently of prices. In his view such comparisons can only be carried out with 'sufficient precision' if the exchange values of commodities are known.

4. What is profitable is 'productive'

Hermann criticizes the conventional distinction between 'productive' and 'unproductive' labour which derives from Smith and was advocated in one form or another by contemporary German economists, including Rau (1826, sections 103–5). The characterization of services and trade as 'unproductive' is rejected by Hermann on the grounds that the only criterion for deciding the 'productivity' of a business is whether it is *profitable*, that is, pays the ordinary profits on the capital invested. On this count services and trade, being profitable, have to be considered productive on a par with agriculture and manufactures. Hermann follows McCulloch and Say and extends Smith's generalization of the Physiocratic concept of productivity to all profitable activities in the economy.

To this he adds two observations. First, in line with his three-dimensional specification of a 'good', he considers transport and storage activities as productive because they generate new goods by moving given use values through space and time (Hermann, 1832, p. 27). In this way, as well as by material production, the supply of goods is adjusted to the wants of consumers. Second, in conditions of free competition there is a tendency towards a uniform rate of profit. Hermann (ibid., p. 40) expressly subscribes to Robert Torrens's dictum that the articles produced by capitals of the same magnitude, together with the residues of the capitals, have the same value (cf. Torrens, 1826, p. 71). Let K_i denote the capital advanced in industry $i (i = 1, 2, \ldots, n)$ at the beginning of the period of production, Y_i the value of the product, R_i the value of the 'residue of capital', and r the (uniform) rate of profit, then we have

$$(1 + r)K_i = Y_i + R_i \quad (i = 1, 2, \ldots, n)$$

In this perspective an old fixed capital item can be treated as a kind of by-product, or joint output, of the main product.

Torrens's argument has impressed Hermann. He takes it to have overthrown the classical labour quantity-based approach to the explanation of exchange values and credits Torrens with having developed 'the more correct rule' that after the separation of worker and capitalist commodities exchange according to the quantities of capital employed (Hermann, 1832, p. 134, fn.). However, while he subscribes to the formal aspect of Torrens's construction, he finds its material aspect wanting.

The main shortcoming of the classical English authors, including Torrens, is said to be that they 'do not consider the *capital services* [*Kapitalnutzung*] an *independent element* of the products'; he adds: 'As far as we can see, this is the main achievement in political economy we owe J. B. Say' (ibid., pp. 31–2, fn.). This passage foreshadows Hermann's own theory of profits, centred around the notion of 'capital services'. A first important aspect of his theory is the redefinition of the notion of capital.

5. Hermann's notion of 'capital'

Hermann deviates from Adam Smith's definition of capital in two important respects:

(1) Smith treated land and natural resources as an independent factor of production, Hermann subsumes them under 'capital';
(2) Smith treated human capital as a part of capital, Hermann regards it as a separate factor.

In what follows, the emphasis will be on the first aspect.

While Smith is said to have correctly seen that only those valuable things count as capital which, while they exist, yield their proprietors an income, Hermann accuses him of not consequently applying this insight: 'In particular it is astonishing that he does not reckon land amongst the capitals, although it is a good which continues to exist while it yields an income' (ibid., p. 48). However, Hermann himself does not appear to have been very clear about the concepts he uses when he observes that in civilized nations plots of land have generally been modified by capital investments and *therefore* have gradually assumed the nature of capital.

Hermann's redefinition of capital has met with considerable criticism. Roscher (1874, p. 864) accused him of 'confounding the rent of land and the profits on capital'. In fact, the category of natural resources such as land does not lose its distinctness just because it is possible to modify within limits the quality and yield of natural resources. For example, the classification of plots of land according to their 'fertility' still makes sense, as does the explanation of rents in terms of (extensive) diminishing returns. Interestingly, defining away land and natural resources as a separate kind of factor of production does not lead Hermann to abandon the principles developed by earlier authors, most notably Ricardo, to explain the income obtained by the proprietors of this kind of resources: the principles of extensive and intensive rent. On the contrary, the gist of his argument consists of an attempt to generalize these principles to the explanation of *all* distributive variables, including profits and wages.[14] Scrutiny shows that it is not so much land that he subsumes under capital, but rather (fixed) capital that he subsumes under

---

14 Hermann was not the first author to attempt this generalization of the principle of rent to other factors of production. In German-speaking economics he was anticipated to some extent by Hufeland and Storch, among others.

land. Profits on fixed capital items are accordingly conceived of as a scarcity rent in complete analogy with the rents obtained on different qualities of land that are in short supply. Hermann's analysis can be said to contain one of the most important anticipations of marginal productivity theory in the history of our subject.

In terms of *method*, Hermann's approach to the theory of distribution implies a shift away from the long-period method of Smith and Ricardo to some short-period method. As is well known, Smith and Ricardo focused attention on positions of the economic system characterized by a full reciprocal adjustment of productive capacity in the different lines of production and 'effectual demand' so that a uniform rate of profit obtains.[15] These positions were seen to act as 'centres of gravitation', given the actions of profit-seeking producers who allocate their capital in search of the highest rate of return. By increasing (decreasing) the production of those capital goods which paid high (low) rates of profit, discrepancies between productive capacity and demand would be abolished and a tendency towards a uniform rate of profit manifest itself. Hermann does not abandon this notion. He rather relegates it to the status of a benchmark and in much of what he writes rather concentrates on the short and medium run in which the capital stock has not yet had enough time to adjust fully to the other data of the economic system in order for a competitive long-run 'equilibrium' with a uniform rate of profit to become established. This shift away from the long period is justified in terms of the observation that the economic system is continuously exposed to changes of a more or less exogenous nature, so that the system will hardly ever be in a long-period position. This becomes clear in chapter 4, in which Hermann puts forward his price theory.

6. Price theory

In 'civil exchange', Hermann argues, 'the price is the result of the struggle between two parties with opposed interests and under the influence of competition'. The 'market price' is defined as that price at which the two parties are 'in equilibrium', that is, 'when the same amount of the commodity is wanted and offered' (Hermann, 1832, p. 67). This definition conveys the impression as if Hermann was exclusively concerned with the actual price, whereas the 'natural' price of the classical economists plays no role in his argument. However, throughout his work the classical notion lingers in the background and frequently comes to the fore. The exchange value of a commodity is said 'to cover in addition to the value of circulating capital contained in it the exchange value of all the capital services forgone in its production, or the *ordinary profit*' (ibid., p. 79; emphasis added). The reference is to that amount of profits which could be obtained in alternative

---

15 Alternatively, a relatively stable structure of differential rates of profit, reflecting persistent causes affecting profitability in different employments of capital, was contemplated by these authors; see, for example, Smith (*WN*, I.x.b).

employments of capital (ibid., pp. 81–2), that is, Hermann has recourse to the principle of *opportunity benefit* (or *cost*).[16]

In the sequel, Hermann moves freely between the long-run and the short-run notion of price. He makes it clear that for the most part he does not follow Smith and Ricardo but rather J. B. Say and especially Malthus (ibid., p. 96, fn.). Accordingly, both actual and normal price are taken to be determined by 'demand and supply' (*Ausgebot und Nachfrage*).[17] As is well known, Ricardo in a letter to Malthus dated 9 October 1820 objected: 'You say demand and supply regulates value – this, I think, is saying nothing' (Ricardo, *Works*, VIII, p. 279). Hermann could not know this objection, but he was aware of the necessity to render the two words *analytical categories*. To this effect he studied the determinants of demand and supply. He saw three factors at work on each side. It should be mentioned that in places his reasoning is rather clouded.

From the point of view of *demand*, the price of a commodity is said to depend on

(1) the use value of the good, that is, the position in the hierarchy of wants of the respective want that is satisfied by means of the good;[18]
(2) the purchasing power of those who desire the good, that is, what matters is their 'effectual' (*wirksame*) demand;[19] and
(3) the additional costs of purchasing the commodity, that is, 'natural' and 'social' factors that constrain competition and prevent the price from falling to cost of production (inclusive of ordinary profits) (Hermann, 1832, p. 66–76).

While the consumer is assumed to be predominantly interested in the use value of a commodity, the producer is said to be exclusively interested in its exchange value or, more precisely, the difference between the exchange value and total unit costs. The three factors at work on the *supply* side contemplated by Hermann are

(1) the cost of production of the commodity;
(2) the 'natural' and 'social' factors that constrain competition and thus exert an influence on price; and

16 John, E. Cairnes is commonly credited with establishing the concept of opportunity costs in economics and of basing the theory of value on it. Cairnes introduced in particular the notion of disutility as a criticism to Ricardo. As will become clear in the following, he was partly anticipated by Hermann.

17 It has been widely acknowledged that the major novelty in Mountifort Longfield's approach to the problem of value and distribution in his *Lectures on Political Economy* (Longfield, [1834] 1971) consisted in his attempt to determine the price of a product as well as the price of a factor service by the opposing forces of 'demand' and 'supply'. It may be said that in this regard Hermann anticipated Longfield by two years. Longfield has also been credited with building up the notion of a demand schedule on an argument that can be interpreted as an early statement of marginal utility theory (cf. Schumpeter, 1954, p. 465). As we have seen, in this regard Hermann cannot claim priority.

18 Hermann's view of needs and wants may be compared to the concept of lexicographic preferences.

19 It is in the context of an investigation of (2) that Hermann refers to Bernoulli *via* Laplace's *Essai philosophique sur les probabilités*, published in 1825; cf. Hermann (1832, p. 73, fn.). For a discussion of the way Hermann dealt with the problem and its relationship to Bernoulli's argument, see Baloglou (1995, pp. 34–9).

(3) the 'exchange value of price goods', by which Hermann appears to mean the terms of trade between the commodity under consideration and all the other commodities or, broadly speaking, the purchasing power, in terms of the standard of value, of the proceeds from selling one unit of the commodity (ibid., pp. 76–96).

As regards the supply side, the emphasis is on item 1 (ibid., pp. 76–88). In what follows we shall exclusively deal with this factor because it is here that Hermann comes up with his most interesting insights. In modern parlance, Hermann defines the long-run supply price of a commodity as unit costs plus profit at the ordinary rate on the capital advanced at the beginning of the production period:

> It can thus be said in brevity that the costs of a product are equal to the sum of all capitals passed on to the product [i.e., circulating capital] plus the value of the services of all capitals employed in production. Calling A the circulating capital, which passes on to the product, and B the fixed capital, which is employed in production, and assuming that the value of the capital service is on average $p/100$ of the capital, then costs equal: $A + (A + B)p/100$.
>
> (ibid., pp. 79–80)

This is a price = cost equation. Let p_i $(i = 1, 2, \ldots, n)$ denote the ordinary or normal price of commodity i and r the ordinary rate of profit. Adding subscripts to the symbols for the two kinds of capital, we have

$$(1+r)A_i + rB_i = p_i \quad (i = 1, 2, \ldots, n) \tag{4.1}$$

It should be noted that in Hermann the circulating capital includes the wages of workers and the hypothetical wages of the entrepreneur. The uniformity of the rate of profit is expressly tied to the condition of 'freedom of trade' (*Freiheit des Verkehrs*), that is, free entry and exit in all industries (ibid., p. 82).

Before we continue, a slip in Hermann's price equations should be pointed out. Hermann assumes the fixed capital to be advanced at the beginning of the period and in addition reckons fixed capital consumption, depreciation, C_i, as a part of the circulating capital (ibid., p. 79). C_i is therefore discounted forward twice. The corrected version of Hermann's price equation is

$$(1+r)A_i - rC_i + rB_i = p_i \quad (i = 1, 2, \ldots, n)^{20} \tag{4.2}$$

---

20 If old fixed capital were to be treated as a joint product, as suggested by Hermann (see Section 4), then still another formulation would be appropriate. With A_i^* as circulating capital per unit of output exclusive of depreciation, the price equation would be

$$(1+r)A_i^* + (1+r)B_i = p_i + (B_i - C_i)$$

or

$$(1+r)A_i^* + rB_i + C_i = p_i \quad (i = 1, 2, \ldots, n)$$

Although his formalization is quite primitive, it is to be noted that Hermann was one of the first economists to envisage the interdependence of prices and to hint at the possibility of studying this interdependence in terms of a system of *simultaneous* equations. In his discussion of the impact of changes in one of the determinants of supply and demand on the price of the commodity he aims at taking into account the repercussions of the change of one price on itself via its impact on the prices of other commodities which enter the production of the commodity under consideration. In this framework of analysis Hermann extends the law of diminishing returns, which Ricardo had developed for agriculture, to all productive activities in the economy. He stresses that in long-period competitive 'equilibrium', that is, after all the necessary adjustments have taken place, the price of a commodity equals its marginal cost inclusive of the ordinary profits on capital: the price will rise or fall to that level of costs, 'below which that part of the total quantity demanded which is provided by the least effective means of production cannot be produced' (ibid., p. 84). Implicit in Hermann's argument is the concept of a relationship between the quantities of the different commodities produced and their long-period prices, given technical alternatives. In Hermann we encounter the idea of *long-run supply functions* for the different industries of the economy.

Hermann's discussion of the choice of technique of cost-minimizing producers is of particular interest to us. Apparently inspired by Ricardo's analysis of the conditions in which (new) improved machinery will be introduced, Hermann is one of the first authors to approach this problem in terms of *inequalities*. Unit costs, he argues, may be reduced

(1) by economizing on circulating capital,
(2) as a consequence of a reduction in the ordinary rate of profit, and
(3) 'by a change in the composition of costs, especially by replacing circulating capital by fixed capital' (ibid., p. 87).

As regards the third possibility, the question is whether a newly invented machine will be employed, that is, become an innovation. Hermann approaches the problem as follows. Assume that in the original situation price equation (4.1) applies. Now an invention is made which allows one to save a part of the circulating capital, a, by employing a machine, whose value is B' and whose yearly wear and tear amounts to b. Then, Hermann argues,

the new costs are

$$A - a + b + (A - a + b + B + B') \left(\frac{p}{100} \right)$$

and these must be smaller than the previous costs, that is

$$b + (B' + b) \left(\frac{p}{100} \right) < a + a \left(\frac{p}{100} \right)$$

The change is advantageous, if

$$p < \frac{100(a - b)}{B' + b - a}$$

or

$$b < \frac{a(100 + p) - B'p}{100 + p}$$

or

$$a > \frac{b(100 + p) + B'p}{100 + p}$$

or

$$B' < \frac{(a - b)(100 + p)}{p}$$

It can be seen, among other things, that this kind of cost reduction depends on the rate of profit and is the more effective, the lower are the ordinary profits. It is therefore indeed seen to be carried out mostly in countries in which the rate of profit is low relative to the wage rate.

(ibid., pp. 87–8)

This algebraic demonstration reflects Hermann's analytical ingenuity and his capability to put mathematics at the disposal of economic theory.[21] He corroborates Ricardo's view (cf. *Works* I, p. 395) that the choice of technique cannot generally be decided independently of income distribution. The second of the inequalities in the quotation provides a comparison between the profitability of the old and the new method of production and thus informs about whether the new method is able to pay extra profits or incurs extra costs.

Hermann's approach to the problem of the choice of technique in terms of inequalities was anticipated by one year by the Cambridge mathematician William Whewell (1831) who attempted to put the argument in Ricardo's *Principles* in a mathematical form.[22] There is no presumption that Hermann was familiar with Whewell's essay. We may therefore credit him with the independent formulation of an approach that was to become prominent in later theory.[23]

---

21 Roscher (1874, p. 866) was one of the few authors who saw the importance of Hermann's finding, whereas Baloglou (1995, p. 35), who calls Hermann's contribution to mathematical economics 'unimportant', missed it. Unfortunately, the posthumously published second edition of Hermann's book does not contain the above algebraic discussion. It is not clear whether it was dropped by Hermann himself or the editors, Helferich and Mayr.

22 For a summary statement of Whewell's treatment of the choice of technique, see Kurz and Salvadori (1995, chapter 13, section 5); on Whewell and the group of mathematical economists around him, see the literature referred to there.

23 We encounter this approach for example in Ladislaus von Bortkiewicz; it found its most sophisticated expression in John von Neumann's famous paper on growth in a linear system of production. See Kurz and Salvadori (1993).

Hermann concludes the chapter with a summary statement of what he considers to be the main shortcoming of Ricardo's theory of value. He maintains

> that the price of those commodities which are regularly brought to the market in any desired quantity is not exclusively determined by cost, as Ricardo and his pupils teach. In any case the first and most important factor of price is rather demand, which has its main roots in the use value of the good and in the purchasing power of the buyers. From demand and from what those who want the good are willing to abstain from derives the cost of the least efficient production that may be undertaken to satisfy the demand.
>
> (Hermann, 1832, p. 95)[24]

While Hermann places a lot of emphasis on the factors affecting the demand for commodities and, deriving from that, the demand for factor services, he did not develop the concept of a 'demand function'. The reason for this is that he did not have a clear notion of *substitution* in consumption or production. While he showed some awareness that demand and supply are responsive to changes in relative prices, and thus income distribution, he failed to provide a theoretical expression of these interdependences.[25] As we shall see in the next section, this is also the reason why Hermann's explanation of income distribution in terms of demand and supply is left hanging in the air and is at best a halfway house between classical theory and marginalist theory.

7. Theory of profits

Both in his view and in that of many of his commentators, Hermann's main contribution consisted of a fresh attempt at explaining the origin and the level of profits.

24 There is a close resemblance between Hermann's and Malthus' position. In a letter dated 26 October 1820 Malthus had answered Ricardo's earlier letter: 'No wealth can exist unless the demand, or the estimation in which the commodity is held exceeds the cost of production: and with regard to a vast mass of commodities does not the demand actually determine the cost? How is the price of corn, and the quality of the last land taken into cultivation determined but by the state of the population and the demand. How is the price of metals determined?' (in Ricardo, *Works* VIII: 286). Ricardo replied in a letter dated 24 November 1820, saying: 'I shall not dispute another proposition in your letter "No wealth['] you say "can exist unless the demand, or the estimation in which the commodity is held exceeds the cost of production" '. I have never disputed this. I do not dispute either the influence of demand on the price of corn and on the price of all other things, but supply follows close at its heels, and soon takes the power of regulating price in his own hands, and in regulating it he is determined by cost of production. I acknowledge the intervals on which you so exclusively dwell, but still they are only intervals' (ibid., p. 302). This shows that the dispute between Ricardo and Malthus was partly a dispute about method, that is, whether the theory of value should be short or long-period: while Ricardo was in favour of the latter, Malthus opted for the former. Hermann can be said to have sided more with Malthus.

25 As regards production, Hermann's discussion of the choice of technique problem contains of course the germs of some concept of substitution. Yet Hermann does not appear to have been aware of the wider implications of his argument.

The main chapters of the *Staatswirthschaftliche Untersuchungen* to consult in this regard are the long chapter 5 and chapter 6. However, several of Hermann's ideas are anticipated in previous passages of the book, especially in the section devoted to the problem of the measure of value in the chapter on price theory. Apparently inspired by Malthus's thoughts on the matter, there Hermann confronts Ricardo's concept of the quantity of 'labour embodied' (l.e.) in a commodity and Smith's concept of the quantity of 'labour commanded' (l.c.) by it. Hermann points out that 'goods commonly buy more labour or the produce of more labour [l.c.] than has been necessary in their production [l.e.]; without this surplus the capitalist would have no profit and would refrain from advancing his capitals' (Hermann, 1832, p. 132). Hence, it is a necessary (but not sufficient) condition for profits to be positive that l.c. > l.e. This is obviously true and was not questioned by Ricardo. Yet Hermann seems to think that it contradicts Ricardo's labour theory of value. He maintains that acknowledging a difference between l.c. and l.e. is tantamount to conceding 'that in addition to labour another element is necessary in order to produce the good, namely the services of capitals, and if the good has an exchange value that is larger than the labour it contains, then this shows precisely that these services not only have use value, but also exchange value.' This seems to be an expression of the usual confusion encountered at the time between labour as the sole cause of value and labour as the sole cause of wealth. Hermann concludes with the rhetorical question: 'But if the finished product has, besides labour, another component part, which just like labour assumes an exchange value due to demand and scarcity [*Seltenheit*], does it *cost* only *labour*?' (ibid., pp. 133–4).

Clearly, the explanation of relative prices in terms of relative quantities of l.e. in the different commodities is not contradicted by the mere existence of profits. (However, when capital–labour ratios differ across industries it is contradicted by the rule that in competitive conditions profits tend to be distributed in proportion to the capital invested; Ricardo, it is known, grappled with this problem.) A difference between l.c. and l.e. is simply an expression of the existence of profits; their explanation is an entirely different matter. We must therefore turn to Hermann's further thoughts on the matter.

In the chapter on profits Hermann stresses first that in competitive conditions there will be a tendency towards the uniformity of profit rates. The self-interest of capitalists will make them seek the highest rate of return on their invested capital; this will tend to equalize profitability across sectors. In reality, this tendency is said to be clearly discernible. People who maintain the opposite often have made mistakes in their calculations of the capital advances. In particular, there is the widespread error of not subtracting 'entrepreneurial wages' from profits (ibid., pp. 146–7). However, Hermann admits, strictly speaking the 'law of the equalization of profits' relates only to circulating capital and not to fixed capital. While the former is seen to return to its owner after each cycle of production and circulation in the fluid or 'indifferent form of money, which allows any kind of employment', fixed capital cannot quickly be transmuted into the most profitable form (ibid., p. 149). Hence, while circulating capital can be said to earn its proprietor the ordinary rate of profit, fixed capital earns him a scarcity rent. Hermann thus anticipates Wicksell's 'Rent goods' (*Rentengüter*) (cf. Wicksell, 1893, p. 80) and Marshall's concept of 'Quasi-rent' (cf. Marshall, [1890] 1977, p. 341 and 516–22).

What role is played by capital in the process of production and valuation of commodities? Hermann denies that commodities cost only labour, the reason being that the role of *durable* capital (as opposed to circulating capital, such as raw materials) cannot be reduced to the transfer of labour embodied in it in proportion to its wear and tear:

> Although the machine itself contains labour, this labour is totally different from the labour contained in the material that enters the product; only to the extent to which the machine is consumed does it behave like material; taken as a whole, the works and services combined in it enter into circulation, are only the *basis of a service* which then becomes an element of the product.
>
> (Hermann, 1832, p. 133)

This passage contains the essence of Hermann's 'use' or 'services theory of profits' (*Nutzungstheorie*), as Böhm-Bawerk ([1884] 1921, pp. 180–6) was to dub it. Hermann's explanation revolves around a concept which conceives of a fixed capital item as representing two separate goods: on the one hand the physical capital good and on the other its use or services. In a passage which is reminiscent of John Bates Clark's later distinction between 'concrete capital goods', each of which is destructible and has to be destroyed in order to serve its productive purpose, and 'true capital', a permanent abiding fund of productive wealth, Hermann states:

> It is of the utmost importance to distinguish between the object in which a capital is materialized and capital itself. Capital is the basis of permanent services which have a certain exchange value; it continues to exist undiminished as long as the services do have this value, and it makes no difference whether the goods, which form the capital, are useful only as capital or otherwise, indeed in which form capital presents itself.
>
> (Hermann, 1832, pp. 335–6)

Hermann credits Jean-Baptiste Say with the finding that capital services are exchange values that are separate from the capital goods proper (ibid., p. 270, fn.).

Böhm-Bawerk was to denounce Clark's above distinction as 'dark, mystical rhetoric' (Böhm-Bawerk, 1907). His characterizations of Hermann's services theory of profits and of the more elaborate form it had assumed in the hands of his former teacher Carl Menger were hardly more favourable (cf. Böhm-Bawerk, [1884] 1921; chapter VIII).[26] We may thus ask: What made Hermann postulate a service rendered by a fixed capital item that is independent of and available in

---

26 For a discussion of Böhm-Bawerk's criticism of the services theories of interest, see Kurz (1994, pp. 72–9).

addition to the item's wear and tear? What made him envisage durable capital as providing *two* kinds of economic goods?

The key to an answer to these questions is to be found in Hermann's concept of capital which conceives of capital as a rent-bearing asset on a par with scarce land. In a sense Hermann generalizes the Physiocratic idea of *produit net* due to the productivity of land to profits due to the productivity of capital. In this perspective machine power can be compared to land power (and labour power) and just like the latter is the source of a surplus product and (non-Marxian) surplus value. A first way to increase the productive powers of society is in terms of an increase of the amount of arable land by ameliorating given plots or, in the extreme, gaining new land from the sea by way of empoldering it. While this is a possibility, Hermann argues that in advanced states of the economy the accumulation of capital is a more efficient device in order to increase the wealth of a nation: 'Most important for an economy are capitals of the *second* kind, since their multiplication is fully under the control of man, who is thus possessed of a means continuously to open up new and lasting sources which generate the instruments to satisfy wants growing with education and population towards a boundary that is rather far off' (1832, p. 282). Just like adding a piece of land, adding a capital good to the existing stock implies 'a new and permanently consumable commodity for exchange, namely its services' (ibid., p. 282). This explains also Hermann's idiosyncratic concept of 'capital'. In order to be able to speak of capital's permanent or perennial nature he confounded it with land, the (stylised) characteristic of which is that it is everlasting.

It explains also why Hermann rejects two doctrines, one of which was still prominent when he wrote, while the other was just about to gain momentum:

(1) Turgot's idea that society's surplus, though *generated* in agriculture, in competitive conditions will tend to be *appropriated* in proportion to the capital advanced in the various spheres of production; and
(2) the wage fund doctrine.

Hermann finds fault with both doctrines because they amount, explicitly or implicitly, to a denial of a separate productivity of a factor called 'capital'. In the first case this is obvious, as Hermann points out in his *magnum opus* and in a review article of J. Dutens' *Philosophie de l'économie politique*, published in 1835 (Hermann, 1837a). In his *Réflexions sur la formation et la distribution des richesses* Turgot had indicated that the *produit net*, which in Physiocratic authors was conceived of as a *pur don de la nature*, need not be exclusively distributed in the form of ground rent. With land freely tradable, the owners of money capital may choose among various alternatives to invest their capital, including the acquisition of a rent-bearing piece of land. In conditions of free competition there will be a tendency to a uniform rate of return on capital, which implies that the surplus product will be distributed in proportion to the capitals invested in all sectors of the economy (see on this Faccarello, 1990). While Hermann adopts Turgot's view of land as capital, he rejects the idea that only landed capital (or rather those employed in agriculture) is productive. It is his contention that (fixed) capital in general is productive. In chapter 6 of the *Untersuchungen*, under the heading of 'effects of capital', he criticizes Smith, Ricardo, Malthus, McCulloch and Rau for not having singled out the 'service of capital as such' as an independent 'economic good', that is, a 'good with a separate use value'. Smith is accused of having overlooked that 'in agriculture the larger product [i.e. wages, profit and rent] is due to the cooperation of the productive powers of land, for which the proprietor demands a part of the product [i.e., rent]' (Hermann, 1832, p. 276). Profits can be regarded on a par with rents as the fructification of an original productive power. Similarly, in his review of the book by Dutens, Hermann asks the rhetorical question: 'What else is the interest on capital but an excess of the price of the product over its cost, a *produit net*, which the consumer of the product grants the capitalist in the same way as he grants the landlord the rent of land? Both are high or low in proportion to the scarcity of land and capital and the demand for products, in the production of which they are needed' (Hermann, 1837a; column 349). Here profits on capital are seen in complete analogy to the rent of land and are explained in terms of the relative scarcity of capital.

In the second case Hermann's reasoning goes as follows. According to the advocates of the wage fund doctrine – Hermann mentions Malthus, McCulloch and Rau – 'the number of those seeking employment and the quantity of capital, designed to be applied in the employment of labour in profitable firms, determine the wage' (Hermann, 1832, p. 280). Let W denote the wage fund, L the number of people seeking employment, and w the wage rate, then we have

$$w = W/L$$

In this version the wage fund doctrine is a theory that determines the wage rate in conditions of *full* employment. The rate of profit is ascertained residually as the ratio of the net product (exclusive of total wages) and the value of the social capital. Hermann is opposed to this theory, since it contradicts his view of the independent forces determining profits. He admits that 'the capital as a whole and its increase are of the utmost importance for the level of wages'. Yet, he adds, this is not 'because workers are paid a wage from it, but because each new capital brings a new consumable and permanently revolving [*ein neues beliebig verzehrbares und sich dauernd wiederholendes*] exchange good to the market, namely its service' (ibid., p. 282). New capital puts into existence new productive power, that is, increases the productive potential of the economy. Additional demand for goods will not fail to come forth, thanks to Say's Law of markets, which Hermann adopts. This additional demand for goods will lead to an additional demand for labour, which, in conditions of full employment, will push up wages: 'The wage does not rise because the capital used to pay wages is increased, but because as a consequence of the increase in freely disposable values the demand for labour increases.' The wage fund doctrine is said to take 'a side effect for the cause' (ibid., p. 282).

We may conclude this section by going back to Hermann's treatment of land as capital. Hermann stresses that a *ceteris paribus* increase of the product of land, say corn, and thus of rent, increases the price of land (ibid., p. 153). Let σ_j denote the rent per acre of a given quality j of land, π_j the price of that quality of land per acre, and r the general rate of profit, then the expression for a perpetual rent is

$$\pi_j = \sigma_j / r \tag{4.3}$$

We may now follow Hermann's suggestion and reckon land among the capital advanced at the beginning of the production period. Under the simplifying assumption that there is no durable capital other than land, and assuming that land is not subject to qualitative change in the course of the production process, we may write the following price equation for product i which is produced by means of land of quality j:

$$(1 + r)(A_i + \pi_j b_{ij}) = p_i + \pi_j b_{ij} \tag{4.4}$$

where A_i gives the value per unit of output of the circulating capital (inclusive of the wages of workers and the hypothetical wage of the entrepreneur) and b_{ij} the amount of land of the j-th quality needed per unit of output. In this formulation, which is in agreement with Torrens's suggestion, land is considered both an input into production and a joint output with commodity i. Rewriting the equation gives

$$(1 + r)A_i + \sigma_j b_{ij} = p_i \tag{4.5}$$

where $\sigma_j = r\pi_j$. While equation (4.4) may be said to reflect a situation in which the producer has acquired the land, equation (4.5) has him rent it from the landowner (cf. ibid., pp. 167–77). This shows that Hermann's treatment of land as a capital good does not, in itself, involve an abandonment of the classical theory of value and distribution. Nor does it necessarily imply, as Roscher had argued, that rent and profits are confounded.

8. Hermann's criticism of Senior

In 1836 Hermann published an extensive review article in the *Gelehrte Anzeigen* edited by the Royal Bavarian Academy of Sciences on Nassau W. Senior's *Political Economy* and the French edition of his *Lectures* both of which had come out earlier in the year (cf. Hermann, 1836a). As Bowley stressed, 'Hermann was the only economist who seems to have had any influence on his [Senior's] later work' (1937, p. 94; see also, pp. 132–4, 152–80). This influence is clearly expressed in Senior's Lectures, 1847–52, Course II, in which Senior changed his definition of capital and his theory of profits in response to and substantially along the lines suggested by Hermann in his review. However, the review is not only interesting because of the impact it had on Senior, but also because of the clarity with which some of Hermann's own ideas are spelled out.

Hermann contends that since the writings of that 'ingenious thinker' by the name of Ricardo (Hermann, 1836a; column 194) there have been only a few authors with an independent point of view on economic matters, one of which is said to be Senior. Hermann adds that several of Senior's findings, although arrived at in a different way, are in harmony with the results put forward by Hermann himself in his book. Hermann takes this fact to be an expression of the 'inner necessity' of his own research (ibid.; column 195). His main criticisms of Senior are the following. First, in his concept of wealth Senior includes the feelings of those providing services, for example, the emotional satisfaction a doctor derives from being able to help a patient. Hermann objects that what counts are only the results of the mental and emotional forces at work, that is, the usefulness of the goods generated, and not the forces themselves. Second, he accuses Senior of advocating a naive view of 'demand and supply', in particular of not seeing 'that there is neither an absolute supply of commodities nor an unlimited demand for them; a certain supply rather presupposes already a price expected by the sellers, just as a certain demand presupposes a definite price at which buyers are willing to purchase' (ibid.; column 206). Demand and supply thus have to be conceived of as functional relationships between the quantity and price of a commodity.[27] The maximum price is that price which the buyers would be willing to pay at most and equals the cost they would incur if they were to produce the commodity themselves, whereas the minimum price is given by the cost of production (exclusive of profits) incurred by the sellers. This is said to refute the 'error' repeated once and again since Ricardo that cost of production determines the price. Third, Senior is criticized for not distinguishing carefully between the technical and the economic aspects of production (ibid.; column 214).

Most important, however, are Hermann's objections to Senior's theory of capital and profits. The received distinction between productive and unproductive consumption, which Senior adopts, is taken to make no sense both with regard to the sphere of production and that of consumption. As to the former, 'the using up of a machine means *to the producer*, who employs it, only a *change in form* of his capital, whose value continues to exist due to the making good of the wear and tear in the price of the product, but it does not mean consumption'. As to the latter, Senior is said to be wrong in considering those who do not work but live on the proceeds of their wealth as 'unproductive consumers': 'He overlooks that they leave the *use* of their wealth to society as a full compensation for their consumption' (ibid.; column 220). Senior's distinction between three agents of productions – labour, natural agents and 'abstinence' – and his theory of distribution are considered problematic essentially for two reasons. First, Hermann stresses that capital and natural agents form a single category of factors of production whose characteristic feature is that they earn their proprietors a rent. Second, he emphasizes that 'from an economic point of view a product is made up of nothing but costs' (ibid.; column 231). While according to Hermann Senior deserves to be credited with seeing that these costs do not only comprise labour costs, as was maintained by Smith and others, but also 'sacrifices' on the part of the capitalists, he is said to not really understand the nature of these 'sacrifices'. Hermann stresses: 'Profits are a compensation of the

27 This view was of course advocated, among others, by Hermann's teacher Rau.

objective collaboration of capital in production and not of the *subjective* abstinence of the capitalist' (ibid.; column 222, emphases added). What really matters is the productive 'use' made of the capital stock; hence 'a product is nothing but a sum of labours and uses of wealth' (ibid.; column 231). This 'objective' aspect, Hermann maintains, is well captured in his own 'use theory of profits'.[28]

Hermann then discusses the principle of rent as applied indiscriminately to land, labour and capital. Interestingly, in investigating the impact of additions to the stock of capital Hermann begins with a remark on the *division of labour* as it was discussed by Adam Smith and then by Charles Babbage (ibid.; column 229). In this *dynamic* notion the accumulation of capital is seen to be the key to what nowadays are called economies of scale. The reference is to an environment characterised by a change in technological and organizational knowledge which is envisaged to be intimately intertwined with the accumulation of capital. He then switches to the *static* notion of virtual changes in the proportion of factor inputs as it was to become prominent with marginal productivity theory, which presupposes an environment in which the set of technical alternatives from which producers can choose is given and constant. He does not seem to feel the potential tension between these two notions: Whereas in the former view increments to the capital stock enhance capital productivity, in the latter they are the cause of its decline.

It is within the latter framework that Hermann compares a change in output caused by an increase in the employment of labour-cum-capital per unit of land, or rather 'land capital', as he calls it, with a change in output caused by an increase in labour-cum-raw materials per unit of fixed capital. He argues:

> Land capital has the decisive advantage that it offers a greater variety of its utilization, especially if combined with more or less of the other means of production, than the other fixed capitals; its cultivation with a larger capital may at the beginning even provide a more than proportional increase in the products, a possibility that is inconceivable with regard to other fixed capitals. Put more workers on a given workfloor with given machinery and tools and provide them with more raw materials, then the limit is very close, at which this additional input ceases to be compensated [*vergelten*] by an additional output, whereas this limit is farther away with regard to land.
>
> (Hermann, 1836a; column 229–30)

This is a clear statement of the idea that the marginal product of labour-cum-raw materials will fall rapidly as more labour-cum-raw materials is employed per unit of fixed capital. There is also the idea of an equality between marginal revenue and marginal cost which gives the optimum amount of employment of the single firm. Hermann's argument can thus be interpreted as a contribution to identifying

---

28 Apparently, as a result of Hermann's criticism, Senior 'did emphasize the whole influence of productivity more in 1847 than earlier' (Bowley, 1937, p. 133). In addition he accepted Hermann's view that land and capital were really the same genus (ibid., pp. 156–9).

the short-run cost-minimizing porportions of the variable inputs (labour and raw materials) relative to the fixed ones (land, machinery and tools). As regards the relationship between output and labour-cum-capital per unit of homogeneous land, he reiterates the view expressed, for example, by Thünen that the marginal (and the average) product may first rise and then fall. He does not point out, however, that the segment of the productive relationship in which the average product per unit of land is rising is irrelevant since it contradicts cost-minimization.

While production processes using perennial capital, that is, land, are taken to exhibit a *slowly* falling marginal product of the variable factors, this kind of capital cannot easily be multiplied. Things are said to be different with regard to fixed capital of a less longlived nature, that is, machinery and tools. Interestingly, at this point, Hermann shifts back to the dynamic notion of increments to the capital stock: He starts from the assumption that the accumulation of capital is naturally associated with improvements in the methods of production: 'Each improvement . . . is to be considered like an increase in the productivity of capital, which substitutes the land of a country in the production of agricultural products' (ibid.; column 231). Without this assumed 'endogenous' improvement in the productive powers consequent upon an increase in the capital stock, the system would get stuck due to diminishing returns in agriculture. Thus, Hermann wants to have it both ways: falling marginal products and rising productive powers. He does not discuss whether or not these two notions are compatible with one another.

Next Hermann criticizes Senior's concept of 'monopoly' in the theory of distribution. Senior had argued along Smithian lines that the share of the product appropriated by the landed gentry is not due to some sacrifice on their part and therefore must be attributed to a monopoly position which allows them 'to harvest, where they never sowed'. Hermann observes that this leaves out alternative uses of land. Rather than letting it to farmers to cultivate it, landowners could use it themselves in one or another of a variety of different ways. Hermann concludes that the rent of land is a scarcity price just like the profits on (fixed) capital; in the determination of both the concept of opportunity cost (or use) plays an important role (ibid.; column 233–4). It is also interesting that in this context Hermann points out with reference to Ricardo that the principle of rent can be developed without assuming different qualities of land (ibid.; column 237). The theory of *intensive* diminishing returns with regard to homogenous land was indeed to provide the analytical nucleus around which marginalist theory was to be built. Given his scarcity approach to the explanation of wages, profits and rents, it should come as no surprise that Hermann, commenting on Senior, would take issue with Ricardo's concept of an inverse relationship between the real wage rate and the rate of profit. In Hermann's view there is no such relationship: at any moment of time there is rather a particular constellation of the wage rate and the rate of profit compatible with the givens of the economic system, that is, the needs and wants of consumers, the endowment of the economy with labour and capital, broadly defined, and the technical and organizational conditions of production (ibid.; column 239). While the so-called 'Ricardian socialists' are said to have interpreted the inverse relationship as indicating a 'degree of freedom' in the distribution of income which could and should be fixed in a way that is favourable to workers, factory owners in Britain who testified in committees set up by the Parliament tried to use it in support of their own interests, arguing that high wages endanger the profitability and competitiveness of British firms.

9. Innovations and technological change

One of Hermann's main concerns in the *Untersuchungen* is the origin, diffusion and economic and social effects of innovations and technological change. Attention focuses on two aspects: the innovative dynamism generated endogenously by systems based on self-interested behaviour, and the impact of different forms of technological change on the distribution of income. As regards the first aspect, Hermann's starting point is obviously Smith's metaphor of the 'invisible hand' which, in conditions of 'natural liberty', is taken to be responsible for the generation of a variety of positive external effects. He ties this idea to his notion of the 'productivity of capital':

> The totality of employments and the relationship of the product to the expenses form what is called the *productivity of capital*. In industrious nations the latter grows continuously as a result of the activity of industrial entrepreneurs. It is a most beneficial consequence of the ceaseless need for industry [*Erwerbtrieb*] that those are offered a secure reward, who *first* introduce improvements in the production of goods, and that in this way there is a permanent encouragement of ingenuity and talent. At the same time it is clear that in the long run the advantage of each new and improved method of production accrues to the whole, which with the less expensive product henceforth enjoys the fruit of the talent and diligence, the fruit of the spirit [*Geist*] in general, that is, a public good, without any further compensation .... Improvements in the economy and cost reductions in general are first beneficial to the entrepreneur and later only to the consumer, and all inventions and improvements will only for some time pay the entrepreneurs, whereas in the end they only increase the general productivity of the national capitals.
>
> (Hermann, 1832, pp. 212–13)

Accordingly, the market economy stimulates a wide range of decentralized and uncoordinated attempts at innovation. Those innovations that succeed are coordinated by the market process, which proves to be an institution adapted to absorbing the opportunities for growth offered by innovation. These innovations at first involve some monopoly rents, which competition will sooner or later erode.[29]

---

29 However, if entrepreneurs 'are able to keep the improvements secret or if they are protected by a privilege against competition, they are able to pocket more than the ordinary profits for a longer time' (ibid., pp. 210–11).

In the long run they have the tendency to become, in the words of Ricardo, a 'general good' (*Works*, I, p. 386).[30]

While at the time of the first edition of his *magnum opus* Hermann envisages substantial positive externalities of selfish behaviour, he hardly shows awareness of any negative externalities. He plays down the possibility that a change in relative prices consequent upon revolutions in techniques may be detrimental to the interest of some groups in society. As is well known, in the newly added chapter 31 of the third edition of the *Principles*, published in 1821, Ricardo had questioned Smith's overly optimistic view as to the socially beneficial consequences of profit-seeking behaviour. He showed that the introduction of improved machinery in search of extra profits may lead to the displacement of workers that cannot be compensated in the short run. While Hermann admits that there is the possibility of labour displacement in some lines of production, he expresses his conviction that this will quickly be made good by an increase of employment in other lines. His argument is reminiscent of McCulloch's doctrine of automatic compensation (McCulloch, 1821).[31] Later in his life he seems to have become more sensitive to the problem under consideration (cf. Hermann, 1837a, 1838) and advocated an active economic policy to fight unemployment and mitigate the misery of the labouring classes.[32] He also seems to have lost some of his earlier confidence in Say's Law and the impossibility of general gluts of commodities. Notwithstanding these changes of opinion, Hermann held an essentially harmonist view of society.

Hermann's second important concern is the impact of different forms of technological change on the distribution of income. In accordance with his theory of production, which knows only two kinds of factors, labour and capital, he distinguishes between two broad forms of technological change: one which increases the 'efficiency' (*Ergiebigkeit*) of labour, the other that of capital (Hermann, 1832, p. 242). As regards the second form, Hermann sees further

30 Growth in the classical economists and Hermann is clearly *endogenous*. In this context it deserves to be mentioned that all the basic ideas that play a prominent role in the literature on the so-called 'new' growth theory were anticipated in the writings of these authors. For example, the notion of technology as a good that is or tends to become a public good, that is, non-rival and non-excludable, is foreshadowed in Hermann's above reasoning.

31 It is surprising to see Hermann maintain as late as 1837 that so far the machinery problem had not been given much attention in the literature (Hermann, 1837a; column 350–1) – as if Barton, Ricardo or Malthus had never written on the subject. It is also surprising that he does not refer to McCulloch's essay: as the *Untersuchungen* and his book reviews document, Hermann was a regular and attentive reader of the *Edinburgh Review*, in which McCulloch's essay had been published.

32 Hermann's paternalist-etatist attitude towards the emerging social question (*Soziale Frage*) shares many of the characteristic features of the policy propagated later by the so-called 'socialists of the chair' (*Kathedersozialisten*) (see Kurz, 1998). It should be noted that Hermann also felt the challenge to the established political order coming from the 'Ricardian socialists' on the one hand and what Marx was to call the French 'utopian socialists', Fourier, Saint-Simon and their followers, on the other. He was one of the first academic economists to enter into a critical discussion of their ideas (see, e.g., Hermann, 1835). He anticipated several of the arguments put forward later by A. E. F. Schäffle and Böhm-Bawerk in their attacks on socialist ideas.

reason to attack Ricardo and his followers, who are said to have repeated like an 'axiom' that 'the increase in the efficiency of capital raises the rate of profit' (ibid., p. 256, fn.). Hermann's objection that this is the opposite of the truth shows that he had neither fully grasped Ricardo's doctrine nor the principle of marginal productivity. Böhm-Bawerk ([1884] 1921, pp. 185–6) had no difficulty to point out the flaw in Hermann's argument (see also Kurz, 1994, pp. 102–4).

10. Concluding remarks

Hermann was a remarkable theoretical economist of the German language, without doubt one of the best in the first half of the nineteenth century. Coming from mathematics, the abstract propositions of classical political economy, especially in the form in which they had been handed down by Ricardo, were accessible to him. Hermann attempted to generalize them in various ways. He extended the principle of diminishing returns, which Ricardo had limited to agriculture and mining, to all lines of production, including services. Hermann also managed to render precise the principle of cost minimization in his original discussion of the problem of the choice of technique. And he showed some awareness of the interdependences between different sectors of production and the need to determine prices in a general framework.[33]

While there are several elements in Hermann's analysis which contributed to the development of classical theory, there are also important elements which involved a sharp break with it and pointed in the direction of marginalism.[34] In particular, Hermann abandoned the asymmetric treatment of the distributive variables advocated by Ricardo, which implies that all shares of income other than wages are considered residual claims to the social product. Hermann rather advocated the idea that wages and profits ought to be explained symmetrically in terms of the supply of and the demand for the services of labour and capital. In his view all economic explanation was to be rooted in a single, universally applicable principle: the principle of scarcity. In the theory of income distribution this implied an

---

33 The above discussion has shown that Hermann envisaged Ricardo's analysis as the real challenge any contemporary economic theorist had to face. It has also been shown to what extent Hermann borrowed from and was influenced by Ricardo and other English political economists, in particular Malthus. Therefore, Blaug's opinion that the *Staatswirthschaftliche Untersuchungen* 'owed much to *The Wealth of Nations* but little to the writings of either Malthus or Ricardo' (Blaug, 1987, p. 639) is difficult to sustain. Paul Mombert's characterisation of Hermann as the 'German Ricardo' (cf. Schachtschabel, 1971, p. 78) is likewise dubious. The main evidence that can be put forward in its support is perhaps the statement by Hermann's student Knapp that Hermann considered himself as someone 'who continued and completed Ricardo's system' (cf. Weinberger, 1925, p. 466, fn.). However, as we have seen, in terms of substance this is only partly true. Schumpeter's judgement is more reliable in this regard (cf. Schumpeter, 1954, p. 503).

34 It may be argued that Marshall's high esteem for Hermann had to do with the fact that he saw in him an important precursor of his own point of view. It was particularly Hermann's attempt to complement the classical cost of production or supply perspective with a use value or demand perspective which Marshall may have found appealing (cf. Marshall, [1890] 1977, p. 657).

explanation in terms of the marginal productivities of the factors of production. While the 'natural' price of the classical economists still served him as a benchmark, Hermann often focused attention on the short run, in which the composition of plant and equipment is not fully adjusted to demand. Hence, fixed capital items will not normally yield their proprietors the general rate of profit, but a return, which is explained in the same way as the rent of some particular quality of land that is in short supply. Almost everywhere he looked, Hermann saw cost and profit rate differentials, reflecting diminishing productivity as output increases. He anticipated Marshall's concept of 'Quasi-rent' and Wicksell's concept of 'Rent goods'. His achievements concern essentially the supply side, whereas his work on the demand side did not go beyond received wisdom in contemporary German economics.

Hermann's writings reflect a period in travail – both theoretically and socioeconomically. It is a period of transition between classical and marginalist, or neoclassical, economics, and a period in which the 'social question' became ever more pressing, fed political unrest and endangered the old order. Hermann struggled with both challenges: he was a theoretical economist trying to understand the working of commercial society and a politician and public administrator seeking to ward off the destructive tendencies accompanying the emerging industrial capitalism. Hermann did not provide a complete and logically coherent system but a host of penetrating thoughts, discerning observations and several original findings, some of which are valuable both to the classical and the neoclassical traditions of economic thought.

This brings us back to the question raised at the beginning of the paper: Why did Hermann's achievements fall into oblivion? The following factors might have played a role. First, Hermann's contribution sits uncomfortably between classical analysis on the one hand and marginalist analysis on the other. This may explain why the advocates of neither of the two traditions did care too much to keep alive the memory of his achievements. To the economist working in the classical tradition, Hermann was a revisionist, whereas to the marginalist economists he was still too much of a dyed-in-the-wool classicist. When in the final quarter of the last century the 'showdown' (Böhm-Bawerk) between the two alternative theories of value and distribution had allegedly come, people that were considered to be sitting on the fence had a good chance to be ignored by both camps. Second, Hermann's heavy engagement in politics and public administration prevented him from playing a more active role in intellectual debates and developing his analysis. Third, his numerous book reviews were most certainly not conducive to gain him friends in academic circles, to say the least.[35] Fourth, the purging of the second edition of his *Staatswirthschaftliche Untersuchungen* of some of the analytically more demanding, and innovative, parts was detrimental to the perception of Hermann as an important economic theorist of last century. Finally, Hermann, like several of his colleagues, suffered from the rise to dominance of the Historical School.

---

35 His book reviews culminated often in a merciless demolition of the respective author's project, peppered with polemics; see Kurz (1998).

While the early historicists such as Roscher combined a concern with economic and social history with a vivid interest in economic theory, many of the later historicists were decidely anti-theoretical. In such an environment there is no reason to expect the achievements of an economic theorist to be allocated a prominent place in the collective memory of the scientific community.

Acknowledgements

This chapter developed from a larger work on Hermann (see Kurz, 1998), which was part of a project initiated by Manfred Pix, Munich, to commemorate Hermann's life and work on the occasion of the bicentenary of his birth (1995). An earlier version of the chapter was given at the European Conference on the History of Economics, Erasmus University Rotterdam, Rotterdam, 10–11 February 1995. I am grateful to Bertram Schefold, who served as a discussant of the chapter, for valuable hints and suggestions. I should also like to thank Karl Brandt, Christian Gehrke, Hans Möller (†), Ian Steedman and Richard Sturn for useful discussions. I benefited especially from the comments I received from Giancarlo De Vivo and Gilbert Faccarello. Manfred Pix generously provided me with details of Hermann's life and work. The comments of two anonymous referees are gratefully acknowledged.

References

Baloglou, C. (1995). *Die Vertreter der mathematischen Nationalökonomie in Deutschland zwischen 1838 und 1871*. Marburg: Metropolis.
Blaug, M. (1962). *Economic Theory in Retrospect*. Homewood, IL: Richard D. Irwin. Fifth edn, Cambridge: Cambridge University Press (1997).
Blaug, M. (1987). Hermann, Friedrich Benedict Wilhelm von. In J. Eatwell, M. Milgate and P. Newman (eds), *The New Palgrave. A Dictionary of Economics*, London, Vol. 2: 639–40.
Böhm-Bawerk, E. v. (1907). Capital and Interest Once More, Part II. *Quarterly Journal of Economics*, 21: 247–82.
Böhm-Bawerk, E. v. (1921). *Kapital und Kapitalzins. Erste Abteilung: Geschichte und Kritik der Kapitalzins-Theorien*. 1st edn Innsbruck (1884). Quoted after the 4th edn, Jena (1921).
Bowley, M. (1937). *Nassau Senior and Classical Economics*. London: George Allen & Unwin.
Brandt, K. (1992). *Geschichte der deutschen Volkswirtschaftslehre*, Vol. 1: *Von der Scholastik bis zur klassischen Nationalökonomie*. Freiburg im Breisgau: Haufe.
Brems, H. (1986). *Pioneering Economic Theory, 1630–1980. A Mathematical Restatement*. Baltimore and London: The Johns Hopkins Press.
Crook, J. W. (1898). *German Wage Theories. A History of Their Development*. New York: Columbia University Press.
Debreu, G. (1959). *Theory of Value. An Axiomatic Analysis of Economic Equilibrium*. New Haven and London: Wiley.
Ekelund, R. B. and Hébert, R. F. (1983). *A History of Economic Theory and Method*. Singapore: McGraw-Hill.

Faccarello, G. (1990). Le legs de Turgot: aspects de l'économie politique sensualiste de Condorcet à Roederer. In G. Faccarello and Ph. Steiner (eds), *La Pensée économique pendant la révolution française*. Grenoble: Presses Universitaires de Grenoble.

Helferich, J. A. v. (1878). Fr. B. W. Hermann als nationalökonomischer Schriftsteller. *Zeitschrift für die gesamte Staatswissenschaft*, 34: 637–51.

Hermann, F. B. W. (1823). *Sententiae Romanorum ad oeconomiam universam sive nationalem pertinentes*, PhD thesis and Habilitation, Erlangen: Kunstmann. A German translation was provided by M. and B. H. Overbeck (mimeo).

Hermann, F. B. W. (1832). *Staatswirthschaftliche Untersuchungen*. Munich: Anton Weber. A reprint was edited by Karl Diehl in 1924. A facsimile edition was published in 1987; see Recktenwald (1987).

Hermann, F. B. W. (1835). review article of L. F. Huerne de Pommeuse, *Des colonies agricoles etc.* (Paris 1832), M. le Baron de Morogues, *Du Paupérisme* (Paris 1834), and M. le Vicomte Alban de Villeneuve-Bargemont, *Économie politique chrétienne*, three vols (Paris 1834). In *Jahrbücher für wissenschaftliche Kritik*, 36: columns 287–296.

Hermann, F. B. W. (1836a). review of Nassau W. Senior, *An Outline of the Science of Political Economy* (London 1936) and of *Principes fondamentaux de l'économie politique, tirés de leçons édites et inédites de Mr. N. W. Senior etc. par le Cte. Jean Arrivabene* (Paris 1836). In *Gelehrte Anzeigen*, Vol. II: columns 193–8, 201–206, 209–214, and 217–48.

Hermann, F. B. W. (1836b). review of K. S. Zachariä, *Abhandlungen aus dem Gebiete der Staatswirthschaftslehre* (Heidelberg 1835). In *Gelehrte Anzeigen*, Vol. II: columns 417–22.

Hermann, F. B. W. (1836c). review of E. Baumstark, *Kameralistische Encyklopädie* (Heidelberg and Leipzig 1835). In *Jahrbücher für wissenschaftliche Kritik*, 13: columns 97–104.

Hermann, F. B. W. (1837a). Review of J. Dutens, *Philosophie de l'économie politique* (Paris 1835). In *Gelehrte Anzeigen*, Vol. V: columns 345–51, 358–60.

Hermann, F. B. W. (1837b). Review of L. Say, *Etudes sur la richesse des nations et réfutation des principales erreurs en économie politique* (Paris 1836). In *Jahrbücher für wissenschaftliche Kritik*, 6: columns 41–6.

Hermann, F. B. W. (1838). Review of 'Trades, Unions and Strikes', essay in the *Edinburgh Review*, April 1838, 208–259. In *Gelehrte Anzeigen*, Vol. VII: columns 199–208, 215–6.

Hermann, F. B. W. (1870). *Staatswirthschaftliche Untersuchungen*. 2nd edn, edited by J. v. Helferich and G. v. Mayr, Munich: A. G. Fleischmann.

Ingram, J. K. (1967). *A History of Political Economy*. 1st edn 1888; new and enlarged edn with a supplementary chapter by W. A. Scott and an introduction by Richard T. Ely 1915. Reprint, New York: Kelley.

Kautz, J. (1860). *Theorie und Geschichte der Nationalökonomik. Propyläen zum volks- und staatswirthschaftlichen Studium*, second part: *Die geschichtliche Entwicklung der National-Oekonomik und ihrer Literatur*. Vienna: Carl Gerold's Sohn.

Kurz, H. D. (1986). Classical and Early Neoclassical Economists on Joint Production. *Metroeconomica*, 38: 1–37.

Kurz, H. D. (1994). Auf der Suche nach dem 'erlösenden Wort': Eugen von Böhm-Bawerk und der Kapitalzins. In B. Schefold (ed.), *Eugen von Böhm-Bawerks 'Geschichte und Kritik der Kapitalzins-Theorieen'. Vademecum zu einem Klassiker der Theoriegeschichte*. Düsseldorf: Verlag Wirtschaft und Finanzen, 45–110.

Kurz, H. D. (1995). *Theory of Production. A Long-Period Analysis*. Cambridge: Cambridge University Press.

Kurz, H. D. (1998). *Hermanns Beitrag zur Kapital- und Verteilungstheorie*. In H. D. Kurz, *Ökonomisches Denken in Klassischer Tradition*. Marburg: Metropolis, 147–214.

Kurz, H. D. and Salvadori, N. (1993). Von Neumann's Growth Model and the 'Classical' Tradition. *European Journal of the History of Economic Thought*, 1: 129–60.

Longfield, M. (1971). *Lectures on Political Economy*; first published in 1834. In R. D. Collison Black (ed.), *The Economic Writings of Mountifort Longfield*. New York: Augustus M. Kelley.

McCulloch, J. R. (1821). The Opinions of Messrs Say, Sismondi, and Malthus, on the Effects of Machinery and Accumulation, Stated and Examined. *Edinburgh Review*, March: 102–23.

Marshall, A. (1977). *Principles of Economics*; 1st edn 1890. 8th edn 1920; reprint, reset. London: Macmillan.

Menger, C. (1871). *Grundsätze der Volkswirthschaftslehre*. Vienna: Braumüller; 2nd edn 1923. English translation of the 2nd edn by J. Dingwall and B. T. Hoselitz entitled *Principles of Economics*, New York and London 1981: New York University Press.

Niehans, J. (1990). *A History of Economic Theory. Classic Contributions, 1720–1980*. Baltimore and London: The Johns Hopkins University Press.

Pix, M. (1995). *Friedrich Benedikt Wilhelm Hermann*, Vol. 1, *Darstellung*. Munich: mimeo.

Pribram, K. (1983). *A History of Economic Reasoning*. Baltimore: The Johns Hopkins University Press.

Rau, K. H. (1826). *Grundsätze der Volkswirthschaftslehre*. Heidelberg, 8th edn 1869.

Recktenwald, H. C. (1987). Hermanns 'Untersuchungen' – Ein Pionier dynamischer Wettbewerbsmärkte und Eigentumsrechte. In H. C. Recktenwald (ed.), *Vademecum zu einem unterbewerteten Klassiker der ökonomischen Wissenschaft*, Düsseldorf: Verlag Wirtschaft und Finanzen, 15–68.

Ricardo, D. (1951–73). *The Works and Correspondence of David Ricardo*. Edited by Piero Sraffa with the collaboration of M. H. Dobb, 11 vols. Cambridge: Cambridge University Press. In the text quoted as *Works*, volume number, page.

Rima, I. H. (1991). *Development of Economic Analysis*. 5th edn, Homewood, IL: Richard D. Irwin.

Roscher, W. (1874). *Geschichte der National-Oekonomik in Deutschland*. Munich and Berlin: Oldenbourg.

Routh, G. (1975). *The Origin of Economic Ideas*. London: Macmillan.

Schachtschabel, H. G. (1971). *Geschichte der volkswirtschaftlichen Lehrmeinungen*. Stuttgart and Düsseldorf: Kohlhammer.

Schäffle, A. E. F. (1870). Ueber den Gebrauchswerth und die Wirthschaft nach den Begriffsbestimmungen Hermann's. *Zeitschrift für die gesamte Staatswissenschaft*, 26: 122–79.

Schneider, E. (1962). *Einführung in die Wirtschaftstheorie*. Part IV. Tübingen: J. C. B. Mohr.

Schumpeter, J. A. (1914). Epochen der Dogmen- und Methodengeschichte. In *Grundriss der Sozialökonomik, I. Abteilung: Wirtschaft und Wirtschaftswissenschaft*. Tübingen: J. C. B. Mohr, 19–124.

Schumpeter, J. A. (1954). *History of Economic Analysis*. New York and Oxford: Oxford University Press.

Smith, A. (1976). *An Inquiry into the Nature and Causes of the Wealth of Nations*. 1st edn 1776. In *The Glasgow Edition of the Works and Correspondence of Adam Smith*, eds R. H. Campbell and A. S. Skinner. Oxford: Oxford University Press.

Spiegel, H. W. (1971). *The Growth of Economic Thought.* Englewood Cliffs, NJ: Prentice-Hall.

Stavenhagen, G. (1957). *Geschichte der Wirtschaftstheorie.* 2nd edn, Göttingen: Vandenhoeck & Ruprecht.

Streissler, E. W. (1994). *Friedrich B. W. von Hermann als Wirtschaftstheoretiker.* University of Vienna, mimeo.

Thünen, J. H. v. (1990). *Der isolierte Staat in Beziehung auf Landwirtschaft und Nationalökonomie.* First published in 1826 and 1850. Edited by H. Lehmann with the collaboration of L. Werner. Berlin: Akademie Verlag.

Torrens, R. (1820). *An Essay on the Influence of the External Corn Trade upon the Production and Distribution of National Wealth.* 3rd edn. London: Hatchard (1826).

Weinberger, O. (1925). Friedrich Benedikt Wilhelm Hermann. *Zeitschrift für die gesamte Staatswissenschaft,* 79: 464–519.

Whewell, W. (1831). Mathematical Exposition of Some of the Leading Doctrines in Mr. Ricardo's 'Principles of Political Economy and Taxation'. In *Transactions of the Cambridge Philosophical Society.* 1–44. Reprint in W. Whewell, *Mathematical Exposition of Some Doctrines of Political Economy.* New York 1971: Augustus M. Kelley.

Wicksell, K. (1893). *Über Wert, Kapital und Rente nach den neueren nationalökonomischen Theorien.* Jena: G. Fischer. English translation as *On Value, Capital and Rent,* London: Macmillan (1954).

5 Burgstaller on classical and neoclassical theory[*]

Giuseppe Freni and Neri Salvadori

Property and Prices (Burgstaller, 1994) is a book of great interest and the reader who takes the time to read it carefully will not regret his decision. Burgstaller points out several similarities between the classical analysis of value *à la* Ricardo, Marx, and Sraffa on one side and the neoclassical theory of prices *à la* Walras, Hicks, and Arrow–Debreu on the other. The analysis he provides is designed to show that these two theories (or rather these two groups of theories) have many elements in common and, in particular, that once the stock market is incorporated into general equilibrium theory both groups of theories can be seen to possess the same mathematical structure.

The book consists of eight chapters in which eleven models are analysed (each model is labelled with the name of one or two prominent contributors to economics in block letters, like von Neumann, Ricardo, Marx, Walras, and Sraffa), an extensive introduction, supplements to some chapters, and mathematical appendices to some other chapters. The eight chapters are organized in two parts. Part I contains models in which all resources are reproducible. The model introduced in Chapter 1 is used in Chapter 2 to discuss some aspects of the Arrow–Debreu model. Chapter 3 extends the same model to cover non storable commodities – which the author misleadingly calls 'non-basic commodities' – and adjustment costs. Finally, reproducible labour is introduced in Chapter 4. Part II begins with the analysis of primary land, shows that some kinds of optimal growth models comprising nonreproducible labour are isomorphic to Ricardian models, examines models in which multiple capital goods coexist with primary resources, and concludes with the analysis of intersectoral transfer of primary resources. The Walrasian pure exchange model is shown to be symmetric to the model introduced in Chapter 1 and to rely for its dynamics, as do all the other models in the book, upon a perfectly functioning stock market. A figure gives a useful taxonomy of the models investigated.

Classical economists focus on the long term and generally pay little attention to the short term. Neoclassical economists also started their theorizing, in the 1870s,

* Reprinted with permission from *Economics and Philosophy*, 1996.

by analysing the long term, but they soon found difficulties that prompted them to switch, beginning in the late 1920s, to intertemporal analysis. Until one or two decades ago the time horizon was considered finite and, therefore, arbitrary. The introduction of an infinite horizon is critical, as Burgstaller (1994, pp. 43–8) shows. It pushes the analysis inevitably toward the long term. This is clearly spelled out, for instance, by Lucas who observed that 'for *any* initial capital $K(0) > 0$, the optimal capital-consumption path $(K(t), c(t))$ will converge to the balanced path asymptotically. That is, the balanced path will be a good approximation to any actual path "most" of the time', and that 'this is exactly the reason why the balanced path is interesting to us' (1988, p. 11). Lucas is thus (re-)switching from an intertemporal analysis to a long-term one. Since the balanced path of the intertemporal model is often the only path fully analysed, the intertemporal model is but a way to obtain a rigorous long period setting. Moreover Lucas is giving up one of the characteristic features of neoclassical theories, that is, income distribution is determined by supply and demand of factors of production: if we concentrate on the 'balanced path', capital in the initial period cannot be taken as given along with other 'initial endowments'.

Careful examination shows that contributions to the 'classical' theory of value and distribution – notwithstanding the many differences that exist between authors – share a common feature: in investigating the relationship between the system of relative prices and income distribution they start from the same set of *data*. These data concern:

(i)   the technical conditions of production of the various commodities;
(ii) the size and composition of the social product;
(iii) one of the distributive variables: either the ruling wage rate(s) or the ruling rate of profit; and
(iv) the quantities of available natural resources.

In correspondence with the underlying long-term competitive position of the economy, the capital stock is assumed to be fully adjusted to these data. Hence the 'normal' desired pattern of utilization of plant and equipment would be realized and a uniform rate of return on its supply price obtained. The data or independent variables from which neoclassical theories typically start are the following. They take as given:

(a) the initial endowments of the economy and the distribution of property rights among individual agents;
(b) the preferences of consumers; and
(c) the set of technical alternatives from which cost-minimizing producers can choose.

It can be easily verified that the given (c) is not very different from the given (i), whereas the given (ii) could be thought to be determined by the given (b). What makes the two theories really different are the data (iii) and (a). However, if there is no labour in the economy – and therefore the given (iii) is automatically deleted – the given (a) is not very different from the given (iv). Hence the main difference between the two theories is the way in which labour is dealt with. Burgstaller remarks rightly that 'The central idea of the recent neoclassical theory of endogenous growth (Romer (1986), Lucas (1988), Sala-i-Martin (1990)) – that human capital is a reproducible input which may be accumulated (or allowed to depreciate) like physical capital – is formally indistinguishable from the classical concept of labor' (1994, p. 71n; see also pp. 190–1).

However, classical and neoclassical economists have quite different ideas on the sort of dynamics they are interested in. The literature on 'Gravitation of market prices to prices of production', which is the dynamics in which classical economists are mainly interested, considers that during the dynamical process the rates of profit are different in the different sectors. This is so because the appropriate rentals on the available resources are not calculated, as is the case in an equilibrium dynamics, which is the special dynamics in which neoclassical intertemporal analysis is mainly interested. Burgstaller has seen with great clarity that neoclassical theorizing is moving back to long-term problems and, therefore, to a framework which is very close to the classical one. But he does not seem to have paid the same attention to the modern literature developing classical ideas: the vast literature on the classical approach published since Sraffa's *Production of Commodities by Means of Commodities* appears to have been largely ignored.

The book contains a number of interesting observations and challenging propositions. The reader who completes the eight chapters will certainly also enjoy reading the four supplements which enrich the book. These supplements deal with an interpretation of the Arrow–Debreu model, the dynamical Ricardo model, a critique of Walras's capital theory and an insightful note on the neoclassical theory of endogeneous growth. These supplements show how powerful is the taxonomy of models presented. Because of its controversial nature and its new perspective on the relationship between competing schools of thought the book is certainly to be recommended to all economic theorists.

Finally, a comment on the formalism of the book seems appropriate. In principle, it is not difficult as a two-sector framework is used throughout. However, since the assumptions are often not clearly stated and the procedures used are not explicated, at best one has to work hard in order to grasp the scope of the models and the connections with the existing literature. A few examples can illustrate the point. In VON NEUMANN I, it is not straightforward to see how a four-dimensional system is reduced to a planar one. As regards the price equations, since they are linear, no problem rises. But what about the quantity equations? After some work it can be discovered that the author is exploiting a property of the utility function adopted: instead of jumping directly from the usual necessary conditions of the 'maximum principle' to the sufficient ones, he takes an intermediate step by adding the *further* necessary condition that saving has to be a given fraction of the value of capital. Similar criticisms apply to VON NEUMANN II, in which it is not clear if there are three or four different commodities, and to MARX-SRAFFA, in which the intrinsic jointness of the production process is never mentioned. To sum up, one cannot avoid the feeling that if the author had spent more time in writing the book, the reader would have spent much less time in reading it. This criticism should not be taken to imply that major tasks such as the one attempted by the author are not worth undertaking. On the contrary, the author deserves praise for his boldness. However, given the magnitude of the task it is not surprising that its execution is less than perfect.

References

Burgstaller, A. 1994. *Property and Prices. Toward a Unified Theory of Value.* Cambridge, Cambridge University Press.

Lucas, R. E. 1988. 'On the Mechanisms of Economic Development', *Journal of Monetary Economics*, 22: 3–42.

Romer, P. M. 1986. 'Increasing Returns and Long-run Growth', *Journal of Political Economy*, 94: 1002–37.

Sala-i-Martin, X. 1990. Lecture notes on economic growth (II): Five prototype models of endogenous growth, NBER Working Paper No. 3564, Cambridge, Mass.: NBER.

Part II

Growth theory and
the classical tradition

6   Theories of 'endogenous' growth in historical perspective[*]

Heinz D. Kurz and Neri Salvadori

1. Introduction

Whenever someone claims a major intellectual breakthrough, this claim should be subject to close scrutiny. Economics is no exception. Throughout history, economists have carefully examined the novelty of ideas in economics. In fact, one of the main objectives of the history of economic thought as an academic discipline is to critically examine claims to originality in economic analysis.

Our concern in this chapter is one such case: the so-called theory of 'endogenous' growth. The idea underlying that theory took off in the mid-1980s and has experienced a remarkable boom since, reflected in a formidable industry of theoretical and empirical research on economic growth. Also described as 'new' growth theory (NGT) to indicate the claim to orginality, some advocates (see e.g. Grossman and Helpman, 1994, p. 42), are quite explicit in their view that NGT will revolutionize the way economists think about certain problems. They also claim that the revolution will not be peripheral to economic analysis but will affect its core. In their view, NGT is a basic innovation in the way economists theorize that will leave its mark on virtually every aspect of analytical economics. Whilst other authors are more cautious in their claims, there appears to be widespread agreement in the profession that the contributions of the NGT are both novel and important. This assessment should be sufficient for the historian of economic thought to delve more deeply into the matter and confront the scope, method, content and results of the 'new' growth models (NGMs) with earlier attempts at explaining economic growth.

This chapter places the NGT in historical perspective, although we can only look at endogenous growth theory from a bird's-eyes perspective, which hides from view many of the important details and differences between different approaches and which can only deal with a small selection of authors. It is impossible to elaborate in sufficient detail the recent literature on growth or the received and much larger body of literature since Adam Smith. Instead, we only consider certain characteristic features of the NGMs, and a few aspects of the theories elaborated

* Reprinted with permission from *Economic Behaviour and Design*, St Martin's Press, 1999.

by earlier authors. Hence, this chapter consists, of a couple of observations, not more. We do not claim to do full justice to the approaches under consideration; completeness is not our goal. We hope, however, that the argument and the evidence put forward questions the claim to originality of the 'new' growth literature. Also, space limitations force us to set aside the post-Keynesian approach to growth and distribution, although some of these models are clearly endogenous growth models.

We have adopted the idea of 'endogeneity' employed in the NGT. According to Barro and Sala-i-Martin (1995), the characteristic feature of the NGT is that long-run growth is determined '*within the model*, rather than by some exogenously growing variables like unexplained technological progress' (p. 38, emphasis added). They add: 'The key property of endogenous-growth models is the absence of diminishing returns to capital' (p. 39). Therefore, the way or mechanism by means of which diminishing returns to capital are avoided provides a criterion to classify the NGMs (see Kurz and Salvadori, 1995b). The following discussion focuses on alternative mechanisms contemplated in the growth literature, old and new. Concerning earlier authors, attention centres on those elements of their analyses that compare with crucial features of the NGMs. In particular, we investigate those factors that counteract any tendency of the general rate of profit to fall. We found that different assumptions concerning saving behaviour were not essential to the argument. That is, it does not matter whether the propensity to save is exogenously given or whether it is determined via inter-temporal utility maximization. A rate of return on capital larger than the rate of 'time preference' is both necessary and sufficient for positive endogenous growth to obtain in both kinds of NGMs.

Section 2 summarizes some crucial features of Adam Smith's views on capital accumulation and economic growth. The emphasis is on two contradictory effects of capital accumulation contemplated by Smith: a tendency of the rate of profit to fall due to the intensification of competition among capital owners; and a tendency of the rate of profit to rise due to the increase in productivity associated with the division of labour. Section 3 turns to David Ricardo's approach to the theory of distribution and capital accumulation. We argue that in Ricardo the growth rate is endogenous and may fall to zero when, during capital accumulation and population growth, the rate of profit tends to fall due to diminishing returns in agriculture. Section 4 deals with linear models of economic growth: the authors discussed include Robert Torrens, Karl Marx, Georg von Charasoff and John von Neumann. Section 5 provides a taxonomy of 'classical' cases in which the rate of profit, and thus the rate of growth, need not fall to zero. We consider three cases: (i) the absence of scarce non-accumulative factors of production; (ii) the existence of a 'backstop technology' and (iii) increasing returns to capital that are external to firms. Section 6 discusses 'neoclassical' ideas or models of exogenous growth, especially those of Alfred Marshall, Gustav Cassel, Knut Wicksell, Frank Ramsey, Robert Solow, Trevor Swan and James Meade. Section 7 classifies the 'new' growth literature into three groups according to the route by which they try to avoid diminishing returns to capital. Section 8 draws some conclusions and argues that NGT shares some crucial elements of the classical approach to the problem of growth and distribution. Hence, it can be said that there is a 'revolution' in the proper sense of the word, that is, present-day growth theory is partly returning to the roots of the classical approach.

2. Adam Smith on growth

A characteristic feature of the classical approach is the view that production involves labour, produced means of production and natural resources. In contrast to some contributions to modern growth theory none of these factors – labour, capital and land – were considered negligible other than in thought experiments designed 'to illustrate a principle' (Ricardo). To understand real growth processes one had to come to grips with the interrelated laws governing the growth of population, the pace of accumulation and the rate and bias of technical innovation in an environment characterized by the scarcity of natural resources. At stake was an understanding of the working of a highly complex system.

2.1. Capital accumulation and the division of labour

Adam Smith viewed the growth process as endogenous. Adolph Lowe (1954) considered this to be *the* major distinguishing feature of classical as opposed to neoclassical growth theory:

> It is only fair to say that [the] modern notion of 'endogeneity' is but a dim reflection of a much more ambitious method of analysis that dominated an earlier epoch of theoretical economics. As a matter of fact, upon this issue of endogeneity versus exogeneity, rather than upon conflicting theories of value, hinges the main difference between genuine classical theory and post-Millian economic reasoning, including all versions of neoclassical analysis.
>
> (Lowe, [1954] 1987, p. 108)

Lowe's observation predates Solow's growth model by two years and Paul Romer's doctoral thesis by thirty years. Walter Eltis (1984, p. 69) also stressed that Smith had developed

> a line of argument about the positive association between capital accumulation and productivity growth which modern theory has only recently begun to redis-cover. Astonishingly, in much of twentieth-century growth theory, the rate of investment is predicted to have no effect at all on an economy's *long-term* rate of growth of output and living standards. This is true of all neoclassical growth theory and of a good deal of Keynesian growth theory in addition.[1]

According to these two interpreters, classical growth theory in general and Smith's analysis in particular are theories of endogenous growth placing special emphasis on the impact of capital accumulation on productivity.

---

1 Unless otherwise stated, the emphases in quotations are the author's.

Smith began his inquiry into *The Wealth of Nations* (1976, first published 1776; the abbreviation *WN* is used for references below) by stating that income per capita

> must in every nation be regulated by two different circumstances; first, by the skill, dexterity, and judgment with which its labour is generally applied; and, secondly, by the proportion between the number of those who are employed in useful labour, and that of those who are not so employed.
>
> (*WN* I.3)

Denoting (net) income by Y, the size of the population by P, total employment by N and the number of workers employed 'productively' by L, we have

$$\frac{Y}{P} = \frac{Y}{L}\frac{N}{P}\frac{L}{N} \quad \text{or} \quad p = yqu$$

where p is income per capita (Y/P), y is labour productivity (Y/L), q is the participation rate (N/P), and u is the ratio between the number of productive workers and total employment (L/N). In terms of proportionate growth rates we have

$$\hat{p} = \hat{y} + \hat{q} + \hat{u}$$

Implicitly, Smith took the participation rate as given and fairly constant over time ($\hat{q} = 0$). As u increases, output increases in a given period, improving the potential for growth. There is an upper limit to u, which is unity. In steady-state analysis $\hat{u}$ must be set equal to zero. There is no upper limit to y: labour productivity can rise without boundary. This is why Smith maintained that an investigation of the growth of income per capita is first and foremost an inquiry into 'The causes of this improvement, in the productive powers of labour, and the order, according to which its produce is naturally distributed among the different ranks and conditions of men in the society' (*WN* I.5).

Smith's attention focused accordingly on the factors determining the growth of y, that is, the factors affecting 'the state of the skill, dexterity, and judgment with which labour is applied in any nation' (*WN* I.6). At this point the accumulation of capital enters into the picture, because of Smith's conviction that the key to the growth of labour productivity is the division of labour which in turn depends on the extent of the market and thus upon capital accumulation. 'The greatest improvement in the productive powers of labour', we are told, 'seem to have been the effects of the division of labour' (*WN* I.i.1), both *within* given firms and industries and, even more significantly, *between* them. In his analysis in the first three chapters of Book I of *The Wealth of Nations*, Smith established the idea that there are increasing returns which are largely *external* to firms, that is, broadly compatible with the classical hypothesis of a uniform rate of profit. In the first chapter he made clear how powerful a device the division of labour is in increasing labour productivity, and analysed in some detail its major features: (i) the improvement of the dexterity of workers; (ii) the saving of time which is otherwise lost in passing from one sort of work to another and, most significantly, (iii) the invention of specific machinery (cf. *WN* I.i.6–8). In the second chapter he argued that there is a certain propensity in human nature 'to truck, barter and exchange one thing for another', which appears to be rooted in 'the faculties of reason and speech', that gives occasion to the division of labour (*WN* I.ii.1–2). In the third chapter the argument is completed by stressing that the division of labour is limited by the extent of the market (cf. *WN* I.iii.1): a larger market generates a larger division of labour among people and, therefore, among firms, and a larger division of labour generates a larger productivity of labour for all firms.

Despite the presence of increasing returns, Smith retained the concept of a *general* rate of profit. His argument appears to be implicitly based on the hypothesis that each single firm operates at constant returns, while total production is subject to increasing returns. Even though some examples provided by Smith relate more to the division of labour within firms than to the division of labour among firms, Smith appears to be correct in sustaining that some of the activities which were originally a part of the division of labour within the firm may eventually become a different 'trade' or 'business', so that the division of labour *within* the firm is but a step towards the division of labour *amongst* firms. In the example of pin making at the beginning of his Chapter I, Smith pointed out that 'in the way in which this business is now carried on, not only the whole work is a peculiar trade, but it is divided into a number of branches, of which the greater part are likewise peculiar trades' (*WN* I.i.3).

Smith's analysis foreshadows the concepts of induced and embodied technical progress, learning by doing, and learning by using. The invention of new machines and the improvement of known ones is said to be originally due to the workers in the production process and 'those who had occasion to use the machines' (*WN* I.i.9). At a more advanced stage of society, making machines 'became the business of a peculiar trade', engaging

> philosophers or men of speculation, whose trade it is, not to do any thing, but to observe every thing; and who, upon that account, are often capable of combining together the powers of the most distant and dissimilar objects.

Research and development of new industrial designs becomes 'the principal or sole trade and occupation of a particular class of citizens' (ibid.). New technical knowledge is systematically created and economically used, with the sciences becoming more and more involved in that process. The accumulation of capital propels this process forward, opens up new markets and enlarges existing ones, increases effectual demand and is thus the main force behind economic and social development:

> The increase of demand ... never fails to lower [prices] in the long run. It encourages production, and thereby increases the competition of the producers, who, in order to undersell one another, have recourse to new

divisions of labour and new improvements of art, which might never otherwise have been thought of.

(*WN* V.i.e.26)

Here we have a dynamic notion of competition which anticipates in important respects the views on competition of authors such as Marx and Joseph Schumpeter. Smith also anticipates the following two ideas that are prominent within the NGT literature:

(1) 'new improvements of art' are generated within the economic system by specialized activities and
(2) new technical knowledge is or eventually will become a *public good*, that is, non-rival and non-excludable.

However, whilst, as we shall see, the advocates of the NGT are bold enough to postulate a production function of new technical knowledge – for example, the concept of 'research technology' in Romer (1986) – that is, a definite quantitative relationship between output (additional knowledge) and some inputs, and to provide a formalization of the positive externality, Smith did not put his ideas into algebra.

2.2. Are there clear and obvious limits to growth in Smith?

Did Smith expect the endogenous growth factors to lose momentum as capital accumulates? He considered three potential limits to growth: an insufficient supply of workers, the scantiness of nature, and an erosion of the motives of accumulation. Because of our concern with the NGT we set aside the third limit and treat the second one only cursorily. Smith saw that the scarcity of renewable and the exhaustion of depletable resources may constrain human productive activity and the growth of the economy, and pointed out that 'useful fossils and minerals of the earth, &c. naturally grow dearer as the society advances in wealth and improvement' (*WN* I.xi.i.3; see also I.xi.d). Yet, it cannot be claimed that he paid a lot of attention to the scarcity of natural resources and its impact on economic growth. At the time when he wrote, the limits to growth deriving from nature were apparently still considered rather distant and thus negligible. This was to change soon, with authors like West, Malthus and Ricardo placing emphasis on the scarcity of land as the main barrier to economic growth. But in Smith there are not yet clear signs of any growth pessimism.[2]

Smith also saw no danger that the process of accumulation might come to an end because of an insufficient supply of labour and the ensuing diminishing returns to

---

2 According to Eltis (1984, p. 70), Smith 'clearly believed that growth would eventually cease when a country's potential for development was fully realised'. However, in Smith it is not sufficiently clear how a country's potential is defined. Ultimately, a falling trend in the rate of profit is taken to indicate that the potential is getting exhausted. Yet, as we shall see, Smith's explanation of that trend is difficult to sustain.

capital. He rather advocated a view which was to become prominent amongst the classical economists: the supply of labour is generated within the socioeconomic system, that is, *endogenously*. Interestingly, Smith was of the opinion that the size of the workforce is regulated by the demand for labour. He drew an analogy between the multiplication of animals and that of the inferior ranks of people. He wrote: 'Every species of animals naturally multiplies in proportion to the means of their subsistence, and no species can ever multiply beyond it' (*WN* I.viii.39). A similar principle is said to govern the multiplication of men: the 'liberal reward of labour', by enabling workers to provide better for their children, adjusts the workforce

> as nearly as possible in the proportion which the demand for labour requires...It is in this manner that the demand for men, like that for any other commodity, necessarily, regulates the production of men; quickens it when it goes too slowly, and stops it when it advances too fast. It is this demand which regulates and determines the state of propagation in all the different industries of the world.
>
> (*WN* I.viii.40)

Smith envisaged the growth of the labour force as endogenous, the determinant being the rate of capital accumulation. Real wages are higher, the more rapidly capital accumulates. As to the impact of high and rising real wages on the rate of profit, it appears that we cannot say anything definite, given Smith's opinion that 'the same cause . . . which raises the wages of labour, the increase of stock, tends to increase its productive powers, and to make a smaller quantity of labour produce a greater quantity of work' (*WN* I.viii.57). However, surprisingly, Smith came up with a definitive answer in chapter IX of book I. He introduced the chapter in the following terms: 'The rise and fall in the profits of stock depend upon the same causes with the rise and fall in the wages of labour, the increasing or declining state of the wealth of the society; but those causes affect the one and the other very differently' (*WN* I.ix.1). He added:

> The increase of stock, which raises wages, tends to lower profit. When the stock of many rich merchants are turned into the same trade, their mutual competition naturally tends to lower its profit; and when there is a like increase of stock in all the different trades carried on in the same society, the same competition must produce the same effect in them all.
>
> (*WN* I.ix.2)

This explanation of a falling tendency of the rate of profit in terms of 'competition' does not stand up to close examination.[3] First, since Smith commonly presupposed free competition, a fall in profitability cannot be traced back to

---

3 For a different, interesting view placing special emphasis on Malthus's interpretation of Smith according to which Smith had ruled out constant and diminishing returns, see Negishi (1993).

an intensification of competition. Second, Smith erroneously tried to carry an argument that is valid in a partial framework over to a general framework. A shift of capital from one trade to another, other things equal, will tend to reduce the rate of profit obtained in the latter (and increase it in the former); this mechanism was referred to by Smith in his explanation of the 'gravitation' of market prices to 'natural' prices, and has been discussed by Kurz and Salvadori (1995a; chapter 1). An increase in the economy's capital stock as a whole need not have an adverse effect on the general rate of profit. It all depends on how the real wage rate and the technical conditions of production are affected in the course of the accumulation of capital. This problem was tackled by David Ricardo.

Adam Smith explained economic growth thoroughly as an *endogenous* phenomenon. The growth rate depends on the decisions and activities of agents. Special emphasis is placed on the endogenous creation of new knowledge that can be used economically. New technical knowledge is treated as a good, which is or in the long run tends to become a public good. There are no clear and obvious limits to growth. The additional work force required in the process of accumulation is generated by that process itself: labour power is a commodity the quantity of which is regulated by the effectual demand for it. Diminishing returns due to scarce natural resources are set aside or taken to be compensated by the increase in productivity due to the division of labour.

3. David Ricardo on diminishing returns

Ricardo set aside what may be called *statically and dynamically increasing returns*. The beneficial effects of capital accumulation on productivity mediated through the extension of the division of labour play hardly any role in his analysis. In modern parlance, the problems of externalities which figured prominently in Smith's analysis are given only sparse attention. Much of Ricardo's argument was developed in terms of the implicit assumption that the set of (constant returns to scale) methods of production from which cost-minimizing producers can choose, is given and constant. In such a framework the question then is how scarce natural resources, such as land, affect profitability as capital accumulates. The resulting vision is reflected in what Ricardo called the 'natural course' of events.

3.1. Diminishing returns in agriculture

As capital accumulates and population grows, and assuming the real wage rate of workers given and constant, the rate of profit is bound to fall; due to extensive and intensive diminishing returns on land, 'with every increased portion of capital employed on it, there will be a decreased rate of production' (Ricardo, [1817] 1951, p. 98). Since profits are a residual income based on the surplus product left after the used up means of production and the wage goods in the support of workers have been deducted from the social product (net of rents), the 'decreased rate of production' involves a decrease in profitability. On the assumption that there are only negligible savings out of wages and rents, a falling rate of profit involves a falling rate of capital accumulation. Hence, Ricardo's 'natural course' of events will necessarily end up in a stationary state.

3.2. Technical progress: a counteracting factor

This path should not be identified with the *actual* path the economy is taking because technical progress will repeatedly offset the impact of the 'niggardliness of nature' on the rate of profit:

> The natural tendency of profits then is to fall; for, in the progress of society and wealth, the additional quantity of food required is obtained by the sacrifice of more and more labour. This tendency, this gravitation as it were of profits, is happily checked at repeated intervals by the improvements in machinery, connected with the production of necessaries, as well as by the discoveries in the science of agriculture which enable us to relinquish a portion of labour before required, and therefore to lower the price of the prime necessary of the labourer.
>
> (Ricardo, 1951, p. 120)

By contrast, Smith was of the opinion that the accumulation of capital will systematically lead to improvements in the productive powers. Ricardo did not see an intimate connection; he rather treated those improvements as the outcome of singular events – special scientific discoveries and the like – not necessarily tied up with capital accumulation. Put more strongly, whereas Smith considered technological progress essentially an endogenous phenomenon, Ricardo treated it as largely exogenous. There is, however, also an important similarity: neither of them was of the opinion that technical progress will always be such that any tendency of the rate of profit to fall will be effectively counteracted. The classical authors' view is perfectly compatible with phases of falling and phases of rising profitability in any particular economic system. Ricardo was one of the first to stress that technological progress can take several forms associated with different implications for the performance of the system, its growth, employment and the sharing out of the product between wages, rents and profits.[4] The idea of 'neutrality' of technical progress as it is necessarily entertained in steady-state growth theory was alien to Ricardo's thinking.

3.3. The endogeneity of growth

Like Smith, Ricardo thought that saving and investment, that is, accumulation, would largely come from profits, whereas wages and rents played a negligible role.

---

4 See in particular Ricardo's discussion of what he called the 'gross produce reducing' form of technical progress in chapter 31 of the third edition of the *Principles*.

Hence, as regards the dynamism of the economy attention should focus on profitability. Assuming that the marginal propensity to accumulate out of profits, s, is given and constant, a 'classical' accumulation function can be formulated:

$$g = \begin{cases} s(r - r_{min}) & \text{if } r \geq r_{min} \\ 0 & \text{if } r \leq r_{min} \end{cases}$$

where $r_{min} \geq 0$ is the minimum level of profitability, which, if reached, will arrest accumulation (cf. Ricardo, 1951, p. 120).

Ricardo saw the rate of accumulation as endogenous. The demand for labour is governed by the pace at which capital accumulates, the long-term supply of labour by the 'Malthusian Law of Population'. Real wages may rise, that is, the 'market price of labour' may rise above the 'natural' wage rate. This is the case in a situation in which capital accumulates rapidly, leading to an excess demand for labour. As Ricardo put it, 'notwithstanding the tendency of wages to conform to their natural rate, their market rate may, in an improving society, for an indefinite period, be constantly above it' (Ricardo, 1951, pp. 94–5). If such a constellation prevails for some time it is even possible that 'custom renders absolute necessaries' what in the past had been comforts or luxuries. Hence, the natural wage is driven upward by persistently high levels of the actual wage rate. Accordingly, the concept of 'natural wage' in Ricardo is a flexible one and must not be mistaken for a physiological minimum of subsistence.

3.4. A graphical illustration

Setting aside the complex wage dynamics in Ricardo's theory, that is, assuming a given and constant real wage rate and setting the minimum rate of profit equal to zero, we may illustrate Ricardo's view of the long-run relationship between profitability and accumulation and thus growth. Figure 6.1, originally used by Kaldor (1955–6), shows the marginal productivity of labour-cum-capital curve *CEGH*. It is decreasing since land is scarce: when labour-cum-capital increases, either less fertile qualities of land must be cultivated or the same qualities of land must be cultivated with processes which require less land per unit of product, but are more costly in terms of labour-cum-capital. Let the real wage rate equal *OW*. Then, if the amount of labour-cum-capital applied is L_1, the area $OCEL_1$ gives the product, $OWDL_1$ gives total capital employed, and *BCE* the total rent.

Profit is determined as a residual and corresponds to the rectangle *WBED*. As a consequence, the *rate* of profit can be determined as the ratio of the areas of two rectangles which have the same basis and, therefore, it equals the ratio *WB/OW*. Let us now consider the case in which the amount of labour-cum-capital is larger, that is, L_2. Then $OCGL_2$ gives the product, $OWFL_2$ the capital, *ACG* the rent and *WAGF* the profits. The rate of profit has fallen to *WA/OW*. Obviously, if a positive profit rate implies a positive growth rate, the economy will expand until labour-cum-capital has reached the level $\bar{L}$. At that point the profit rate is equal to zero

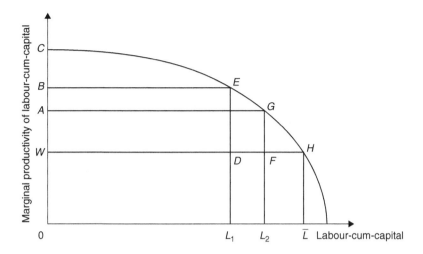

Figure 6.1 Diminishing returns to labour-cum-capital.
Source: Kaldor (1955–6).

and so is the growth rate. The system has arrived at the so-called stationary state: growth has come to an end because profitability has.

For both Smith and Ricardo the required size of the workforce is essentially generated by the accumulation process itself. In other words, labour power is treated as a kind of producible commodity. It differs from other commodities in that it is not produced in a capitalistic way in a special industry on a par with other industries, but is the result of the interplay between the growth of the working population and socioeconomic conditions. In the most simple conceptualization possible, labour power is seen to be in elastic supply at a given real wage basket. Increasing the number of baskets available in the support of workers involves a proportional increase of the workforce. In this view the rate of growth of labour supply adjusts to any given rate of growth of labour demand without necessitating a variation in the real wage rate.

In a slightly more sophisticated conceptualization, higher rates of growth of labour supply presuppose higher levels of the real wage rate. But the basic logic remains the same: in normal conditions the pace at which capital accumulates regulates the pace at which labour, a non-accumulable factor of production, grows. Thus labour cannot put a limit to growth because it is generated within the growth process. The only limit to growth can come from other non-accumulable factors of production: as Ricardo and others made clear, these factors are natural resources in general and land in particular. In other words, there is only endogenous growth in Ricardo. This growth is bound to lose momentum as the system hits its natural barriers, especially as soon as extensive and intensive diminishing returns make themselves felt. There is no exogenous growth in Ricardo. Despite the fact that he turned a blind eye to Smith's idea of increasing returns and positive externalities of selfish behaviour, Ricardo's theory fulfills the criterion of an endogenous explanation of growth. This shows also that it is not a necessary condition for a theory to be considered a theory of endogenous growth that it assumes some kind of increasing returns. The following section illustrates this point.

4. Linear classical models of production

Central elements of classical analysis are the concept of production as a circular flow and the related concept of *surplus* product left after the wage goods and what is necessary for the replacement of the used up means of production have been deducted from the annual output. This surplus can be consumed or accumulated. With constant returns to scale and setting aside the problem of scarce natural resources, the notion of an economy expanding at a constant rate of growth was close at hand. In this section we shall summarize some contributions to what may be called linear growth theory with a classical flavour.

4.1. Robert Torrens

Robert Torrens (1820) in his *Essay on the External Corn Trade* clarified that the concept of surplus provides the key to an explanation of the *rate* of profit. He put forward a 'corn model' in which the rate of profit can be determined as the ratio of two quantities of corn: the surplus product and the corn advanced as seed and as food in the support of workers (Torrens, 1820, p. 361). Torrens acknowledged his indebtedness to Ricardo's 'original and profound inquiry into the laws by which the rate of profit is determined' (ibid., p. xix). One year later he published his *Essay on the Production of Wealth*, in which he generalized the argument to the case of two sectors, each of which produces a commodity that is either needed as a means of production or as a means of subsistence in both sectors. In the numerical example provided by him the surplus and the social capital consisted of the same commodities in the same proportions, so that the rate of profit can be determined without having recourse to the system of relative prices (Torrens, 1821, pp. 372–3).

Torrens made it clear that the physical schema of the production of commodities by means of commodities is not only important for the determination of the rate of profit and relative prices – it also provides the basis for assessing the growth potential of the economy. As Torrens stressed, 'this surplus, or profit of ten per cent they [that is, the cultivators and manufacturers] might employ either in setting additional workers to work, or in purchasing luxuries for immediate enjoyment' (Torrens, 1820, p. 373). If in each sector the entire surplus were to be used for accumulation purposes in the same sector, then the rates of expansion of the two sectors would be equal to one another and equal to the rate of profit. Champernowne (1945, p. 10) in his commentary on von Neumann's growth model was later to call a constellation of equi-proportionate growth a 'quasi-stationary state'.

4.2. *Karl Marx*

Growth in Torrens' model is both linear and endogenous; the rate of growth depends on the general rate of profit and the propensity to accumulate. The same can be said of Marx's theory of accumulation and expanded reproduction in chapter 21 of volume II of *Capital* (Marx, [1885] 1956). There Marx studied the conditions under which the system is capable of reproducing itself on an upward spiralling level. The expansion of the economy at an endogenously determined rate of growth is possible. This rate depends on the proportion of the surplus value ploughed back into the productive system to increase the scale of operation. Marx stressed that the accumulation of capital is 'an element *immanent* in the capitalist process of produc- tion' (Marx, 1956, p. 497, emphasis added). For, 'the aim and compelling motive of capitalist production' is 'the snatching of surplus-value and its capitalisation, i.e., accumulation' (Marx, 1956, p. 507).

Marx illustrated his argument in terms of numerical examples relating to an economy with two departments, one which produces the means of production, while the other produces the means of consumption. Commodities are exchanged according to their labour values and the accumulation of surplus value takes place within the same department in which the surplus value has been 'produced' and appropriated. Given the real wage rate, the rates of profit in the two sectors assessed on the basis of labour values are known magnitudes. Designating these rates of profit with π_1 and π_2, respectively, and the sectoral shares of surplus-value saved and invested with s_1 and s_2, a uniform rate of growth g involves

$$g = \pi_1 s_1 = \pi_2 s_2 \quad \text{and thus} \quad s_1/s_2 = \pi_2/\pi_1$$

that is, a definite proportion between the two sectoral propensities to accumulate (cf. Marx, 1956, p. 516).

4.3. *Georg von Charasoff*

The Russian mathematician Georg von Charasoff elaborated on Marx's analysis and was possibly the first to provide a clear statement of the fundamental duality relationship between the system of prices and the rate of profit on the one hand, and the system of quantities and the rate of growth on the other, in von Charasoff (1910). He developed his main argument within the framework of an interdependent model of (single) production exhibiting all the properties of the later input–output model, and which is fully specified in terms of use values (rather than labour values as in the case of Marx) and labour needed per unit of output. Let $\mathbf{C}$ be the $n \times n$ matrix of material inputs, let $\mathbf{d}$ be the n vector giving the real wage rate, and let $\mathbf{l}$ be the n vector of direct labour inputs in the different production processes. The $n \times n$ input matrix $\mathbf{A}$ used by Charasoff includes the means of subsistence in the support of workers and is therefore given by

$$\mathbf{A} = \mathbf{C} + \mathbf{l}\mathbf{d}^{\mathrm{T}}$$

that is, it equals what later became known as the 'augmented input matrix'. For a given real wage rate he showed that the rate of profit and relative prices are simultaneously determined and that the former equals the maximum rate of growth of the system compatible with the given conditions of production (cf. ibid., p. 124). Although Charasoff refrained from using mathematics in his argument, it is clear from his verbal argument that the rate of profit is determined by

$$r = G = (1 - \lambda)/\lambda$$

where r is the rate of profit, G is the maximum rate of growth and λ is the dominant real eigenvalue of matrix $\mathbf{A}$. He thus anticipated, albeit in a much less general framework, an important result of John von Neumann.

4.4. John von Neumann

The most sophisticated linear model of endogenous growth was elaborated by John von Neumann (1945) in a paper first published in German in 1937 and then translated into English in 1945. In it von Neumann assumed there are n goods produced by m constant returns-to-scale production processes. There is a problem of the choice of technique which consists of establishing which processes will actually be used and which not, being 'unprofitable'. Von Neumann (1945, pp. 1–2) took the real wage rate, consisting of the 'necessities of life', to be given and paid at the beginning of the uniform period of production, that is, he considered wages as a part of the capital advanced. In addition, he assumed 'that all income in excess of necessities of life will be reinvested'. The characteristic features of the model include:

(1) 'Goods are produced not only from "natural factors of production", but in the first place from each other. These processes of production may be circular'.
(2) Primary factors of production can be expanded 'in unlimited quantities'.
(3) The processes of production 'can describe the special case where good G_j can be produced only jointly with certain others, viz. its permanent joint products'.
(4) Both circulating and fixed capital can be dealt with: 'wear and tear of capital goods are to be described by introducing different stages of wear as different goods, using a separate P_i [process i] for each of these'.
(5) The Rule of Free Goods is applied to all primary factors of production, with the exception of labour, and to overproduced goods.

(von Neumann, pp. 1–2)

To see the basic argument, let $\mathbf{A}$ and $\mathbf{B}$ be the $m \times n$ input and output matrices, respectively, where $\mathbf{A}$ includes, as in Charasoff's case, the means of subsistence in the support of workers. At the going real wage rate, labour is taken to be in perfectly elastic supply, that is, available in whichever amount is required by the growth of the system. Von Neumann demonstrated that there is a solution to his model, which determines (i) which processes will be operated; (ii) at what rate the economic system will grow; (iii) what prices will obtain; (iv) what the rate of interest (rate of profit) will be and (v) that, given the special assumptions employed, the rate of interest equals the rate of growth.

In von Neumann's model the rate of growth is determined *endogenously*. This is one of the reasons why the conventional interpretation of that model as belonging to the tradition established by the so-called 'Walras–Cassel model' cannot be sustained (see Kurz and Salvadori, 1993). Cassel took as exogenously given the rates of growth of all primary factors, and assumed their continuous full employment, which is discussed in Section 6. Von Neumann never made this assumption. He set aside the problem of scarcity of all non-accumulable factors of production: while all primary factors other than labour were taken to be available at whichever amount was needed at zero price, labour was assumed to be available at the required amount at a given real wage rate.

5. A typology of cases

We can now classify some broad cases in which the rate of profit, and therefore the rate of growth, does not fall to zero. There is perpetual growth provided that the premises underlying the different cases hold infinitely. It will be seen that while the cases discussed are all derived from a classical framework of the analysis as it was developed by Adam Smith and David Ricardo, the cases exhibit some striking similarities to the types of NGMs discussed in Section 7.

5.1. Constant returns to capital

The main ingredient to obtain a stationary state in the Ricardian model is the existence of land available in limited supply. If there were no land needed in production, then the graph giving the marginal productivity of labour-cum-capital would be a horizontal line, and therefore the rate of profit would be constant whatever the amount of labour-cum-capital. This case is illustrated in Figure 6.2. As a consequence, the growth rate would also be constant.

Yet to assume that there is no land needed at all or that it is available in given quality and unlimited quantity is unnecessarily restrictive. With the system growing infinitely, the point will come where land of the best quality will become scarce. This brings us to a case similar to one discussed in the economics of exhaustible resources, in which there is an ultimate 'backstop technology'. For example, some exhaustible resources are used to produce energy. In addition, there is solar energy which may be considered an undepletable resource. A technology based on the use of solar energy defines the backstop technology mentioned. Let us translate this assumption into the context of a Ricardian model with land.

5.2. A backstop technology

The case under consideration corresponds to a situation in which 'land', although useful in production, is not indispensable. In other words, there is a technology that allows the production of the commodity without any 'land' input; this is the

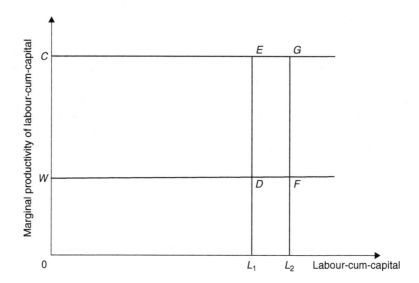

Figure 6.2 Constant returns to labour-cum-capital.

backstop technology. With continuous substitution between labour-cum-capital and land, the marginal productivity of labour-cum-capital would be continuously decreasing, but it would be bounded from below. This case is illustrated in Figure 6.3, with the dashed line giving the lower boundary. In this case the profit rate and thus the growth rate are falling, but they could never fall below certain positive levels. The system would grow indefinitely at a rate of growth that asymptotically approaches the product of the given saving rate multiplied by the value of the (lower) boundary of the profit rate. In Figure 6.3 the latter is given by *WR/OW*.

5.3. Increasing returns to capital

The final case is that of increasing returns to labour-cum-capital (see Figure 6.4), as it was discussed, following Adam Smith, by Allyn Young (1928) and Nicholas Kaldor (1957, 1966). Taking the wage rate as given and constant, the rate of profit and the rate of growth will rise as more labour-cum-capital is employed. (In Figure 6.4 it is assumed that there is an upper boundary to the rise in output per unit of labour-cum-capital given by *OR*.) To preserve the notion of a uniform rate of profit, it is necessary to assume that the increasing returns are *external* to the firm and exclusively connected with the expansion of the market as a whole and the social division of labour. This implies that while in the case of decreasing returns due to the scarcity of land (cf. Figures 6.1 and 6.3) the product was given by the area under the marginal productivity curve, now the product associated with any given amount of labour-cum-capital is larger than or equal to that amount multiplied by

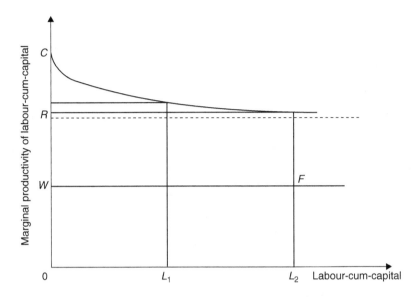

Figure 6.3 Diminishing returns to labour-cum-capital, bounded from below.

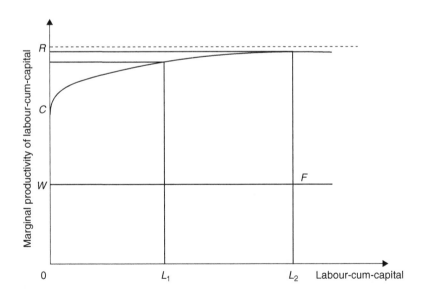

Figure 6.4 Increasing returns to labour-cum-capital, bounded from above.

the corresponding level of output per unit of labour-cum-capital. It is larger if there is still scarce land; it is equal to it if there is not. In any case, the sum of profits and wages equals the product of the given amount of labour-cum-capital multiplied by the corresponding level of output per unit of labour-cum-capital.[5] Hence, in the case in which labour-cum-capital is L_2, the product is given by the corresponding rectangle. As a consequence, the product is larger than the area under the marginal productivity curve. The cases of decreasing and increasing returns are therefore not symmetrical: with increasing returns a rising real wage rate need not involve a falling general rate of profit.

6. Models of exogenous growth

The marginalist or 'neoclassical' school of economic thought attempts to explain income distribution in a symmetrical way via the relative scarcities of the factors of production, labour, 'capital' and land. Interestingly, the idea of *exogenous* growth which classical theory did not entertain is the starting point of important early works in the marginalist tradition.

6.1. Alfred Marshall and Gustav Cassel

The idea of an economic system growing exclusively because some exogenous factors make it grow has variously been put forward in the history of economic thought as a standard of comparison. For example, in chapter V of book V of his *Principles*, first published in 1890, Alfred Marshall ([1890] 1977, p. 305) introduced the 'famous fiction of the "Stationary state" ... to contrast the results which would be found there with those in the modern world'. By relaxing one after another of the rigid assumptions defining the stationary state, Marshall sought to get gradually closer to the 'actual conditions of life'. The first relaxation concerned the premise of a constant (working) population:

> The Stationary state has just been taken to be one in which population is stationary. But nearly all its distinctive features may be exhibited in a place where population and wealth are both growing, provided they are growing at about the same rate, and there is no scarcity of land: and provided also the

---

5 Let $x = f(L, L^*)$ be the product of the last unit of labour-cum-capital, when L represents the amount of labour-cum-capital employed and the division of labour is artificially kept fixed at the level appropriate when the amount of labour-cum-capital employed is L^*. Obviously, $f(L, L^*)$ as a function of L alone is either decreasing as in Figures 6.1 and 6.3 (if land is scarce), or constant as in Figure 6.2 (if land is not scarce). The product at L^* equals $\int_0^L f(L, L^*) dL$, that is, the area under the curve $f(L, L^*)$ in the range $[0, L^*]$. If $(\partial f/\partial L^*) > -(\partial f/\partial L)$ for $L = L^*$, then the curve $x = f(L, L^*)$, which is the curve depicted in Figure 6.4, is increasing, but the product is, as stated in the text, larger than or equal to the sum of profits and wages, which equals the product of the given amount of labour-cum-capital times the corresponding level of output per unit of labour-cum-capital.

methods of production and the conditions of trade change but little; and above all, where the character of man himself is a constant quantity. For in such a state by far the most important conditions of production and consumption, of exchange and distribution will remain of the same quality, and in the same general relations to one another, though they are all increasing in volume.

(Marshall, [1890] 1977, p. 306)

The resulting economic system grows at a constant rate which equals the exogenous rate of growth of population.[6] Income distribution and relative prices are the same as in the stationary economy. In modern parlance: the system expands along a steady-state growth path.

We encounter essentially the same idea in Gustav Cassel's ([1918] 1932) *Theory of Social Economy*. The model of exogenous growth delineated by Cassel can be considered the proximate starting point of the development of neoclassical growth theory. In chapter IV of book I of his treatise Cassel presented two models, one of a stationary economy, the other of an economy growing along a steady-state path.

In his first model Cassel assumed that there are z (primary) factors of production. The quantities of these resources and thus the amounts of services provided by them are taken to be in given supply. The n goods produced in the economy are pure consumption goods, that is, there are no produced means of production or capital goods contemplated in the model: goods are produced exclusively by combining primary factor services at fixed technical coefficients of production. There are as many single-product processes of production as there are goods to be produced, that is, there is no choice of technique. General equilibrium is characterized by the following sets of equations:

(1) equality of supply and demand for each factor service;
(2) equality of the price of a good and its cost of production, that is, the sum total of factor service payments incurred in its production, and thus the absence of extra profits and
(3) equality of supply and demand for each good produced, where the demand for each good is conceived as a function of the prices of all goods.

The resulting sets of equations constitute what is known as the 'Walras–Cassel model' (Dorfman *et al.*, 1958, p. 346). It satisfies the then-going criterion of completeness: there are as many equations as there are unknowns to be ascertained.[7]

---

6 It should be noted that Marshall (1977, book IV, chapter 4) saw reason to suppose that the growth of population depended, among other things, on socioeconomic factors and thus could not sensibly be treated, other than in a first step of the analysis, as exogenous.

7 As is well known, the approach to the theory of general equilibrium in terms of equations was attacked by Knut Wicksell, Hans Neisser, Heinrich von Stackelberg, Frederick Zeuthen, Karl Schlesinger and Abraham Wald and led to the development of the neoclassical theory of general equilibrium in terms of *in*equalities coupled with the introduction of the Rule of Free Goods (or free disposal assumption); see Kurz and Salvadori (1995a, chapter 13, section 7).

Cassel (1932, pp. 152–3) then turned to the model of a uniformly progressing economy. Although described only verbally, he introduced the model in the following way:

> we must now take into consideration the society which is progressing at a uniform rate. In it, the quantities of the factors of production which are available in each period . . . are subject to a uniform increase. We shall represent by [g] the fixed rate of this increase, and of the uniform progress of the society generally.

In Cassel's view this generalization to the case of an economy growing at an exogenously given and constant rate does not cause substantial problems. The previously developed set of equations can easily be adapted appropriately, 'so that the whole pricing problem is solved'. Cassel thus arrived at basically the same result as Marshall.

6.2. Knut Wicksell

Prior to Cassel, Knut Wicksell had dealt with the problem of growth and income distribution in volume I of his *Lectures* (Wicksell, [1901] 1934). Wicksell assumed that production is carried out by means of labour, land and 'capital', that is, produced means of production, and that there was the possibility of substitution between these factors. He was very clear about the deficiency of the notion of 'capital' in marginal productivity theory. With heterogeneous capital goods, 'social capital' had of necessity to be conceived of as a *value* magnitude. Trying to explain the rate of interest in terms of the marginal product of (value) capital implied 'arguing in a circle' (ibid., p. 149), since capital and the rate of interest enter as a cost in the production of 'capital' itself. Hence the value of the capital goods inserted in the production function depends on the rate of interest and will generally change with it. Nevertheless Wicksell thought that the theory could be used in order to explain the long-run trend of profitability.

In the first two parts of volume I of the *Lectures* it is established that an increase in the amount of 'capital', given the amount of labour employed and the amount of land available, tends to diminish the marginal product of capital and thus the rate of interest. More precisely, different states of the economy characterized by different endowments of factors of production are compared. This, Wicksell (1934, p. 7) expounded, is the 'static point of view, that is, we shall assume, in principle, a society which retains unchanged from year to year the same population, the same area of territory and the same amount of capital, and remains on the same level of technical achievement'. There is on the other hand 'a more dynamic point of view' which focuses attention on 'the problem of saving or *accumulation of capital*'. Wicksell confronted this problem by first reformulating the findings of the static theory in the new 'dynamic' framework. He started from the premise that 'the progressive accumulation of capital must be regarded as economical so long as any rate of interest, however low, exists',[8] and added:

> Under such conditions, we should therefore expect a continual accumulation of capital – though at a diminishing rate – and, at the same time, a continual fall in the rate of interest.
>
> (Wicksell, 1934, p. 209)

Here we have a clear expression that in neoclassical models without exogenous factors that make the system grow, the economy will asymptotically converge to a stationary state *strictu sensu*.

6.3. Frank Ramsey

Frank Ramsey (1928) went beyond the Cassellian formulation in his 'A Mathematical Theory of Saving'. He assumed a one-good economy, in which homogeneous labour with a stock of (durable) capital would produce a flow of output, part of which is consumed. The remaining part is saved and thereby added to the capital stock. There is a choice of technique, that is, output can be produced with different proportions of capital and labour, where $F(K, L)$ gives the macroeconomic production function. Ramsey set aside population growth and technical progress; his concern was essentially normative. The main question was how much should a society save in order to achieve the 'maximum *obtainable* rate of enjoyment', or *bliss*. Ramsey postulated an additive intertemporal social welfare function as the objective to be maximized: enjoyment was the utility of consumption less the disutility of working, summing over all time and assuming a zero discount rate. The thrust of his argument was the Keynes–Ramsey rule of saving, according to which the rate of saving times the marginal utility of consumption should at all times be equal to the difference between the maximum possible rate of enjoyment and the total net rate of enjoyment of utility.[9]

Given the premises of Ramsey's model, any process of capital accumulation and thus income growth can only be transitory until the point of bliss has been reached: the long-term rate of growth of the system is necessarily equal to zero, because there is no endogenous mechanism to engender growth and because the exogenous factors (population and technology) are 'frozen in'. Hence, Ramsey's model has some feature in common with the Walras–Cassel model: the exogeneity of the long-term rate of growth. At the same time, the model improves on Wicksell's contribution by analysing explicitly the equilibrium dynamics of the model. This anticipates later neoclassical models that ask whether the dynamic equilibrium in

---

8 Wicksell (1934, p. 169) implicitly assumes a zero rate of time preference. In an earlier part of his book he had rejected Böhm-Bawerk's arguments in favour of a positive rate of time preference as 'evidently untenable'.

9 The result also bears Keynes's name because he gave a non-technical interpretation of the result.

which an economic system is taken to be at any given moment of time converges to
a steady-state equilibrium characterized by the system's full attuning to the growth
of the exogenous factors.

6.4. Robert Solow, Trevor Swan and James Meade

The neoclassical growth models of the 1950s and early 1960s (and partly also
Ramsey's 1928 model) differ from the growth version of the Walras–Cassel model
in five important respects:

(1)   they are macro-models with a single produced good only which could be used
      both as a consumption good and as a capital good;
(2)   the number of primary factors of production is reduced to one, homogeneous
      labour (as in Solow, 1956 and 1963; Swan, 1956); or two, homogeneous
      labour and homogeneous land (as in Swan, 1956; Meade, 1961);
(3)   the all-purpose good is produced by means of labour, capital, that is, the good
      itself, and possibly land;
(4)   there is a choice of technique, where technical alternatives are given by
      a macroeconomic production function, which is homogenous of degree
      one with neoclassical features, that is, positive and decreasing marginal
      productivities with respect to each factor of production and
(5)   planned saving, which is taken to be equal to planned investment at all times, is
      proportional to net income, that is, a 'Keynesian' saving function is assumed.

Focusing attention on the models with a single primary factor (labour), in steady-
state equilibrium:

$$sf(k) = gk$$

where s is the (marginal and average) propensity to save, $f(k)$ is the per unit
of labour or *per capita* production function, k is the capital–labour ratio (where
labour is measured in terms of efficiency units), and g is the steady-state growth
rate of capital (and labour, and income, etc.). In steady-state equilibrium, output
expands exactly as the exogenous factors make it grow. Note that assuming $s > 0$
presupposes that the exogenous factors are growing at some positive rate. In the
case of two primary factors of production where the second factor, land, is available in given and constant supply, the system is bound to end up in a stationary
state unless land-saving technical progress counteracts the tendency to diminishing
returns due to the scarcity of land. In these models the steady-state rate of growth
is exogenous. Outside steady-state equilibrium the rate of growth can be shown
to depend also on the behavioural parameter of the system, that is, the propensity
to save (and invest), but that parameter plays no role in determining the long-term
rate of growth.

While these models are aptly described as models of *exogenous* growth, they
can also be described as models of *endogenous* profitability. Since in the one-good
framework adopted by the authors under consideration the rate of profit r equals

the marginal productivity of capital:

$$r = f'(k)$$

the two equations are able to determine a relationship between the rate of profit and the steady-state rate of growth. The following section shows that the NGMs essentially reverse what is endogenous and what is exogenous. In other words, they are models of *endogenous* growth and *exogenous* profitability.

7. The 'new' models of endogenous growth

One of the key properties of the NGMs emphasised by their advocates is the limitation of diminishing returns to capital. The first generation of NGMs defined the confines within which subsequent contributions to NGT were carried out. The attention focuses on the mechanism that prevents the returns to capital from falling – below a certain level.[10]

7.1. Constant returns to capital

The first class of models set aside all non-accumulable factors of production such as labour and land and assume that all inputs in production are accumulable, that is, 'capital' of some kind. The simplest version of this class is the so-called 'AK model', which assumes that there is a linear relationship between total output, Y, and a single factor capital, K, both consisting of the *same* commodity:

$$Y = AK \qquad (6.1)$$

where $1/A$ is the amount of that commodity required to produce one unit of itself. Because of the linear form of the aggregate production function, these models are also known as 'linear models'. This model is immediately recognized as the model dealt with in subsection 5.1 on the assumption that the technology to produce corn is the one illustrated in Figure 6.2. The rate of return on capital r is given by

$$r + \delta = Y/K = A \qquad (6.2)$$

where δ is the exogenously given rate of depreciation. There is a large variety of models of this type in the literature. In the two-sector version in Rebelo (1991) it is assumed that the capital good sector produces the capital good by means of itself and nothing else. It is also assumed that there is only one method of production to produce the capital good. Therefore, *the rate of profit is determined by technology alone*. The consumption good is produced by means of the capital good and nothing else. Then the saving–investment mechanism jointly with the

---

10 For a more detailed treatment of these models, see Kurz and Salvadori (1995b).

assumption of a uniform rate of growth, that is, a steady-state equilibrium, determines a relationship between the growth rate, g, and the rate of profit, r. Rebelo
(1991, pp. 504, 506) obtains either

$$g = (A - \delta - \rho)/\sigma = (r - \rho)/\sigma \qquad (6.3)$$

or

$$g = (A - \delta)s = sr \qquad (6.4)$$

Equation (6.3) is obtained when savings are determined on the assumption that
there is an immortal representative agent maximizing the following intertemporal
utility function:

$$\int_0^\infty e^{-pt} \frac{1}{1-\sigma} [c(t)^{1-\sigma} - 1]\, dt$$

subject to the constraint of equation (6.1), where ρ is the discount rate, or rate of
time preference, and $1/\sigma$ is the elasticity of substitution between present and future
consumption $(1 \neq \sigma > 0)$, and where $Y = c(t) + \dot{K}$. Equation (6.4) is obtained
when the average propensity to save, s, is given. Hence, in this model the rate of
profit is determined by technology alone and the saving–investment mechanism
determines the growth rate.

King and Rebelo (1990) essentially followed the same avenue. Instead of one
kind of 'capital' they assumed that there are two kinds, real capital and human
capital, both of which are accumulable. There are two lines of production, one
for the social product and the real capital, which consist of quantities of the same
commodity, and one for human capital. The production functions relating to the two
kinds of capital are assumed to be homogeneous of degree one and strictly concave.
There are no diminishing returns to (composite) capital for the reason that there is
no non-accumulable factor such as simple or unskilled labour that enters into the
production of the accumulable factors, investment goods and human capital.[11] As
in Rebelo's model the rate of profit is uniquely determined by the technology (and
the maximization of profits which, because of the Non-substitution Theorem,[12]
implies that only one technique can be used in the long run); the growth rate of
the system is then endogenously determined by the saving–investment equation.
The larger the propensities to accumulate human and physical capital, the larger
is the growth rate.

11 The assumption that the formation of human capital does not involve any unskilled labour as an
   input is not convincing: the whole point of education processes is that a person's capacity to perform
   unskilled labour is gradually transformed into his or her capacity to perform skilled labour. Adam
   Smith, for example, was perfectly aware of this. For an analytical treatment of the problem of human
   capital, taking Smith's discussion as a starting point, see Kurz and Salvadori (1995a, chapter 11).
12 We need a special case of the Nonsubstitution Theorem, because no primary factor (or a primary
   factor with a zero remuneration) is assumed; see Kurz and Salvadori (1995c).

7.2. Returns to capital bounded from below

The second class of models preserve the dualism of accumulable and non-accumulable factors, but restrict the impact of an accumulation of the former on their returns by a modification of the aggregate production function. Jones and Manuelli (1990), for example, allow for both labour and capital and even assume a convex technology, as in the Solow model. However, a convex technology requires only that the marginal product of capital is a decreasing function of its stock, not that it vanishes as the amount of capital per worker tends towards infinity. Jones and Manuelli assume that:

$$h(k) \geqslant bk \quad \text{each } k \geqslant 0$$

where $h(k)$ is the per capita production function and b is a positive constant. The special case contemplated by them is

$$h(k) = f(k) + bk \tag{6.5}$$

where $f(k)$ is the conventional per capita production function. As capital accumulates and the capital–labour ratio rises, the marginal product of capital will fall, asymptotically approaching b, its lower boundary. With a given propensity to save, s, and assuming capital never wears out, the steady-state growth rate g is endogenously determined: $g = sb$. Assuming, on the contrary, intertemporal utility maximization, the rate of growth is positive provided the technical parameter b is larger than the rate of time preference ρ. In the case in which it is larger, the steady-state rate of growth is given by equation (6.3) with $r = b$.

It is not difficult to recognize that the difference between the model of Jones and Manuelli (1990) and that of Rebelo (1991) is the same as the one existing between the cases illustrated by Figures 6.3 and 6.2.

7.3. Factors counteracting diminishing returns to capital

Finally, there is a large class of models contemplating various factors counteracting any diminishing tendency of returns to capital. These can be grouped in two subclasses: human capital formation, and knowledge accumulation. In both kinds of models *positive external effects* play an important part; they offset any fall in the marginal product of capital.

7.3.1. Human capital formation

Models of the first sub-class attempt to formalize the role of human capital formation in the process of growth. Elaborating on some ideas of Uzawa (1965), Lucas (1988) assumed that agents have a choice between two ways of spending their (non-leisure) time: to contribute to current production or to accumulate human capital. It is essentially the allocation of time between the two alternatives contemplated that decides the growth rate of the system. For example, a decrease in the time spent producing goods involves a reduction in current output; at the same time it speeds up the formation of human capital and thereby increases output growth. With the accumulation of human capital there is said to be associated an externality: the more human capital society as a whole has accumulated, the more productive each single member will be. This is reflected in the following macroeconomic production function:

$$Y = AK^\beta (uhN)^{1-\beta} h^{*\gamma} \tag{6.6}$$

where the labour input consists of the number of workers, N, times the fraction of time spent working, u, times h which gives the labour input in efficiency units. Finally, there is the term h^*. This is designed to represent the externality. The single agent takes h^* as a parameter in his or her optimizing by choice of c and u. However, for society as a whole the accumulation of human capital increases output both directly and indirectly, that is, through the externality. Here we are confronted with a variant of a *public good* problem, which may be expressed as follows. The individual optimizing agent faces constant returns to scale in production: the sum of the partial elasticities of production of the factors he or she can control, that is, his or her physical and human capital, is unity. Yet for society as a whole the partial elasticity of production of human capital is not $1 - \beta$, but $1 - \beta + \gamma$.

Lucas's conceptualization of the process by means of which human capital is built up is the following:

$$\dot{h} = vh(1 - u) \tag{6.7}$$

where v is a positive constant. (Note that equation (6.7) can be interpreted as a 'production function' of human capital.)

Interestingly, it can be shown that if the externality mentioned above is *not* present, that is, if γ in equation (6.6) equals zero, and therefore returns to scale are constant and, as a consequence, the Non-substitution Theorem holds, endogenous growth in Lucas's model is obtained in essentially the same way as in the models by Rebelo (1991) and King and Rebelo (1990): the rate of profit is determined by technology and profit maximization alone; and for the predetermined level of the rate of profit the saving–investment mechanism determines the rate of growth. Yet, as Lucas himself pointed out, the endogenous growth is positive *independently* of the fact that there is the above-mentioned externality, that is, independently of the fact that γ is positive.[13] *Therefore, while complicating the picture increasing returns do not add substantially to it: growth is endogenous even if returns to scale are constant.* If returns to scale are not constant then the Non-substitution Theorem does not apply, implying that neither the competitive technique nor the associated rate of profit are determined by technical alternatives and profit maximization alone. Nevertheless, these two factors still determine, in steady states, a relationship between the rate of profit and the rate of growth. This relationship together with the relationship between the same rates obtained from the saving–investment mechanism determines both variables. Although the analysis is more

---

13 For a demonstration of this, see Kurz and Salvadori (1995b, pp. 13–19).

complex, essentially the same mechanism applies as in the models dealt with in Subsection 7.1.

7.3.2. Technical change

Models of the second sub-class attempt to portray technological change as generated endogenously. The proximate starting point of this kind of model was Arrow's (1962) paper on 'learning by doing'. Romer (1986) focuses on the role of a single state variable called 'knowledge' or 'information' and assumes that the information contained in inventions and discoveries has the property of being available to anybody to make use of it at the same time. In other words, information is considered essentially a non-rival good. Yet, it need not be totally non-excludable, that is, it can be monopolized at least for some time. It is around the two different aspects of publicness – non-rivalry and non-excludability – that the argument revolves. Discoveries are made in research and development departments of firms. This requires that resources be withheld from producing current output. The basic idea of Romer's (1986, p. 1015) model is 'that there is a trade-off between consumption today and knowledge that can be used to produce more consumption tomorrow'. He formalizes this idea in terms of a 'research technology' that produces 'knowledge' from forgone consumption. Knowledge is assumed to be cardinally measurable and not to depreciate: it is like perennial capital.

Romer stipulates a research technology that is concave and homogeneous of degree one:

$$\dot{k}_i = G(I_i, k_i) \tag{6.8}$$

where I_i is an amount of forgone consumption in research by firm i and k_i is the firm's current stock of knowledge. (Note that the forgone consumption good is a capital good utilized in the production of 'knowledge'.) The production function of the consumption good relative to firm i is

$$Y_i = F(k_i, K, \mathbf{x}_i) \tag{6.9}$$

where K is the accumulated stock of knowledge in the economy as a whole and $\mathbf{x}_i$ are all inputs different from knowledge. The function is taken to be homogeneous of degree one in k_i and $\mathbf{x}_i$, and homogeneous of a degree greater than one in k_i and K. Romer (1986, p. 1019) assumes that 'factors other than knowledge are in fixed supply'. This implies that 'knowledge' is the only capital good utilized in the production of the consumption good. Spillovers from private research and development activities increase the public stock of knowledge K.

Assuming, contrary to Romer, that the above production function of equation (6.9) is homogeneous of degree one in k_i and K involves a constant marginal product of capital: the diminishing returns to k_i are exactly offset by the external improvements in technology associated with capital accumulation. In this case it can be shown that, similar to the NGMs previously dealt with, the rate of profit is determined by technology and profit maximization alone, provided, as is assumed by Romer, that the ratio K/k_i equals the (given) number of firms.

The saving–investment relation then determines endogenously the growth rate. Once again endogenous growth does not depend on an assumption about increasing returns with regard to accumulable factors. Growth would be no more endogenous if increasing returns were to be assumed: such an assumption would only render the analysis a good deal more complicated. In particular, a steady-state equilibrium does not exist, and in order for an equilibrium to exist the marginal product of capital must be bounded from above. This is effected by Romer in terms of an *ad hoc* assumption regarding equation (6.8) (ibid., p. 1019). This assumption is not different from the one used in drawing Figure 6.4, where the marginal product of corn is shown to be increasing with the scale of production, but is bounded from above.

8. Conclusion

The NGMs revolve around a few simple and rather obvious ideas which have been anticipated by earlier economists, most notably Adam Smith and David Ricardo. We hope to have shown that many of the interesting aspects of the NGMs are related to the classical perspective their authors (unwittingly) take on the problem of growth, whereas some of their shortcomings derive from the lack of solutions to the problems of the neoclassical theory of growth which were put into sharp relief during the 1960s and 1970s. It has also been hinted that in some non-neoclassical approaches to the theory of accumulation and growth, the endogeneity of the growth rate has always been taken for granted. A brief look into the history of economic thought shows that from Adam Smith via David Ricardo, Robert Torrens, Thomas Robert Malthus, Karl Marx up to John von Neumann, both the equilibrium and the actual rate of capital accumulation and thus both the equilibrium and the actual rate of growth of output as a whole, were seen to depend on agents' behaviour, that is, endogenously determined. In this regard there is indeed nothing new under the sun.

Barro and Sala-i-Martin (1995, p. 39) suggest that the AK model 'becomes more plausible if we think of K in a broad sense to include human capital'. We advocate an alternative interpretation: in this model, as in the NGT more generally, endogenous growth is obtained by assuming that there is a technology producing labour, as in the classical economists. Following the later neoclassical tradition, Solow considered labour a non-accumulable factor: this factor is now referred to as 'human capital' or 'knowledge'. These names are simply evocations of this fundamental transposition.

Acknowledgements

We are grateful to Walter Eltis, the discussant of our paper at the meeting of the International Economic Association in Tunis in 1995, Erich Streissler and Mark Knell for helpful comments and suggestions. Neri Salvadori also thanks MURST (the Italian Ministry of University and Technological and Scientific Research) and the CNR (the Italian National Research Council) for financial support. The usual caveats apply.

References

Arrow, K. J. (1962) 'The Economic Implications of Learning by Doing', *Review of Economic Studies*, vol. 29, pp. 155–73.

Barro, R. J. and X. Sala-i-Martin (1995) *Economic Growth* (New York: McGraw-Hill).

Cassel, G. (1932) *The Theory of Social Economy* (first German edn 1918) (New York: Harcourt Brace).

Champernowne, D. G. (1945) 'A Note on J. v. Neumann's Article on "A Model of Economic Growth" ', *Review of Economic Studies*, vol. 13, pp. 10–18.

Charasoff, G. von (1910) *Das System des Marxismus: Darstellung und Kritik* (Berlin: H. Bondy).

Dorfman, R., P. A. Samuelson and R. M. Solow (1958) *Linear Programming and Economic Analysis* (New York: McGraw-Hill).

Eltis, W. (1984) *The Classical Theory of Economic Growth* (London: Macmillan).

Grossman, G. M. and E. Helpman (1994) 'Endogenous Innovation in the Theory of Growth', *Journal of Economic Perspectives*, vol. 8, pp. 23–44.

Jones, L. E. and R. Manuelli (1990) 'A Convex Model of Equilibrium Growth: Theory and Policy Implications', *Journal of Political Economy*, vol. 98, pp. 1008–38.

Kaldor, N. (1955–56) 'Alternative Theories of Distribution', *Review of Economic Studies*, vol. 23, pp. 83–100.

Kaldor, N. (1957) 'A Model of Economic Growth', *Economic Journal*, vol. 67, pp. 591–624.

Kaldor, N. (1966) *Causes of the Slow Rate of Growth of the United Kingdom* (Cambridge: Cambridge University Press).

King, R. G. and S. Rebelo (1990) 'Public Policy and Economic Growth: Developing Neoclassical Implications', *Journal of Political Economy*, vol. 98, pp. 126–50.

Kurz, H. D. and N. Salvadori (1993) 'Von Neumann's Growth Model and the "Classical" Tradition', *The European Journal of the History of Economic Thought*, vol. 1, pp. 129–60.

Kurz, H. D. and N. Salvadori (1995a) *Theory of Production. A Long-period Analysis* (Cambridge, Melbourne and New York: Cambridge University Press).

Kurz, H. D. and N. Salvadori (1995b) 'What is "New" in the New Theories of Economic Growth? Or: Old Wine in New Goatskins', revised version of a paper presented at the workshop 'Endogenous Growth and Development' of *The International School of Economic Research*, University of Siena, Italy, 3–9 July 1994, in F. Coricelli, M. Di Matteo and F. H. Hahn (eds), *Growth and Development: Theories, Empirical Evidence and Policy Issues* (London: Macmillan, 1998).

Kurz, H. D. and N. Salvadori (1995c) 'The Non-substitution Theorem: Making Good a Lacuna', *Journal of Economics*, vol. 59, pp. 97–103.

Lowe, A. (1954) 'The Classical Theory of Economic Growth', *Social Research*, vol. 21, pp. 127–58, reprinted in A. Oakley (ed.) (1987), *Essays in Political Economics: Public Control in a Democratic Society* (Brighton: Wheatsheaf).

Lucas, R. E. (1988) 'On the Mechanics of Economic Development', *Journal of Monetary Economics*, vol. 22, pp. 3–42.

Marshall, A. (1890) *Principles of Economics*, 8th edn 1920; variorum edn, C. W. Guillebaud (ed.) 1961 (London: Macmillan).

Marx, K. (1956) *Capital*, vol. II (Moscow: Progress Publishers). English translation of *Das Kapital*, vol. II, F. Engels (ed.) (1885) (Hamburg: Meissner).

Meade, J. E. (1961) *A Neoclassical Theory of Economic Growth* (London: Allen & Unwin).

Negishi, T. (1993) 'A Smithian Growth Model and Malthus's Optimal Propensity to Save', *The European Journal of the History of Economic Thought*, vol. 1, pp. 115–27.

Neumann, J. von (1945) 'A Model of General Economic Equilibrium', *Review of Economic Studies*, vol. 13, pp. 1–9. English translation of 'Über ein ökonomisches Gleichungssystem und eine Verallgemeinerung des Brouwerschen Fixpunktsatzes', in *Ergebnisse eines mathematischen Kolloquiums*, vol. 8 (1937), pp. 73–83.

Ramsey, F. P. (1928) 'A Mathematical Theory of Saving', *Economic Journal*, vol. 38, pp. 543–59.

Rebelo, S. (1991) 'Long Run Policy Analysis and Long Run Growth', *Journal of Political Economy*, vol. 99, pp. 500–21.

Ricardo, D. (1951) *On the Principles of Political Economy and Taxation*, 1st edn 1817, 3rd edn 1821; in vol. I of *The Works and Correspondence of David Ricardo*, edited by Piero Sraffa with the collaboration of Maurice H. Dobb (Cambridge: Cambridge University Press).

Romer, P. M. (1986) 'Increasing Returns and Long-run Growth', *Journal of Political Economy*, vol. 94, pp. 1002–37.

Smith, A. (1976) *An Inquiry into the Nature and Causes of the Wealth of Nations* (first published in 1776) *The Glasgow Edition of the Works and Correspondence of Adam Smith*, two vols (Oxford: Oxford University Press).

Solow, R. M. (1956) 'A Contribution to the Theory of Economic Growth', *Quarterly Journal of Economics*, vol. 70, pp. 65–94.

Solow, R. M. (1963) *Capital Theory and the Rate of Return* (Amsterdam: North-Holland).

Swan, T. W. (1956) 'Economic Growth and Capital Accumulation', *Economic Record*, vol. 32, pp. 334–61.

Torrens, R. (1820) *An Essay on the Influence of the External Corn Trade upon the Production and Distribution of National Wealth*, 2nd edn (London: Hatchard).

Torrens, R. (1821) *An Essay on the Production of Wealth* (London: Longman, Hurst, Rees, Orme and Brown); reprint: J. Dorfman (ed.) 1965 (New York: Kelley).

Uzawa, H. (1965) 'Optimum Technical Change in an Aggregate Model of Economic Growth', *International Economic Review*, vol. 6, pp. 18–31.

Wicksell, K. (1934) *Lectures on Political Economy* (first Swedish edn 1901) (London: Routledge).

Young, A. A. (1928) 'Increasing Returns and Economic Progress', *Economic Journal*, vol. 38, pp. 527–42.

7   What could the 'new' growth theory teach Smith or Ricardo?*

Heinz D. Kurz

1. Introduction

In many countries, departments of economics as well as other departments are nowadays subject to recurrent assessments of the quality of their work, especially the research performed by their members. In Britain this activity is known as the Research Assessment Exercise. While there appears to be fairly wide agreement within the profession that such assessments might be a good thing, at least in principle, there is much less agreement about how they should be carried out and whether the way in which they are in fact done can be expected to yield a fair judgement on the strengths and weaknesses of economics departments. It would of course be very unwise for me to enter into a discussion of this hot topic, of which I understand so little, and I can assure you that I will not do so. I shall rather deal with a first attempt to realize a proposal of which you may not yet have heard. It has been suggested that the now common cross-section assessment should be complemented by a time-series assessment aimed at evaluating the relative speeds with which the different scientific disciplines and their various branches progress. Applied to our subject, the question is what can be said about the advancement of economic knowledge in general and in special fields in particular.

Next the questions were addressed which area to examine and whom to commission to the intertemporal assessment of economics. Growth theory was chosen for obvious reasons and just at this point someone drew attention to a fundamental breakthrough in medicine which had made it possible to bring dead people back to life. On mature deliberation it was then easy to select Adam Smith and David Ricardo. Reanimated, the two economists, after some hesitation, accepted to serve on a committee 'On the Advancement of Knowledge in Growth Economics, Paying Special Attention to the Contribution of "New" Growth Theory'.

Smith and Ricardo met in a place mid-way between Glasgow and Gloucester, in a charming town by the name of Stoke-on-Trent, where they were offered an impressive chamber in which they could work and had access to all the relevant literature. After some weeks of reading they decided to structure their following

* Reprinted with permission from *Economic Issues*, Vol. 2, Part 2, 1997.

discussion. They wanted to begin with a brief investigation of the *scope* of 'new' growth theory, then turn to the *method* in terms of which the problem was studied, and finally approach the *content* of the theory. As regards the latter task they agreed to deal first with major building blocks of the theory and subsequently to study how these blocks were combined. They decided to concentrate on fundamentals and set aside what may be considered peripheral to the main argument. This also made them focus attention on what may be called the first generation of contributions to 'new' growth theory, because these defined the confines within which the resulting avalanche of theoretical literature was to unfold.

By inexplicable luck it fell upon me to report on their conversations while working on the assessment. In the following I provide a summary account of what I had the privilege to hear and see. It goes without saying that none of the views put forward in the sequel are my responsibility. If you should dislike them you must not put the blame on me; I am only the messenger. The unfortunate habit in antiquity of decapitating those who brought bad news (and were generally good at running) may have been one of the causes of the eventual decline of those nations.

My report is in the form of a dialogue between Smith and Ricardo. This keeps close to what actually happened. It goes without saying that I am bound to read out what they said. If I didn't you might be inclined to think that what follows is an invention of my mind. So please forgive me for not speaking freely to you; it is in the interest of undiluted scholarship and truth.

2. They and us

SMITH: On the whole I was rather disappointed how little the majority of modern authors know about what we have done. Whilst there are occasional references to our works . . .

RICARDO: There are many more to yours than to mine!

SMITH: It's kind of you to say this, my dear David, but being referred to more often doesn't mean much. I have the feeling that to praise an author is sometimes just a pretext *not* to take into account what he has written. There are also statements that I found amazing. Listen, for example, to the following dictum of Martin Weitzman of Harvard University: 'Before Robert Solow and his co-conspirators did serious growth accounting[,] economists did not think too systematically about the sources of economic growth . . . ' (Weitzman, 1996, p. 207). What does he think we were doing?

RICARDO: I understand your disenchantment, Adam, but don't forget that the judgement came from an American, and, as we know, they occasionally have a tendency to grossly exaggerate things and present their ideas as if they were totally original and novel. British people are different.

SMITH: I wonder! But let's get back to our main topic and discuss the scope of the 'new' growth models.

3. Scope

SMITH: As you know, Adam Ferguson coined the beautiful phrase that history is 'the result of human action, but not the execution of any human design' (Ferguson, [1767] 1793, p. 205). We considered the explanation of human history one of the most important, if not *the* most important problem of the social sciences. The explanation sought included an investigation of the nonintended consequences of purposeful action and a discussion of the possibilities and limits of statesmanship. What was at stake was, in the words of John Hicks (1969), the development of a 'theory of economic history'. We accepted this challenge and, I dare say, with some little success.

RICARDO: I think this is a fair description of what *you* did. My concern was much more limited.

SMITH: You're a modest man, David. Be that as it may, the grandiose question of what shapes the long-term development of the economy is again high on the agenda. This should be some comfort to us. We may ask now: Has growth theory progressed since our days? Or: What could the 'new' growth theory teach us?

4. Method

RICARDO: As I see things there is not only a revival of interest in the old questions but also in the method of analysis proposed by us, namely, the method of *long-period* positions, or 'equilibria', in the language of the 'new' growth theorists, characterised by a *uniform* rate of profit. More precisely, these authors focus attention on what is but a very special case of such positions, that is, *steady states* of the economy. As you will have read, the long-period method which was used by essentially all economists, classical and neoclassical alike, until the late 1920s was then replaced by the new methods of *temporary* and *intertemporal equilibrium*, pioneered by Hayek, Lindahl and Hicks. There is no time to go into the details of this break with the traditional method here. Suffice it to say that in temporary equilibrium theory in general and in intertemporal equilibrium theory until a few decades ago the time horizon was assumed to be finite and, therefore, arbitrary. The introduction of an *infinite* horizon turned out to be critical (see also Burgstaller, 1994, pp. 43–8). It pushed the analysis inevitably towards the long period. This was clearly spelled out, for instance, by Robert Lucas, who observed that

> for *any* initial capital $K(0) > 0$, the optimal capital-consumption path $(K(t), c(t))$ will converge to the balanced path asymptotically. That is, the balanced path will be a good approximation to any actual path 'most' of the time.

and that 'this is exactly the reason why the balanced path is interesting to us' (Lucas, 1988, p. 11).

Lucas thus advocated a *(re-)switching* from an intertemporal analysis to a long-period (steady-state) one. Since the balanced path of the intertemporal model is the only path analyzed by Lucas, the intertemporal model may be regarded simply as a step to obtain a rigorous long-period setting (see also King and Rebelo, 1993). (Paraphrasing a dictum put forward by Paul Samuelson in a different context, we may say that intertemporal analysis is a *detour* with regard to long-period analysis.) Moreover, concentrating on the 'balanced path', capital in the initial period *cannot* be taken as given alongside other 'initial endowments'. As a consequence, income distribution cannot be determined by demand and supply of the respective factors of production.

SMITH: What you said is very interesting. Whilst I am not at all happy with the narrowing of our notion of long period to steady states, in terms of scope and method I already begin to feel somewhat at home. But what about the content of the theory? Since the saving-investment mechanism is at the heart of every theory of accumulation and growth. I suggest we start with that.

5. Consumption, saving and investment

RICARDO: I must confess that I was very surprised to see that these models know essentially only a single agent. You will remember that our approaches were criticized for being insufficiently microeconomic, because we knew only three kinds of agents and economic roles associated with them – workers, capitalists and landlords. Yet many if not the majority of contemporaries seem to find nothing wrong with the single-agent abstraction mongering. It is even assumed – can you believe it? – that the 'representative agent' is immortal and immutable, which follows from his – or is it her? – concern with maximizing an intertemporal utility function over an infinite time horizon. The exercise then consists of choosing the path of consumption that maximizes the integral of instantaneous utility:

$$\int_0^\infty e^{-\rho t} \frac{1}{1-\sigma} [c(t)^{1-\sigma} - 1] \, dt \tag{7.1}$$

subject to $Y = c(t) + \dot{K}$, where Y is net national income, $c(t)$ is consumption at time t, $\dot{K}$ is net investment which is the derivative of the capital stock K with respect to time, ρ is the rate of time preference or discount rate, and $1/\sigma$ is the elasticity of substitution between present and future consumption $(1 \neq \sigma > 0)$. In the literature, the discount rate is occasionally dubbed 'required rate of return', since it gives the break-even level of the profit rate: with the rate of profit larger (smaller) than the discount rate, savings will be positive (negative). As becomes already clear at this stage, the models generally know only a single consumption good, which is commonly taken to be identical with the physical capital good.

SMITH: This is indeed an amusing way of dealing with the complex issue of 'microfoundations'. It seems to me that the 'representative agent' could claim with greater authority than Louis XIV: 'L'État c'est moi!' Setting aside a variety of behaviour and thus selection strikes me as neglecting some of the most important aspects of any real process of growth and development. It should also be pointed out that this optimizing approach leads to various difficulties, logical and other, which raise serious doubts about its usefulness. For example, no allowance is made for the fact that consumption takes time; as income per capita rises, the problem of *when* to consume ever larger quantities of the single consumption good cannot be evaded (cf. Steedman, 2001). Robert Solow, for perfectly good reasons, it seems, maintained: 'the use made of the inter-temporally-optimizing representative agent . . . adds little or nothing to the story anyway, while encumbering it with unnecessary implausibilities and complexities' (Solow, 1994, p. 49).

What I also find peculiar is that ρ – which, as we shall see, plays a crucial role in the argument – is commonly assumed to be given from outside the system and constant. In contradistinction, John Stuart Mill and after him many others, including John Maynard Keynes, stressed that 'The minimum rate of profit varies according to circumstances' (Mill, [1848] 1965, p. 736). Considerations of this kind made me advocate the view that a fall in the rate of profit need not necessarily entail a fall in the rate of accumulation.

RICARDO: It should also be noted that because there is no real distinction between savers and investors there is none between savings and investment. Say's law is taken to hold full sway. The problem of effective demand and unemployment is simply set aside, whereas in my controversy with Malthus I was at least keen to argue my case, perhaps overkeen, I now recognize. Indeed, I am in sympathy with the thrust of a statement by Edmond Malinvaud put forward only a few years before the take-off of 'new' growth theory. *Vis-à-vis* the unemployment figures in the OEEC he wrote:

> Students of economic growth will easily accept two ideas put forward . . . , namely that some disequilibria may be sustained over rather long periods, and that the existence of these disequilibria significantly reacts on the growth process, to speed it up, slow it down or change its course. . . . [A]n essential part of any theory of economic growth should be the representation of investment, and it seems to me that both excess capacity and profitability have an important role to play in this representation.
>
> (Malinvaud, 1983, p. 95)

6. Production

SMITH: I think Malinvaud has a good point. And there are others. Did you notice, David, that in this literature production as a whole is represented in terms of what are called *aggregate production functions*?

RICARDO: I did indeed and was baffled, because I could not believe that all the different productive activities in any real economy can be portrayed in such a way. How do you aggregate lorries, conveyor belts, personal computers etc. to a 'quantity of capital' for the economy as a whole, and similarly with

regard to the social product? Looking up the modern literature on capital theory and aggregation I saw my scepticism fully corroborated. Franklin Fisher
(1993), for example, has made it abundantly clear that there is no such thing
as an aggregate production function. And Andreu Mas-Colell stressed that
'modelling the world as having a single capital good is not *a priori* justified'
(Mas-Colell, 1989, p. 508), and I doubt that it can be justified *a posteriori.*
However, these results don't seem to be taken seriously in the literature under
consideration.

SMITH: Well, there are at least occasional hints that something is dubious. After
having discovered that an earlier formulation of his is inconsistent with the
assumption that research is a nonrival good, Paul Romer added that this

> may seem a trifling matter in an area of theory that depends on so many
> other short cuts. After all, if one is going to do violence to the complexity
> of economic activity by assuming that there is an aggregate production
> function, how much more harm can it do to be sloppy about the difference
> between rival and nonrival goods?
>
> (Romer, 1994, p. 15)

I kept wondering where to stop this process.

RICARDO: I came across an even more puzzling passage by the same author. In the
context of a discussion of some people's opposition to mathematical formalism
he stated:

> Only 30 years ago many economists still objected to a mathematical
> statement of the relationship between output and capital in terms of an
> aggregate production function and an aggregate stock of capital, $Y =
> f(K, L)$.
>
> (Romer, 1996, p. 202)

I hope he doesn't imply that Fisher is not a good mathematical economist. As
if the question was against pro or con mathematical formalism as such and
not pro or con cases of silly mathematical formalism.

SMITH: I agree. More generally, I found that many modern writers have a pronounced concern for *spurious* precision. They put into algebra what perhaps
cannot yet be put into mathematical language because the phenomena under
consideration have not yet been studied with sufficient care. Faith does not
seem to be a scarce good in contemporary economics. Are 'microfoundations'
not required in production theory?

7. A falling rate of profit

SMITH: But let's get to the core of the matter. We are told that 'The key property of
endogenous-growth models is the absence of diminishing returns to capital'
(Barro and Sala-i-Martin, 1995, p. 39), that is, the absence of any falling

long-term tendency of the rate of profit. Since you did not approve of my explanation of the falling tendency of the profit rate for reasons which I think I now understand, it would be good if you could summarize what, in your view, is responsible for any such tendency. Your argument may then serve as a foil against which we can discuss the mechanisms invoked by the 'new' growth theorists to prevent the rate of profit from falling.

RICARDO: This is very kind of you. I shall try to set the stage for our discussion in terms of a highly stylised representation of what I called the 'natural' course of the economy. By this I meant the purely hypothetical path an economic system would take in the absence of any technical progress. For simplicity, and perfectly in line with much of 'new' growth theory, I shall assume a one-commodity economy. The only commodity produced is dubbed 'corn'. You may have heard that there is some controversy whether in my lost papers on Profits of 1814 I held such a 'corn model'. Unfortunately, I have forgotten whether I did or didn't, which however is of no import for the rest of my argument. With corn of a given quality as the only capital good there simply cannot arise the problem of what is meant by a given 'quantity of capital' or by an 'increase' of that quantity.

Assuming, in addition, the real wage rate of workers to be given and constant, the rate of profit is bound to fall due to extensive and intensive diminishing returns on land. On the premise that there are only negligible savings out of wages and rents, a falling rate of profit involves a falling rate of capital accumulation. Assuming that the marginal propensity to accumulate out of profits, s, is given and constant, a 'classical' accumulation function can be formulated:

$$g = \begin{cases} s(r - r_{\min}) & \text{if } r \geq r_{\min} \\ 0 & \text{if } r \leq r_{\min} \end{cases} \tag{7.2}$$

where $r_{\min} \geq 0$ is the minimum level of profitability which, if reached, will arrest accumulation (cf. *Works*, I, p. 120). My 'natural' course will necessarily end up in a stationary state. Notice that the rate of accumulation is *endogenously* determined. The demand for labour is governed by the pace at which capital accumulates, whereas the long-term supply of labour is regulated by a population mechanism.[1]

---

1 To this Ricardo added: 'Real wages may rise, that is, the "market price of labour" may rise above the "natural" wage rate. This is the case in a situation where capital accumulates rapidly, leading to an excess demand for labour. As I put it, "notwithstanding the tendency of wages to conform to their natural rate, the market rate may, in an improving society, for an indefinite period, be constantly above it" (ibid., pp. 94–5). If such a constellation prevails for some time it is even possible that "custom renders absolute necessaries" what in the past had been comforts or luxuries. Hence, the natural wage is driven upward by persistently high levels of the actual wage rate. Accordingly, in my analysis the concept of "natural wage" is a flexible one and must not be mistaken for a physiological minimum of subsistence. I take it that your view on wages and the growth of the work force is similar, Adam.'

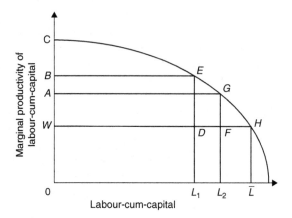

Figure 7.1 Diminishing returns.

Let me illustrate the case with the help of the familiar Figure 7.1 (cf. Kaldor, 1956). For simplicity I set aside seed capital: capital consists only of wages. In the most simple conceptualization possible, the one entertained here, labour is seen to be in long-run elastic supply at a given real wage rate, which is taken to equal *OW*. The curve *CEGH* is the marginal productivity of labour-cum-capital. Then, if the amount of labour-cum-capital applied is L_1, the area $OCEL_1$, gives the product, $OWDL_1$ gives total capital employed, and *BCE* total rent. Profit is determined as a residual and corresponds to the rectangle *WBED*. The *rate* of profit can be determined as the ratio of the areas of two rectangles which have the same basis and, therefore, it equals the ratio *WB/OW*. Obviously, if a positive profit rate implies a positive growth rate (i.e. $r_{min} = 0$), the economy will expand until labour-cum-capital has reached the level $\bar{L}$.

The important point to note here is that the work force needed in a given moment of time is considered to be generated by the accumulation process itself. In your words, Adam: 'the demand for men, like that for any other commodity, necessarily, regulates the production of men: quickens it when it goes on too slowly, and stops it when it advances too fast. It is this demand which regulates and determines the state of propagation in all the different countries of the world' (*WN*, I.viii.40).[2] Labour can thus put no limit to growth because it is 'generated' within the growth process. The only limit to growth can come from other *nonaccumulable* factors of production, that is, natural

---

2 To this Ricardo added the following qualification: 'In the more sophisticated conceptualizations underlying the arguments of you and myself, higher rates of growth of labour supply presuppose higher levels of the real wage rate. But the basic logic remains the same: in normal conditions the pace at which capital accumulates regulates the pace at which labour grows.'

resources in general and land in particular. It is the 'niggardliness of nature' which is responsible for the falling tendency of the rate of profit.

8. Solow's model

SMITH: Well done, David! I think I now also understand Solow's model much better (cf. Solow, 1956). Whilst you and I put forward an approach which subsumed the supply of labour under the needs of capital accumulation, Solow subsumed land (and natural resources) under capital. Therefore, labour assumes in his model a position that may be compared to that of land in yours. And very much as in your argument the rate of profit is taken to fall as the accumulable factor – capital – grows relatively to the nonaccumulable factor. Outside the steady state, both the actual rate of growth and income distribution are *endogenously* determined, whereas in the steady state the rate of growth equals the *exogenously* given natural rate of growth. But the rate of profit as well as the real wage rate are still *endogenous*. I may illustrate this in terms of the very familiar Figure 7.2. The endogenously determined steady-state rate of profit $r(k^*)$ is given by the slope of the tangent at P.

Now let me ask you a question and add a speculation. The question is: Would it be very misleading to say that compared to the Solovian model in the 'new' growth literature the situation is reversed in the following sense: *the steady-state rate of profit is exogenous, whereas the steady-state rate of growth is endogenous*? And the speculation is: With the rate of profit at centre stage of the 'new' growth models, in order to have perpetual growth, the rate of profit must not fall to r_{min} or ρ. Hence, in terms of Figure 7.1 I see essentially three research strategies: provide arguments that guarantee *either* that the curve giving the marginal product of labour-cum-capital does not fall,

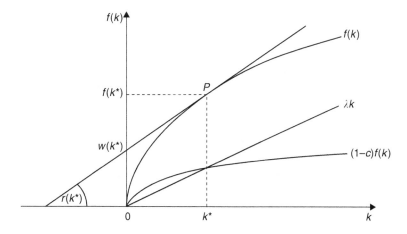

Figure 7.2 Endogenous steady-state rate of profit.

but is a line parallel to the abscissa, *or* falls, but its fall is bounded from below, *or* instead of falling rises.

RICARDO: As regards your question: No, it wouldn't be *very* misleading. As regards your speculation: it provides a most useful systematic framework for the following discussion. Let me begin with the so-called 'linear' or '*AK* models'.

9. 'AK' models

RICARDO: If in Solow's model there was no labour needed in production, or if labour was a free good, then the marginal product of capital could not fall as capital accumulates. This is precisely the route taken by one class of 'new' growth models: whereas Solow had only removed land from the scenery, they remove also labour, that is, all nonaccumulable factors, and assume that all inputs are 'capital' of some kind. You could say that these are Solovian models *sans travail*. Beauty is sought in simplicity. The most elementary version of this class of models assumes that there is a linear relationship between total gross output, Y, and a single factor capital, K, both consisting of the same commodity:

$$Y = AK \tag{7.3}$$

where $1/A$ is the amount of that commodity required to produce one unit of itself. The *surplus product* or net output equals $Y - \delta K$, where δ is the exogenously given rate of depreciation. The surplus is assumed to be appropriated entirely in the form of *profits*. The net rate of return on capital r is what my friend Malthus would have called a 'material rate of produce' and is given by:

$$r = \frac{Y}{K} - \delta = A - \delta \tag{7.4}$$

The saving-investment mechanism jointly with the assumption of a uniform rate of growth then determines a relationship between the growth rate g and the profit rate. Rebelo (1991, pp. 504 and 506) obtains either:

$$g = \frac{A - \delta - \rho}{\sigma} = \frac{r - \rho}{\sigma} \tag{7.5}$$

or

$$g = (A - \delta)s = sr \tag{7.6}$$

Equation (7.5) is obtained when savings are determined on the basis of intertemporal utility maximization, whereas equation (7.6) is obtained when the average propensity to save s is treated as a given parameter. Hence, in this model the rate of profit is given *by technology*, that is, exogenously, just as you said, Adam, and the saving-investment mechanism determines the growth rate.

SMITH: The model strikes me as a simplified version of the (in)famous 'corn model' and a replica ($\delta = 0$) of Frank Knight's 'Crusonia plant model':

> We may think of our Crusonia as living on the natural growth of some perennial which grows indefinitely at a constant (geometric) rate, except as new tissue is cut away for consumption. We assume that it requires no cultivation or other care, and we must ignore any 'labour' which may be involved in gathering or simply 'eating' the product.
>
> (Knight, 1944, p. 30)

Knight stressed that 'The resource must, of course, be of the nature of capital' and added: 'In an economy of the type postulated, the only problem of choice presented to the "management" will be the determination of the rate of consumption, which is the same as saying the rate of saving and investment or of disinvestment' (ibid., p. 30).

RICARDO: This is a valid observation, Adam. Compared with the 'corn model' there are two differences: (i) the input of 'corn' in the AK model is treated as a durable capital good and (ii) land is a free good. As regards the problem of depreciation, let me mention in passing that I find the assumption of an exogenously given rate of depreciation highly problematic. But let me turn immediately to the implicit assumption that land is a free good. When I once engaged in the fancy thought experiment of what would happen if land and natural resources of the best quality were available in unlimited amount, I did not of course think I could thereby anticipate what towards the end of the twentieth century would be considered an innovative idea. Let me remind you of what I wrote:

> Profits do not *necessarily* fall with the increase of the quantity of capital because the demand for capital is infinite and is governed by the same law as population itself. They are both checked by the rise in the price of food, and the consequent increase in the price of labour. If there were no such rise, what could prevent population and capital from increasing without limit?
>
> (Ricardo, *Works*, VI, p. 301)

With land as a *free good*, costs of production of the amount of corn constituting the given real wage rate would be constant. In this case – see Figure 7.3 – the graph giving the marginal productivity of labour-cum-capital would be a horizontal line and therefore the rate of profit would be constant whatever the amount of labour-cum-capital. As a consequence, the system could grow forever provided $r > r_{min}$.

The AK model is now immediately recognized as describing a world similar to the one contemplated in my thought experiment, provided that labour is set aside and $\delta = 1$. Even the saving-investment mechanism is essentially the same: in the case of equation (7.5) $\sigma = 1/s$ and $\rho = r_{min}$ (provided that

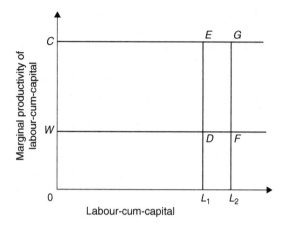

Figure 7.3 Land as a free good.

$r > r_{\min}$); in the case of equation (7.6) $r_{\min} = 0$. Hence, the version of the 'new' growth theory under consideration is but a further simplification of the most elementary of my growth models. I, for one, can hardly be accused of having taken that case too seriously. Schumpeter (1954, pp. 472–3) used to chastise what he dubbed the 'Ricardian Vice', that is, the habit of applying results derived from simple 'one-way relations' to the 'solution of practical problems'. What would he have said about the policy recommendations that abound in the 'new' growth literature?

SMITH: You appear to dislike the idea of *Ricardian* vice – perhaps because compared with you Schumpeter was not exactly what one would call successful, *financially* speaking?

RICARDO: Well, may be . . . Since you don't seem to show signs of boredom as yet may I take one more minute and talk briefly about the set of linear models that differentiate between physical and human capital? I refer particularly to a paper by King and Rebelo (1990).

SMITH: How could I stop you?

10. Physical and human capital

RICARDO: In the context of a discussion of the labour displacing effects of machinery I once went to the extreme and imagined a world in which machine power has entirely replaced labour power. I wrote:

> If machinery could do all the work that labour now does, there would be no demand for labour. Nobody would be entitled to consume any thing who was not a capitalist, and who could not buy or hire a machine.
>
> (*Works*, VIII, pp. 399–400)

SMITH: So what you are alluding to is that in some of the 'new' growth models all people are in fact capitalists of sorts.

RICARDO: Exactly. This is also why the idea of a 'representative agent' is somewhat congenial to these kinds of models. On the other hand, the existence of different kinds of agents cannot sensibly be denied. In particular, there *are* workers. The 'new' growth theorists seem to feel entitled to subsume workers under capitalists as a consequence of conceiving of the capacity to work as a *special* kind of capital: 'human capital'.

SMITH: This appears to me to be an important point. Authors like King and Rebelo (1990) draw indeed a strict analogy between an item of fixed capital and skilled labour. The production functions relating to the two kinds of capital have the two kinds of capital as the only inputs and are assumed to be homogeneous of degree one and strictly concave. There are no diminishing returns to (composite) capital for the reason that there is no nonaccumulable factor such as simple labour that enters into the production of the accumulable factors. In contradistinction to the above model of Rebelo there is a *choice of technique problem*. The rate of profit is now uniquely determined by the technology and the maximization of profits.[3] With the rate of profit ascertained in this way, the growth rate of the system is then determined in the usual way by the saving-investment equation.

RICARDO: Are you happy with this conceptualization of human capital?

SMITH: Hardly. First, the assumption entertained in this model, but also in that of Lucas (1988), that the formation of human capital does not involve any unskilled labour as an input is difficult to sustain: the whole point of education processes is that a person's capacity to perform unskilled labour is gradually transformed into capacity to perform skilled labour. Second, more than two centuries ago I wrote:

> A man educated at the expence of much labour and time to any of those employments which require extraordinary dexterity and skill, may be compared to one of those expensive machines. The work which he learns to perform, it must be expected, *over and above the usual wages of common labour*, will replace to him the whole expence of his education, with at least the ordinary profits of an equally valuable capital.
>
> (*WN*, I.x.b.6, emphasis added)

While I also drew a parallel between fixed (physical) capital and human capital, I was careful to keep a reference to the wage rate paid to workers performing 'common labour'. I don't see how that kind of labour could be made to vanish. And if it cannot, then assuming that there is no such thing as 'common labour' amounts to assuming that it is a free good . . .

---

3 Smith added in parenthesis: 'It is easily checked that if the production functions are "well-behaved", then there is one and only one solution to the system.'

11. Nonsubstitution theorem

RICARDO: . . . which in turn amounts to assuming that the wage rate is given from outside. This procedure bears a close resemblance to the *asymmetric* treatment of the distributive variables characteristic of our approach in which profits emerge as a residual. Yet there is a substantial difference here. The notion that in conditions of free competition the services of certain factors of production, such as some qualities of land, which are in excess supply assume a zero price – the so-called 'Rule of Free Goods' – was a standard element in what is known as classical rent theory. However, with respect to labour we only allowed an excess of labour to drive the wage to a *positive* minimum, reflecting social, historical and moral elements.

This brings me to a further observation. The authors of these models don't seem to be aware that they have simply put forward special cases of the so-called *nonsubstitution theorem* (see, e.g. Samuelson, 1961). The theorem states that with (i) constant returns to scale, (ii) a single primary factor of production only (homogeneous labour) and (iii) no joint production, and taking the real wage rate as given from outside the system, the price of human capital in terms of the consumption good and the rate of profit are uniquely determined. The theorem implies that generally only one technique can be used in the long run. The growth models under consideration satisfy conditions (i) and (iii). As regards condition (ii), a special form of the Theorem is needed because of the absence of any primary factor (or a primary factor with a zero remuneration).[4] It hardly needs to be stressed that compared to these models the famous von Neumann growth model (von Neumann, [1937] 1945) is a *good* deal more general.

SMITH: Let me summarize. In the class of models considered so far the role played by 'human capital' may be compared to the role played by 'labour' in our approaches: both factors of production are taken to be generated *endogenously*. The linear models thus replicate in elementary terms the *logic* of some two centuries old theory.

12. A convex technology with returns to capital bounded from below

RICARDO: True. Let me add, as an afterthought, a constellation that is mildly less fancy than the one depicted in Figure 7.3. Assume that land is differentiated into infinitely many classes: there is a continuum of different qualities – and all qualities superior to quality m are available in limited supply, whereas land of quality m is available in unlimited supply. Then the old story can be told anew except for a small modification. With the system growing forever and assuming continuous substitutability between labour-cum-capital and land, lands of

---

4 For a treatment of this special case of the nonsubstitution theorem, see Kurz and Salvadori (1994).

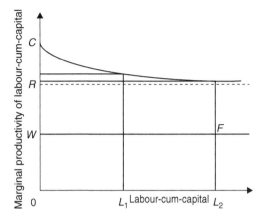

Figure 7.4 Returns to labour-cum-capital bounded from below.

quality 1 to $m - 1$ will eventually become scarce and the rate of profit will gradually fall to the level associated with land of quality m – given by the dashed line in Figure 7.4. On the assumption that the corresponding rate of profit is larger than $r_{min} \geq 0$, the system would grow indefinitely at a rate of growth which would asymptotically approach its lower boundary.

Interestingly, the properties of this case have recently been mimicked by Jones and Manuelli (1990). They preserved the dualism of an accumulable and a nonaccumulable factor as in Solow, but restricted the impact of an accumulation of the former on its returns by an *ad hoc* modification of the aggregate production function. The special case contemplated by them is:

$$\varphi(k) = f(k) + bk \qquad (7.7)$$

where $f(k)$ is the previously hallowed, but no longer sacrosanct Solovian production function, and b is a positive parameter. As capital accumulates and the capital-labour ratio rises, the marginal product of capital will fall, approaching asymptotically its lower boundary b. With a given propensity to save s and assuming capital to be everlasting, the steady-state growth rate g is endogenously determined: $g = s(b - r_{min})$. Assuming on the contrary intertemporal utility maximization, the steady-state rate of growth is given by $g = (b - \rho)/\sigma$. The rate of growth is positive, provided the technical parameter b is larger than r_{min} or ρ.

This prompts me to the following observation. All the papers referred to have been published in so-called 'core' journals. The term 'Diamond list' is said to be one of the most often heard terms these days in economics departments in the UK. But it would seem to me that one had better *read* what is commonly praised before passing a judgement on whether it is in fact praiseworthy.

SMITH: You may recall the 'paradox of value' which I illustrated in terms of the water and diamond example. There I wrote that diamonds – that is, things 'which have the greatest value in exchange have frequently little or no value in use' (*WN*, I.iv.13). *Frequently*, not always. Still there are the problems of deception and pressures to conformity. But this is too big a theme to be dealt with now.

13. Increasing returns to capital bounded from above

SMITH: So far we have seen two types of models: one in which decreasing returns to capital – a falling rate of profit – are prevented by juggling away *any* nonaccumulable factors, the other in which the impact of those factors is contained by some *ad hoc* assumption concerning technology. Let us now turn to a further class of models. These have recourse to *positive external effects* associated with self-seeking behaviour: these externalities are taken to offset any fall in the rate of profit as capital accumulates. The basic idea underlying these kinds of models can easily be illustrated in terms of another modification of the basic diagram used so far: the remaining possibility is increasing returns to capital, depicted in Figure 7.5. Clearly, if these returns were rising and unbounded from above, the growth rate might rise over time and tend towards infinity, which is not a very sensible thing to assume. The steady-state framework adopted by the 'new' growth theorists requires them to introduce *ad hoc* some upper boundary to returns to capital.

RICARDO: Externalities is clearly your field, not mine. However, whilst in your discussion of the division of labour you allowed both positive and negative externalities, in many models now there are only positive ones.

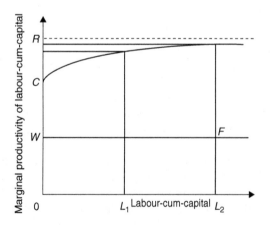

Figure 7.5 Increasing returns.

SMITH: This is indeed the case with regard to the models of Lucas (1988) and Romer (1986) which we must now investigate. But before we do that let me add a remark on Figure 7.5. In order to be able to preserve the notion of a *uniform* rate of profit, it has to be assumed that the increasing returns are *external* to the firm and exclusively connected with the expansion of the market as a whole and the social division of labour. This implies that whereas in the case of decreasing returns due to the scarcity of land (cf. Figures 7.1 and 7.4) the product was given by the area under the marginal productivity curve, now the product associated with any given amount of labour-cum-capital is larger than the area under that curve.[5] The cases of decreasing and increasing returns are thus not symmetrical.

I begin with a first subgroup of models contemplating the role of positive externalities for economic growth, that is, models in the tradition of Lucas (1988), which emphasize spillovers from human capital formation.

14. Human capital formation and externalities

SMITH: Lucas assumed that agents have a choice between two ways of spending their (non-leisure) time: to contribute to current production or to accumulate human capital. It is essentially the allocation of time between these two alternatives that decides the growth rate of the system. Lucas conceptualizes the process by means of which human capital is built up *ad hoc* by:

$$\dot{h} = \upsilon h^{\xi} (1 - u) \tag{7.8}$$

where u and ξ are positive constants. Whilst he indeed begins with equation (7.8), he quickly finds himself obliged to consider equation (7.8) with $\xi = 1$, because this is the only assumption consistent with steady-state growth. Equation (7.8) is thus a kind of 'production function' of human capital by means of human capital, where the average product is constant and equal to υ. It has been shown (Baldassari *et al.*, 1994) that if in Lucas's model leisure is included in the utility function, the system degenerates to a model of exogenous growth in which the rate of expansion equals the exogenous rate of growth of population. This relates somewhat to the earlier objection that consumption takes time and that it does not make sense to assume that 'corn' income per capita grows without saying *when* the exponentially rising amount of 'corn' can be consumed by the 'representative agent'.

But let us see how the story goes on. With the accumulation of human capital there is said to be associated an externality: the more human capital society as a whole has accumulated, the more productive each single member

---

5 See Kurz and Salvadori (1997), p. 342, n.6.

will be. This is reflected in the following macroeconomic production function:

$$Y = AK^{\beta}(uhN)^{1-\beta}h^{*\gamma} \tag{7.9}$$

where the labour input consists of the number of workers, N, times the fraction of time spent working, u, times h which gives the labour input in efficiency units. Finally, there is the term h^*. This is designed to represent the externality. The single agent takes h^* as a parameter when optimizing by choice of c and u. However, for society as a whole the accumulation of human capital increases output both directly and indirectly, that is, through the externality. The individual optimizing agent faces constant returns to scale in production: the sum of the partial elasticities of production of the factors he can control, that is, his physical and human capital, is unity. Yet for society as a whole the partial elasticity of production of human capital is not $1 - \beta$, but $1 - \beta + \gamma$.

Now I would like to pose a problem to you, David. Known for your 'taste for abstract and general reasoning' (*Works*, X, p. 4), could you kindly tell me what happens if we set aside the externality, that is, put γ in equation (7.9) equal to zero?

RICARDO: In this case returns to scale are constant and as a consequence, the nonsubstitution theorem holds. Accordingly endogenous growth in Lucas's model is obtained in essentially the same way as in the 'linear' models above: the rate of profit is determined by technology and profit maximization alone; and for the predetermined level of the rate of profit the saving-investment mechanism determines the rate of growth. Hence, growth is endogenous and positive *independently* of the fact that there is the above mentioned externality.[6] Therefore, though complicating the picture, increasing returns do not add substantially to it: growth would be no less endogenous if returns to scale were constant. In fact, after a little calculation we obtain that

$$r = \upsilon + \lambda \tag{7.10}$$

where λ is the exogenous rate of growth of population. There is only one meaning that can be given to the dependence of r on λ: it is a consequence of the remarkable fact that in Lucas's model the growth of 'population' means simply that the immortal consumer grows 'bigger' at rate λ. Otherwise one would have to assume the existence of another type of externality: costless socio-cultural transmission, that is, to new generations the existing knowledge is a free good. As far as I recall, my children and their teachers saw things somewhat differently.

SMITH: Well, let's now assume a positive γ (but lower than $(1 - \beta)\sigma$). In this case returns to scale are not constant and consequently the nonsubstitution theorem does not apply. Therefore, neither the competitive technique nor the corresponding rate of profit is determined by technical alternatives and

6 See Kurz and Salvadori (1995b), pp. 13–19.

profit maximization alone. The simple 'recursive' structure of the model is thereby lost. Nevertheless, technical alternatives and profit maximization still determine, in steady states, a relationship between the rate of profit and the rate of growth. This relationship together with the relationship between the same rates obtained from the saving-investment equation determines both variables. Thus, although the analysis is more complex, essentially the same mechanism applies as in the 'linear' models. Once again the concept of 'human capital' has assumed a role equivalent to the role of the concept of 'labour' in our approaches.

15. Research and development and endogenous technical change

RICARDO: This concludes the chapter on human capital formation. We should proceed to approaches that attempt to endogenise technical progress, paying special attention to a paper by Romer (1986). As we shall see, this literature revolves around the idea that technical knowledge is, or tends to become, a *public good*, that is, nonrival and nonexcludable. To put the discussion in perspective, let me recall two facts. First, technical progress in Solow's model was taken to be costless and equally beneficial to all firms – like 'manna from heaven'. Technology in this model is a pure public good of a special kind, because it does not cause, in modern parlance, any problem of 'market failure'. The 'new' growth theory dispenses with this assumption and, therefore, in principle with the assumption of perfect competition. Second, I dare say that all the ideas that play a prominent role in this kind of literature were anticipated in our writings. In our perspective the market economy on the one hand stimulates a wide range of decentralized and uncoordinated attempts at innovation, many of which fail and appear wasteful *post factum*, while on the other hand, those innovations which succeed are coordinated by the market process, which proves to be an institution adapted to absorbing the opportunities for growth offered by innovation (cf. *WN*, I.x.b.43). We were also well aware of the fact that innovations generally involve some kind of monopolistic competition, reflected – in my words – in the 'great profits', the succesful innovator could pocket 'for a time' (*Works*, I, p. 387), and that these innovations had the tendency to become – again in my words – a 'general good' (ibid., p. 386).

SMITH: Well put, David. Now to the theoretical 'innovators': In Romer (1986) attention focuses on the role of a single state variable called 'knowledge' or 'information'. It is assumed that the information contained in inventions and discoveries has the property of being available to anybody to make use of it at the same time. Poor von Hayek! In other words, information is considered essentially a nonrival good. However, it need not be totally nonexcludable, that is, it can be monopolized at least for a time. Discoveries are made in research and development departments of firms. This requires that resources be withheld from producing current output. The basic idea of Romer's model is 'that there is a trade-off between consumption today and knowledge that can be used to produce more consumption tomorrow' (ibid., p. 1015). Knowledge is assumed to be cardinally measurable and not to depreciate: it is like perennial capital. No comment!

Romer then stipulates for each firm *i* *ad hoc* a 'research technology' that produces 'knowledge' from forgone consumption; the technology is concave and homogeneous of degree one:

$$\dot{k}_i = G(I_i, k_i) \tag{7.11}$$

where I_i is an amount of forgone consumption in research by firm i and k_i is the firm's current stock of knowledge. Equation (7.11) can be interpreted as a production function describing the production of 'knowledge' by means of 'knowledge' and the forgone consumption good. The production function of the consumption good relative to firm i is:

$$Y_i = F(k_i, K, \mathbf{x}_i) \tag{7.12}$$

where K is the accumulated stock of knowledge in the economy as a whole and $\mathbf{x}_i$ is a vector of inputs different from knowledge. Romer assumes that 'factors other than knowledge are in fixed supply' (ibid., p. 1019). This implies that 'knowledge' is the only capital good utilized in the production of the consumption good. Spillovers from private research and development activities increase the public stock of knowledge, K. It is assumed that the function is homogeneous of degree one in k_i and $\mathbf{x}_i$ and homogeneous of a degree greater than one in k_i and K.

RICARDO: Apparently, function (7.11) performs in Romer's model what function (7.8) does in Lucas's.

SMITH: This is true. We may carry out also the same thought experiment as in the case of Lucas's model. I ask you: Assume, unlike Romer, that production function (7.12) is homogeneous of degree one in k_i and K; what follows?

RICARDO: This implies constant returns to capital: the diminishing returns to k_i are exactly offset by the external improvements in technology associated with capital accumulation. In this case it can be shown that, just as in the models previously dealt with, the rate of profit is determined by technology and profit maximization alone, provided, as is assumed by Romer, that the ratio K / k_i equals the (given) number of firms. The rest is by now well known: given the rate of profit, the saving-investment relation then determines endogenously the growth rate. Once again endogenous growth does not depend on an assumption about increasing returns with regard to accumulable factors. Assuming increasing returns renders the analysis a good deal more complicated. In particular, a steady-state equilibrium does not exist unless the marginal product of capital is taken to be bounded from above. This is done by Romer in terms of an *ad hoc* assumption regarding equation (7.11) (ibid.). This assumption is not different from the one used in drawing Figure 7.5.

By that time the two economists were growing weary, but Smith bravely made an attempt to summarize their discussion.

16. Conclusion

SMITH: I think I have now understood at least two things. First, Weitzman may have been right in accusing us of not having thought 'too systematically about the sources of economic growth'. If we had, we might have been reduced to producing trivial little models. Second, seen from the perspective of our analyses, the *main* contribution of the 'new' growth theory boils down to the suggestion that there is a technology producing a surrogate for what we called 'labour'. That factor has merely been given new names and enters the stage either as 'human capital' or 'information' or 'knowledge'. If there is such a technology and if it fulfils certain properties, then the rate of profit is either technologically given or results from the cost-minimizing behaviour of producers. For a given saving behaviour the rate of growth is endogenously determined. In a sense, these authors have rediscovered what we already knew or were close to knowing.

RICARDO: So much for the realism of the assumption that knowledge can never be lost.

SMITH: The problem is that the contemporary economics profession as a whole does not appear to be overly keen to economize on its scarce resources, especially time. Otherwise precautions would be taken to prevent energy from being lost in 're-inventing the wheel', so to speak.

RICARDO: What kind of precautions do you have in mind?

SMITH: It seems to me that during the past decades the history of economic thought has been marginalised in the education of economists, with sometimes detrimental effects, as we have seen. Maybe it would be good to make students read some of the old masters. At any rate, I still believe that there is some truth in the following statement of mine:

> One who reads a number of modern books, altho they be very excellent, will not get thereby the Character of a learned man: the acquaintance of the ancients will alone procure him that name.
>
> (*LRBL* ii.215)

RICARDO: But you don't imply that you and I should be reckoned amongst the ancients?

SMITH: Well . . .

And here the dialogue came to a close.

17. Acknowledgements

The present chapter draws freely on the fruits of a most pleasant collaboration with Neri Salvadori over the past couple of years. See, in particular, Kurz and Salvadori (1995a, 1995b, 1995c, 1997). I should like to thank Christian Gehrke and Christian Lager for useful comments on an earlier version of the paper. I am also grateful to the organisers of the Royal Economic Society Conference, especially Peter Reynolds. Ian Steedman kindly took pains to render my English (and my economics) less imperfect. It goes without saying that the responsibility for everything in the chapter is mine.

References

Baldassari M., De Santis P. and Moscarini G. (1994) 'Allocation of Time, Human Capital and Endogenous Growth' in M. Baldassari, L. Paganetto and E. Phelps (eds), *International Differences in Growth Rates: Market Globalization and Economic Areas*, London: Macmillan, 95–110.

Barro R. J. and Sala-i-Martin X. (1995) *Economic Growth*, New York: McGraw-Hill.

Burgstaller A. (1994) *Property and Prices: Toward a Unified Theory of Value*, Cambridge: Cambridge University Press.

Ferguson A. (1793) *An Essay on the History of Civil Society*, 6th edn (1st edn 1767), reprint 1966, Edinburgh: Edinburgh University Press.

Fisher F. M. (1993) 'Aggregation: Aggregate Production Functions and Related Topics' in J. Monz (ed.), *Collected Papers by Franklin M. Fisher*, Cambridge, Mass.: MIT Press.

Hicks J. R. (1969) *A Theory of Economic History*, Oxford: Clarendon Press.

Jones L. E. and Manuelli R. (1990) 'A Convex Model of Equilibrium Growth: Theory and Policy Implications', *Journal of Political Economy*, 98, 1008–38.

Kaldor N. (1956) 'Alternative Theories of Distribution', *Review of Economic Studies*, 23, 83–100.

King R. G. and Rebelo S. (1990) 'Public Policy and Economic Growth: Developing Neoclassical Implications', *Journal of Political Economy*, 98, 126–50.

King R. G. and Rebelo S. (1993) 'Transitional Dynamics and Economic Growth in the Neoclassical Model', *American Economic Review*, 83, 908–31.

Knight F. H. (1944) 'Diminishing Returns from Investment', *Journal of Political Economy*, 52, 26–47.

Kurz H. D. and Salvadori N. (1994) 'The Non-substitution Theorem: Making Good a Lacuna', *Journal of Economics*, 59, 97–103.

Kurz H. D. and Salvadori N. (1995a) *Theory of Production. A Long-period Analysis*, Cambridge: Cambridge University Press.

Kurz H. D. and Salvadori N. (1995b) 'The "New" Growth Theory: Old Wine in New Goatskins', revised version of a paper given at the workshop 'Endogenous Growth and Development' of The International School of Economic Research, University of Siena, Italy, 3–9 July 1994. Published in F. Coricelli, M. Di Matteo and F. H. Hahn (eds), *Growth and Development: Theories, Empirical Evidence and Policy Issues*, London: Macmillan 1998, pp. 63–94.

Kurz H. D. and Salvadori N. (1995c) 'Theories of "Endogenous" Growth in Historical Perspective', paper given at the Eleventh World Congress of the International Economic Association, 17–22 December 1995, Tunis, Tunisia. Published in Murat R. Sertel (ed.), *Contemporary Economic Issues. Proceedings of the Eleventh World Congress of the International Economic Association, Tunis*. Volume 4: *Economic Behaviour and Design*, London: Macmillan and New York: St Martin's Press, 1999, 225–61.

Kurz H. D. and Salvadori N. (1997) 'In the Beginning All the World Was Australia . . . ', in P. Arestis, G. Palma and M. Sawyer (eds), *Capital Controversy, Post-Keynesian*

Economics and the History of Economics. Essays in Honour of Geoff Harcourt, London: Routledge. vol. 1, 425–43.

Lucas R. E. (1988) 'On the Mechanics of Economic Development', *Journal of Monetary Economics*, 22, 3–42.

Malinvaud E. (1983) 'Notes on Growth Theory with Imperfectly Flexible Prices', in J.-P. Fitoussi (ed.), *Modern Macroeconomic Theory*, Oxford: Basil Blackwell, 93–114.

Mas-Colell A. (1989) 'Capital Theory Paradoxes: Anything Goes', in G. R. Feiwel (ed.), *Joan Robinson and Modern Economic Theory*, London: Macmillan, 505–20.

Mill J. S. (1965) *Principles of Political Economy With Some of Their Applications to Social Philosophy*, in J. M. Robson (ed.), *Collected Works of John Stuart Mill*, introduced by V. W. Bladen, vol. III, Toronto: University of Toronto Press.

Neumann J. von (1945) 'A Model of General Economic Equilibrium', *Review of Economic Studies*, 13, 1–9. English translation of 'Über ein ökonomisches Gleichungssystem und eine Verallgemeinerung des Brouwerschen Fixpunktsatzes', in *Ergebnisse eines mathematischen Kolloquiums*, 8 (1937), 73–83.

Rebelo S. (1991) 'Long Run Policy Analysis and Long Run Growth', *Journal of Political Economy*, 99, 500–21.

Ricardo D. (1951 *et seq.*) *The Works and Correspondence of David Ricardo*, edited by Piero Sraffa with the collaboration of Maurice H. Dobb. Cambridge: Cambridge University Press, 11 vols, referred to as *Works*, vol., page.

Romer P. M. (1986) 'Increasing Returns and Long-Run Growth', *Journal of Political Economy*, 94, 1002–37.

Romer P. M. (1994) 'The Origins of Endogenous Growth', *Journal of Economic Perspectives*, 8, 3–22.

Romer P. M. (1996) 'Why, Indeed, in America? Theory, History, and the Origins of Modern Economic Growth', *American Economic Review. Papers and Proceedings*, 86, 202–6.

Samuelson P. A. (1961) 'A New Theorem on Nonsubstitution', in *Money, Growth and Methodology*, Lund Social Science Studies, vol. 20, Lund: C. W. K. Gleerup, 407–23. Reprinted in G. E. Stiglitz (ed.), *The Collected Scientific Papers of P. A. Samuelson*, vol. 1, Cambridge, Mass.: MIT Press, 1966.

Schumpeter J. A. (1954) *History of Economic Analysis*, New York: Oxford University Press.

Smith A. (1976a) *An Inquiry into the Nature and Causes of the Wealth of Nations*, first published in 1776. *The Glasgow Edition of the Works and Correspondence of Adam Smith*, vol. I, Oxford: Oxford University Press. In the text referred to as *WN*, book, chapter, etc.

Smith A. (1976b) *Lectures on Rhetoric and Belles Lettres*, vol. IV of *The Glasgow Edition of the Works and Correspondence of Adam Smith*, Oxford: Oxford University Press. In the text referred to as *LRBL*, part, paragraph.

Solow R. M. (1956) 'A Contribution to the Theory of Economic Growth', *Quarterly Journal of Economics*, 70, 65–94.

Solow R. M. (1991) 'Growth Theory', in D. Greenaway, M. Bleaney and Ian M. T. Stewart (eds), *Companion to Contemporary Economic Thought*, London: Routledge, 393–415.

Solow R. M. (1994) 'Perspectives on Growth Theory', *Journal of Economic Perspectives*, 8, 45–54.

Steedman I. (2001) *Consumption Takes Time. Implications for Economic Theory*. The Graz Schumpeter Lectures, vol. 4, London: Routledge.

Weitzman M. L. (1996) 'Hybridizing Growth Theory', *American Economic Review. Papers and Proceedings*, 86, 207–12.

Appendix

Comment by Kenneth J. Arrow[1]

Dear Heinz,

This is a belated comment on your paper, 'What Could the "New" Growth Theory Teach Smith or Ricardo?' It is a very clever format, and your exposition is indeed excellent. I have only one comment on the format; surely Smith and Ricardo would not have used first names in their day. (I riffled through Ricardo's letters in Sraffa's edition. Almost invariably, the salutation was, 'Dear Sir', or, 'My Dear Sir'. This was true even with such frequent correspondents and occasional house guests as Malthus and Mill. The only exception was the interchange with Ricardo's good friend, Hutches Trower; here, they address each other, 'Dear Trower', and, 'Dear Ricardo'.) But since you have resurrected them in the present era, perhaps they talk in current language.

In some of the passages, you seem to argue that just because some of the conclusions of modern growth theory are couched as balanced growth paths, they are pretty much the same as classical results. But the variables are different, as you indeed scrupulously note. Does not a reinterpretation constitute a creative act?

Let me turn to more specific points. On p. 138, you criticize Weitzman's claim that no one before Solow thought 'systematically about the sources of economic growth'. But, as I think I pointed out in Naples, the crucial point is *intensive* growth. In the basic structure of Ricardo's theory, *per capita* income converges to a limit, and indeed, a minimal limit at that. It is of course true that Smith in his opening chapters was indeed talking about growth, and, to be fair, most 'new' growth theorists take Smith as their starting point, as indeed did Allyn Young in his 1928 paper. It is also easy to point to predecessors to Solow's empirical analyses, particularly Tinbergen in 1942 (*Weltwirtschaftliches Archiv*) and Abramovitz in 1956. But I am not sure that Weitzman is entirely wrong when one adds the word, 'systematically'. No intelligent observer could fail to note that people, at least the English, really were getting off, and Smith was emboldened to advance some views, though one can hardly say the same for Ricardo. I do not take such vague statements as those cited by you on p. 155 as a theory of any kind. One aspect of the new growth economics is that innovation occurs in response to profitability; statements that the returns on innovations are, initially, different from (not necessarily greater than) those on established investments are not the same.

On pp. 140–1, you (I mean, of course, Smith and Ricardo) ridicule the representative-agent intertemporal optimization model. Smith quotes Solow, but Solow's model is certainly a representative-agent model, though not intertemporally optimizing. I agree with their implicit argument that heterogeneity of

1 This comment is contained in a letter to the author dated 23 December 1999. It is printed with the kind permission of Professor Arrow. (The page references have been adapted to the present reprint of the paper.)

consumption and savings behavior (and heterogeneity in other ways) is an essential and omitted factor in all economic processes, including growth. On the other hand, Smith has little to complain about; his emphasis was on the identity of human beings; for example, his explanation of wage differences as due to net advantages depends on similarity of individuals, as, indeed, does his explanation of trade as the result of specialization (rather than inherent differences, as in Ricardo's theory of international trade). Ricardo did have, perhaps, a threefold class differentiation but homogeneity within classes.

On the same page (p. 141), Smith slips, it seems, in discussing whether the parameter ρ is exogenous or endogenous. ρ, as it appears in equation (7.1), is a discount rate for utilities, not a rate of return on capital, and it can be a datum representing the tastes of savers at the same time that the required rate of return on capital varies.

On p. 141 Ricardo sniffs at the failure of growth models to take account of effective demand. I should have thought that Ricardo would be the last to talk, since all of his analysis assumes that saving equals capital formation. For my own part, I agree with you and Malinvaud that effective demand variations are certainly important in the short run. Whether they play a significant role in growth is not empirically clear, nor do I know of any serious attempt to study this question.

Your characters make fun of an aggregate production function (p. 142). Let me spell out what you are saying. Under perfect competition, production functions of individual firms aggregate perfectly well. What is incorrect (and what Fisher argued) is that you can't aggregate different kinds of inputs without unrealistic assumptions. In particular, there is no aggregate measure of capital. By the same argument, there is no aggregate measure of labor, once it is recognized that there are skill differences. But Ricardo certainly aggregates labor, and, in fact, he really has only one kind of capital (food advances to labor) until he finally introduces machinery in an afterthought. With regard to labor, he realizes he is in difficulty and makes a vague stab at assuming that the relative prices of different kinds of labor are fixed (an assumption that, as I recall, Marx echoes). But this is precisely the kind of unrealistic assumption under which aggregation is legitimate. In short, I don't think the classics differ in any way on this point from the neoclassicals, and indeed all the models you analyze are based on the same aggregation (you have to to present them in diagrams). Multi-commodity versions of growth models along the same lines are possible and even easy to write down, satisfying the heart of any follower of Lindahl and Hicks. They do give rise to new phenomena, as Mordecai Kurz showed long ago.

The idea that labor has the same role as land (p. 145) is already in the founding neoclassicals, Jevons, Menger, and Walras. It was the consequent multiplicity of primary factors that was, in my view, the essential component of neoclassicism. It followed that relative prices were determined in part by demand.

I agree with your view that the production of human capital (whose importance you do not appear to deny) must require 'raw labor' as an input. Pure labor is certainly of diminishing importance in industry proper, but it still enters as an input into the educational process and, some analysts have emphasized, into the research and development process. This has led to the view, which is compatible, I think, with that which you are implying, that in the long run intensive growth will be brought to a halt by the scarcity of labor. My 'learning-by-doing' model had the uncomfortable implication that, in the steady state, the rate of intensive growth was an increasing function of the rate of population growth and would fall to zero if population were stationary.

I agree with your analysis of the limitations of the Lucas model (pp. 153–5). But your critique seems to me to point in a very non-classical direction. You begin to emphasize concepts like costs of transmission of knowledge from generation to generation (and, I would add, across individuals at a moment of time). One cannot reduce these to classical concepts. I agree (see your discussion on p. 155) that the assumption of pure nonrivalry in information is extreme. It is costly to transmit and above all to receive. But it is frequently true that information is much more costly to produce than to reproduce, and that is the essential point in Romer's models. We can see how quickly generic drugs appear when drug patents expire. We can argue this back and forth; but my point is the terms of the discussion have no classical or indeed neoclassical counterparts. Information economics is something new.

I must question Smith's conclusion (p. 157) that 'human capital' or 'knowledge' play the role that 'labor' did in Smith and Ricardo. If we take the Malthusian model for labor supply, as Ricardo did, then labor is produced out of goods. The analogy would be that knowledge is produced out of goods. But there are two important differences; knowledge is permanent, not a flow, and there are externalities associated with it. These differences are too big to be referred to as 'trvial little models'. I don't see that Ricardo was anywhere 'close to knowing this'; I will concede that Smith did have an inkling.

A final remark on your footnote 1: I did not find in Ricardo the idea that if real wages are above subsistence for a long time, the subsistence level will rise, though perhaps I missed it. This theory is very explicit in John Stuart Mill.

As you can see, by omission, at least, I found your exposition of the different models very clear. But I do have a different view of the current relevance of the classics. The greatness of Smith and Ricardo and, to my mind, any scholar is measured in good part by the stimulus it gives to their followers to transcend them.

I hope we meet again soon. Our meeting in Naples was a source of great pleasure.

Sincerely yours,
Kenneth J. Arrow

8 A linear multisector model of 'endogenous' growth and the problem of capital*

Neri Salvadori

1. Introduction

The 1960s could be seen as the 'golden age' of Solovian growth economics: they brought a host of theoretical and empirical studies. However, in the controversy over the theory of capital, foreshadowed by a paper of Joan Robinson in the early 1950s (Robinson, 1953) and inspired by Piero Sraffa's book (Sraffa, 1960), it was conclusively shown that traditional (i.e. long period) neoclassical theory was based on an untenable concept of capital. According to this concept the 'quantity of capital' as a factor of production could be given independently of relative prices and prior to the determination of the rate of profit. With the quantity of capital in given supply, the rate of profit (or rate of interest) was envisaged as the 'price' of capital obtained when confronting the given supply with a demand function for capital, derived from an analysis of the choice of technique of cost-minimizing producers. The demonstration that this was not possible except in singularly special cases implied that neoclassical long-period theory was no reliable guide to understanding the laws governing growth and distribution. This insight, which gradually filtered into the economics profession, concurred to lead to a situation, in the 1970s and early 1980s, in which growth economics as a whole was marginalized.

The situation changed dramatically in the mid-1980s, when growth economics started to boom again, following the lead of Paul Romer and Robert Lucas. A formidable industry of theoretical and empirical research on economic growth sprang up like a mushroom. Also described as 'new' growth theory (NGT) to indicate the claim to originality, some advocates were quite explicit in their view that NGT will revolutionize the way economists think about certain problems (see Grossman and Helpman, 1994, p. 42). The emphasis is on 'endogenous' mechanisms generating economic growth, that is, long-term growth is determined 'within the model, rather than by some exogenously growing variables like unexplained technological progress' (Barro and Sala-i-Martin, 1995, p. 38). This is considered the main distinguishing feature between NGT and old, Solovian, growth theory.

* Reprinted with permission from *Metroeconomica*, 49: 3, 1998.

In previous papers Heinz D. Kurz and I attempted to relate some of the most prominent models of the NGT literature to the 'classical' tradition of economic thought (Kurz and Salvadori, 1996, 1997, 1998, 1999; Kurz, 1997). We argued that in a very precise sense the NGT can be said to involve a return to modes of thought and the method of analysis characteristic of the classical authors. In terms of method, the NGT is essentially a variant of *long-period* theory, originally advocated by Adam Smith and then developed by David Ricardo. In terms of content, many of the 'new' growth models (NGMs) dispense with the traditional neoclassical determination of the rate of profit in terms of the supply of and demand for 'capital'. This implies that *by construction* the models under consideration circumnavigate the capital theory criticisms levelled at the traditional long-period neoclassical theory. The purpose of this chapter is to clarify this issue by building up a multisector model with heterogeneous capital goods.[1]

The structure of the chapter is as follows. In Section 2, I specify in some greater detail what we mean by the 'classical' as opposed to the traditional 'neoclassical' approach. Section 3 shows why in our view crucial aspects of the NGT point in the direction of the classical tradition. Section 4 develops the model. The model is built up in such a way as to facilitate a comparison with the current literature on endogenous growth. For example, it is well known that in a long-period framework it would be simpler and more in line with the observed facts to treat time as a discrete variable. However, since a large part of the literature on endogenous growth starts from continuous time, I adopted the same assumption. Other features of the present model also reflect the aim of facilitating a comparison with the growth literature under consideration. However, no attempt will be made to allow for increasing returns in the model. Therefore, there is no rising income *per capita*. Nevertheless, the model is an endogenous growth model in the sense specified above. Section 5 contains some conclusions.

2. 'Classical' and 'neoclassical' approaches

Scrutiny shows that the contributions to the theory of value and distribution of 'classical' derivation share a common feature: in investigating the relationship between the system of relative prices and income distribution they start from the same set of *data* (see, e.g. Kurz and Salvadori, 1995, chapter 1). These data concern:

(i) the set of technical alternatives from which cost-minimizing producers can choose;
(ii) the size and composition of the social product;

---

1 It should be stressed from the outset that in the model developed the set of heterogeneous capital goods does not change over time. Therefore an important aspect of any real process of capital accumulation, and the capital theoretic problem posed by it (i.e. the introduction of entirely new capital goods and the disappearance of old ones), is set aside.

(iii) one of the distributive variables – either the ruling wage rate(s) or the ruling rate of profit; and

(iv) the quantities of available natural resources, such as land.

In correspondence with the underlying long-period competitive position of the economy the capital stock is assumed to be fully adjusted to these data. Hence, the 'normal' desired pattern of utilization of plant and equipment would be realized and a uniform rate of return on its supply price obtained.

The data or independent variables from which neoclassical theories typically start are the following. They take as given:

(a) the set of technical alternatives from which cost-minimizing producers can choose;

(b) the preferences of consumers; and

(c) the initial endowments of the economy and the distribution of property rights among individual agents.

It is easily checked that the given (a) is the same as the given (i), whereas the given (b) could be thought of as expressing elements of the given (ii). What makes the two theories really different are the data (iii) and (iv) on the one hand and the given (c) on the other: while classical theory takes as given only the endowment of natural resources, neoclassical theory assumes that the endowments of labour and capital are also given. However, there is a special case in which the difference is strongly reduced. This is the case in which natural resources are set aside and there is no distinct factor 'labour' in the economy, because it is subsumed under 'capital'. Therefore, as regards classical theory, the given (iii) and (iv) are automatically deleted because natural resources are set aside and the rate of profit would be endogenously determined and could not be given from outside the system. Similarly, as regards neoclassical theory, the given endowment of 'capital' has no role to play in the determination of the long-period rate of profit, that is, the given (c) is superfluous in this regard: the decisions of cost-minimizing producers who can choose from a set of technical alternatives (a) decided the long-period rate of profit independently of the 'quantity of capital' available in the economy.

In previous papers Heinz D. Kurz and I showed that the special case just mentioned is indeed underlying some of the most prominent contributions to the modern literature on endogenous growth. These models eliminate labour from the picture and put in its stead 'human capital' or 'knowledge', that is, something that a twentieth century audience can be expected to accept as a producible (and accumulable) factor of production. However, from an analytical point of view the conditions of production of this surrogate of labour play essentially the same role as the assumption of a given real wage rate in classical theory: they define the (physical) costs at which additional units of the respective factor are available.

Whilst previous papers by Heinz D. Kurz and myself were devoted to a clear statement of this fact and thus focused attention on the *analytical structure* of the NGT, we were aware of the fact that there are other elements in the NGT with a decidedly classical flavour. The insistence on increasing returns, for example, bears a close resemblance to Adam Smith's treatment of the division of labour.

It was indeed Smith's contention that the accumulation of capital is a prerequisite of the emergence of new, and the growth of many of the existing, markets which is intimately intertwined with an ever more sophisticated division of labour, and which in turn is seen to be the main source of a continual increase in labour productivity. In Smith's view the division of labour leads to the discovery of new methods and means of production – new machines – and new goods and is generally associated, at least temporarily, with forms of monopolistic competition which allow the successful innovators to reap extra profits for some time (see, e.g. Smith, *WN*, I.x.b.43; see also Ricardo, *Works*, vol. I, chapter 31; Young, 1928). Hence, in Smith the endogeneity of the rate of growth is the result not so much of the features of some *given* technology as of the continuous *revolution* of the technological, organizational and institutional conditions of production, that is, a process of the development of the 'productive powers of society'. Whilst we are aware of the similarities between this view and some of the ideas developed in more recent contributions to NGT,[2] our main concern in our previous papers was not with them but with showing that the data set from which the majority of NGMs start is that typical of the classical and not that of the neoclassical approach.

The following section describes the general framework to which the models developed in the subsequent sections belong. I begin with a remark on the long-period method and then turn to a brief discussion of alternative views of the interplay between income distribution and growth.

3. Setting the stage

Classical economists focused on the long period and generally paid little attention to the short period. Neoclassical economists also started their theorizing, in the 1870s, by analysing the long period. Later generations of neoclassical authors encountered serious difficulties that prompted them to switch, beginning in the late 1920s, to intertemporal analysis (see, e.g. Kurz and Salvadori, 1995, chapter 14). Until a few decades ago the time horizon in intertemporal general equilibrium theory was assumed to be finite and, therefore, arbitrary. The introduction of an infinite horizon pushed the analysis inevitably towards the long period (see also Burgstaller, 1994, pp. 43–8). This was clearly spelled out, for instance, by Robert Lucas, who observed that 'for *any* initial capital $K(0) > 0$, the optimal capital-consumption path $(K(t), c(t))$ will converge to the balanced path asymptotically. That is, the balanced path will be a good approximation to any actual path 'most' of the time', and that 'this is exactly the reason why the balanced path is interesting to us' (Lucas, 1988, p. 11). Lucas thus advocated a (*re-*)*switching* from an intertemporal analysis to a long-period steady-state one. Since the balanced path of the intertemporal model is the only path analysed by Lucas, the intertemporal model may be regarded simply as a step to obtain a rigorous long-period setting.

---

2 See, for example, Yang and Borland (1991), Becker and Murphy (1992), Rodriguez-Clare (1996); see also the so-called neo-Schumpeterian models, for example, Aghion and Howitt (1992).

(Paraphrasing a dictum of Paul A. Samuelson, we may say that intertemporal analysis is, in this case, a *detour* with regard to long-period steady-state analysis.) Moreover, Lucas abandoned one of the characteristic features of all neoclassical models, that is, income distribution is determined by demand and supply of factors of production: if we concentrate on the 'balanced path', capital in the initial period *cannot* be taken as given along with other 'initial endowments'. In this chapter, I will present the main result in two different ways, one by using the usual procedure followed in the literature on NGT, the other by simply assuming that a long-period position exists and studying its properties. It will be shown that the two procedures obtain exactly the same result. Hence, if one is not interested in the intertemporal analysis itself, but just the steady state of that analysis, then the use of the long-period method may speed up the elaboration of new scientific results (and avoid undesirable assumptions).

Readers of *Production of Commodities by Means of Commodities* (Sraffa, 1960) will recall that when, at the beginning of chapter II (§§4 and 5), wages are regarded as entering the system 'on the same footing as the fuel for the engines or the feed for the cattle', the profit rate and the prices are determined by technology alone. To the contrary, when the workers get a part of the surplus, the quantity of labour employed in each industry has to be represented explicitly, and the profit rate and the prices can be determined only if an extra equation determining income distribution is introduced into the analysis. The additional equation generally used by advocates of neoclassical analysis is the equality between the demand for and the supply of 'capital', which requires the homogeneity of this factor. But no extra equation is required in the NGT since, as in Ricardo and in §§4 and 5 of Sraffa's book, there is a mechanism, or 'technology', producing 'labour'. In the model presented here, we will simply assume that all inputs are (re)producible. We shall not attempt to interpret or rationalize this assumption. For our purpose it suffices to point out that it is widely used in the NGT. What matters is that this assumption is enough to ensure that the rate of profit is determined by technology alone.

The core of every growth theory is the relationship between saving and investment, or the saving–investment mechanism. In the models advocated by Robert Solow (1956, 1963), Trevor Swan (1956) and James Meade (1961), this relationship is given by

$$sf(k) = gk$$

where s is the (marginal and average) propensity to save, $f(k)$ is the per capita production function, k is the capital–labour ratio (labour is measured in terms of efficiency units and capital is taken to consist of a single commodity), and g is the steady-state growth rate of capital (and labour and income). Since in the one-commodity analysis used by these economists the rate of profit r equals the marginal productivity of capital:

$$r = f'(k)$$

the two equations are able to determine a relationship between the rate of profit and the rate of growth. In these models the growth rate is exogenously given and these equations are used to determine the rate of profit, that is, the income distribution.[3] Alternatively, had income distribution been taken as given, the relationship between saving and investment would have determined the growth rate.

The exogenously given saving rate was taken to reflect a multiplicity of factors shaping consumers' behaviour. Most of the NGMs have done away with this approach. In the alternative approach a 'microfoundation' of that behaviour is attempted. It is assumed that there exists an immortal 'representative agent' who is concerned with maximizing an intertemporal utility function, $u = u(c(t))$, over an infinite time horizon. Choosing the path that maximizes consumption involves maximizing the integral of instantaneous utility:

$$\int_0^\infty e^{-\rho t} u(c(t)) \, dt \tag{8.1}$$

where ρ is the discount rate. In order to obtain a steady state with a growth rate that is constant over time (see Barro and Sala-i-Martin, 1995, p. 64), a special instantaneous utility function is assumed:

$$u(c(t)) = \frac{1}{1-\sigma} [c(t)^{1-\sigma} - 1] \tag{8.2}$$

where $1/\sigma$ is the elasticity of substitution between present and future consumption ($1 \neq \sigma > 0$). This gives the following relationship between the growth rate g and the profit rate r:

$$g = \frac{r - \rho}{\sigma} \tag{8.3}$$

Now, if the reader is ready to accept equation (8.3) as a postulate, then he could dispense with the assumptions concerning the saving–investment mechanism (including the dubious assumption of an immortal representative agent). These assumptions, in fact, serve only a single purpose: they allow one to determine relationship (8.3). In this chapter, when it is postulated that a long-period position holds, equation (8.3) has also the character of a postulate; in this case we do not need any assumption about a representative agent. Since, as mentioned above, the technology is such as to determine the rate of profit, then equation (8.3) will determine the growth rate. To the contrary, when the paper presents the results using the approach commonly adopted in the NGT, the immortal representative

---

3 The 1950s and 1960s actually saw the confrontation of two approaches: the post-Keynesian and the neoclassical. According to the former, championed by Nicholas Kaldor (1955–6), Joan Robinson (1956) and Luigi Pasinetti (1962), savings tend to adjust to investment through changes in income distribution, since workers and capitalists are assumed to have different saving habits. Yet despite the difference in the route chosen, both schools of economic thought obtained a relationship between the growth rate on the one hand and income distribution on the other. Since in both of them the growth rate was considered as given from outside the system, in both theories what was to be determined endogenously was income distribution.

agent makes an appearance, whereas equation (8.3) plays no role in the derivation of the results, even if it is implicit in the results obtained.

The model presented here can be considered to be a generalization of the linear growth model, known also as the '*AK* model' (Rebelo, 1991). Actually, that model is not all that new – in fact, it dates back decades (see, e.g. the discussion in Takayama, 1974, section 5.D.b). It has rightly been dubbed 'the simplest endogenous growth model' (Barro and Sala-i-Martin, 1995, p. 38; see also, pp. 39–42 and 141–4). Its characteristic feature is that there is only one commodity whose production function has the form $Y = AK$, where Y is the output and K is the input, both consisting of quantities of the same commodity, and A is a positive constant reflecting the level of technological knowledge. In the following I will generalize the *AK* model to the case of any number of commodities, assuming in accordance with the general thrust of the original model that all inputs are themselves produced. I have chosen the *AK* model because it is simple and yet can be said to convey the main message of the NGT.

4. The model

There are n commodities, but only one of them is consumed, say commodity 1. (Alternatively, commodities available at the same time can be considered perfect complements in consumption so that they are consumed in given proportions.) Technology is fully described by an $n \times n$ instantaneous capital goods matrix $\mathbf{A}$, the corresponding $n \times n$ instantaneous output matrix $\mathbf{I} + (1-\delta)\mathbf{A}$, where $\mathbf{I}$ is the $n \times n$ identity matrix and δ is the uniform rate of depreciation of capital goods, $0 \leqslant \delta < 1$; that is, no primary factor is used in production and there is no choice of technique.[4] Matrix $\mathbf{A}$ is assumed to be non-negative and indecomposable. Its eigenvalue of maximum modulus (also known as the Frobenius eigenvalue, cf. Takayama, 1974, chapter 4; Kurz and Salvadori, 1995, pp. 509–19), λ, is assumed to satisfy the following inequalities:

$$(\delta + \rho)\lambda \leqslant 1 \tag{8.4a}$$

$$1 - (\delta + \rho)\lambda < (1 - \delta\lambda)\sigma \tag{8.4b}$$

---

4 In a framework assuming discrete time it would be possible to assume $\delta = 1$. In such a framework this would mean that all capital is consumed in one unit of time, that is, all capital is circulating capital. This would not be possible in a continuous time framework, because in it $\delta = 1$ would mean that capital is consumed at the same instant of time at which produced commodities appear: with no time elapsing between inputs and outputs, there would actually be no capital! Moreover, to allow for a situation in which a capital good is consumed in a finite amount of time, we would need to introduce an infinite number of commodities for each capital good, each of these infinite commodities representing the capital good at the appropriate (continuous) vintage. With continuous time, then, the idea that a capital good depreciates in the sense that a part of it evaporates is not only the simplest one available to capture the idea of capital, but also the only one which, as far as I know, avoids the need to have recourse to an infinite number of capital goods.

In the presentation following the usual procedure it will also be assumed for simplicity that **A** is invertible and has n distinct eigenvalues.

4.1. The long-period solution

Let some agent own the commodities $\mathbf{e}_j^T \mathbf{A}$ at time 0 and use them to produce continuously commodity j from time 0 to time t, so that at time t he owns the commodities $e^{-\delta t} \mathbf{e}_j^T \mathbf{A}$ and at each time τ, $0 \leqslant \tau < t$, he has a flow of product of $e^{-\delta \tau}$ units of commodity j which is invested in another business. If all investments earn a nominal rate of profit i (to be determined), then:

$$\int_0^t e^{(t-\tau)i} e^{-\delta \tau} \mathbf{e}_j^T \mathbf{p}_\tau \, d\tau + e^{-\delta t} \mathbf{e}_j^T \mathbf{A} \mathbf{p}_t = e^{it} \mathbf{e}_j^T \mathbf{A} \mathbf{p}_0 \tag{8.5}$$

In a long-period position relative prices are constant and the rate of inflation is also constant, so that for each t:

$$\mathbf{p}_t = e^{\pi t} \mathbf{p}$$

where $\mathbf{p}$ is a vector to be determined and π is the rate of inflation (or deflation). Hence, if long-period conditions are assumed to hold (and if $i \neq \pi - \delta$), from equation (8.5) we obtain:

$$[e^{it} - e^{(\pi-\delta)t}] \left[\frac{1}{i - \pi + \delta} \mathbf{e}_j^T \mathbf{p} - \mathbf{e}_j^T \mathbf{A} \mathbf{p} \right] = 0$$

which can be written as

$$[e^{(r+\pi)t} - e^{(\pi-\delta)t}] \left[\frac{1}{r + \delta} \mathbf{e}_j^T \mathbf{p} - \mathbf{e}_j^T \mathbf{A} \mathbf{p} \right] = 0$$

where r is the real rate of profit ($r = i - \pi$).[5] Since this equation must hold for each j and since $\mathbf{p}$ must be semipositive, then we have from the Perron–Frobenius Theorem that $\mathbf{p} > 0$ is the right eigenvector of matrix **A** corresponding to the

---

5 If $i = \pi - \delta$, then from equation (8.5) we would obtain

$$t e^{it} \mathbf{e}_j^T \mathbf{p} = 0$$

which can hold for each t only if $\mathbf{e}_j^T \mathbf{p} = 0$. And since this equation should hold for each j, $\mathbf{p}$ could not be semipositive.

eigenvalue of maximum modulus $\lambda > 0$, and

$$r = \frac{1 - \delta\lambda}{\lambda} > 0$$

the inequality being a consequence of inequality (8.4a). Moreover, because of equation (8.3):

$$g = \frac{1 - \delta\lambda - \rho\lambda}{\lambda\sigma} \tag{8.6}$$

Note that inequalities (8.4a) and (8.4b) imply

$$0 \leqslant g < r$$

Finally, since only commodity 1 is consumed and the economy grows at the rate g, the consumption C_t, and the intensity vector $\mathbf{x}_t$ must satisfy the following equations:

$$C_t = C_0 \, e^{gt}$$
$$\mathbf{x}_t^T = C_0 \mathbf{e}_1^T [\mathbf{I} - (\delta + g)\mathbf{A}]^{-1} \, e^{gt}$$

provided that $\delta + g < \lambda^{-1}$, which is certainly the case, since inequality (8.4b) holds.

4.2. The solution using the usual procedure

We now turn to the usual procedure. Here saving (and investment) derives from the consumption decisions of a representative agent concerned with maximizing functional (8.1) (where the instantaneous utility function is defined by equation (8.2)) under the constraints defined by the available technology, The agent is then faced with the following problem ($t \in \mathbb{R}$):

$$\max \int_0^\infty e^{-\rho t} \frac{C_t^{1-\sigma} - 1}{1 - \sigma} \, dt \tag{8.7a}$$

$$\text{s.t. } \mathbf{x}_t^T (\mathbf{I} - \delta\mathbf{A}) \geq C_t \mathbf{e}_1^T + \dot{\mathbf{x}}_t^T \mathbf{A} \tag{8.7b}$$

$$\mathbf{x}_t \geq \mathbf{0}, \quad \mathbf{x}_0^T \mathbf{A} \leq \bar{\mathbf{x}}, \quad C_t \geqslant 0 \tag{8.7c}$$

where $\dot{\mathbf{x}}$ is the derivative of $\mathbf{x}$ with respect to time, and $\bar{\mathbf{x}}$ is the given positive vector of initial stocks of commodities. Inequality (8.7b) corresponds to the description of technology given above, but free disposal has also been introduced. Obviously, in the long-period solution this assumption is superfluous because joint production is set aside, but free disposal can be used in the short run, if the initial conditions are such that some commodity is available in excess supply.

The problem (8.7) can be tackled in two steps. First, the following optimal control problem (subscript t has been omitted) is solved:

$$y(\mathbf{x}_0) = \max \int_0^\infty e^{-\rho t} \frac{C^{1-\sigma} - 1}{1 - \sigma} dt \tag{8.8a}$$

$$\text{s.t. } \dot{\mathbf{x}}^T = \mathbf{x}^T (\mathbf{I} - \delta \mathbf{A}) \mathbf{A}^{-1} - C \mathbf{e}_1^T \mathbf{A}^{-1} - \mathbf{z}^T \mathbf{A}^{-1} \tag{8.8b}$$

$$\mathbf{x} \geq \mathbf{0}, \quad C \geqslant 0, \quad \mathbf{z} \geq \mathbf{0} \tag{8.8c}$$

where $\mathbf{x}$ are the state variables and $\mathbf{z}$ and C are the control variables. Let $(\hat{\mathbf{x}}, \hat{\mathbf{z}}, \hat{C})$ be a solution to the problem, then $\hat{\mathbf{x}}$ is a continuous function of time, whereas $\hat{\mathbf{z}}$ and $\hat{C}$ may have a finite number of discontinuous points. Second, the following problem has to be solved:

$$\max y(\mathbf{x}_0)$$

$$\text{s.t. } \mathbf{x}_0^T \mathbf{A} \leq \bar{\mathbf{x}}$$

$$\mathbf{x}_0 \leq \mathbf{0}$$

The following proposition (whose proof is provided in the appendix) explores the steady-state solution(s) to problem (8.8).

Proposition 1. *There are scalars g and $C_0 = 0$ such that $\hat{\mathbf{x}} = \mathbf{x}_0 \, e^{gt}$, $\hat{\mathbf{z}} = \mathbf{0}$ and $\hat{C} = C_0 \, e^{gt}$ if and only if equation (8.6) holds and there is a scalar $\theta > 0$ such that*

$$\mathbf{x}_0^T = \theta \mathbf{e}_1^T [\mathbf{I} - (\delta + g)\mathbf{A}]^{-1} \tag{8.9}$$

Therefore a steady-state solution to problem (8.7) is obtained along the ray

$$\bar{\mathbf{x}} = \theta \mathbf{e}_1^T [\mathbf{I} - (\delta + g)\mathbf{A}]^{-1} \mathbf{A}$$

5. Concluding remarks

In this chapter we have built up a linear multisector model of growth with heterogeneous capital goods. The purpose of this exercise is to show that this kind of NGM is not subject to the capital theory critique put forward against the conventional long-period neoclassical growth model. This confirms a previous claim by Heinz D. Kurz and myself that at least some of the NGMs are somewhat extraneous to neoclassical analysis and actually exhibit the logical structure of classical theory. In addition it has been shown that the use of an intertemporal analysis to establish a correct long-period position is not necessary and that the use of the long-period method may speed up the process of elaboration of new scientific results (although a truly dynamical analysis is required if the stability of the long-period position is to be established).

Appendix

It is easily checked that the value function of problem (8.8) is finite since inequality (8.4b) holds. This allows the analysis of the problem in terms of the following procedure. The current value Hamiltonian for (8.8) is

$$H(\mathbf{x}, C, \mathbf{z}, \mathbf{v}) = \frac{C^{1-\sigma} - 1}{1 - \sigma} + \left[\mathbf{x}^T (\mathbf{I} - \delta \mathbf{A}) - C \mathbf{e}_1^T - \mathbf{z}^T \right] \mathbf{A}^{-1} \mathbf{v}$$

and the Lagrangian for (8.8) is

$$L(\mathbf{x}, C, \mathbf{z}, \mathbf{v}, \mathbf{w}, \alpha, \mathbf{u}) = H(\mathbf{x}, C, \mathbf{z}, \mathbf{v}) + \mathbf{x}^T \mathbf{w} + \alpha C + \mathbf{z}^T \mathbf{u}$$

Hence $(\hat{\mathbf{x}}, \hat{\mathbf{z}}, \hat{C})$ is a solution to problem (8.8) if there are (vector) functions of t, $\hat{\mathbf{w}}, \hat{\alpha}, \hat{\mathbf{u}}, \hat{\mathbf{v}}$ such that $\hat{\mathbf{x}}, \hat{\mathbf{z}}, \hat{C}, \hat{\alpha}, \hat{\mathbf{u}}, \hat{\mathbf{v}}$ are solutions to the system:

$$\dot{\mathbf{v}} = -[\mathbf{I} - (\delta + \rho)\mathbf{A}]\mathbf{A}^{-1}\mathbf{v} - \mathbf{w} \tag{8.10a}$$

$$C^{-\sigma} = \mathbf{e}_1^T \mathbf{A}^{-1} \mathbf{v} - \alpha \tag{8.10b}$$

$$\mathbf{A}^{-1}\mathbf{v} = \mathbf{u} \tag{8.10c}$$

$$\dot{\mathbf{x}}^T = \mathbf{x}^T (\mathbf{I} - \delta \mathbf{A})\mathbf{A}^{-1} - C \mathbf{e}_1^T \mathbf{A}^{-1} - \mathbf{z}^T \mathbf{A}^{-1} \tag{8.10d}$$

$$\mathbf{x}^T \mathbf{w} = 0, \quad \alpha C = 0, \quad \mathbf{z}^T \mathbf{u} = 0 \tag{8.10e}$$

$$\mathbf{x} \geq 0, \quad C \geqslant 0, \quad \mathbf{z} \geq 0, \quad \mathbf{w} \geq 0, \quad \alpha \geqslant 0, \quad \mathbf{u} \geqq 0 \tag{8.10f}$$

$$\lim_{t \to \infty} \mathbf{x}^T \mathbf{v} e^{-\rho t} = 0 \tag{8.10g}$$

Conditions (8.10a)–(8.10f) are also necessary if the usual constraint qualification holds (see e.g. Seierstad and Sydsæter, 1987, pp. 380–1). By eliminating the slack variables, system (8.10) can be stated as

$$\dot{\mathbf{v}} \leq -[\mathbf{I} - (\delta + \rho)\mathbf{A}]\mathbf{A}^{-1}\mathbf{v} \tag{8.11a}$$

$$\mathbf{x}^T \dot{\mathbf{v}} = -\mathbf{x}^T [\mathbf{I} - (\delta + \rho)\mathbf{A}]\mathbf{A}^{-1}\mathbf{v} \tag{8.11b}$$

$$C^{-\sigma} \leqslant \mathbf{e}_1^T \mathbf{A}^{-1}\mathbf{v} \tag{8.11c}$$

$$C^{1-\sigma} = C \mathbf{e}_1^T \mathbf{A}^{-1}\mathbf{v} \tag{8.11d}$$

$$\dot{\mathbf{x}}^T \mathbf{A} \leq \mathbf{x}^T (\mathbf{I} - \delta \mathbf{A}) - C \mathbf{e}_1^T \tag{8.11e}$$

$$\dot{\mathbf{x}}^T \mathbf{v} = \mathbf{x}^T (\mathbf{I} - \delta \mathbf{A})\mathbf{A}^{-1}\mathbf{v} - C \mathbf{e}_1^T \mathbf{A}^{-1}\mathbf{v} \tag{8.11f}$$

$$\mathbf{x} \geq 0, \quad C \geqslant 0, \quad \mathbf{A}^{-1}\mathbf{v} \geq 0 \tag{8.11g}$$

$$\lim_{t \to \infty} \mathbf{x}^T \mathbf{v} \, e^{-\rho t} = 0 \tag{8.11h}$$

Then we prove the 'if' part of proposition 1. From equality (8.6) and inequality (8.4b) we obtain that $\delta + g < \lambda^{-1}$ and therefore matrix $[\mathbf{I} - (\delta + g)\mathbf{A}]$ is invertible and its inverse is positive (see e.g. Takayama, 1974, chapter 4; Kurz and Salvadori, 1995, p. 517). Hence vector $\mathbf{x}_0$ is well defined by the equality (8.9). Then we obtain by substitution that:

$$\mathbf{x} = \theta \mathbf{e}_1^T [\mathbf{I} - (\delta + g)\mathbf{A}]^{-1} e^{gt}$$
$$C = \theta \, e^{gt}$$
$$\mathbf{v} = \theta^{-\sigma} \lambda \mathbf{p} \, e^{-g\sigma t}$$

is a solution to system (8.11), $\mathbf{p}$ being the left eigenvector of matrix $\mathbf{A}$ associated with the eigenvalue λ and normalized by the condition $\mathbf{e}_1^T \mathbf{p} = 1$.

Next we prove the 'only if' part of proposition 1. Let us first prove that $C_0 > 0$ and $\mathbf{x}_0 > \mathbf{0}$. If $C_0 = 0$, then $C = 0$ and the functional (8.8a) would equal zero, and therefore it cannot be a maximum. If $\mathbf{x}_0 \geqslant \mathbf{0}$ but not $\mathbf{x}_0 > \mathbf{0}$, then inequality (8.11e) cannot have a solution since $\dot{\mathbf{x}} = g\mathbf{x}$ and $\mathbf{A}$ is non-negative and indecomposable (see e.g. Kurz and Salvadori, 1995, p. 516). Since $\mathbf{x} = \mathbf{x}_0 \, e^{gt} > \mathbf{0}$, inequality (8.11a) is satisfied as an equation, and $C = C_0 \, e^{gt} > 0$, the constraint qualification holds. Moreover, we obtain from system (8.11a)–(8.11g) that:

$$\dot{\mathbf{v}} = -[\mathbf{I} - (\delta + \rho)\mathbf{A}]\mathbf{A}^{-1}\mathbf{v} \tag{8.12a}$$

$$C = [\mathbf{e}_1^T \mathbf{A}^{-1} \mathbf{v}]^{-1/\sigma} \tag{8.12b}$$

$$\mathbf{x}^T[\mathbf{I} - (\delta + g)\mathbf{A}] \geq C\mathbf{e}_1^T \tag{8.12c}$$

$$\mathbf{x}^T[\mathbf{I} - (\delta + g)\mathbf{A}]\mathbf{A}^{-1}\mathbf{v} = C\mathbf{e}_1^T\mathbf{A}^{-1}\mathbf{v} \tag{8.12d}$$

$$\mathbf{A}^{-1}\mathbf{v} \geqq \mathbf{0}. \tag{8.12e}$$

From differential equation (8.12a) we obtain

$$\mathbf{v} = \mathbf{T} \, e^{[(\delta+\rho)\mathbf{I} - \mathbf{L}^{-1}]t}\mathbf{h}$$

where $\mathbf{T}$ is the matrix of the right eigenvectors of matrix $\mathbf{A}$, $\mathbf{L}$ is the diagonal matrix with the eigenvalues of matrix $\mathbf{A}$ on the main diagonal ($\mathbf{A}\mathbf{T} = \mathbf{T}\mathbf{L}$), $\mathbf{h}$ is a vector of constants which depends on the initial conditions $\mathbf{x}_0$. With no loss of generality assume that $\mathbf{T}\mathbf{e}_1 = \mathbf{p} > \mathbf{0}$ and $\mathbf{e}_1^T \mathbf{L}\mathbf{e}_1 = \lambda$. Then for $j \neq 1$ the real part of vector $\mathbf{T}\mathbf{e}_j$ has negative and positive entries and $\mathbf{e}_j^T \mathbf{L}\mathbf{e}_j$ is not larger in modulus than λ. Since C is an exponential function of t, all the non-zero entries of vector $\mathbf{h}$ belong to the same eigenvalue λ_0 because of equation (8.12b). Moreover, since inequality (8.12e) holds, λ_0 must be the Frobenius eigenvalue, that is, $\lambda_0 = \lambda$ and therefore vector $\mathbf{h}$ has only one non-zero entry which is the first one. Hence

$$\mathbf{v} = h_1 \mathbf{p} \, e^{[(\delta+\rho)-\lambda^{-1}]t} = h_1 \mathbf{p} \, e^{-g\sigma t}$$

$$C = [\lambda^{-1} h_1 \mathbf{e}_1^T \mathbf{p}]^{-1/\sigma} \, e^{-gt} = C_0 \, e^{gt}$$

where g is defined by equation (8.6) and $C_0 = h_1^{-1/\sigma} \lambda^{1/\sigma}$ is a positive constant which depends on the initial conditions $\mathbf{x}_0$. Since

$$\mathbf{A}^{-1}\mathbf{v} = \lambda^{-1} h_1 \mathbf{p} \, e^{-g\sigma t} = C_0^{-\sigma} \mathbf{p} \, e^{-g\sigma t} > \mathbf{0}$$

we obtain from inequality (8.12c) and equation (8.12d) that:

$$\mathbf{x}_0^T[\mathbf{I} - (\delta + g)\mathbf{A}] = C_0\mathbf{e}_1^T$$

Since $(\delta + g)^{-1} > \lambda$, because of inequality (8.4b), matrix $[\mathbf{I} - (\delta + g)\mathbf{A}]$ is invertible and its inverse is positive. Hence $\mathbf{x}_0$ satisfies equality (8.9) with $\theta = C_0$.

Acknowledgements

I thank Giuseppe Freni, Fausto Gozzi, Sergio Parrinello, Ian Steedman and, above all, Heinz D. Kurz for useful comments on a previous draft, and the MURST (the Italian Ministry of the University and Technological and Scientific Research) and the CNR (the Italian National Research Council) for financial support.

References

Aghion P. and Howitt P. (1992) 'A Model of Growth through Creative Destruction', *Econometrica*, 60, pp. 323–51.

Barro R. J. and Sala-i-Martin X. (1995) *Economic Growth*, McGraw-Hill, New York.

Becker G. S. and Murphy K. M. (1992) 'The Division of Labour, Coordination Costs, and Knowledge', *Quarterly Journal of Economics*, 106, pp. 501–26.

Burgstaller A. (1994) *Property and Prices: Toward a Unified Theory of Value*, Cambridge University Press, Cambridge.

Grossman G. M. and Helpman E. (1994) 'Endogenous Innovation in the Theory of Growth', *Journal of Economic Perspectives*, 8, pp. 23–44.

Kaldor N. (1955–6) 'Alternative Theories of Distribution', *Review of Economic Studies*, 23, pp. 83–100.

Kurz H. D. (1997) 'What Could the "New" Growth Theory Teach Smith or Ricardo?', *Economic Issues*, 2, pp. 1–20. Here reprinted as Chapter 7.

Kurz H. D. and Salvadori N. (1995) *Theory of Production: A Long-Period Analysis*, Cambridge University Press, Cambridge, New York, Melbourne.

Kurz H. D. and Salvadori N. (1996) 'In the Beginning All the World Was Australia...', in P. Arestis, G. Palma, M. Sawyer (eds): *Capital Controversy, Post-Keynesian Economics and the History of Economic Thought. Essays in Honour of Geoff Harcourt*, vol. 1, Routledge, London, pp. 425–43.

Kurz H. D. and Salvadori N. (1997) ' "Endogeneous" Growth Models and the "Classical" Tradition', chapter 4 of Kurz H. D., Salvadori N., *Understanding 'Classical' Economics: Studies in Long-period Theory*, Routledge, London and New York.

Kurz H. D. and Salvadori N. (1998) 'What is New in the "New" Theories of Economic Growth? Or: Old Wine in New Goatskins', in F. Coricelli, M. Di Matteo, F. H. Hahn (eds): *Growth and Development: Theories, Empirical Evidence and Policy Issues*, Macmillan, London, pp. 63–94.

Kurz H. D. and Salvadori N. (1999) 'Theories of "Endogenous" Growth in Historical Perspective', in Murat R. Sertel (ed.): *Contemporary Economic Issues*. Proceedings of the Eleventh World Congress of the International Economic Association, Tunis. Volume 4: *Economic Behaviour and Design*, London (Macmillan) and New York (St Martin's Press), pp. 225–61. Here reprinted as Chapter 6.

Lucas R. E. (1988) 'On the Mechanics of Economic Development', *Journal of Monetary Economics*, 22, pp. 3–42.

Meade J. E. (1961) *A Neoclassical Theory of Economic Growth*, Allen & Unwin, London.

Pasinetti L. L. (1962) 'Rate of Profit and Income Distribution in Relation to the Rate of Economic Growth', *Review of Economic Studies*, 29, pp. 267–79.

Rebelo S. (1991) 'Long Run Policy Analysis and Long Run Growth', *Journal of Political Economy*, 99, pp. 500–21.

Ricardo D. (1951 ssq.) *The Works and Correspondence of David Ricardo*, 11 volumes, edited by P. Sraffa in collaboration with M. H. Dobb, Cambridge University Press, Cambridge. In the text referred to as *Works*, volume number and chapter number.

Robinson J. V. (1953) 'The Production Function and the Theory of Capital', *Review of Economic Studies*, 21, pp. 81–106.

Robinson J. V. (1956) *The Accumulation of Capital*, Macmillan, London.

Rodriguez-Clare A. (1996) 'The Division of Labour and Development', *Journal of Development Economics*, pp. 3–32.

Seierstad A. and Sydsæter K. (1987) *Optimal Control Theory with Economic Applications*. North Holland, Amsterdam.

Smith A. (1976) *An Inquiry into the Nature and Causes of the Wealth of Nations*, 1st edn 1776, vol. II of *The Glasgow Edition of the Works and Correspondence of Adam Smith*, edited by R. H. Campbell, A. S. Skinner and W. B. Todd, Oxford University Press, Oxford. In the text quoted as *WN*, book number, chapter number, section number, paragraph number.

Solow R. M. (1956) 'A Contribution to the Theory of Economic Growth,' *Quarterly Journal of Economics*, 70, pp. 65–94.

Solow R. M. (1963) *Capital Theory and the Rate of Return*, North Holland, Amsterdam.

Sraffa P. (1960) *Production of Commodities by Means of Commodities. Prelude to a Critique of Economic Theory*, Cambridge University Press, Cambridge.

Swan T. W. (1956) 'Economic Growth and Capital Accumulation', *Economic Record*, 32, pp. 334–61.

Takayama A. (1974) *Mathematical Economics*, Cambridge University Press, Cambridge, New York, Melbourne.

Yang X. and Borland J. (1991) 'A Microeconomic Mechanism for Economic Growth', *Journal of Political Economy*, 99, pp. 460–82.

Young A. (1928) 'Increasing Returns and Economic Progress', *Economic Journal*, 38, pp. 527–42.

9 A linear multisector model of 'endogenous' growth

A post-script

Giuseppe Freni and Neri Salvadori

The structure of the multisector AK model introduced by Salvadori (1998), here reprinted as previous chapter, has been further investigated by Freni *et al.* (2001, 2003); see also Gozzi and Freni (2001). The starting point of these papers was a criticism of the formulation used in the previous chapter in stating the optimal control problem (8.7) of the representative agent within 'the solution using the usual procedure'. This analysis led to the slightly different formulation of the model developed by Freni *et al.* (2001), and to the various generalisations that are studied by Gozzi and Freni (2001) and by Freni *et al.* (2003). In this post-script we first try to clarify the difference between the original article and the most recent works. Then we provide the 'long-period solution' for the Classification Theorem by Freni *et al.* (2001).

1.

The previous chapter uses inequality (8.7b), or equivalently equation (8.8b), in order to describe the accumulation process in the version of the single production multisector AK model depicted there. This formulation of the accumulation process can be easily rationalised in discrete time by assuming that capital goods cannot be stored, which in continuous time is equivalent to assuming that the speed of disposal is infinite. To clarify this point, suppose that the production process as described in the previous chapter takes place within a discrete time setting. Assume also that consumption takes place at the end of each period, that the capital stock available at time t, s_t^T, consists of commodities which can be either used in production or stored, that commodities used in production decay at the uniform rate δ, $0 \le \delta \le 1$, and that stored commodities decay at the uniform rate μ, $0 \le \mu \le 1$. Of course, if $\mu = 1$, a stored commodity is actually disposed of (free of charge). Under these assumptions the following equations hold:

$$s_{t+1}^T = x_{t+1}^T A + z_{t+1}^T \tag{9.1}$$

$$x_t^T + (1 - \delta)x_t^T A + (1 - \mu)z_t^T = s_{t+1}^T + c_{t+1}e_1^T \tag{9.2}$$

in which c is consumption, and x^T and z^T are the non-negative intensity vectors of the production and the 'storage' processes, respectively. From equations (9.1) and (9.2) we obtain:

$$(\mathbf{x}_{t+1}^T - \mathbf{x}_t^T)\mathbf{A} + \mathbf{z}_{t+1}^T = \mathbf{x}_t^T(\mathbf{I} - \delta\mathbf{A}) + (1 - \mu)\mathbf{z}_t^T - c_{t+1}\mathbf{e}_1^T \qquad (9.3)$$

If $\mu = 1$, then equation (9.3) and the non-negativity of the storage intensity vector $\mathbf{z}_{t+1}^T$ clearly imply:

$$(\mathbf{x}_{t+1}^T - \mathbf{x}_t^T)\mathbf{A} \leqq \mathbf{x}_t^T(\mathbf{I} - \delta\mathbf{A}) - c_{t+1}\mathbf{e}_1^T \qquad (9.4)$$

which is the discrete time analogue of inequality (8.7b). If $\mu < 1$, inequality (9.4) does not need to hold and inequality (8.7b) is not obtained. Note that if in discrete time the rate of depreciation is μ, then the corresponding instantaneous rate is $-\ln(1 - \mu)$ and therefore the instantaneous rate corresponding to $\mu = 1$ is infinite.

2.

In a framework treating time as a discrete variable free disposal is introduced in terms of the assumption that there is a process which has the commodity to be disposed of as an input and no output. As all other processes disposal requires time. Alternative formulations are also possible, but in all of them disposal requires a finite time, generally one period. (Similarly for costly disposal: in this case some other inputs are required, which constitute the 'cost' of the disposal.) In a continuous time framework, in order to have a finite time to obtain (complete) disposal we need to introduce a number of technicalities because, instead of the usual differential equations, we need difference-differential equations. An alternative could be the assumption of an infinite speed of disposal, and this was the way followed by stating inequality (8.7b), as we have just shown. But this solution contrasts not only with the simple fact that disposal requires time but also introduces the need for other technicalities since the path of stocks can jump down. A better alternative consists in assuming that the rate of decay of 'disposed' commodities is a very high number, but still finite. For our purposes it is enough to assume that $\mu > \delta$. This is the way followed by Freni *et al.* (2001). They considered the capital stocks as the state variables of the system and by stating equation (9.1) as

$$\mathbf{x}_t^T\mathbf{A} + \mathbf{z}_t^T = \mathbf{s}_t^T \qquad (9.1')$$

they obtained from (9.1') and (9.2) the difference equation:

$$(\mathbf{s}_{t+1}^T - \mathbf{s}_t^T) = \mathbf{x}_t^T(\mathbf{I} - \delta\mathbf{A}) - \mu\mathbf{z}_t^T - c_{t+1}\mathbf{e}_1^T$$

which survives the 'passing to the limit' operation involved in modelling production as a continuous process. Freni *et al.* (2001) therefore stated the optimal control problem of the representative consumer in the following way:

$$
\max \int_0^\infty e^{-\rho t} u(c) \, dt
$$

$$
\text{s.t. } \mathbf{s}^T = \mathbf{x}^T \mathbf{A} + \mathbf{z}^T
$$

$$
\dot{\mathbf{s}}^T = \mathbf{x}^T (\mathbf{I} - \delta \mathbf{A}) - \mu \mathbf{z}^T - c \mathbf{e}_1^T \tag{9.5}
$$

$$
\mathbf{x} \geq \mathbf{0}, \quad \mathbf{z} \geq \mathbf{0}, \quad c \geq 0
$$

$$
\mathbf{s}_0^T = \hat{\mathbf{s}}^T \ (> \mathbf{0}^T)
$$

where, as usual, the instantaneous utility function $u(c)$ takes the form:

$$
u(c) = \begin{cases} \dfrac{c^{1-\sigma}}{1-\sigma} & \sigma \neq 1 \\[2mm] \log(c) & \sigma = 1 \end{cases}
$$

Gozzi and Freni (2001) and Freni *et al.* (2003) show how this model can be generalised to deal with problems such as joint production, multiple consumption goods and choice of technique.

3.

Salvadori (1998) characterises the steady-state solutions of the multisector AK model under the restrictions given by inequalities (8.4a) and (8.4b). He also implicitly assumes that the discount rate is positive and this allows him to obtain $r > 0$ from inequality (8.4a). An analytic result proved under these restrictions in the previous chapter is the extension of a non-substitution theorem to the endogenous growth AK model, a result that is not startling for the readers of Sraffa's book, as mentioned in p. 167,[1] and to the conoisseurs of the early literature on optimal growth (see, e.g. Atsumi, 1969), but that has been often forgotten in the new growth literature (see, however, Kaganovich, 1998; McKenzie, 1998). According to such a theorem, the long-run rate of profit and relative prices are independent of the intertemporal preferences, whose changes affect only the intensities of operation and the rate of growth.

With some qualifications given below, the main comparative statics results contained in the above version of the non-substitution theorem carry over to the framework developed by Freni *et al.* (2001). However, these authors showed that inequality (8.4b) is both necessary and sufficient for the existence of both a finite value solution and a steady-state solution of problem (9.5), and hence that side parameter restrictions, such as inequality (8.4a) or positive discounting (i.e. $\rho > 0$), can be dropped without affecting the main results. Nevertheless, there

---

1 All page references are to the previous chapter and not to the original paper.

is a cost in dropping all side parameter restrictions. It consists in the enlargement of the set of steady states the model allows.

The problem surfaces already in the framework of the previous chapter under the particular parameters $\delta = 0$ and $1 - \lambda\rho = 0$. For this case, Freni *et al.* (2001) show that the equilibrium prices are still those given by the dominant eigenvector of the matrix $\mathbf{A}$. This, however, is not the effect of the complementary slackness condition (8.11b), that in this case is not able to obtain equation (8.12a) since the intensity vector $\mathbf{x}$ is proportional to $\mathbf{e}_1$ and therefore is not positive.

The main result of Freni *et al.* (2001) on the structure of the steady-state equilibria is a Classification Theorem in which three different regimes are distinguished, depending on the values of the involved parameters. The first regime is the one emphasised in the previous chapter and arises whenever:

$$(\lambda^{-1} - \delta)(1 - \sigma) < \rho < \lambda^{-1} - \delta(1 - \sigma)$$

If

$$\lambda^{-1} - \delta(1 - \sigma) \leq \rho \leq a^{-1} - \delta(1 - \sigma)$$

where $a = (\mathbf{e}_1^T \mathbf{A} \mathbf{e}_1)$, then there is a different kind of steady state in which $g = -\delta$, the profit rate varies in the range $[\lambda^{-1} - \delta, a^{-1} - \delta]$ and relative prices are constrained but not determined. Finally, if

$$a^{-1} - \delta(1 - \sigma) < \rho$$

then there is a steady state in which r is constant again and equals $a^{-1} - \delta$, whereas g varies in the range $(-\infty, -\delta)$. In this case, all commodities used in the production of commodity 1 except commodity 1 itself have a zero price. In other words, production is reduced to the production of commodity 1 by means of commodity 1 and free goods.

4.

The reader of the previous chapter might wish to ask whether the Classification Theorem stated and proved by Freni *et al.* (2001) can be proved by following the long-period procedure used in that chapter. This is indeed the case, as will be seen in the following.

If and only if $g > -\delta$, all commodities need to be produced and therefore equation (8.5) must hold for each j, $1 \leq j \leq n$. This determines r and $\mathbf{p}$, as shown in the previous chapter. In this regime prices are proportional to the right eigenvector of matrix $\mathbf{A}$ corresponding to the eigenvalue of maximum modulus λ. Then, from inequality (8.4b), equation (8.6), and the condition that $g > -\delta$ we obtain that this regime holds if and only if

$$(\lambda^{-1} - \delta)(1 - \sigma) < \rho < \lambda^{-1} - \delta(1 - \sigma)$$

If and only if $g < -\delta$, the inputs required for the operation of prosess 1 (i.e. the process producing commodity 1) are produced jointly by process 1 itself at a rate $(-\delta)$ larger than the growth rate. As a consequence, (i) all commodities used in the production of commodity 1 except commodity 1 itself are overproduced and have a zero price, and (ii) all processes except process 1 do not need to be operated in the long period. Since the only process which is relevant is the process producing commodity 1, equation (8.5) needs to hold only for $j = 1$. This is enough to determine the rate of profit (since the prices of inputs in terms of commodity 1 are known):

$$r = a^{-1} - \delta$$

which implies, with equation (8.3) and the condition $g < -\delta$, that this regimes holds if and only if

$$a^{-1} - \delta(1 - \sigma) < \rho$$

If and only if $g = -\delta$, the inputs required for the operation of prosess 1 are produced jointly by process 1 itself at a rate equal to the growth rate and, therefore, these commodities (except commodity 1) may have either a positive or a zero price. Those with a positive price cannot be separately produced or stored (otherwise they would be overproduced and their prices would be zero) and their existing stocks can be regarded as stocks of 'renewable' resources for which a growth rate of $-\delta$ is granted in the production of commodity 1. In these conditions equation (8.5) needs to hold only for $j = 1$, whereas for $2 \leq j \leq n$ we must have:

$$\int_0^t e^{(t-\tau)i} e^{-\delta\tau} \mathbf{e}_j^{\mathrm{T}} \mathbf{p}_\tau \, d\tau + e^{-\delta t} \mathbf{e}_j^{\mathrm{T}} \mathbf{A} \mathbf{p}_t \leq e^{it} \mathbf{e}_j^{\mathrm{T}} \mathbf{A} \mathbf{p}_0 \tag{9.6}$$

since no investor can get a larger profit by operating a process different from process 1. The rate of profit is determined by equation (8.3) and by the condition that $g = -\delta$:

$$r = \rho - \delta\sigma$$

Once again the only relevant process is that producing commodity 1, but this process is not able to determine prices, but only to constrain them by determining the price of the bundle of commodities used in the production of commodity 1 except commodity 1 itself: an economy characterised by a larger ρ must have lower prices of the inputs of commodity 1 in order to allow the higher rate of profit which compensates exactly the larger ρ to leave the growth rate unchanged. In this regime the rate of profit r is bounded by the inequalities:

$$\lambda^{-1} - \delta \leq r \leq a^{-1} - \delta$$

In fact, when the first inequality is satisfied as an equation, the inequalities (9.6) are also satisfied as equations and for lower values of r they cannot be all satisfied. Similarly, when the second inequality is satisfied as an equation all commodities used in the production of commodity 1 except commodity 1 itself have a zero price and for higher values of r such prices cannot be all non-negative. From these inequalities, with equation (8.3) and the condition $g = -\delta$, we obtain that this regimes holds if and only if

$$\lambda^{-1} - \delta(1 - \sigma) \leq \rho \leq a^{-1} - \delta(1 - \sigma)$$

5.

The reader of the previous chapter might wish to ask whether the long-period procedure used in that chapter can suggest a generalisation of the Classification Theorem. This is indeed the case, as will be shown in the following. Proofs are either analogous to those stated in the previous section or obvious to those who know the technicalities of the long period analysis (those who do not can consult the book by Kurz and Salvadori, 1995, especially chapter 5) and are here omitted. The aim of this section is to show once again both the powerfulness of the long period procedure and of the reformulation of the problem investigated in previous chapter developed by Freni *et al.* (2001).

Let us replace the state equation of problem (9.5) with the equation:

$$\dot{\mathbf{s}}^{\mathrm{T}} = \mathbf{x}^{\mathrm{T}}(\mathbf{B} - \delta\mathbf{A}) - \mu\mathbf{z}^{\mathrm{T}} - c\mathbf{e}_1^{\mathrm{T}}$$

where each row of matrix $\mathbf{B}$ has one and only one positve element (the others being nought) and matrices $\mathbf{A}$ and $\mathbf{B}$ are non-negative $m \times n$ matrices ($m \geq n$) such that for each $\varepsilon > 0$:

$$(\mathbf{u}^{\mathrm{T}}(\mathbf{B} - \varepsilon\mathbf{A}) \geqq \mathbf{0}, \mathbf{u} \geq \mathbf{0}) \quad \Rightarrow \quad \mathbf{u}^{\mathrm{T}}\mathbf{A} > \mathbf{0}$$

In this way we have introduced choice of technique, but we have mantained that jount production is avoided and that all commodities *always* enter directly or indirectly into the production of all commodities. These assumptions are enough to prove that:

$$\mathrm{Inf}\,\{\mu \in \mathbb{R} | \exists \mathbf{x} \in \mathbb{R}^m : \mathbf{x} \geq \mathbf{0} \text{ and } \mathbf{x}^{\mathrm{T}}[\mu\mathbf{B} - \mathbf{A}] > \mathbf{0}^{\mathrm{T}}\}$$

$$= \mathrm{Min}\{\mu \in \mathbb{R} | \exists \mathbf{x} \in \mathbb{R}^m : \mathbf{x} \geq \mathbf{0} \text{ and } \mathbf{x}^{\mathrm{T}}[\mu\mathbf{B} - \mathbf{A}] \geqq \mathbf{0}^{\mathrm{T}}\}$$

$$= \mathrm{Max}\{\rho \in \mathbb{R} | \exists \mathbf{y} \in \mathbb{R}^n : \mathbf{y} \geq \mathbf{0} \text{ and } [\rho\mathbf{B} - \mathbf{A}]\mathbf{y} \leqq \mathbf{0}\}$$

and that the:

$$\mathrm{Arg\,max}\{\rho \in \mathbb{R} | \exists \mathbf{y} \in \mathbb{R}^n : \mathbf{y} \geq \mathbf{0}, \mathbf{e}_1^{\mathrm{T}}\mathbf{y} = 1, [\rho\mathbf{B} - \mathbf{A}]\mathbf{y} \leqq \mathbf{0}\}$$

is uniquely determined. Then by stating:

$$\lambda = \mathrm{Max}\{\rho \in \mathbb{R} | \exists \mathbf{y} \in \mathbb{R}^n : \mathbf{y} \geq \mathbf{0} \text{ and } [\rho\mathbf{B} - \mathbf{A}]\mathbf{y} \leqq \mathbf{0}\},$$

$$\mathbf{p} = \mathrm{Arg\,max}\{\rho \in \mathbb{R} | \exists \mathbf{y} \in \mathbb{R}^n : \mathbf{y} \geq \mathbf{0}, \mathbf{e}_1^{\mathrm{T}}\mathbf{y} = 1, [\rho\mathbf{B} - \mathbf{A}]\mathbf{y} \leqq \mathbf{0}\}$$

$$a = \mathrm{Min}_{j \in J_1} a_{1j},$$

where J_1 is the set of the indices of the processes producing commodity 1, the Classification Theorem holds with the new meanings of the symbols.

References

Atsumi, H. (1969). 'The Efficient Capital Programme for a Maintainable Utility Level', *Review of Economic Studies*, 36, pp. 263–87.

Freni, G., Gozzi, F. and Salvadori, N. (2001). 'A Multisector "AK Model" with Endogenous Growth: Existence and Characterization of Optimal Paths and Steady-state Analysis', *Studi e Ricerche del Dipartimento di Scienze Economiche dell'Università di Pisa*, n. 75.

Freni, G., Gozzi, F. and Salvadori, N. (2003). 'Endogenous Growth in a Multi-sector Economy', in N. Salvadori (ed.), *The Theory of Economic Growth: A 'Classical' Perspective*, Cheltenam: Edward Elgar, pp. 60–80.

Gozzi, F. and Freni, G. (2001). 'On a Dynamic Non-Substitution Theorem and Other Issues in Burgstaller's "Property and Prices" ', *Metroeconomica.*, 52, 2, 2001, pp. 181–96.

Kaganovich, M. (1998). 'Sustained Endogenous Growth with Decreasing Returns and Heterogeneous Capital', *Journal of Economic Dynamics and Control*, 22, pp. 1575–603.

Kurz, H. D. and Salvadori, N. (1995). *Theory of Production. A Long-period Analysis*, Cambridge, Melbourne and New York: Cambridge University Press.

McKenzie, L. W. (1998). 'Turnpikes', *American Economic Review*, 88, pp. 1–14.

Salvadori, N. (1998). 'A Linear Multisector Model of "Endogenous" Growth and the Problem of Capital', *Metroeconomica*, 49, pp. 319–35. Here reprinted as Chapter 8.

Part III
On Sraffa's contribution

10 Sraffa and the mathematicians*

Frank Ramsey and Alister Watson

Heinz D. Kurz and Neri Salvadori

1. Introduction

In the Preface of *Production of Commodities by Means of Commodities* Sraffa mentions John Maynard Keynes, pointing out that in 1928 he had shown him 'a draft of the opening propositions of this paper' (Sraffa, 1960, p. vi). Yet, there is no expression of gratitude to any of his fellow economists for comments, suggestions or assistance during the long period over which the book had been in preparation. There is no mention of Maurice Dobb, Richard Kahn, Nicholas Kaldor, Joan Robinson or of any other economist, whether Cantabrigian or not. The only people Sraffa thanks are three mathematicians: 'My greatest debt is to Professor A. S. Besicovitch for invaluable mathematical help over many years. I am also indebted for similar help at different periods to the late Mr Frank Ramsey and to Mr Alister Watson' (ibid., pp. vi–vii). In a provisional draft of the book's preface, written in Rapallo on 3 January 1959, Sraffa had also thanked David Champernowne amongst his 'mathematical friends' (*Sraffa Papers (SP)* D3/12/46: 49).[1] However, at a later stage his name was dropped from the list. We can only speculate why Sraffa did this. Perhaps the presence of the name of Champernowne, who was a mathematician by training, but then had become a statistician and economist, would have rendered the absence of the names of other economists even more glaring. This Sraffa may have wanted to avoid. Sraffa's papers also show that he benefited from Champernowne, the mathematician, not Champernowne the economist. To avoid a possible irritation on the part of his other fellow economists Sraffa then may have decided to mention only pure mathematicians.

In this chapter we shall ask what was the role of some of Sraffa's 'mathematical friends' in the genesis of the propositions of his book. This question could not sensibly be approached, let alone answered, prior to the opening of Sraffa's unpublished papers and correspondence in the Wren Library of Trinity College, Cambridge. The available material provides evidence as to the kinds of problem

* Reprinted with permission from *Piero Sraffa's Political Economy. A Centenary Estimate*, Routledge, 2000.

1 We are grateful to Pierangelo Garegnani, literary executor of Sraffa's papers and correspondence, for granting us permission to quote from them. References to the papers follow the catalogue prepared by Jonathan Smith. Unless otherwise stated, all emphases are in the original.

Sraffa was concerned with and when, and which of these problems he would com-
municate to his mathematical colleagues, seeking their assistance to solve them.
It is hardly an exaggeration to say that without the help of Ramsey, Watson and
especially Besicovitch Sraffa could not have accomplished his task.

In the various drafts of the Preface of his 1960 book Sraffa composed, he consistently singled out Besicovitch as the mathematician whom he owed the greatest
intellectual debt. In fact, Besicovitch can be said to have taken a crucial part in
the development of Sraffa's thought in the second and third phase of his work on
Production of Commodities, that is, basically in the first half of the 1940s and in the
second half of the 1950s. Sraffa consulted Besicovitch on virtually all problems of
a mathematical nature he was confronted with. There are numerous documents in
his unpublished papers reflecting their close collaboration. A proper treatment of it
is beyond the scope of this chapter: the material is too huge and complex and ought
to be dealt with separately. Confronted with the alternative of entirely setting aside
Sraffa's collaboration with Besicovitch or of providing just a few illustrations of
it, we opted for the former solution. This is a serious limitation of the chapter,
which we hope to be able to make good in another work. Hence, apart from a few
remarks in this chapter attention will exclusively focus on Sraffa's collaboration
with Frank Ramsey and Alister Watson.

The composition of the chapter is as follows. Section 2 provides some hints as
to Sraffa's training in mathematics. Section 3 gives information about his meetings
with his mathematical friends, our main source being his diaries. The diaries are
also used in Section 4 in order to give an idea about the community of scholars
involved in reading and commenting on the manuscript of his book. After the
stage has been set we enter, beginning with Section 5, into a discussion of Sraffa's
collaboration with the mathematicians. Section 5 reconstructs Frank Ramsey's
contribution. Sections 6 and 7 turn to Sraffa's collaboration with Alister Watson
during the period when Sraffa was writing the book and at the time of the correction
of the galley-proofs, respectively. Section 8 is an excursus to the main argument.
Its starting point is the correction of a slip in Sraffa's book by Harry Johnson and
Sraffa's response to it. The reconstruction of this story is here reported because it
sheds additional light on the relationship between Sraffa, David Champernowne
and Alister Watson. Section 9 contains some conclusions.

2. Sraffa's training in mathematics

Sraffa had no special training in mathematics: he had been exposed to the ordinary dose of mathematics common in Italian secondary schools, but no more, and
during his studies at Turin University the classes he attended were mathematically
not demanding. When Sraffa moved to Cambridge he apparently brought with him
two books by Pradella (1915a and 1915b) on the mathematics which were then
used in secondary schools. Sraffa's annotations in the first of the two document
that he must have studied the volume carefully. Pradella's book on algebra and
arithmetic is mentioned a few times in his notes. For instance, he refers to it
in a document titled 'First equations: on linear homogeneous equations'

(*SP* D3/12/10: 33). Another book to which Sraffa referred in his first papers on systems of production equations is Chini (1923). In particular there are two documents dated 'End of Nov. 1927' in which Sraffa calculated two numerical examples relative to equations without a surplus and with a surplus (see *SP* D3/12/2: 33). In the example with a surplus he found that there was no solution (since the two equations were contradictory). There is a big question mark added on the document, but then follows the remark:

V. Chini p. 41 (le equazioni sono contraddittorie quindi non esiste

alcuna soluzione)

$$\text{Le equaz. devono essere} \begin{cases} \text{non contradditorie} \\ \text{indipendenti} \end{cases}$$

$\Big[$See Chini p. 41 (the equations are contradictory and as a consequence

there is no solution)

$$\text{The equations must be} \begin{cases} \text{non contradictory} \\ \text{independent} \end{cases} \Big]$$

A copy of the book by Chini (1923) is in Sraffa's Library (No. 3204), but there are only a few annotations, mainly on pages 41 and 42, where the mentioned property is dealt with.

Another book to which Sraffa refers sometimes is Vivanti (*Complementi di Matematica*): see, for instance, *SP* Dl/11: 79, where with the help of this book Sraffa calculates some simple derivatives and the maximum of a simple function. Vivanti is referred to in another document in which Sraffa expressed some concern about the possibility that his system of equations has '*infinite* soluz. proporzionali' (*SP* D3/12/11: 86). However, Vivanti's book is not in Sraffa's Library (in all probability Sraffa referred to Vivanti 1903). In his papers there are also references to G. Chrystal's book on *Algebra*, part I, published in 1889, which Sraffa consulted on the solution of systems of equations (see *SP* D3/12/6: 23; see also *SP* D3/12/8: 1 and 30); there is no copy of the book in Sraffa's library.[2]

3. Sraffa's meetings with his 'mathematical friends'

In his *Cambridge Pocket Diaries* Sraffa used to note his appointments and the meetings he attended. The diaries provide a useful skeleton of his activities over time. They also provide useful information about his meetings and collaboration with his mathematical friends which gets some confirmation from the material contained in his unpublished papers. There is no presumption, of course, that

---

2 Nerio Naldi kindly informed us that in Sraffa's former flat in Rapallo there are several mathematical exercise and high school books. We still have to check this material.

this information is complete, nor can we be sure that the meetings were mainly or at least partly devoted to discussing the problems Sraffa encountered in his attempt to reformulate the Classical approach to the theory of value and distribution. However, cross-checking the dates listed and the dates of some of his unpublished manuscripts in which he refers to the discussions he had with Frank Ramsey, Alister Watson and A. S. Besicovitch reveals that there are close connections between the two. Therefore it might be of some interest to begin by providing the details of the respective information available in Sraffa's diaries.

As is well known, Sraffa's work on what was eventually to become his 1960 book fell in three periods: the first broadly comprised the years from (late) 1927 to 1930,[3] the second the 1940s, with the main activities in the first half of the decade,[4] and the third the second half of the 1950s.

In the first of the aforementioned periods the following meetings with Frank Ramsey are listed in Sraffa's diaries; during this period there is no information about meetings with other mathematicians. The first appointment with the young mathematician is dated 28 June 1928. The two meet again on 11 November 1928, on 10 and 30 May, and on 29 November 1929. There are no other appointments listed with Ramsey, who died from an attack of jaundice on 19 January 1930 in a London hospital.

In the second period there are four meetings with David Champernowne noted in Sraffa's diaries, two at the beginning of the 1940s, 27 October 1940 and 1 February 1942, and two in the second half, that is, 26 November and 11 December 1947. However, Sraffa's writings in that period do not seem to reflect an impact of Champernowne on the progress of his project. Things are different with regard to Besicovitch. The following meetings with him are listed in the diaries: 29 October and 7 and 11 November 1942, 13 May 1943, 5 June 1944. Besocovitch's collaboration with Sraffa is also vividly reflected in the latter's unpublished papers.[5] From 1945 onward Sraffa also met with Alister Watson. The diaries list the following appointments: 1 May and 30 July 1945, 19 January 1947, 31 January 1948, 4 and 7 January 1949.

The 1950s show these appointments. Both before and after his completion of the main body of the Ricardo edition Sraffa met with Alister Watson and David

---

3 In February 1930 Sraffa was assigned by the Royal Economic Society the task of editing David's Ricardo works and correspondence. As we know, Sraffa immediately took up the work and put a lot of effort into it. However, for a while he appears to have been of the opinion that he could carry on with his constructive work, albeit at a much reduced speed. Therefore, we find some documents also after February 1930 up until 1932. Yet soon Sraffa appears to have been overwhelmed with the new task, which absorbed all his energy and forced him to interrupt his constructive work. It goes without saying that his editorial work generated noticeable positive externalities to his constructive work, both conceptually and analytically.

4 The discovery of Ricardo's letters to James Mill in 1943 and their full availability in 1945 directed Sraffa's attention away from his constructive work and toward his editorial work, with the main body of *The Works and Correspondence of David Ricardo* being published between 1951 and 1955.

5 On 24 January 1950 Sraffa noted in his diary: 'Besicovitch elected prof. (on his birthday)'.

Champernowne. According to his diary Watson visited Sraffa in Cambridge from 25 to 27 July 1952 and from 13 to 14 January 1953. He had an appointment with Champernowne on 15 February 1953. Watson visited Sraffa again from 29 to 30 April 1955. The date of this latter visit is significant, because it took place only a few days after Sraffa's return from Majorca and Spain, where he had begun, in Majorca, to resume his constructive project and to draft parts of his book. Apparently, he was keen to discuss with Watson some of the difficulties he encountered. On 14 June of the same year Sraffa noted in his diary: 'Besicovitch returned from America'. Obviously, he was also eager to get Besicovitch's assistance. A few days later, on 18 June, he wrote: 'Trovato il trick per ridurre il sistema a linearità (utilizzando relaz. lineare fra w e r) con soluzione lineare generale di R' [Found the trick to reduce the system to linearity (using a linear relation between w and r) with a general linear solution for R]. His meeting with Besicovitch had to be postponed, however, because on 5 June Sraffa left for continental Europe, where he stayed until 4 October.[6] His diary notes 'passegg. Besicovi[t]ch' [walk with Besicovitch] on 18 November of the same year. In mid-December Sraffa had to undergo an operation because of a hernia and spent several weeks in the Evelyn Nursing Home. Besicovitch visited him twice, on 21 December 1955 and on 4 January 1956. On 21 April Sraffa's diary notes 'walk Besicovitch'; then there are meetings listed on 25 July, 6 August and 19 October. In the second half of 1957 Sraffa had several meetings with David Champernowne, who was then still affiliated with Oxford University. The first meeting of the two in that year is dated 20 July. On 19 August Sraffa noted in his diary: 'written to Champernowne & booked room', and an entry on 24 August says: 'Champernowne arrives'. Apparently Champernowne stayed until 28 August and had every day long discussions with Sraffa. Most importantly, as Sraffa noted on 26 August: 'Champernowne (legge il mio lavoro. Tutto Part I, §1–47' [Champernowne (reads my work. The whole Part I, §1–47], and on the following day: 'e 2 Appendices' [and two appendices]. Champernowne's reading continued the following days. On 28 August Sraffa noted in his diary: 'Champernowne ritorno a Oxford' [Champernowne back to Oxford]. Three days later, on 31 August, he had every reason to be happy because he could note in his diary: 'Besicovitch offre di aiutarmi nei miei problemi matematici' [Besicovitch offers to help me with my mathematical problems]. Yet the following day, on 1 September, we find the sober observation: 'Besicovitch (pochino!)' [Besicovitch (not much!)]. Two other meetings appear to have taken place that month, one on 7 September, about which we find the remark: 'Besicovitch risponde a domanda' [Besicovitch answers to question], and one on 13 September.

It must have come as a shock to Sraffa when around the turn of the month Besicovitch told him that he could not help him any more. On 1 October 1957 an understandably depressed Sraffa noted in his diary: 'Besicovitch non ce la fa'

---

6 On 3 October 1955, 10.30–13, he met Togliatti in Rome. In his diary Sraffa noted in brackets: 'dettagli del mio libro: con. Marx restato all '800' [details of my book: with Marx left in the XIX century].

[Besicovitch cannot do it]. Yet, the pending tragedy did not unfold: just one day later we find the relieving message: 'Bes. si ri-interessa' [Besicovitch gets interested again]. One can only wonder what has made the mathematician radically change his mind twice in so short a time. Then the speed at which Sraffa's work progressed accelerated tremendously. He had another meeting with Besicovitch on 5 October. On the following day Sraffa jotted in his diary that the mathematician 'Swinnerton-Dyer guarda il mio problema' [Swinnerton-Dyer looks at my problem].[7] On 17 October he noted: 'Besicovitch manda il mio problema a Todd' [Besicovitch sends my problem to Todd].[8] On 22 October, we read: 'Bes. mi da una soluz. del non-basic' [Besicovitch gives me a solution for non-basics], and on 1 November: 'Besicovitch (ultime prove)' [Besicovitch (last proofs)]. Sraffa had further meetings with his elder friend on 2 November and on 8 December. (On 17 December, in a session that lasted for five hours, he discussed with Nicholas Kaldor 'Capital theory – depreciation'.) On 25 December we read: 'Besicovitch (prova non-basics in multiple syst.)' [Besicovitch (proves non-basics in multiple system)]. After another meeting with his mathematical friend on 26 January 1958 and some hard work we find on the 29th of that month the triumphant exclamation: 'Filled last gap in my work (Rent) FINIS'.

4. Reading the manuscript and the proofs

On 5 February 1958 Sraffa wrote to Alister Watson inviting him to see his work in Cambridge. Before that visit took place, other people were involved in reading the manuscript. On 7 February he had lunch with Kaldor in College, who afterwards 'legge 17 pp. mio lavoro' [reads 17 pages of my work]. On 12 February he reported: 'Maurice [Dobb] legge 10 p. mio lavoro' [Maurice reads 10 pages of my work]. On the same day Sraffa wrote again to Watson, anxious to get his younger friend's reaction. Watson came to Cambridge for the weekend from 15 to 17 February. On 15 February Sraffa noted in his diary: '12 [o'clock] Alister Watson arrives for week-end to read my work'; on the 16th: '10.30–1 Watson reads[;] 2–4 walk to Coton[;] 5–8 reads on[;] 8 Watson in hall (Master's lodge Besicovitch)'; and on the 17th: '1 Watson lunch, poi riparte' [1 o'clock Watson lunch, then he leaves]. On 19, 21 and 27 February Maurice Dobb continued his reading to arrive at p. 75 of the manuscript. On 6 March Sraffa noted: '4.30–6 Maurice (discussion, no reading)'. On 11 March Sraffa reported the receipt of a letter by Watson announcing his coming on Wednesday of that week. On 11 and 12 March there were altogether four meetings between Sraffa and Watson dedicated to 'mio lavoro' [my work]. On 21 and 22 March Champernowne was involved in reading and discussing the manuscript. On 25 March Sraffa left for Paris and then Milan, where Sergio Steve

---

7 Peter Swinnerton-Dyer (born in 1927) was a Research Fellow in Mathematics in Trinity College, 1950–4, and later became a Professor of Mathematics at Cambridge University.
8 John Arthur Todd (1908–98) was a Lecturer in Mathematics in the University of Cambridge, 1937–60, and a Reader in Geometry; he was a Fellow and then the Master of Downing College.

read the work between 9 and 12 April; on 12 April Sraffa noted in his diary in brackets: 'S. consiglia pubblicare con prefaz. che spieghi attaches storici' [Steve advises to publish with a preface explaining historical backgrounds]. After his return to Cambridge on 15 April there were two further meetings with Champernowne on 18 and 19 April. On 3 May Sraffa went on a walk with Besicovitch. On the 23rd of that month he wrote to Champernowne. Apparently, Sraffa had doubts about whether to publish the work. These were effectively dispelled, it seems, by his Trinity College mathematical friend; on 31 May we find the following entry in Sraffa's diary: 'Besicovitch insiste che io pubblichi[;] il fatto che ho potuto prevedere risultati matematici interessanti mostra che c'è qualcosa nella teoria' ['Besicovitch insists that I publish; the fact that I was able to forsee interesting mathematical results shows that there must be something in the theory].

Later that year Sraffa attended (together with Champernowne and Kaldor) the famous conference on capital theory in Corfu, 4–11 September 1958 (see Lutz and Hague, 1961), where he met, among others, John Richard Hicks, Edmond Malinvaud, Paul A. Samuelson and Robert Solow. There are no indications in his diary that he spoke to his fellow economists about his book. However, from private conversations with Paul A. Samuelson we know that in Corfu Sraffa had told him that he was about to publish a book on capital theory.[9]

On the occasion of a visit to Italy during Christmas vacation of 1958 Sraffa prepared drafts of the Preface of his book, but was unsatisfied; in addition he carried out corrections of Part III. He sent copies to his friend Mattioli in Rome. Back in Cambridge he gave Pierangelo Garegnani the opportunity to read the manuscript between 14 and 19 January 1959. On 1 March he noted in his diary: '1 Birch – rimette a posto il mio esempio numerico' [Birch – fixes my numerical example].[10] The following day we read: 'dato a Dobb da leggere Part I del mio MS' [given to Dobb to read Part I of my MS]. On 16 March Sraffa had a 'seduta con Dobb: sue osservazioni dopo letto tutto il mio lavoro' [session with Dobb: his remarks after having read the whole work]. On 31 March he reported, in brackets: 'Consegnato MS per estimate' [manuscript has been presented for the estimate], and on 3 April an appointment with Burbridge, the man at CUP in charge of his book: 'accepted estimate U.P.' On 22 April he noted with some irritation, in brackets: 'Champernowne riparte senza avermi visto' [Champernowne leaves without having seen me]. (Champernowne, who had applied for a position in Cambridge, had visited the Faculty.) In a letter dated 2 May 1959 he was informed that people in the Department of Applied Economics of Cambridge University would check the calculations for the numerical examples contained in the book (see *SP* D3/12/112: 78). On 9 May Sraffa wrote a letter to Roy F. Harrod and on 10 May one to Champernowne. On 19 May he was informed by the Press: 'Burbridge: "Prod. of Com." comincia in settimana: bozze fra un mese o 6 sett'.

---

9 See also Samuelson's recollection of the event in Kurz (2000, p. 113).
10 Bryan Birch was a fellow of Trinity between 1956 and 1960 and had the set of rooms above Sraffa's in Neville's Court. He is presently Professor at the Mathematical Institute, Oxford.

[Burbridge: "Prod. of Com." starts within a week: proofs in a month or six weeks]. On 22 May we read: '1.45 phoned Champ. (Council has appointed him).' In the period from 29 May to 3 June Garegnani is reported to have read the entire manuscript. On 28 July Maurice Dobb is said to have provided 'correz. al mio MS' [corrections to my manuscript].

On 7 September 1959 Sraffa received from Burbridge, 'in segreto' [in secret], a set of proofs before they were corrected inhouse (this set seems to correspond to item No. 3371 of Sraffa's books). Next day a meeting with Champernowne is reported. The following day Sraffa left for Paris and then Milan, where on the 26th of the month he could happily note in his diary: 'Ricevuto 1ª bozza corretta completa di "P. of C. by C."' [Received the first corrected complete proofs of 'P. of C. by C.']. On the following day he wrote: 'rivisto bozze in albergo' [checked proofs in the hotel].

Back in Cambridge he had a 'seduta con Champernowne' [session with Champernowne] during the afternoon of 29 September. On 2 October he received four additional copies of the proofs from the binders. On the 9th of that month there is a note '9 Maurice (mie bozze)' [9 o'clock: Dobb (my proofs)]. Amartya Sen read the proofs on 22, 24, 25 and 28 October. On the following day Sraffa went on a walk with Carlo Brunner and noted in his diary: 'ridatogli bozze P. of C. by C.' [I gave him again the proofs of P. of C. by C.].[11]

On 3 November Sraffa reported to have 'phoned to Alister Watson & sent him proof to read'. In brackets he added: 'recd. 18th', which replicates the information given on the 18th of that month: 'received proofs with comments from A. Watson.' In the meantime Sraffa had another meeting with C. Brunner, on 8 November, concerning a 'report su [on] P.C.C.'; and two days later he reports 'p. 16 correction to Watson Brunner e Matt. [Mattioli]' – the reference being apparently a correction sent to the people mentioned. On 20 November Sraffa met Robert Neild at 7.30 p.m.; in his diary he noted: '9.30–12.30 Robert legge mie bozze' [9.30–12.30 Robert reads my proofs], an activity that is continued on the following two days: on the 21st between 11 a.m. and 1 p.m. and between 2.45 and 6 p.m.; and on the 22nd between 10.30 and 12 a.m. and between 3 and 6 p.m., where, as Sraffa did not fail to notice in brackets, Neild 'Salta i 3 cap. J.-P.' [Skipped chapters VII–IX]. On 13 December he noted: 'sent [my]self proofs Milan', that is, to Mattioli.

On 16 December Sraffa left for Paris and then Milan, where on the morning of the 19th he began to dictate an Italian translation of his book to a secretary in Mattioli's office. This work and the correction of the text, which was carried out in long sessions, assisted by Mattioli, was finished at 5 a.m. on 12 January 1960. To celebrate the event, Sraffa, Mattioli and Giulio Einaudi (the publisher of the Italian edition of Sraffa's book, a son of Sraffa's former teacher Luigi Einaudi) had champagne.

---

11 Unfortunately, we have not yet been able to identify Carlo Brunner.

Back in Cambridge Sraffa noted in his diary on 17 January: 'bozze' [proofs], referring presumably to the second set of proofs. On the 20th of that month he sent the English proofs to his friend and fellow economist Sergio Steve 'per confrontare con le ital.' [for a comparison with the Italian proofs]. On the same day he received the blurb for his book which he showed to Dobb and sent by express mail to Mattioli. On 24 January he noted: 'mandato 2^0 bozze ingl. a Steve (espresso) e lettera id[;] scritto Matt. (con bozze indice)' [I sent second proofs of the English version to Steve by express with a letter; I wrote to Mattioli (with proofs of the index)]. Two days later we read: '9 Maurice (queries on last doubts)'. On 18 February Sraffa noted: 'Handed in final proofs *for press!*' However, an entry of 20 March reads: 'espresso a [express to] Burbridge con [with] stoppress corrections.' Back in Italy (Rapallo) Sraffa received on 7 April '2 copie mio libro in fogli (di 32 pagine)' [two copies of my book in folio (of 32 pages)]. The following day he got from Einaudi the second set of proofs of the Italian version of his book and started working on them, assisted by Steve and Mattioli.

On 13 April he met Rosenstein-Rodan in Milan. Sraffa noted in his diary: 'Rosenstein has seen, in Boston, 2 or 3 weeks ago, my proofs: disagrees on "marginal" in Preface but not with the rest. Also Solow and Samuelson have seen and approved.'[12]

Back in Cambridge, Sraffa on 16 April noted in his diary: 'A Dennis [Robertson], a sua richiesta, le bozze del mio libro' [To Dennis, at his request, the proofs of my book]. The following day carries the entry: 'Dennis has read my Ch. I, will read no more. "A wicked book, ought to be burnt" '. And on 18 April we read: 'Dennis: "Not ashamed of yourself! an immoral book. Neo-ricardian & Neo-marxist" '. On 12 May Sraffa noted: 'To Joan, advance copy of my book'. While Sraffa, Joan Robinson and Richard Kahn ('Joan & Kahn', as Sraffa used to refer to them in his diary) had had numerous walks together during the last couple of years, the evidence suggests that Sraffa did not inform the two about the precise content and progress of his work. It was only after he had completed the book that he would break his silence.[13]

On 27 May 1960 we read: 'Pubblicaz. ediz. inglese "Production of Commodities" '. And on 6 June: 'Produzione Merci a 1/2 Merci pubblicato in Italia'.[14] On the front cover of Sraffa's copy of the 1959–60 *Cambridge Pocket Diary* these two important events are abbreviated as: 'P.C. x C 27/5 e P.M. 1/2 M. 6/6 pubblicato'.

---

12 We know from Paul Samuelson that in the spring of 1960 he received from Cambridge University Press page proofs of Sraffa's book. In the letter accompanying the proofs he was asked: 'Shall we bring out a separate American publication?', to which he replied 'in enthusiastic affirmation'. We also know from Samuelson that he showed the proofs to Solow, who, however, did not really study the book at that time. See again Samuelson's recollection in Kurz (2000, p. 113).

13 On 29 May he and Joan went for a long walk. Sraffa's diary notes: '2–7. Joan walk Hardwick e discusso, ahimè, il mio lavoro!' [and talk about, alas, my work]'. However, all's well that ends well: as Sraffa added, later that day they had 'champagne in hall'.

14 The correct Italian title is *Produzione di merci a mezzo di merci*. The Italian word 'mezzo' has both the meaning of 'means' and that of 'half': Sraffa has taken advantage of this.

5. Frank Ramsey

Sraffa began to formulate what he was later to call the 'conditions of production' or the 'production system' in terms of systems of simultaneous equations in the second half of the 1920s. Sraffa's 'first equations' refer to systems of production without a surplus, whereas his 'second equations' refer to systems with a surplus. At the end of November 1927 he put down equations representing two industries without and with a surplus (see *SP* D3/12/2: 32–5). One of the systems with a surplus is given by

$$11A = 3A + 9B$$
$$13B = 7A + 3B$$
$$S = 1A + 1B$$

where A and B indicate the prices of the two commodities and S the volume of the surplus product of the system as a whole. Sraffa observes that these equations are 'contradictory' (ibid.) and that 'the problem is overdetermined' (*SP* D3/12/11: 17).

On 26 June 1928 Sraffa summarized what Ramsey appears to have told him on the occasion of their meeting earlier that day:

(1) Equations with surplus: Exact solutions can be found for up to 4 equations. Approximate solutions can probably be found for any number of equations.
(2) It can probably be proved that, whatever the number of equations only *one* set of solutions is significant.
(3) Equations without surplus: each quantity must be expressed by *two* letters, one being the number of units, the other the unit of the commodity. Otherwise, if I use only one letter, this would stand for heterogeneous things and the sum would be meaningless.

(*SP* D3/12/2: 28)

This note should probably be seen in conjunction with another note in the same folder, which, however, has no date on it, but appears to have come out of the same meeting (ibid.: 29). The first three lines of the second document are in Sraffa's hand in pencil and the rest is in Ramsey's hand in ink. Sraffa put down the following system of equations:

$$v_a A = (v_a a_1 + v_b b_1 + c_1)r$$
$$v_b B = (v_a a_2 + v_b b_2 + c_2)r$$
$$C = (v_a a_3 + v_b b_3 + c_3)r$$

The interpretation is obvious: A, B and C are the gross outputs of commodities a, b and c, respectively, the a_is, b_is and c_is are the inputs of the three commodities in the production of commodity i ($i = 1, 2, 3$; where, obviously, 1 stands for a,

2 for b and 3 for c), and v_j is the value of commodity j ($j = a, b$), commodity c serving as numeraire; r is the interest factor. The part written by Ramsey is the following:

$$v_a \left(a_1 - \frac{A}{r} \right) + v_b b_1 + c_1 = 0$$

$$v_a a_2 + v_b \left(b_2 - \frac{B}{r} \right) + c_2 = 0$$

$$v_a a_3 + v_b b_3 + \left(c_3 - \frac{C}{r} \right) = 0$$

$$\begin{vmatrix} \left(a_1 - \dfrac{A}{r} \right), & b_1 & , & c_1 \\[2mm] a_2 & , & \left(b_2 - \dfrac{B}{r} \right), & c_2 \\[2mm] a_3 & , & b_3 & , & \left(c_3 - \dfrac{C}{r} \right) \end{vmatrix} = 0$$

As already stated, in our interpretation the two documents refer to the same meeting, but chronologically the order is to be reversed: the one containing the three remarks was a memo prepared by Sraffa after the meeting summarizing its results, whereas the other document was produced during the meeting. At first Sraffa appears not to have explicitly distinguished between the quantity and the price or value of a commodity, a fact to which Ramsey immediately seems to have objected. Sraffa then appears to have introduced the distinction during the conversation with Ramsey, as is shown by the second document. Ramsey then reformulated the system first by putting the system of homogeneous linear equations in its canonical form, then by setting the determinant of coefficients equal to zero in order to get a non-trivial solution. This was enough for him to recognize what became the first remark in Sraffa's memo of the meeting. This remark, in fact, says that although there are solutions for any number of equations (i.e. processes and therefore produced commodities), their computation is possible only for a number of commodities smaller than or equal to 4. There is no doubt that this refers to the fact that algebraic equations of a degree larger than 4 are not solvable in terms of radicals and, as a consequence, with the exception of some special cases, only approximate solutions can be found. Ramsey, in fact, calculated what in the spectral analysis of a matrix is called the characteristic equation (whether he knew this literature or not) and found that it is an algebraic equation whose degree is equal to the number of commodities involved.

As regards the second remark, as reported by Sraffa, we do not know, of course, what was at the back of Ramsey's mind. However, had the starting point of his remark been the Perron-Frobenius Theorem, then things would have been crystal clear. Yet in this case he could have been expected to draw Sraffa's attention to the existence of this theorem, which is a most powerful tool to solve the kind of problems Sraffa was interested in. There is no evidence to this effect; on the contrary, Sraffa's papers would seem to imply that none of his mathematical friends referred him to this theorem.[15]

The reference in the third remark to 'Equations without a surplus' was perhaps meant as a reminder that back home Sraffa had to carry out the change with regard to the equations with a surplus also with regard to the equations without a surplus.[16]

6. Alister Watson's help during the writing of *Production of Commodities*

Before we enter into a discussion of the details of how Watson assisted Sraffa in solving some of his mathematical problems, it is perhaps worth mentioning that Watson felt honoured by being asked to lend a helping hand. This is neatly expressed in the following letter by Watson dated 13 February 1958 (*SP* C 333):

> Dear Sraffa,
> Many thanks for your letter. I hope to get up to Cambridge on Saturday by midday. It will be very good to see you & I am very grateful to you for asking me.
>
> Yours sincerely,
> Alister Watson

Unfortunately, there is no record of the meeting (which is also mentioned in the diary).

The first note we came across referring to Alister Watson is entitled 'Alister Watson's visit to Cambridge' on 19 January 1947.[17] It is a memo by Sraffa about the content of the discussions they had (*SP* D3/12/44: 4, 6). Apparently, the main question was the uniqueness of the maximum rate of profits R:

> I. Q-system: several all-positive solutions. The only solution I have considered gives a value 0 to the qs of all *non-basic* processes.
>   However, suppose that one (or more) of the non-basic commodities [wheat] uses itself in its own production in a proportion greater than that of the basics taken as a whole (in other words, its own internal R is *smaller* than the R of the basic group), then there is another solution: for this non-basic commodity uses in its own production some basic ones, thus diminishing the ratio of basic means of production to basic products.

15 One is inclined to say that Sraffa was forced to develop that theorem himself. As we have argued elsewhere, Sraffa's demonstration of the existence and uniqueness of the 'Standard commodity' in the case of single production can be considered a (not fully complete) proof of this theorem (see Kurz and Salvadori, 1993).

16 In *SP* D3/12/2 there are three small sheets with symbols and figures in Ramsey's hand, but they seem to be of no use in the present context.

17 In Sraffa's papers there do not seem to be records of the meetings between the two in 1945, 1948 and 1949.

If, on the other hand, the internal R of the non-basic is larger than the R of the basic group, there is only one all-positive solution, with the q's for non-basics $= 0$.

[N.B. This has its symmetrical case in the P-system. If some of the non-basics have an own internal R *larger* than the basics group, there are alternative solutions with all the basic p's $= 0$, and bigger values of R.]

(*SP* D3/12/44: 4)

The note continues on page 6, whereas page 5 includes a note added by Sraffa on 23 February 1955. Let us report first the end of the note of 1947:

We can thus sum up:
There are several non-negative systems of roots of the Q-system. The system with the largest value for R has all zero values for the qs of the non-basic processes.

There are several non-negative systems of roots of the P-system. All these systems, except the one with the smallest value for R, have all zero values for the ps of the basic commodities.

[N.B. (1) The largest R of the Q-system is equal to the smallest R of the P-system. – (2) The proposition referring to the Q-system assumed that non basics have a *smaller* internal own ratio than r-basic; that referring to P-system assumes it *larger*]

(*SP* D3/12/44: 6)

The Q-system mentioned in this memo is certainly the system of equations which determine the Standard commodity

$$\mathbf{q}^T[\mathbf{I} - (1 + R)\mathbf{A}] = \mathbf{0}^T$$

where $\mathbf{q}$ is the vector of multipliers, $\mathbf{A}$ is the square matrix of material inputs, $\mathbf{I}$ is the identity matrix, and R is the maximum rate of profits. If there are non-basic commodities and if matrix $\mathbf{A}$ is in the canonical form, then the above equation can be stated as

$$\mathbf{q}_1^T[\mathbf{I} - (1 + R)\mathbf{A}_{11}] = (1 + R)\left[\mathbf{q}_2^T\mathbf{A}_{21} + \mathbf{q}_3^T\mathbf{A}_{31} + \cdots + \mathbf{q}_s^T\mathbf{A}_{s1}\right]$$

$$\mathbf{q}_2^T[\mathbf{I} - (1 + R)\mathbf{A}_{22}] = (1 + R)\left[\mathbf{q}_3^T\mathbf{A}_{32} + \cdots + \mathbf{q}_s^T\mathbf{A}_{s2}\right]$$

$$\vdots$$

$$\mathbf{q}_s^T[\mathbf{I} - (1 + R)\mathbf{A}_{ss}] = \mathbf{0}^T$$

It is clear from Sraffa's memo that he had arrived at the solution obtained by setting $\mathbf{q}_i = \mathbf{0}$ ($i = 2, 3, \ldots, s$), $R = (1 - \lambda_1)/\lambda_1$ (where λ_i is the Perron-Frobenius eigenvalue of matrix $\mathbf{A}_{ii}$), and $\mathbf{q}_1 = \mathbf{x}_1$ (where $\mathbf{x}_i$ is the left eigenvector of matrix $\mathbf{A}_{ii}$ corresponding to λ_i). But Watson showed him that if the Perron-Frobenius eigenvalue of submatrix $\mathbf{A}_{jj}$, λ_j, is larger than the Perron-Frobenius eigenvalues of matrices $\mathbf{A}_{11}, \mathbf{A}_{22}, \ldots, \mathbf{A}_{j-1,j-1}$, then another non-negative solution is found by setting $\mathbf{q}_i = \mathbf{0}$ $(i = j+1, j+2, \ldots, s)$, $R = (1 - \lambda_j)/\lambda_j$, $\mathbf{q}_j = \mathbf{x}_j$, and

$$\mathbf{q}_i^\mathrm{T} = (1 + R)\left[\mathbf{q}_{i+1}^\mathrm{T}\mathbf{A}_{i+1,i} + \mathbf{q}_{i+2}^\mathrm{T}\mathbf{A}_{i+2,i} + \cdots + \mathbf{q}_j^\mathrm{T}\mathbf{A}_{ji}\right]\left[\mathbf{I} - (1 + R)\mathbf{A}_{ii}\right]^{-1}$$

$(i = 1, 2, \ldots, j - 1)$. Of course, several of these solutions may exist and to each of them corresponds an R smaller than that found by Sraffa and none of these solutions exists if 'the internal R of the non-basic is larger than the R of the basic group', that is, if $\lambda_1 > \lambda_j$ $(j = 2, 3, \ldots, s)$. These are the results summarized in Sraffa's memo with respect to the 'Q-system'.

Let us turn now to the 'P-system'. This is clearly the price system when the wage rate equals zero and, as a consequence, the rate of profits equals the maximum rate of profits:

$$\mathbf{p} = (1 + R)\mathbf{A}\mathbf{p}$$

where $\mathbf{p}$ gives the price vector. If there are non-basic commodities and if matrix $\mathbf{A}$ is in the canonical form, then the price equation can be stated as

$$\mathbf{p}_1 = (1 + R)\mathbf{A}_{11}\mathbf{p}_1$$
$$\mathbf{p}_2 = (1 + R)(\mathbf{A}_{21}\mathbf{p}_1 + \mathbf{A}_{22}\mathbf{p}_2)$$
$$\vdots$$
$$\mathbf{p}_s = (1 + R)(\mathbf{A}_{s1}\mathbf{p}_1 + \mathbf{A}_{s2}\mathbf{p}_2 + \cdots + \mathbf{A}_{ss}\mathbf{p}_s)$$

It seems that the solution Sraffa had in mind prior to Watson's visit in January 1947 was $R = (1 - \lambda_1)/\lambda_1$, $\mathbf{p}_1 = \mathbf{y}_1$ (where $\mathbf{y}_i$ is the right eigenvector of matrix $\mathbf{A}_{ii}$ corresponding to λ_i), and

$$\mathbf{p}_i = (1 + R)[\mathbf{I} - (1 + R)\mathbf{A}_{ii}]^{-1}[\mathbf{A}_{i1}\mathbf{p}_1 + \mathbf{A}_{i2}\mathbf{p}_2 + \cdots + \mathbf{A}_{i,i-1}\mathbf{p}_{i-1}]$$

$(i = 2, 3, \ldots, s)$. But this solution is semipositive (actually positive) *if and only if* $\lambda_1 > \lambda_i$ $(i = 2, 3, \ldots, s)$. The memo *does not* notice this fact. It *does* notice another fact, that is, that if $\lambda_j > \lambda_i$ $(i = j+1, j+2, \ldots, s)$, then a non-negative solution can be found by setting $\mathbf{p}_i = \mathbf{0}$ $(i = 1, 2, \ldots, j-1)$, $R = (1 - \lambda_j)/\lambda_j$, $\mathbf{p}_j = \mathbf{y}_j$, and

$$\mathbf{p}_i = (1 + R)[\mathbf{I} - (1 + R)\mathbf{A}_{ii}]^{-1}[\mathbf{A}_{ij}\mathbf{p}_j + \mathbf{A}_{i,j+1}\mathbf{p}_{j+1} + \cdots + \mathbf{A}_{i,i-1}\mathbf{p}_{i-1}]$$

$(i = j+1, j+2, \ldots, s)$. Note that in all these solutions the prices of basics are zero and, if $\lambda_1 > \lambda_i$ $(i = 2, 3, \ldots, s)$, the R so determined is larger than $(1 - \lambda_1)/\lambda_1$.

The set of assumptions implicit in the memo is not entirely clear. Certainly it is assumed that there is at least one basic. But all the remarks on the 'P-system' are correct only if $\lambda_1 > \lambda_i$ $(i = 2, 3, \ldots, s)$, whereas in this case the remarks on the 'Q-system' become uninteresting.

Let us now turn to the supplement of 1955. Sraffa wrote:

> We can avoid all these complications by, from the start, removing "manually" all the non-basic equations and dealing with a system composed exclusively of basic commodities [these to be defined, before the removal, as comm.s which directly or indirectly enter all the others](*) and then we can say that there is only one all-positive [and not merely non-negative] solution for the ps and the qs.
>
> [N.B. One point which needs clearing about the Watson alternative solution is this: does it remain true that if we multiply the equations by any pair of solutions of the ps and qs, which is not the all-positive pair of solutions, the sum of all the equations is null?]
>
> (*) For practical application this good enough. But discuss in a note the abstract possibilities of this not being so, for example, of the system falling into two or more self-contained (self-basic) groups of commodities – as if one lumped together the equations of two countries which have no commercial relations (& treating, of course, iron in country A as a different commodity from iron in B).
>
> The more 'elegant' system of solving the complete system (with qs of non-basics = 0) can be discussed here with the Watson difficulties (query, did he derive them from von Neumann?).
>
> > (*SP* D3/12/44: 5)

In this note we find what was to become the expository strategy of *Production of Commodities*. In §35 (the last section of chapter IV), whose title in the table of contents is 'Non-basics excluded', Sraffa argues that 'We may in consequence simplify the discussion by assuming that all non-basic equations are eliminated at the outset so that only basic industries come under consideration' (Sraffa 1960: 25). This is essentially the idea expressed in the note of 1955 of 'removing "manually" all the non-basic equations and dealing with a system composed exclusively of basic commodities' (D3/12/44: 5). In the book the argument justifying this choice is completed with a footnote referring to the 'freak case of the type referred to in Appendix B' (Sraffa 1960, p. 25, fn.), that is, to what in the note above is called 'the Watson alternative solution'.

In the 1955 note, the question in brackets refers to the reason why the proof of the uniqueness of the solution of the 'Q-system' provided in §41 of the book for the case in which the non-basics are excluded does not apply when they are *not* excluded. The point is that now both some p's and some q's can be zero and the zeros can be distributed in such a way that the scalar product of the price vector with a solution of the 'Q-system' different from the Standard one can be zero even if both vectors are semipositive. This possibility can be excluded when one of the two vectors is positive, as is the case in which non-basics are excluded.

On 29 April 1955 Watson visited Sraffa again. In February of that year, apparently in order to prepare for the visit, Sraffa annotated his previous notes. After the visit he produced a memo of their discussions (*SP* D3/12/58: 8–9):

> Points discussed: (Told him the proof of uniqueness of all-positive solution of q's and p's)
>
> (1) The value of R which corresponds to the all-positive p's and q's is the smallest of the values of R. This is proved by the same method by which solution is sought by approximation through successive substitutions. (By the same method Watson proves existence of an all positive solution of ps, which I prove by continuity from $r = 0$.)
>
> (2) All the values of R in p-system are equal to the corresponding values in the q-system. (This is proved by means of the determinant of the coefficients, which is the same in the two systems).
>
> (3) Discussed the possibility of proving uniqueness in case of joint products, when there may be negative qs and ps. Does not regard it as likely.
>
> [Subsequently I have concluded that *if* there is an all-positive solution of the qs (as there *must* be for fixed cap. and there *may* be for joint products) then uniqueness can be proved for any really existent system: for at *some* value of r this must have all positive ps (i.e. at the *actual* value of r); now this r can be represented in terms of R, & then the proof can be applied.]
>
> [With ref. to N. 2 above. My proof of positive prices in the one-process-one-product system is as follows. At $r = 0$ values are proportional to quantities of labour, & these being positive, values must be positive. Now increase gradually r until wages fall to 0. Can any price turn negative as a result? in order to do so, the change being continuous, it must first become 0; but to do so, wages being positive, the price of one of the commod. used in its production must become negative. So no price can become negative first. – This does not apply to joint prod. or Fix. Cap. For the price of a joint prod. can become 0 without need that any other price is negative; it suffices that the price of the other joint product becomes large enough.]

This memo clearly refers to some of the proofs included in *Production of Commodities*, expecially those of chapter V. An echo of the argument (2) in the memo is in §29 where it is proved, among other things, that the maximum rate of profits coincides with the 'Standard ratio'. Interestingly, the proof in the book does not use the determinant argument, but follows from an economic reasoning. In §37 (which is the first paragraph of chapter V, apart from the summary of the chapter presented in §36) Sraffa proves the existence of the Standard system, following a procedure which seems to correspond to that described in the memo as 'by approximation through successive substitutions'.[18] Further, in §39 the positivity

---

18 We will come back to this procedure in the next section.

of prices for each rate of profits between zero and the maximum rate of profits is proved following the procedure illustrated above, based on the fact that no price can become negative before any other. In the book, but not in the memo, the proof is completed with a reference to the fact that the 'prices of basic products cannot become negative through becoming infinite' (Sraffa 1960, p. 28, fn.). The proof of the uniqueness of the Standard system which is sketched in the memo for some possible case of joint production is actually the proof used for single production in §41. Finally, in §42 we find the proof that 'The value of R which corresponds to the all-positive p's and q's is the smallest of the values of R' mentioned above. In §72 of *Production of Commodities* we find also the reason why the proof of the positivity of prices provided in §39 does not apply when there is joint production. Finally, an echo of the above reference to fixed capital is found in §84: 'a system which contained no other element of joint production besides what is implied in the presence of fixed capital would in general have an all-positive Standard commodity, thus reproducing in this respect the simplicity of the system of single-product industries' (Sraffa 1960, p. 73).

7. Alister Watson's help at the time of the corrections of the galley-proofs

Watson was of great help to Sraffa when the galley-proofs of the book manuscript had to be corrected. As mentioned above, on 3 November 1959 Sraffa phoned Alister Watson and 'sent him proofs to read'. In his letter dated 17 November 1959 (*SP* D3/12/112: 71–72), which Sraffa received the following day, Watson wrote:

Dear Piero,
I must start with the most abject apologies for having kept your proofs so long. I found it much more difficult than I had expected to give the necessary time to it, and ended up by going sick.

I have no doubt that it should be published.

I have marked a few corrections in the proofs, in ink. Some of these are points where I suspect that the error was in your copying corrections onto this copy. Other suggestions are on separate sheets enclosed.

There are two general points. First, I think that the general treatment of Multiple-Product Industries, in Chapters VII, VIII and IX, is much the most difficult part of the book, and I fear the reader's interest may flag at this stage. Would it be worth while to explain that in the applications that are to follow many of the points are clearer and that these are merely necessary preliminaries?

Secondly, it seems to me so important that you take the rate of profits as variable from the outside that it should be given even more emphasis and explanation (at the end of Chap. V) than it now has. Otherwise, it might be asked, for example, why in §§50 and 57, we should not assume that the number of processes is one more than the number of products, so that everything, including the rate of profits, is fixed. The answer is given only by the rest of the book, but the dynamic role of the rate of profits might be foreshadowed. Many congratulations on finishing the job!

Yours ever
Alister

Enclosed in the letter was a note containing eleven queries (*SP* D3/12/112: 74–5). These queries concerned, as we will see, all parts of the book. Sraffa replied on 22 November, as we can see from a minute of his reply (*SP* D3/12/112: 77):

Dear Alister,
Thank you so much for your letter & note. I have now gone through the thing again and have adopted your suggestions whenever they could be fitted in easily. One or two are left over, although I entirely accept them, as involving rather more work & more energy than I can muster at the moment.

On looking over this book once more I find it most unsatisfactory, & at the moment I am inclined to suppress it: however, this is a subject on which I have so often fluctuated that I may well change my mind once more & let the printer to go ahead with it.

I am really most grateful for all the trouble you have taken about: whether this thing is to be born or mummified it will be much less bad because of your intervention.

But, when will you come for visit to Cambridge?

The Press received the marked first proofs on 26 November (*SP* D3/12/106). In the Sraffa papers and library there are three sets of first proofs (*SP* D3/12/106–7 and No. 3753; the first is the marked set sent to the publisher, the other two are bound), but in none of them did we find the marks in ink mentioned in Watson's letter. So we cannot compare what Watson really received with the second proofs. Nor can we evaluate the suggested corrections that Watson put directly on the proofs. However, we can analyse the note by Watson and compare the first proofs (*SP* D3/12/106) with the second proofs (*SP* D3/12/108), and, when necessary, with the published book. Sraffa added, in pencil, a question mark to the third and seventh of the queries, a 'no' on the margin of the fourth query, and a typical checking sign to all other queries.

Before we discuss Watson's queries, let us first address the two 'general points' mentioned in his letter. Sraffa took the first one very seriously and, in fact, added a footnote appended to the title of chapter VII:

The next three chapters on Joint Production are in the main a preliminary to the discussion of Fixed Capital and Land in chs. X and XI. Readers who find them too abstract may like to move on to chs. X and XI and to refer back when necessary.

This footnote was first inserted as a note 'in not too small type' under the title of Part II in the title page (p. 41, see *SP* D3/12/107), but then, with a letter sent on 4 January 1960, Sraffa decided to have it as a footnote appended to the title of chapter VII (p. 43, p. 42 being blind). On the contrary, the second general point raised by Watson does not seem to have prompted Sraffa to change the text.

Let us now address Watson's queries. The first query by Watson reads: 'p. 10. §9. Should there not be more discussion of this point?' The published version of §9 is very brief:

> We shall also hereafter assume that the wage is paid post factum as a share of the annual product, thus abandoning the classical economists' idea of a wage 'advanced' from capital. We retain however the supposition of an annual cycle of production with an annual market.

The only difference with respect to the first proofs is that in here the adjective 'annual' to 'product' is missing: it was only added at this stage. This change does not seem to have been prompted by Watson's query; it only implied bringing the expression in line with the expressions 'annual cycle of production' and 'annual market' used in the second sentence of the section.

The second query refers to §12. The preceding section introduces the equations of production with the amounts of labour explicitly represented, and in §12 the 'national income' is taken as numeraire. The section ends with an observation which, in the first proofs, reads: 'The result of adding the wage as one of the variables is that the number of these now exceeds the number of equations by one and the system is free to move along one of the axes'. Watson commented on this: ' "along one of the axes" is inaccurate. Suggest "with one degree of freedom", with perhaps an explanation that if any one of the unknowns is fixed the others will be fixed too'. Sraffa followed the suggestion. In the second proofs as well as in the printed book we read the following sentence, and the appropriate changes are pencilled on the first proofs:

> The result of adding the wage as one of the variables is that the number of these now exceeds the number of equations by one and the system can move with one degree of freedom: and if one of the variables is fixed the others will be fixed too.

The third query refers to the end of §34, but it is not clear; Sraffa in fact added a question mark. The only change we find from the first to the second proofs is a correction of a misprint.

The fourth query refers to §37, that is, the section devoted to prove the existence of the Standard system. As the reader will recall, this proof uses an algorithm which consists of the repetition of two steps until the solution is found. (The algorithm may require an infinite number of steps in order to converge.) The first step consists 'in changing the proportions of the industries', the second 'in reducing in the same ratio the quantities produced by all industries, while leaving unchanged the quantities used as means of production' (p. 26). Watson observed: 'It isn't quite obvious that the first type of step can always be carried out'. There are several changes between the first and the second proofs and between the latter and the printed book, but they do not seem to be related to Watson's query. If we look at Sraffa's description of the algorithm, it is clear that the first step can be carried out, but there are many (actually infinitely many) ways to perform it, and from a mathematical point of view the description of an algorithm needs to be uniquely defined.

The problem is to prove that there is a scalar λ and a semipositive vector $\mathbf{q}$ such that for a given semipositive indecomposable square matrix $\mathbf{A}$

$$\mathbf{q}^{\mathrm{T}}[\lambda \mathbf{I} - \mathbf{A}] = \mathbf{0}^{\mathrm{T}}$$

Sraffa's algorithm can be described in the following way:

[i.0] There are $\mathbf{q}_{i-1}^{\mathrm{T}} \geq \mathbf{0}^{\mathrm{T}}$ and $\lambda_{i-1} \geq 0$ such that $\mathbf{q}_{i-1}^{\mathrm{T}}[\lambda_{i-1}\mathbf{I} - \mathbf{A}] \geq \mathbf{0}^{\mathrm{T}}$.

[i.1] Find $\mathbf{q}_i^{\mathrm{T}} \geq \mathbf{0}^{\mathrm{T}}$ such that $\mathbf{q}_i^{\mathrm{T}}[\lambda_{i-1}\mathbf{I} - \mathbf{A}] > \mathbf{0}^{\mathrm{T}}$ and $\mathbf{q}_i^{\mathrm{T}}\mathbf{1} = \mathbf{q}_{i-1}^{\mathrm{T}}\mathbf{1}$.

[i.2] Find $\lambda_i (< \lambda_{i-1})$ such that $\mathbf{q}_i^{\mathrm{T}}[\lambda_i\mathbf{I} - \mathbf{A}] \not> \mathbf{0}^{\mathrm{T}}$ and $\mathbf{q}_i^{\mathrm{T}}[\lambda_i\mathbf{I} - \mathbf{A}] \geq \mathbf{0}^{\mathrm{T}}$.

[i.3'] If $\mathbf{q}_i^{\mathrm{T}}[\lambda_i\mathbf{I} - \mathbf{A}] = \mathbf{0}^{\mathrm{T}}$, then end of the algorithm: λ_i and $\mathbf{q}_i$ are the required scalar λ and vector $\mathbf{q}$.

[i.3''] If $\mathbf{q}_i^{\mathrm{T}}[\lambda_i\mathbf{I} - \mathbf{A}] \geq \mathbf{0}^{\mathrm{T}}$, then the algorithm can re-start.

Since the sequence $\{\lambda_i\}$ is decreasing and bounded from below ($\lambda_i > 0$), it converges to the requested solution.

The steps [i.l] and [i.2] are the two steps mentioned by Sraffa. The second is well defined since

$$\lambda_i = \max_h \frac{\mathbf{q}_i^{\mathrm{T}}\mathbf{A}\mathbf{e}_h}{\mathbf{q}_i^{\mathrm{T}}\mathbf{e}_h}$$

whereas the first step is not well defined: there are infinitely many ways to perform it. Being a mathematician, Watson was understandably concerned about this fact. It is not clear whether Sraffa understood Watson's concern.[19]

The fifth query by Watson refers to what is now footnote 2 on page 43 of the book. (As we have seen, in order to take account of the first general point raised by Watson, Sraffa added at the stage of the first proofs what is now footnote 1 on page 43.) The footnote in the first proofs reads:

Incidentally, since the proportions in which the two commodities are produced by any one method will in general be different from those in which they are required for use, the existence of two methods of producing them in different

---

19 A simple way to find a well defined algorithm is to set

$$\mathbf{q}_i^T = \frac{\mathbf{q}_{i-1}^T \mathbf{1}}{\mathbf{q}_{i-1}^T (\mathbf{I} - \mathbf{A})^{-1}\mathbf{1}} \mathbf{q}_{i-1}^T (\mathbf{I} - \mathbf{A})^{-1}$$

proportions will make it possible to obtain the required proportion of the two products by an appropriate combination of the two methods.

Watson commented on this: 'For "will make it possible ..." perhaps "may make it possible ..." would be clearer (since negative multipliers may be needed)'.

Sraffa changed the text, but in the opposite direction, rendering the meaning less ambiguous and more determinate. Of course, he was aware that negative multipliers may be needed (see §53), but negative multipliers, while permissible in a fictitious construction such as the Standard system, are not so with regard to the actual requirements for use. In fact, in the second proofs as well as in the printed book we read the following sentence, and the appropriate changes are pencilled on the first proofs:

> Incidentally, considering the proportions in which the two commodities are produced by any one method will in general be different from those in which they are required for use, the existence of two methods of producing them in different proportions will be necessary for obtaining the required proportion of the two products through an appropriate combination of the two methods.

With respect to the sixth query, Sraffa again followed Watson's suggestion. This refers to §63, devoted to the construction of the Standard system in the case of joint production. In the first proofs the comment by Sraffa on the equations defining the multipliers of the Standard system is: 'These equations are of the gth degree, so that there may be up to g possible sets of values or roots for R and the q's; and each set will represent a Standard commodity of different composition.' Watson commented on this: 'Substitute: "These equations give an equation for R of the jth degree, so that there may be up to j possible values of R and corresponding sets of values of the q's; and each set ...".'.

Sraffa carried out the suggested change (which seems to include a change from g and G to j and J also in the equation, unless these corrections were not pencilled by Sraffa in the set of proofs that Watson received) on the first proofs, but both in the second proofs and in the printed book the passage begins with 'The' instead of 'These'.

The seventh query refers to what is now §79 (it was §78 in the first proofs because Sraffa at that stage divided §75 into §§75 and 76). It is devoted to the fact that with fixed capital the reduction to dated quantities of labour is generally impossible. Like the third query also the seventh appears to have been unclear to Sraffa. At any rate, there is no change from the first to the second proofs, and none of the changes from the latter to the book appear to be due to Watson's suggestion.

The eighth query refers to what is now §86 devoted to extensive differential rent. In the first proofs the text was:

> There will therefore be n production-equations, to which must be added the condition that the least productive land pays no rent; and to these equations

there will correspond an equal number of variables representing the rents of the n qualities of land and the price of corn.

Watson commented on this:

> Whence does the definition of 'the least productive land' arise, if the order of fertilities is not defined independently of the rents? The answer is perhaps contained in §87, but, if so, a forward reference should be given.

Sraffa followed the suggestion by changing the text and adding a footnote. In the second proofs as well as in the book we read the following sentence, and the appropriate changes are pencilled on the first proofs:

> There will therefore be n production-equations, to which must be added the condition that one of the lands pays no rent;[1] and to these equations there will correspond an equal number of variables representing the rents of the n qualities of land and the price of corn.
>
> 1 By this token only can it be identified as the least productive land in use (cf. p. 75).

This elicits two remarks. First, an answer to Watson's question was not to be found in §87 (§88 of the printed book), devoted to an explanation of the relation of rent to 'extensive' and 'intensive' diminishing returns. In this section, in fact, the case of lands of different qualities is considered 'readily recognised' and not really dealt with. Second, although Sraffa's wording was misleading and required some change, the formal exposition was correct. In fact, in the first proofs, as well as in the second proofs and in the book, we read in the same section:

> the condition that one of the rents should be zero can be written
>
> $$\rho_1 \rho_2 \ldots \rho_n = 0$$
>
> the relevant solution being always the one in which the ρ's are $\geqslant 0$.

The ninth query by Watson refers to §89 of the printed book (§88 of the first proofs), devoted to the complication introduced by a multiplicity of agricultural products. In the first proofs we read: 'It may however be noticed that only *one* of the crops could be raised by two separate methods; apart from that, the number of processes would have to be equal to the number of products.' Watson commented: 'There is something wrong with the sense of this as corrected'. Sraffa responded by changing the wording, but not the meaning. In fact, there does not seem to be anything wrong with the passage. However, the adjoint 'as corrected' appears to indicate that what was 'wrong' was a correction pencilled by Sraffa on the set of proofs received by Watson (which we have not found, as mentioned). In the second proofs, as well as in the book, we read the following sentence, and the appropriate changes are pencilled on the first proofs: 'It may however be noted that only for *one* of the crops would two separate methods of production be compatible; for the rest, the number of processes would have to be equal to the number of products.'

The last two queries by Watson refer to §95 of the first proofs (§96 of the published book), devoted to the choice of technique in joint production. In this case when an additional method is introduced, it is not clear what is the method which is superseded (in single production it is that which produces the same commodity as the additional method). The sentence in the first proofs is: 'And the problem is how to identify among the pre-existing methods the one to which the new method is an alternative'. The comment is: ' "And the problem . . ." It is not made clear enough why this is the problem. (For example, several methods might be superseded together.)'

In response to the problem raised by Watson Sraffa substituted 'is' with 'arises of', without analysing the question more deeply. The last query concerns the footnote on page 87 of the book (page 86 of the first proofs). In the first proofs the footnote reads: 'We assume here that no commodity's price behaves in the peculiar way described in §§71–2'. The 'peculiar way' consists of the possibility that in joint production a price may fall faster than the wage as a consequence of a change in the rate of profits. Watson commented: 'Why do we have to assume this, and how much of a restriction is it?' Sraffa makes only a small change by adding after 'here' the parenthetical sentence '(and it is essential for the conclusion)'. However, things are much more complex than both Sraffa and Watson were able to recognize at that time (as the following literature has proved; see for instance Salvadori (1985)). It cannot be excluded, of course, that had Sraffa been given the opportunity to pay greater attention to Watson's ultimate two queries, he could have grasped the complexity of the problems involved and found a solution, but this would certainly have been 'involving rather more work & more energy than I can muster at the moment' (*SP* D3/12/112: 77).

The historical reconstruction provided above shows how Sraffa at the stage of the correction of the galley-proofs went about the comments he got from his mathematical friends. He carefully scrutinised their concerns and suggestions, but he did not always follow their advice. There is a set of cases in which he interpreted the suggestions as indicative of the fact that his presentation needed to be changed in order to avoid possible misunderstandings. The remaining cases are those where he either had difficulty in understanding the concerns of his mathematical friends or considered these concerns as uninteresting from the point of view of an economist. In the latter cases he simply set the problems aside.

8. Excursus: Harry Johnson's correction of a slip

In a letter dated 15 May 1961 Harry G. Johnson wrote to Sraffa: 'I have been working over your book with a class of graduates here. We have come across two places in which we think your argument wrong'. Here we are interested only in his first criticism, which relates to a slip in two of Sraffa's mathematical expressions in the book and with regard to which Sraffa, before replying to Johnson, contacted

Watson and Champernowne. (The other criticism refers to the problem of reduction in the case of fixed capital in §79 and derives from a misunderstanding on Johnson's part; it need not concern us.) As regards the slip, Johnson pointed out:

> The two formulas in §47 at the top of p. 37 are wrong.
>
> $$\frac{\mathrm{d}}{\mathrm{d}r}\left(1 - \frac{r}{R}\right)(1 + r)^n = \frac{(1 + r)^n}{R}\left[\frac{(R - r)n}{1 + r} - 1\right]$$
>
> This is zero when $n = (1 + r)/(R - r)$ or $r = (nR - 1)/(n + 1)$, as contrasted with your two formulas. Just as a check, I computed the value of r according to my and your formula at which the curves in Fig. 2 should reach their maxima. The results of my formula checked with the figure, whereas your formula gave too high an r.
>
> (*SP* D3/12/111: 223)

To this Johnson added the numerical calculations referred to.

Sraffa answered Johnson on 21 June (see draft of letter, *SP* D3/12/111: 225–6; see also Johnson's reply of 27 June in which he refers to Sraffa's letter dated 21 June, *SP* D3/12/111: 227–8). Between 15 May and 21 June the only note in Sraffa's diary concerning this question is dated 22 May: 'written Watson'. On 21 June he listed several people in his diary to whom he had written letters, but Johnson's name is absent. Yet there is some further material in Sraffa's papers related to the issue under consideration. There are three communications by Champernowne and a letter by Alister Watson. Besicovitch does not seem to have been involved in this. The reason for this is probably that during most of the period he was in the United States and, as Sraffa noted in his diary, came back only on 18 June.

As stated, the suggested correction concerns §47, which is devoted to the pattern of movement of the individual terms of the reduction to dated quantities of labour as distribution changes, when the Standard commodity is used as numeraire. The reader will recall that §46 introduces the reduction to dated quantities of labour, whereas §48 uses the results of the preceding section to show that the movements of prices are complex (Sraffa provides the example of the 'old wine' and the 'oak chest'). Let us consider §47 more closely. The general form of any nth individual term of the reduction, when the Standard commodity is used as numeraire, is:

$$L_n\left(\frac{R - r}{R}\right)(1 + r)^n$$

It is shown in the section that if $n \leqslant 1/R$, then such a term is a decreasing function of r (in the relevant range $0 \leqslant r \leqslant R$), otherwise it is first increasing and then decreasing. The maximum is obtained for the values of r and n that satisfy the equation obtained by setting the derivative with respect to r equal to zero:

$$\frac{L_n}{R}\left[-(1 + r)^n + n(R - r)(1 + r)^{n-1}\right] = 0$$

The corrected values in the relevant range are those determined by Harry Johnson and his students. Instead the values we find in the 1960 book are:

$$n = \frac{1}{R - r}$$

$$r = R - \frac{1}{n}$$

There appears to be only one way to obtain these wrong expressions, that is, by failing to reduce the power of the second term of the derivative from n to $n - 1$. And Alister Watson thought this could have been the origin of the slip. Confronted with the riddle, he apologised to Sraffa for having overlooked the latter when reading the proofs. In a letter dated 9 June 1961 he wrote:

Dear Piero,
I am sorry I have taken so very long in answering your letter – which is not due to the difficulty of the questions, but only to my delay in getting round to have a proper look at them.
    Johnson is quite right about the first point. I find the formula $r = (nR - 1)/(n + 1)$ in my own notes, but tucked away so that I obviously hadn't thought of drawing your attention to it & it never occurred to me to check the passage in your book. The slip is made rather less important by the fact that the last sentence of the paragraph is, in any case, correct.
    I haven't been able to think of any particularly plausible way in which the slip occurred – it does amount in a way to replacing $n + 1$ by n & this could have been done I suppose by Besicovitch in a hurry.
    As for the last point, I suppose you are right in your interpreatation of Johnson's meaning. I don't know if it would be of interest, either to you or to him, but I have recently come across a paper giving a brief statement and bibliography of the theorems of the type you prove and use that have been dealt with mathematically.[20] This might perhaps help to make clear to him that others besides yourself have thought it necessary to prove such things and that they are distinct from the simpler result he quotes.
    It was good to hear about the reviews: it certainly seems as if some interest is being taken in your work, in particular, that the market hasn't been spoilt by the 'games theory' type of attack that is so fashionable.

Yours ever
Alister Watson
(*SP* D3/12/111: 456–7)

---

20 On the top of the letter Sraffa wrote in pencil: 'yes, send bibliography', but we were not able to trace it in his papers. It is quite possible that the 'bibliography of the type of theorems' Sraffa is said to have proved refers to the Perron-Frobenius Theorem. If so, then Watson's hint may thus be interpreted as rendering some additional support to our above claim that Sraffa did not know that this theorem existed because his mathematical friends had not drawn his attention to it.

Watson's interpretation is not implausible per se: it could have been Besicovitch who, 'in a hurry', had blundered. Watson was willing to assume some responsability for the fact that the slip had crept into the published text. Yet in the light of the further material available to us, Watson's interterpretation cannot be sustained. Let us first turn to Champernowne's reaction when confronted with the problem by Sraffa.

On 31 May Champernowne sent Sraffa the following note (*SP* D3/12/111: 462):

> Dear Sraffa,
> The formula still doesn't seem to come out to $n = 1/(R - r)$ but to $n = (1 + R)/(R - r)$ when wages are advanced: conversely the formula for r becomes
>
> $$r = R - \frac{1 + R}{n}$$

Apparently, Sraffa was not of the opinion that this answer settled the question. On 2 June Champernowne sent another note (*SP* D3/12/111: 460), writing, among other things:

> I return HGJ's letter. He is right on the first point. I can't follow your argument which he attacks in his second point – but I gather from you that you could cope with that one.
>
> I keep trying to get your answer relating to the first point by assuming labour paid in advance but although I keep getting contradictory answers I never seem to get yours.
>
> Tomorrow I get my examination scripts so I would like to stop thinking about the production of commodities by commodities.
>
> Yours sincerely
> D.G. Champernowne

A card from Champernowne to Sraffa dated 20 June 1961 is again on this problem: 'A possible explanation of the R not appearing as denominator in Besicovitch's expression would be that he took as unit of value the total capital or (same thing) total input: where as you took as unit of value the net national income' (*SP* D3/12/111: 230). The reference is not directly to Johnson's letter, but seemingly to an old note by Besicovitch. The idea is close at hand that in that note Besicovitch had put forward a calculation using a different amount of the Standard commodity (i.e., 'total capital') as unit of value. However, also this explanation does not settle the case, because a change of the kind indicated affects the derivative in the sense that it is now multiplied by a positive constant, but this change does not affect the relationship between r and n obtained by the condition that the derivative equals zero.

Champernowne's communications to Sraffa reflect that he and Sraffa took pains to understand the origin of the slip. They first checked what happens if wages are paid *ante factum*. Although the answer is different from the one when wages are paid *post factum*, it is also different from the published one. Then Sraffa, scrutinising his papers, appears to have found an old note in the hand of Besicovitch where R is missing in the denominator. This fact was interpreted, but it did not disclose the origin of the slip.

Folder D3/12/62 contains the material Sraffa had grouped under the heading 'Fluctuations of price with variations of r'. The first part of D3/12/62: 2 is in Besicovitch's hand and provides the calculation starting from the *non-constant* part of the nth individual term of the reduction, which in the document is indicated with letter 'I':

$$I = (R - r)(1 + r)^{n-1}$$

This is clearly the document at which Champernowne hinted: the wages are supposed to be paid *ante factum* and there is no R in the denominator. (This however does not seem to be a consequence of a different amount of the Standard commodity being used as numeraire, but just of setting aside the constants which do not affect the result.) The findings obtained are correct and it was certainly not Besicovitch who 'in a hurry' blundered. This document has no date, but there is an insertion in it dated 1/12/42 whose first part is also in Besicovitch's hand. In the same folder we find two notes written by Sraffa on 28 and 29 December 1956, respectively, which refer to the issue and here we find the origin of the blunder. The first note (28 December 1956) reads:

> The relation of r to w was different in 1942 from what it is in 1956. (r was a linear function of $w(1 + r)$ in 1942 and it is ... [a linear function] of w in 1956).
>
> In 1942 the formula
>
> $$Lw(1 + r)^n = \frac{(R - r)(1 + r)^{n-1}}{R} = \frac{(1 + R)(1 + r)^{n-1} - (1 + r)^n}{R}$$
>
> because not w, $w(1 + r)$ was a linear function of r, and therefore was replaced by
>
> $$\left(1 - \frac{1}{R}\right)$$
>
> In 1956 the formula of the relation is
>
> $$r = R(1 - w), w = 1 - \frac{r}{R}$$
>
> so that [...] $Lw(1 + r)^n$ becomes $(1 - r/R)(1 + r)^n$[...]
>
> (*SP* D3/12/62: 5)

Hence Sraffa was clear that a change of assumption from an *ante factum* to a *post factum* paid wage implied a change in the formula, but apparently he did not ask one of his mathematical friends to obtain the new formula for him. Probably he thought that it would be enough to substitute '$n+1$' for 'n' in the original formula. (If that had indeed been the case he was not consistent in applying that rule.) The second note (29 December 1956) reads:

> The (1942 Besicovitch) rules becomes (1956 form):
>
> (1) In general $Lw(1+r)^n$ has its maximum value when $r = R - \left(\frac{1}{n}\right)$.
> (2) Therefore, when $R - \frac{1}{n} \leqslant 0$, then $Lw(1+r)^n$ has its maximum value for $r = 0$ and decreases steadily as r increases (i.e. when the 'age' of the labour term is equal to, or smaller than, the number of years purchase of the maximum rate of profits) i.e. where $n \leqslant \frac{1}{R}$.
> (3) The term which is at its maximum value when r is a given value, say r_0, is that whose 'age' is
>
> $$ n = \frac{1}{R - r_0} $$
>
> (4) The maximum value of my $Lw(1+r)^n$ is
>
> $$ \frac{1}{Rn} \left(1 + R - \frac{1}{n} \right)^n $$
>
> (5) The rate of profit at which any n-th term reaches its maximum value is equal to the difference between R and the rate of profits of which its own period n is the purchase period, viz. $R - \frac{1}{n}$.
>
> (*SP* D3/12/62: 1)

Now knowing what happened, let us turn to the correspondence with Harry Johnson. In his reply Sraffa left no doubt who was to be blamed for the slip:

> Of course you are right about the formulas in §47, p. 37. I have looked up my notes to see how it came about (it is the digging up of the old notes that has delayed my reply): I find that the correct formula was worked out for me by Besicovitch twenty years ago, but in preparing the book I made a minor change of assumption & in adapting the formula to this I blundered. Fortunately the diagram, as you say, was based on the correct formula; & so is the conclusion in the last sentence of §47.

Sraffa followed essentially the same route when amending the text on the occasion of the 1963 reprint of the book. Here we find the correct formulas on page 37:

$$ n = \frac{1+r}{R-r} $$

$$ r = R - \frac{1+R}{n+1} $$

plus a note appended to the preface (p. vii):

> The only change made in the present reprint (1963) has been to correct
> the expressions for n and r at the end of §47, p. 37, which went wrong in
> a last-moment change of notation. No alteration has been necessary in the
> corresponding text (p. 37) and diagram (fig. 2, p. 36) which were based on
> the correct formulas.

Obviously, one must not interpret Sraffa's remark as meaning that there is a 'notation' for which the formulas in his book would be correct. The meaning rather
appears to be that in adapting the correct formulas to a change in a premiss regarding the payment of wages, Sraffa had slipped.[21] According to our reconstruction
Sraffa correctly described what has happened.

9. Conclusion

The chapter has dealt with Sraffa's collaboration with his mathematical friends
Frank Ramsey and Alister Watson. The assistance of these mathematicians was of
great importance to him. The material presented from Sraffa's hitherto unpublished
papers and correspondence testifies to the independence of Sraffa's mind and his
scepticism as regards all propositions he could not master in his own way. Although
he sought the help of mathematicians, he did not put his lot in their hands, so to
speak. He would carefully listen to them when they talked and jot down summary
accounts of the discussions he had with them; he would ponder over their notes
and proofs, their statements about whether a problem he had put to them was
solvable or not, and what the solution was, if there was one; but he would remain
sceptical until he had finally understood the correctness or otherwise of the answer
given or the fruitfulness of the avenue indicated by them, thinking through the
problem himself and applying his own mental tools and ways of reasoning. He did
not use, or trust per se, abstract mathematical reasoning and would not himself
employ mathematical tools other than elementary ones. Sraffa's fastidiousness, it
seems, was certainly an obstacle to the progress of his work but probably also
a precondition of the latter's excellence.

Acknowledgements

We should like to thank Pierangelo Garegnani and Ian Steedman for valuable
comments on an earlier draft of this chapter. We are also grateful to Jonathan Smith,
archivist at the Wren Library of Trinity College, Cambridge, who catalogued
Sraffa's papers, for his assistance throughout our work on this project.

---

21 It should be noted that in later reprints of the book the note does not reappear.

References

Chini, Mineo (1923). *Corso speciale di Matematiche con numerose applicazioni ad uso principalmente dei chimici e dei naturalisti*, sesta edizione, Livorno: Raffaello Giusti, Editore-Libraio-Tipografo.

Kurz, H. D. and Salvadori, N. (1993). 'The "Standard commodity" and Ricardo's Search for an "invariable measure of value" ', in M. Baranzini and G. C. Harcourt (eds), *The Dynamics of the Wealth of Nations. Growth, Distribution and Structural Change. Essays in Honour of Luigi Pasinetti*, New York: St Martin Press, pp. 95–123. Reprinted in H. D. Kurz and N. Salvadori N. (1998). *Understanding 'Classical' Economics: Studies in Long-Period Theory*. London: Routledge, pp. 123–47.

Kurz, H. D. (ed.) (2000). *Critical Essays on Piero Sraffa's Legacy in Economics*, Cambridge: Cambridge University Press.

Lutz, F. A. and Hague, D. C. (eds) (1961). *The Theory of Capital*, London: Macmillan.

Pradella, P. (1915a). *Algebra ed Aritmetica: ad uso dei licei*, Turin: G. B. Paravia.

Pradella, P. (1915b). *Geometria: ad uso dei licei*, Turin: G. B. Paravia.

Ricardo, D. (1951 ssq.). *The Works and Correspondence of David Ricardo*, 11 volumes, edited by P. Sraffa in collaboration with M.H. Dobb, Cambridge: Cambridge University Press. In the text referred to as *Works*, volume number and page number.

Salvadori, N. (1985). 'Switching in Methods of Production and Joint Production', *The Manchester School*, 53: 156–78.

Sraffa, P. (1960). *Production of Commodities by Means of Commodities*, Cambridge: Cambridge University Press. (Italian version entitled *Produzione di merci a mezzo di merci* published in the same year by Einaudi, Turin.)

11 Sraffa and von Neumann*

Heinz D. Kurz and Neri Salvadori

1. Introduction

The relationship between Piero Sraffa's (1960) *Production of Commodities by Means of Commodities* and John von Neumann's ([1937] 1945) paper on economic growth has given rise to various assessments and comments (see, for e.g., Dore *et al.*, 1988). This is understandable, because the analyses presented by the two authors exhibit several similarities. In particular, they use a similar method of analysis, that is, they are concerned with long-period positions of a competitive economic system characterized by a uniform rate of return; and they study the problem of prices, distribution and the choice of technique, in an intersectoral framework in which production is conceived of as a circular flow. A feature of both contributions is that the distributive variables, the real wage rate and the rate of interest (or rate of profits),[1] are treated asymmetrically: one of these variables is given from outside the system of production, while the other is determined as a residual. Fixed capital is dealt with in a joint products framework. Despite these similarities and common concerns the assessments of the relationship between the two authors differ vastly across different interpretations. While some commentators argue that the analyses of Sraffa and von Neumann are broadly compatible with one another and can be shown to benefit from each other, others maintain that they belong to different traditions of economic thought and are characterized by conceptual incompatibilities.

Von Neumann's paper on economic growth was originally published in German in 1937 in Karl Menger's *Ergebnisse eines mathematischen Kolloquiums* and then, on the initiative of Nicholas Kaldor, translated into English and published in the *Review of Economic Studies* in 1945, accompanied by a commentary by David Champernowne (1945). From Champernowne's commentary, we learn that Sraffa had seen von Neumann's paper when Champernowne prepared his piece.

---

* Reprinted with permission from *Review of Political Economy*, 2001.
1 Von Neumann uses the term 'rate of interest', whereas Sraffa uses the term 'rate of profits'. However, as will become clear later, they mean essentially the same thing. Therefore, the two terms will be considered as synonymous in this chapter.

However, until recently, we did not know whether Sraffa had already worked on problems such as joint production and the choice of technique – problems that figure prominently in von Neumann's contribution – prior to his acquaintance with the paper, and, if he had, what his results had been. We were thus also unable to say whether von Neumann's contribution had left any discernible traces in Sraffa's preparatory manuscripts, which were to grow into his 1960 book.

Since the opening of his unpublished papers and correspondence in the Wren Library at Trinity College, Cambridge, the situation has changed. Since, from an early stage, Sraffa tended to date his manuscripts, we know in most cases precisely when he tackled which question, formulated which hypothesis and arrived at which result. The available material sheds new light on the development of Sraffa's thoughts.

In this chapter we make use of some of this material in order to contribute to a clarification of how Sraffa's reformulation of the 'classical' point of view in the theory of value and distribution relates to von Neumann's model. It should be stated right at the beginning that the available material is enormous and that we were able to review only a part of it. Therefore, it cannot be excluded that the collection contains other documents that are pertinent to the theme under consideration. These may provide additional support to the interpretation given, but they may also throw doubt on it. The reader should be aware of the preliminary character of this chapter.

The composition of the chapter is as follows. Section 2 provides a summary account of our view on the matter put forward in contributions published before we had access to the material (see Kurz and Salvadori, 1993, 1995 (chapter 13)). In these publications we argued that, despite some obvious differences in the mathematico-analytical tools used by von Neumann and Sraffa, there are important conceptual equivalences in their approaches. It would, of course, be a pointless exercise to reiterate our earlier view were we of the opinion that, *vis-à-vis* Sraffa's unpublished manuscripts, this view can no longer be sustained. We will focus on the following issues: (i) the question of returns to scale; (ii) the asymmetrical treatment of the two distributive variables, the real wage rate and the rate of interest; (iii) fixed capital and depreciation; (iv) joint production; (v) the problem of the choice of technique, comparing what may be called the 'direct' and the 'indirect' approach; (vi) the difference between the rule of semi-positive prices (or the Rule of Free Goods), adopted by von Neumann, and the rule of strictly positive prices, adopted by Sraffa; and (vii) the treatment of natural resources, especially land. In Section 3, we take a closer look at the gradual development of Sraffa's approach to the theory of value and distribution. We shall briefly summarize his investigation of 'systems of production' from the time in which he put down his first systems of equations in late 1927 to the publication of his 1960 book. It goes without saying that covering such a long period of time in a few pages necessitates a bird's eye view, focusing attention on a few aspects. Since one of the features of von Neumann's model is the multiple-products framework, we shall be especially concerned with when, and how, Sraffa himself dealt with the problem of joint production. Sections 2 and 3 set the stage for the rest of the argument. Section 4 is devoted to a brief discussion of Sraffa's role in Champernowne's attempt to come to grips with the economics of the von Neumann model in a comment that appeared in the *Review of Economic Studies*. Section 5 discusses some of the material contained in Sraffa's unpublished manuscripts and correspondence in which von Neumann is explicitly mentioned. Section 6 contains some concluding remarks.

2. Mathematical differences and conceptual equivalences[2]

2.1. Returns to scale

Von Neumann explicitly assumes constant returns to scale.[3] Sraffa, on the other hand, stresses that in his analysis 'no such assumption is made', though he adds that 'If such a supposition is found helpful, there is no harm in the reader's adopting it as a temporary working hypothesis' (Sraffa, 1960, p. v). The different approaches to the question of returns follow largely from a difference in perspective: while von Neumann is concerned with a uniformly growing economic system and therefore needs this assumption, Sraffa's investigation 'is concerned exclusively with such properties of an economic system as do not depend on changes in the scale of production' (Sraffa, p. v). Hence, unlike von Neumann, Sraffa does not specify whether the surplus generated by an economy accumulates or is consumed (unproductively): there are no assumptions regarding saving and investment behaviour to be found in his book. Yet there appears to be nothing in Sraffa's approach which, as a matter of principle, would preclude the adoption of constant returns in combination with von Neumann's suppositions regarding saving and investment as a provisional working hypothesis, designed to shed some light on the economic system and its capacity to grow. (This does not mean that Sraffa would endorse such an extension of his equations.) The difference between the two is rather to be seen in the following: whereas von Neumann throughout his paper retains the simplifying assumptions just mentioned, Sraffa makes it clear, sometimes implicitly, that an analysis conducted in these terms is unneccessarily special and cannot cover empirically important cases.[4]

---

2 The title of this section is a metamorphosis of the title of one of Schefold's (1980) papers. However, we do not enter into a discussion of the paper because Schefold does not deal with von Neumann's original article, but only with some of the literature triggered by it. Indeed, von Neumann's article is not cited in the paper. As regards the relationship between the literature under consideration and Sraffa's theory, Schefold sees conceptual differences and mathematical equivalences.

3 This may be considered the twin assumption to his setting aside scarce natural resources (see below Subsection 2.6).

4 As Sraffa's unpublished papers show, Sraffa had a foremost interest in elaborating a theory of accumulation, but first had to solve the problem of value and distribution. The latter turned out to be much more difficult than he expected when he began working on it in the late 1920s. As a matter of fact his constructive work was mainly absorbed by this problem. However, his manuscripts make very clear that, in conditions with ongoing technical progress, the depletion of stocks of exhaustible resources etc., there is no presumption that the economy will follow a steady-state path with the amounts of all capital goods used in the system expanding at a uniform rate of growth.

2.2. Asymmetrical roles of the distributive variables

Von Neumann assumes that at the beginning of the (uniform) period of production, workers are paid a wage that covers no more than the 'necessities of life' (von Neumann, 1945, p. 2). Sraffa, at the very beginning of his book also adopts the assumption of a given subsistence wage, but later drops it. He takes into consideration that workers may receive a share of the surplus product (defined on the basis of a given subsistence wage) and then, after some deliberation, decides to treat wages henceforth as paid *post factum*, that is, at the end of the (uniform) period of production. This is tantamount to assuming wages to be paid entirely out of the surplus product. Sraffa is perfectly aware of the drawback of this approach, which risks losing sight of the indisputable subsistence aspect of wages and prevents one from considering the *real* wage rate as fixed. Hence, if the wage rate were still to be given from outside the system of production, it would have to be 'in terms of a more or less abstract standard, and [would] not acquire a definite meaning until the prices of commodities are determined' (Sraffa, 1960, p. 33), that is, until the system of equations is solved. Hence, Sraffa, unlike von Neumann, does not exclude the possibility of relative prices having an impact on the vector of commodities consumed by workers (and other income recipients). In these circumstances he decides to treat the rate of profits as the independent variable, because, 'as a ratio, [it] has a significance which is independent of any prices, and can well be "given" before the prices are fixed'.

Thus, both analyses share a salient feature of the classical approach: they treat one of the distributive variables as exogenous and the other one (together with relative prices and, in the case of Sraffa, the rents of land) as endogenous. This *asymmetric* treatment of the distributive variables stands in striking contrast to the neoclassical theory of income distribution that attempts to explain wages, profits and rents simultaneously and *symmetrically* in terms of the supply of and the demand for the factors of production: labour, capital and land. This compels neoclassical authors to take the economy's initial endowment of capital (and the other productive factors) as given. No such assumption is to be found in von Neumann or Sraffa. They do not explain distribution in terms of the relative scarcities of 'capital' and labour.

2.3. Fixed capital

Both authors treat fixed capital within a joint production framework. This framework can be traced back to Robert Torrens and is also encountered in the writings of David Ricardo, Thomas Robert Malthus and Karl Marx (see Sraffa, 1960, appendix D). Von Neumann contents himself with the hint that the joint products method is capable of dealing with durable instruments of production: 'wear and tear of capital goods are to be described by introducing different stages of wear as different goods, using a separate [price] for each of these' (von Neumann, 1945, p. 2). Sraffa, on the other hand, devotes a whole chapter to the treatment of fixed capital employing this method (Sraffa, 1960, pp. 63–73). He demonstrates that this powerful method is not restricted to the 'extremely simplified case' of constant efficiency 'but has general validity' (Sraffa, 1960, p. 66); that the method allows one to ascertain the annual charge to be paid for interest and depreciation, and also to ascertain what the results derived imply for the theory of capital.

2.4. Joint production

When we come to the two authors' treatment of pure joint production we are confronted with two closely related issues that appear to indicate substantial differences between the two analyses: (i) while von Neumann adopts the Rule of Free Goods, in Sraffa's book that rule is never mentioned; (ii) in contradistinction to von Neumann, Sraffa formulates his analysis of joint production in terms of equations rather than inequalities and assumes 'that the number of independent processes in the system [is] equal to the number of commodities produced' (Sraffa, 1960, p. 44). This assumption is rationalized in terms of the following argument, referring to a case in which two commodities are jointly produced by two different processes (or methods): 'considering that the proportions in which the two commodities are produced by any one method will in general be different from those in which they are required for use, the existence of two methods of producing them in different proportions will be necessary for obtaining the required proportion of the two products through an appropriate combination of the two methods' (Sraffa, 1960, p. 43, n. 2).[5]

5 It is interesting to notice that an argument in favour of the treatment of joint production in terms of 'square' systems of production, which is similar to Sraffa's, had been put forward by F. Zeuthen in a critical discussion of the limitations and deficiencies of Gustav Cassel's approach (see Zeuthen, 1993). With implicit reference to chapter 16 of Book III of John Stuart Mill's *Principles*, Zeuthen argues: 'It is sometimes emphasized that here [i.e. in the case of joint production] the principle of cost is abrogated. This may be correct in the sense that the distribution of costs between products is not determined by the technical relations alone.... However, on the assumed free mobility ... there will be a complete and automatic determination of prices. This can be imagined as follows. In the example of cattle-breeding there may exist two forms of business, one predominantly concerned with dairy products and requiring a lot of labour, the other predominantly concerned with the production of meat and thus requiring a larger live stock.... [I]t follows that for each new method of production for a commodity there will be an additional magnitude as an unknown and a new cost equation which contributes to the solution of the system' (Zeuthen, 1993, p. 15). And Sraffa, referring to the case in which two products are produced by means of a single method of production, maintains: 'In these circumstances there will be room for a second, parallel process which will produce the two commodities by a different method.... Such a parallel process will not only be possible – it will be necessary if the number of processes is to be brought to equality with the number of commodities so that the prices may be determined.' And later he adds: 'The same result as to the determination of prices which is obtained from the two commodities being jointly *produced* ... could be achieved if the two commodities were jointly produced by only *one* process, provided that they were *used* as means of production to produce a third commodity by two distinct processes; and, more generally, provided that the number of independent processes in the system was equal to the number of commodities produced' (Sraffa, 1960, pp. 43–4, Sraffa's emphases). We have no evidence that Sraffa was familiar with Zeuthen's work.

This elicits the following remarks. First, Sraffa, in accordance with the procedure adopted by the classical economists, in the case of single production and to some extent also in the case of joint production, approaches the theory of value and distribution in two steps. He analyses first the mathematical properties of a *given* system of production and only subsequently addresses the problem of which system will be chosen by cost-minimizing producers from a set of available alternatives. In carrying out the second stage of the analysis Sraffa compares alternative techniques one by one. This approach might be called 'indirect'. Von Neumann, on the other hand, is not concerned with investigating the mathematical properties of a given technique. He tackles at once the problem of the choice of technique from *all* the available alternatives. This approach might be called 'direct'. As is well known, in the case of single production (and in simple cases involving fixed capital), the two approaches produce exactly the same results (see, e.g. Kurz and Salvadori, 1995, chapters 5, 7).

Second, flukes apart, the particular assumptions that underlie von Neumann's model (all interest income is accumulated and the composition of workers' consumption does not depend on prices) generate a situation in which Sraffa's premise holds – in the sense that the number of processes is equal to the number of commodities with a positive price (see Steedman, 1976; Schefold, 1978, 1980; Bidard, 1986). However, with less special assumptions it cannot be presumed that the number of independent processes in the system is always equal to the number of commodities produced. Sraffa's justification of this premise in terms of the 'requirements for use' is valid only in some circumstances.[6]

2.5. *The Rule of Free Goods*

One can distinguish between the application of the Rule of Free Goods (or the assumption of 'free disposal') to 'original' factors of production, in particular different qualities of land, and to produced commodities. Here we shall deal only with the latter case, whereas the former will be touched upon below in the subsection on 'Land'.

Sraffa points out that while, with single production, no price can become negative as a result of the variation of the wage rate between zero and its maximum value, given the system of production, 'it may be said at once, however, that this proposition is not capable of extension to the case of joint-products. . . . The price

---

6 The fact that these aspects of Sraffa's analysis cannot be sustained must not, however, be taken, wrongly, to imply the irrelevance of his approach to joint production. The indirect approach can still be useful when a square cost-minimizing technique obtains, which is necessarily the case in some significant circumstances, but not always (see, for instance, Kurz and Salvadori, 1995, pp. 236–40, and the whole of chapter 9 on jointly utilized machines). Moreover, with universal joint production the indirect approach can be elaborated in such a way that it replicates the results obtained with the direct approach, although in terms of analytical convenience it is inferior to the latter (see Salvadori, 1985).

of one of them might become negative' (Sraffa, 1960, p. 59). Sraffa comments on this possibility as follows:

> This conclusion is not in itself very startling. All that it implies is that, although in actual fact all prices were positive, a change in the wage might create a situation the logic of which required some of the prices to turn negative: and this being unacceptable, those among the methods of production that gave rise to such a result would be discarded to make room for others which in the new situation were consistent with positive prices.
>
> (Sraffa, 1960, p. 59)

This passage witnesses that Sraffa was clear about the fact that the positivity of prices cannot be guaranteed if there is no choice of technique. As to the substance of Sraffa's suggested way out of the impasse arising from the negativity of the price of a joint product, it can be argued that it is tantamount to the *ad hoc* assumption that there is always at least one process of production which, if adopted, makes the phenomenon of negative price disappear. This assumption, as peculiar as it may seem at first sight, is however no less *ad hoc* than the assumption of free disposal. In fact, the latter is equivalent to the assumption that, for each process producing a given product, there is another process that is exactly identical to the first one except that the product under consideration is *not* produced (see Kurz and Salvadori, 1995, section 5 of chapter 7, where *costly disposal* is also introduced along the same lines, and section 2 of chapter 8).

2.6. Land and labour

While the two authors seem to disagree with regard to whether or not the Rule of Free Goods is applicable to produced commodities, they appear to agree with regard to land. Von Neumann assumes that 'the natural factors of production, including labour, can be expanded in unlimited quantities' (von Neumann, 1945, p. 2).[7] Yet, this does not make him treat all these factors alike. Rather, he applies the Rule of Free Goods in the same way as the classical economists. He singles out labour as the only factor that is exempt from that rule; all other primary factors, although needed in production, 'disappear' from the scene because they are taken to

---

7 Assuming that natural resources are non-scarce is, of course, not the same thing as assuming that there are no natural resources at all. Von Neumann's model is frequently misinterpreted in the latter sense. However, with the system growing forever, the point will surely come where some natural resource(s) will become scarce. Surprisingly, von Neumann simply ignores this. As Professor Samuelson has pointed out to us in private correspondence, 'More by inadvertance than conscious intention, v.N. failed to emphasize the basic classical notion of land resources as unproducible or diminishable.' The total neglect of the problem of scarce primary resources such as land distinguishes his analysis in fact from the approaches of both the classical and the neoclassical economists. For a possible explanation of this neglect, see Kurz and Salvadori (1995, chapter 13, section 7).

be non-scarce: they fetch a zero price. Labour is assumed to receive an exogenously given wage bundle that is independent of the degree of employment.[8] Sraffa devotes a whole chapter to 'Natural resources which are used in production, such as land and mineral deposits' (Sraffa, 1960, p. 74), and makes it clear that as long as they are available in abundance they will not yield a rent to their owners. It is only when they are scarce that they assume economic weight. The scarcity of a resource, Sraffa points out, is generally reflected in the coexistence of more than one method utilizing it or more than one method using the product produced by means of it. Sraffa's concern, it should be stressed, is exclusively with land, which is treated as a renewable resource whose quality is taken not to change irrespective of the way it is used, whereas exhaustible resources and general renewable resources are implicitly set aside.

3. The development of Sraffa's analysis

In the preface of his 1960 book, Sraffa points out: 'Whilst the central propositions had taken shape in the late 1920's, particular points, such as the Standard commodity, joint products and fixed capital, were worked out in the 'thirties and early 'forties. In the period since 1955, while these pages were being put together out of a mass of old notes, little was added, apart from filling gaps which had become apparent in the process' (Sraffa, 1960, p. vi). This is confirmed by Sraffa's unpublished manuscripts. In what follows we shall provide a brief account of the development of his thoughts over time, paying special attention to those aspects that are pertinent to the theme of this chapter.

At the beginning of his academic career, economics to Sraffa was essentially Marshallian economics. He was critical of it, but originally appears to have been of the opinion that it was worth attempting to shed its weaknesses and develop its strengths. He despised especially the subjectivist elements of Marshall's theory of value and contemplated the possibility of purging the analysis of them (see D3/12/7:114).[9] His starting point was not, as some commentators have speculated, Marx and the 'transformation problem'. He objected against the labour theory of value that it involved a 'corruption' of the theory of value based on the concept of 'physical real cost', which he considered to provide an appropriate starting point for the theory of value and distribution (cf. D3/12/4: 2; see also D3/12/11: 79–80). In another note he emphasized that there is no 'objective difference' between the labour of a wage earner and of a slave, of a slave and of a horse, of a horse and of a machine, and added: 'It is a purely mystical conception that attributes to labour a special gift of determining value' (D3/12/9: 89).

---

8 'At most, one could say that a "Rule of Zero 'Excess' Wages" is applied because labour is less than fully employed' (Steedman, 1987, p. 419).

9 References to Sraffa's unpublished papers and correspondence follow the catalogue prepared by Jonathan Smith, archivist. We should like to thank Pierangelo Garegnani, literary executor of Sraffa's papers and correspondence, for granting us permission to quote from them.

It was only after he had developed his first systems of equations that Sraffa saw that in special cases the labour theory of value gave essentially the same answers as his own conceptualization. This finding appears to have prompted him to study more carefully the classical economists and Marx.[10] His interest in Marx as an economic theorist thus appears to have been a consequence of, rather than a precondition to, his own thoughts on the matter. The evidence suggests that it was only after the development of his first systems of equations in the second half of 1927 that Sraffa started systematically to study Marx's contributions to political economy. It was not until the early 1940s that he came across Ladislaus von Bortkiewicz's criticism and 'rectification' of Marx's argument concerning the so-called 'transformation' of values into prices of production in the third volume of *Capital*. He excerpted Bortkiewicz's papers with great care and put down numerous critical remarks. By that time, Sraffa had already gone a long way in developing his own point of view.

3.1. Production as a circular flow

Here, we cannot enter into a detailed discussion of the development of Sraffa's views, which changed considerably over time, especially after he had begun to grasp the analytical structure of the classical theory of value and distribution. As a consequence, his understanding of the marginalist theory, and its deficiencies, also underwent a change. While Sraffa retained his critical attitude towards the subjectivist part of that theory, the main target of his criticism now became the explanation of profits in terms of the supply of, and the demand for, a factor called 'capital'. It was in the late 1920s that Sraffa, all of a sudden, must have seen a glimpse of the alternative point of view that fundamentally changed his outlook – a change that is also reflected in his 'Lectures on advanced theory of value' (D2/4). In one place, Sraffa notes that contrary to his earlier opinion, even with constant returns to scale, value in Marshall's theory cannot be assumed as given and constant, because it does not depend only on real physical costs, but also on the distribution of income between wages and profits. His equations indicated that a change in that distribution will generally change relative values.

He appears to have developed his systems of equations from scratch. From the beginning he assumed that commodities are produced by means of commodities, that is, he conceptualized production as a circular flow and not, as the Austrians had done, as a one-way avenue leading from original factors of production to final goods. For example, at the end of November 1927 he put down equations representing two industries without and with a surplus (see D3/12/2: 32–5). In the

---

10 In February 1930, the Royal Economic Society assigned Sraffa to the task of editing David Ricardo's works and correspondence. As we know, Sraffa immediately took up the work and put a great deal of effort into it. However, for a while he appears to have been of the opinion that he could also carry on with his constructive work, albeit at a much reduced speed. Yet soon Sraffa got overwhelmed by the new task, which absorbed all his energy and forced him to interrupt his constructive work.

case where there is no surplus, exchange ratios between commodities are fully determined by the physical scheme of production and reflect physical real costs. When there is a surplus, things are more complicated. One of the systems with a surplus Sraffa discussed is given by

$$11A = 3A + 9B$$
$$13B = 7A + 3B$$
$$S = 1A + 1B$$

where A and B indicate the prices of two commodities and S the value of the surplus product of the system as a whole. Sraffa observed that these equations are 'contradictory' (Sraffa, 1960); in another document he added that 'the problem is overdetermined' (D3/12/11: 17). In the case with a surplus, a rule is needed according to which the surplus is distributed. It is only after this rule has been fixed that relative prices can be ascertained. In conditions of free competition and setting aside the problem of scarce natural resources, such as land, the surplus is distributed according to a uniform rate of return on the capital advanced in each sector of production.

As has already been stressed, in Sraffa's argument, labour values at first played no role whatsoever. There was indeed no analytical scope for them, because, as Sraffa demonstrated, the problem of value and distribution is fully settled in terms of the two sorts of data contemplated: (i) the system of production (and productive consumption) in use; and (ii) the rule governing the distribution of income. The argument could be elaborated without ever referring to labour values. However, Sraffa saw that, in exceedingly special circumstances, that is, essentially those that had already been pointed out by Ricardo and Marx, the exchange ratios are proportional to the relative quantities of labour embodied in the different commodities. The special circumstances are: first, the case in which the rate of profits is equal to zero, and, second, the case in which the proportions of direct labour to labour embodied in the means of production are identical in all industries. In general, the exchange ratios differ from the ratios of labour embodied in the different commodities. Sraffa therefore suggested that the special constellation in which profits vanish might be considered from a different perspective and spoke of the 'Value Theory of Labour' rather than the 'Labour Theory of Value'.

An early concern of Sraffa's was the determination of what he later called the maximum rate of profits of a given system of production; that is, that rate which is compatible with some minimum (subsistence) real wage rate. Next, he began to study systematically the problem that had bothered Ricardo until the end of his life: the impact of a rise (or fall) of the real wage on the rate of profits and relative prices, given the system of production. That problem turned out to be much more intricate than economists had generally realized. Sraffa stressed: 'In such a world, where everything moves in every direction . . . one sympathizes with Ricardo in his search for an "invariable measure of value". In a universe where everything moves we need a rock to which to cling, a horizon to reassure us when we see a brick falling that it is not we who are going up – nor that we are falling when we see a balloon rising' (D3/12/52: 17).

To facilitate the study of changes in prices as distribution changes, Sraffa, in a series of steps, groped his way to the concept of the 'Standard commodity', which proved to be a powerful tool of analysis. As Sraffa stressed, while this particular standard of value 'cannot alter the system's mathematical properties', it is explicitly designed to 'give transparency to a system and render visible what was hidden' (Sraffa, 1960, p. 23). The first important mathematical property of a given system is its maximum rate of profits. The Standard system allows one to ascertain that rate in a straightforward manner. It also provides 'tangible evidence of the rate of profits as a non-price phenomenon' (D3/12/43: 4), an observation which echoes Ricardo's contention that 'the great questions of Rent, Wages and Profits . . . are not essentially connected with the doctrine of value' (Ricardo, 1951–73, *Works*, Vol. VIII, p. 194). The Standard commodity is essentially a tool of analysis that allowed Sraffa to see through the intricacies of the movements of relative prices as income distribution changes, given the technique in use. Sraffa could have obtained the same results by using the Perron–Frobenius theorem; in fact, Sraffa's demonstration of the existence and uniqueness of the Standard commodity can be considered a (not fully complete) proof of this theorem (see Kurz and Salvadori, 1993).

3.2. Joint production

Sraffa had already started to tackle the problem of joint production at an early stage of his work. This is not surprising, given his concern with the difficulty fixed capital introduces into the theory of value: while the circulating part of the capital advances contributes entirely to the annual output, the contribution of the durable part is less obvious and can only be imputed in correspondence with what may be considered the wear and tear of fixed capital items. Sraffa sought to solve the intricate problem by reducing fixed capital to circulating, which implied that each vintage of a particular type of durable capital good had to be treated as a separate commodity. The suggested reduction involved the adoption of a general joint products framework.

In November 1927, Sraffa considered the case of the overproduction of one of the joint products and put forward a clear formulation of the Rule of Free Goods: 'Joint products: they are *always* assumed to be slightly variable, and therefore to have a marg. cost (both cover the whole: Wicksteed, or Euler) [.] – Well, as we are in const. returns, that is the cost of each – If absolutely invariable, probably *only* one would have a price: the one which is not wanted (at whatever price) in that amount, would be gratis' (D3/12/11: 25). However, later he appears to have abandoned that rule. At any rate, he did not adopt it in his book. His preparatory manuscripts document that he contemplated other options. In a note dated 27 October 1943 he discussed the case of 'Joint Products (when only *one* equation exists)'. The reference is to a process that produces jointly two products. Sraffa points out that the conventional approach is to take the aggregate cost as given.

He objects to this assumption on the grounds that if 'one of the products is itself part of the cost . . . the aggregate cost cannot be known in the first instance.' He adds:

> When this difficulty does not arise, the margin[al]ist has two alternative methods at his disposal: 1) Marginal products, when the proportions of production are variable – 2) Marginal utilities, when the proportions are fixed. – The first is out of production, the second out of consumption. *Similarly* with our approach.

He substantiates the latter remark in terms of the following two possibilities. First, there are two joint production methods producing the two products, say A and B, in different proportions. Second, there is only one joint production method, but one of the products is used as a means of production in producing a third product, say C, which is generated by means of a single products process. Now, if there is a second method to produce the third product, but using a different amount of the input per unit of output, we may again, Sraffa contends, get a system in which the problem of overproduction vanishes (D3/12/35: 41).[11]

It deserves also to be mentioned that, as early as around the turn of 1942–3, Sraffa discovered the possibility of negative costs or values in joint production systems (cf. D3/12/28). In addition, in February 1946 he stated that in such systems, 'when we change r [the rate of profits] from its actual value, and make it, say, $= 0$, we may obtain negative values' (D3/12/16: 35).

We may summarize our findings as follows. By the time of the publication of the English translation of von Neumann's paper, Sraffa had already elaborated important elements of his analysis. These concerned, first and foremost, the case of single production, that is circulating capital only, but it was by no means restricted to it. He had already worked for a considerable time on various aspects of joint production and fixed capital and had come up with some remarkable results.

4. Champernowne's commentary

Kaldor, as mentioned above, stimulated the publication of an English version of von Neumann's paper and was also concerned with rendering the mathematically demanding piece attractive to an audience of economists. A first step in the pursuit of this goal appears to have been the adaptation of the paper's title (cf. Kaldor, 1989, p. x), which, in a literal translation of the original German, would have been 'On an economic system of equations and a generalization of Brouwer's fixed point theorem'. The second part of the title, which reflects von Neumann's assessment that the main achievement of the paper consisted of the generalization of a mathematical theorem, was dropped entirely, and the neutral term 'economic system of equations' was replaced by the not-so-neutral term 'model of general economic equilibrium'.

---

11 Sraffa's contention that, in this case, all prices are strictly positive cannot be sustained in general.

The second step consisted of asking David Champernowne, 'the most mathematically-minded economist I knew, to write an explanatory paper *ad usum delphini*, for the use of the semi-numerates, to appear alongside it in the *Review of Economic Studies*' (Kaldor, 1989, p. x).[12] In a footnote to the introduction of his paper Champernowne thanks several people. Interestingly, the footnote in the galley proofs of Champernowne's paper in Sraffa's library is different from the published one. The former reads:

> This note is the outcome of conversations with Mr. N. Kalder [*sic*] and Mr. P. Sraffa, to whom many of the ideas in it are due. I am also indebted to Mr. Crum of New College, Oxford, for his helpful comments on the mathematics in Dr. Neumann's article.
>
> (Sraffa's library, item 4674)

The published version reads as follows:

> This note is the outcome of conversations with Mr. N. Kaldor, to whom many of the ideas in it are due. I am also indebted to Mr. P. Sraffa of Cambridge and to Mr. Crum of New College, Oxford, for instruction in subjects discussed in this article.
>
> (Champernowne, 1945, p. 10, n. 1)

Whereas according to the early version of the footnote Kaldor and Sraffa were to be credited with the ideas in the commentary, now it is only Kaldor. In a letter to Sraffa dated 1 April 1947, accompanied by an offprint of his paper,[13] Champernowne sets the record straight:

> I didn't like to put more than that about you in the footnote, but of course you told me all about (a) cost-theory of value (b) the A.G.D. Watson price-matrix theory: even if my note didn't exactly express your ideas. I think that Neumann's article solves the problem.

We have been unable to pin down what Champernowne meant when referring to the 'A. G. D. Watson price-matrix theory'. Be that as it may, it should come as no surprise that, in his interpretation, von Neumann's model emerges as one characterized essentially by 'classical' features.

In the course of his investigation Champernowne puts forward several concepts and raises a number of issues that we re-encounter in Sraffa (1960). Thus, Champernowne uses the notion of 'system of production' (Champernowne, 1945, p. 14), which figures prominently in Sraffa's analysis. He notes that, in the

---

12 It is interesting to note that in the title of Champernowne's (1945) paper the title of the English version of von Neumann's paper is referred to incompletely: the adjective 'general' is left out.

13 See item 4676 of Sraffa's library; Champernowne's letter is inside the pages of the offprint.

von Neumann model, the role of the 'worker-consumer' can be compared with that of a 'farm animal', for example, a work horse, whose costs consist of his 'fodder, stabling, etc.' (Champernowne, 1945, p. 12), an analogy that recurs in Sraffa's formulation in chapter II of his book: 'We have up to this point regarded wages as consisting of the necessary subsistence of the workers and thus entering the system on the same footing as the fuel for the engines or the feed for the cattle' (Sraffa, 1960, p. 9). The rate of interest, Champernowne stresses, 'depends on the technical processes of production which are available' (Champernowne, 1945, p. 12); Sraffa, on the other hand, elaborates the Standard system with R as the 'Standard ratio or Maximum rate of profits' representing a ratio between quantities of commodities (Sraffa, 1960, p. 22). Champernowne raises the question of what would happen if the real wage were higher than originally assumed and concludes that 'there will be a change in the equilibrium conditions ... with a lower rate of interest and a lower rate of expansion' (Champernowne, 1945, p. 16); this fore-shadows the inverse relationship between the rate of profits and the real wage rate analysed by Sraffa.

In the above-mentioned copy of the galley proofs of Champernowne's paper in Sraffa's library, there are annotations in Sraffa's hand. It is perhaps interesting to note some of the passages marked. These are:

  (i) 'no saving was carried out by the workers whereas the propertied class saved the whole of their income' (p. 12, this is indicated as one of the 'several drastic simplifying assumptions' introduced in order 'to make it possible for quasi-stationary state equilibrium to exist in the model');

 (ii) 'Since Dr. Neumann's results only relate to a quasi-stationary state, the utmost caution is needed in drawing from them any conclusions about the determination of prices, production or the rate of interest in the real world' (p. 15; in the published version 'Dr. Neumann' is substituted by 'v. Neumann');

(iii) with a higher real wage rate 'there will be a change in the equilibrium conditions, and the position of quasi-stationary equilibrium will change to one with a lower rate of interest and a lower rate of expansion' (p. 16);

 (iv) 'The rate of interest will be determined as the greatest rate of expansion possible if all income from property is saved ... [even if part of the income from property were spent on consumption, and not saved, the rate of interest would not necessarily be much affected] it might still be *approximately* equal to the greatest expansion rate that *would* have been possible *if* all income from property had been saved' (p. 16);

  (v) 'here, perhaps for the first time, is a self-contained theory of the determi-nation of prices, ignoring the second approximation' (p. 17, the 'second approximation' refers to the introduction of ' "special cases" such as "the possibility of increasing returns" and "consumers" ' choice as an indepen-dent factor in the direction of productive activity', which 'in traditional economics' are 'at the centre of the theory');

(vi) 'It is expressly assumed that every good is involved (either as input or as output) in every process' (p. 18, Champernowne is critical of this assumption);

(vii) 'It should be noted that although in the model the equilibrium rate of interest is uniquely determined, the system of prices and outputs are not *uniquely* determined: there may be any number of possible equilibrium positions. But each must satisfy the rules set out in section 2 above' (p. 18).

As regards the bold premises (i), (ii) and (vi) that underlie von Neumann's model, Sraffa can safely be assumed to have shared or even inspired Champernowne's critical attitude. Most interesting is perhaps (v). We do not know whether it was due to Sraffa's 'instruction' that Champernowne in his commentary put forward the idea of a 'first' and a 'second approximation' in the theory of prices. Accordingly, factors such as a shift in demand 'may conveniently be considered as the "special cases" of price-theory, to be introduced in the *second approximation*; and not, as is common in traditional economics, at the centre of the theory. For the basic influences determining equilibrium prices v. Neumann's model provides a novel approach; here, perhaps for the first time, is a self-contained theory of the determination of prices, ignoring the second approximation' (Champernowne, 1945, p. 17, emphasis in the original). Champernowne is of the opinion that von Neumann's 'first approximation' is particularly powerful with regard to intermediary goods. In a footnote he adds: 'And even in the case of final consumers' goods, the prices . . . are *largely* to be explained by the technical conditions of production, rather than "marginal utility" '; then follows, in brackets, the adjunct: 'The exceptions being joint products, or commodities with largely increasing or decreasing cost' (Champernowne, 1945, p. 17, fn).

In addition, with respect to the other items, we cannot say whether or not they have been prompted by Sraffa's 'instruction'. However, it should be noted that items (iii) and (iv) concern the fact that the relationship between the wage rate and the rate of interest is decreasing; and that – with constant returns to scale and joint production, as assumed by von Neumann – this relationship is not much affected by the quantities produced. There is evidence that Sraffa was well aware of these facts in the 1940s with respect to single production. (He was perhaps inclined to think that they carry over to systems with joint production, but this needs to be checked.)

Item (vii) is more problematic than the others. In Sraffa's book, a whole chapter is devoted to the 'Uniqueness of the standard system' in single production (chapter V), but there is no attempt to prove the uniqueness of the prices even in the cases in which this proof would be possible (the non-substitution theorem).

5. Sraffa on von Neumann

In the preface to *Production of Commodities*, referring to 'the disproportionate length of time over which so short a work has been in preparation', Sraffa remarks: 'As was only natural during such a long period, others have from time to time independently taken up points of view which are similar to one or other of those adopted in this paper and have developed them further or in different directions from those pursued here' (Sraffa, 1960, p. vi). One of the authors Sraffa may have had in mind when writing these lines was John von Neumann. The question then is, to what extent did Sraffa absorb or reject the ideas put forward by von Neumann?

In this section we take account of statements in Sraffa's papers in which he explicitly mentions von Neumann. Note, however, that it is not claimed that the following discussion exhausts the issue. We shall begin with a discussion of the assistance Sraffa received from Alister Watson, one of Sraffa's 'mathematical friends' (see D3/12/46: 49) whom he thanked in the preface of his book (Sraffa, 1960, p. vii). Watson played a significant part in two periods of Sraffa's work on his book: first in the 1940s; and then in the period since 1955, when Sraffa put together the text out of a mass of old notes, including the proof-reading stage.[14]

5.1. Alister Watson's visits

In January 1947, Alister Watson visited Sraffa in Cambridge; Sraffa took notes of their discussion (D3/12/44: 4, 6). The main question under consideration was the uniqueness of the maximum rate of profits R:

> I. Q-system: several all-positive solutions. The only solution I have considered gives a value 0 to the qs of all *non-basic* processes.
>
> However, suppose that one (or more) of the non-basic commodities [wheat] uses itself in its own production in a proportion greater than that of the basics taken as a whole (in other words, its own internal R is *smaller* than the R of the basic group), then there is another solution: for this non-basic commodity uses in its own production some basic ones, thus diminishing the ratio of basic means of production to basic products.
>
> If, on the other hand, the internal R of the non-basic is larger than the R of the basic group, there is only one all-positive solution, with the q's for non-basics $= 0$.
>
> [N.B. This has its symmetrical case in the P-system. If some of the non-basics have an own internal R *larger* than the basics group, there are alternative solutions with all the basic p's $= 0$, and bigger values of R.]
>
> (D3/12/44: 4)

---

14 For a detailed discussion of the collaboration of Frank Ramsey and Alister Watson with Piero Sraffa, see Kurz and Salvadori (2001).

The notes continue on page 6, whereas page 5 includes a note added by Sraffa on 23 February 1955. Let us first report the end of the note of 1947:

> We can thus sum up:
> There are several non-negative systems of roots of the Q-system. The system with the largest value for R has all zero values for the qs of the non-basic processes.
>   There are several non-negative systems of roots of the P-system. All these systems, except the one with the smallest value for R, have all zero values for the ps of the basic commodities.
>   [N.B. (1) The largest R of the Q-system is equal to the smallest R of the P-system. – (2) The proposition referring to the Q-system assumed that non basics have a *smaller* internal own ratio than r-basic; that referring to P system assumes it *larger*.]
>
> (D3/12/44: 6)

In the note added in 1955, Sraffa mentioned von Neumann:

> We can avoid all these complications by, from the start, removing 'manually' all the non-basic equations and dealing with a system composed exclusively of basic commodities [these to be defined, before the removal, as comm.s which directly or indirectly enter all the others]* and then we can say that there is only one all-positive [and not merely non-negative) solution for the ps and the qs.
>   [N.B. One point which needs clearing about the Watson alternative solution is this: does it remain true that if we multiply the equations by *any* pair of solutions of the ps and qs, which is not the all-positive pair of solutions, the sum of all the equations is *null*?]
>   *For practical application this good enough. But discuss in a note the abstract possibilities of this not being so, e.g. of the system falling into two or more self-contained (self-basic) groups of commodities – as if one lumped together the equations of two countries which have no commercial relations (& treating, of course, iron in country A as a different commodity from iron in B).
>   The more 'elegant' system of solving the complete system (with qs of non-basics $= 0$) can be discussed here with the Watson difficulties (query, did he derive them from von Neumann?)
>
> (D3/12/44: 5)

In April 1955, Watson visited Sraffa again, but in the note concerning that visit (D3/12/58: 8–9) there is no mention of von Neumann. In February, Sraffa was no doubt annotating his previous notes in preparation for the visit of Watson in April. However, we do not know whether Sraffa asked Watson about von Neumann and got an irrelevant answer or whether he himself thought that the question was actually not interesting.

5.2. The correspondence between Hicks and Sraffa

In a letter dated 3 September 1960 (D3/12/111: 267–8), John Richard Hicks commented on *Production of Commodities*, which he had just finished reading. In his comment he referred to von Neumann and pointed out several similarities between the constructions by von Neumann and Sraffa. We quote the letter in full:

> My dear Piero,
> When I got back in mid-July from four months in the Orient, I found your book waiting for me; I did not immediately write to thank you, as I wanted to read it first, and it has taken quite a number of weeks clearing off various kinds of back-logs before I could get down to the attempt to absorb anything new. It is only now that I have been able to read it – not yet in detail but sufficiently to have a general impression and to have something that I very much want to say.
>
> You tell us that your work on the subject goes back a long way – you mention Frank Ramsey; is it possible that it was somehow through you and your mathematical friends that von Neumann got onto what is in so many ways a similar construction (it is understood that his paper was originally given at Princeton in 1932)? I have never been able to understand how he should have hit on it out of the blue. Formally, I believe, your standard system is identical with the von Neumann equilibrium, though it arises in response to a different question. But the model, even to the treatment of fixed capital, is exactly the same.
>
> I am myself intensely interested in the pulling-apart, which you have performed, of the system without and with joint production. I have lately run into this matter myself in two different contexts.
>
> One was over the paper on 'Linear theory' which is to appear as a survey in the December EJ. In the first draft of my paper I followed Dorfman, Samuelson and Solow (Linear Programming chs. 9–10), in a statement of the Samuelson 'substitution theorem' to the effect that (under constant returns to scale), with labour as the only 'outside' – I think you would say 'non-basic' – input, technical coefficients are determined independently of demands, so that the system operates under constant costs. When I sent this in to the editors, Robin Matthews pointed out to me that I had not allowed for joint production. (Had he read your MS?) Then, on my travels, I got to California; there I was told by Arrow that he and Koopmans had noticed the gap in the Samuelson argument, though the mathematics in which they had wrapped up their point (chs. 8–9 of the 'Activity Analysis' book) was too 'opaque' for me to be able to understand it. I have now found a bit of geometry which makes the whole thing fairly clear, and have put it into my revised version.
>
> The other, even more directly relevant, concerns the von Neumann growth model itself and the 'Turnpike Theorem' that Samuelson and Solow have based upon it. Here again I started from the treatment in the Do.S.So. book (chs. 11 and 12), which in this case I did not find at all convincing. In an endeavour

to puzzle the thing out for myself, I made precisely the simplification which you make in your Part I (this was of course not made by von Neumann and the others, but what was true in the general case ought to be true in the special case also, so one could use it, as you use it, as a means of finding one's feet). But when I did so, I got into trouble, and so started quite a controversy (so far consisting only of letters and circulated papers but soon to get into print). I thought at one time that I had found an exception to the Samuelson theorem, and when I was in California last March I still had a paradox for the pundits, to which the answer was not found obvious. In the end, while working with Morishima in Japan, I got it out. What had not been noticed is that under the assumption of no joint production (but not when there is joint production) there is a tendency to constant costs in the von Neumann system (effectively your system with no non-basic elements). This is evidently related to the Samuelson substitution theorem, though it is not the same thing. This Turnpike stuff will be appearing in the February Review of Economic Studies, together with related contributions from Samuelson, Morishima and probably others. Since this has not yet gone to press (unlike the EJ survey, which is out of my hands) I shall certainly add a reference to your work, which is so clearly to the point. But there is certainly much to be done in fitting together your approach with those of others. It will no doubt take much time before that is properly done; it is however quite an exciting job to have before us.

Economic theory (teachable economic theory, at least) was getting just a bit boring lately; for the second time in your life you have livened it up again. Thank you.

Yours ever,
John Hicks.

The draft of Sraffa's reply is dated 8.9.60 (D3/12/111: 269). We have yet to check whether the letter was sent and received by Hicks. Here is the text of the draft.

My dear John,
I was delighted to receive your letter as there was no one whose reaction I was more interested to have.

I have not here the books you refer to on particular points, and I expect to be writing to you again when I get back to Cambridge.

The reason for the analogy between the several constructions seems to me to lie in their having a common source, although by devious ways, in the old classical economists (before their successors introduced the 'cost of production' theories, e.g. Mill, Cairnes etc.: that is undoubtedly the case for the treatment of fixed capital as a joint product. There are however important differences with the von Neumann construction, and the saddle point and the 'free goods' are peculiar to it: I never succeeded in getting quite clear on these points of his but although I am not certain I believe they are related to his treatment of what I call 'non-basic' goods.

The answer to your query concerning the editors of the E.J. is that Austin Robinson read the MS as a Syndic of the Press, but Robin Matthews did not. I really am writing only to say how grateful I am for your having taken so much trouble about my little book and if I can contribute anything on the other matters you refer to, I shall write again.

5.3. Comments

Sraffa was certainly not able to read the mathematics of John von Neumann, but he was able to recognize that von Neumann shared essentially his own outlook. In both models commodities are produced by means of commodities. Profits (interest) are taken to 'come out of the surplus produce', to use Ricardo's expression (*Works*, Vol. II, pp. 130–1): given the real wage rate, profits are a residual left after the wage goods in the support of labourers and what is necessary for the replacement of the used up means of production have been deducted from the annual output. In both models, the rate of profits is not a scarcity index of a factor called 'capital'.

This interpretation is similar to that given by Joan Robinson in a letter to Peter Newman. This letter is dated 29 May 1962; a copy is in the Sraffa papers.

> [Y]our detective work on the influence of von Neumann in Cambridge seems a bit illogical. The reason why Sraffa could explain him to Champernowne was that Sraffa had already made the discovery. Not that I want to be ungrateful to von Neumann. His model is beautiful and it is very useful for dealing with those people who cannot see a simple point unless it is put in a complicated way.
>
> (D3/12/111: 304)

6. Conclusions

This chapter argues that Sraffa's 1960 book and von Neumann's 1937 paper share essentially the same outlook and exhibit remarkable conceptual parallels. Both contributions belong to the 'classical' approach to the theory of value and distribution, characterized by an asymmetric treatment of the distributive variables, the rate of return on capital and the real wage rate. In addition, the chapter presents and discusses some material from Sraffa's hitherto unpublished papers and correspondence which is pertinent to the problem under consideration. From Sraffa's unpublished papers it can be seen that he was not able to understand the mathematics of von Neumann, but also that he understood perfectly well that they started essentially from the same theoretical point of view, that is, the one of the classical economists. This is also why Sraffa was able to discern in von Neumann several aspects which he, Sraffa, had already, at least in part, elaborated himself. When Sraffa came across the von Neumann model his own analysis was already quite advanced.

Acknowledgements

We should like to thank Rodolfo Signorino and an anonymous referee for very valuable comments on an earlier draft of this chapter. The usual disclaimer applies.

References

Bidard, C. (1986) Is von Neumann square?, *Zeitschrift für Nationalökonomie*, 46, pp. 401–19.

Champernowne, D. G. (1945) A note on J. v. Neumann's article on 'A model of economic equilibrium', *Review of Economic Studies*, 13, pp. 10–18.

Dore, M., Chakravarty, S. and Goodwin, R. (Eds) (1989) *John von Neumann and Modern Economics* (Oxford, The Clarendon Press).

Kaldor, N. (1989) John von Neumann: a personal recollection, in: M. Dore, S. Chakravarty, and R. Goodwin (Eds) *John von Neumann and Modern Economics* (Oxford, The Clarendon Press).

Kurz, H. D. and Salvadori, N. (1993) Von Neumann's growth model and the 'classical' tradition, *The European Journal of the History of Economic Thought*, 1, pp. 129–60. Reprinted as Chapter 2 in H. D. Kurz and N. Salvadori, *Understanding 'Classical' Economics. Studies in Long-period Theory*, London, Routledge (1998), pp. 25–56.

Kurz, H. D. and Salvadori, N. (1995) *Theory of Production: A Long-period Analysis* (Cambridge, Melbourne & New York, Cambridge University Press).

Kurz, H. D. and Salvadori, N. (2001) Sraffa and the mathematicians: Frank Ramsey and Alister Watson, in: T. Cozzi and R. Marchionatti (Eds) *Piero Sraffa's Political Economy. A Centenary Estimate* (London, Routledge). Here reprinted as Chapter 10.

Neumann, J. von (1937) Über ein ökonomisches Gleichungssystem und eine Verallgemeinerung des Brouwerschen Fixpunktsatzes, *Ergebnisse eines mathematischen Kolloquiums*, 8, pp. 73–83. Reprinted in K. Menger, *Ergebnisse eines Mathematischen Kolloquiums*, edited by E. Dierker and K. Sigmund (Vienna & New York, Springer-Verlag).

Neumann, J. von (1945) A model of general economic equilibrium, *Review of Economic Studies*, 13, pp. 1–9 [English translation of von Neumann (1937)].

Ricardo, D. (1951–73) *The Works and Correspondence of David Ricardo*, Vols. I–XI (ed. P. Sraffa in collaboration with M. H. Dobb), (Cambridge, Cambridge University Press). Cited as *Works* followed by volume and page numbers.

Salvadori, N. (1985) Switching in methods of production and joint production, *The Manchester School*, 53, pp. 156–78.

Schefold, B. (1978) On counting equations, *Zeitschrift für Nationalökonomie*, 38, pp. 253–85.

Schefold, B. (1980) Von Neumann and Sraffa: mathematical equivalence and conceptual difference, *Economic Journal*, 90, pp. 140–56.

Sraffa, P. (1960) *Production of Commodities by Means of Commodities. Prelude to a Critique of Economic Theory* (Cambridge, Cambridge University Press).

Steedman, I. (1976) Positive profits with negative surplus value: a reply to Wolfstetter, *Economic Journal*, 86, pp. 873–6.

Steedman, I. (1987) Free goods, in: J. Eatwell, M. Milgate and P. Newman (Eds) *The New Palgrave. A Dictionary of Economics*, Vol. 2 (London, Macmillan).

Zeuthen, F. (1933) Das Prinzip der Knappheit, technische Kombination und ökonomische Qualität, *Zeitschrift für Nationalökonomie*, 4, pp. 1–24.

12 Production theory[*]

An introduction

Heinz D. Kurz and Neri Salvadori

1. Introduction

Modern industrial economies are characterized *inter alia* by the following two features: first, commodities are produced by means of commodities (circular flow); and second, production generally requires in addition to circulating capital fixed capital. While the circulating part of the capital goods advanced in production contributes entirely and exclusively to the output generated, that is, 'disappears' from the scene, so to speak, the fixed part of it contributes to a sequence of outputs over time, that is, after a single round of production its items are still there – older though, but still useful. Concerned with the realism of its basic assumptions, Post-Keynesian theory has to take account of these two features. There is another aspect that underscores the importance of fixed capital, especially in a Post-Keynesian framework. In economic systems which are subject to the *principle of effective demand*, as John Maynard Keynes and Michal Kalecki formulated it, there is no presumption that the levels of aggregate effective demand will be such as to allow producers (possibly over a succession of booms and slumps) to utilize the productive capacity installed in the desired way. In particular, aggregate effective demand may fall short of productive capacity, with the consequence of both idle plant and equipment and unemployed workers. The variability in the overall degree of utilization of plant and equipment (and, correspondingly, of the workforce) in combination with countercyclical storage activities is responsible for the remarkable *elasticity* of the modern industrial system, which is able to translate even widely fluctuating levels of effective demand into fluctuating levels of output and employment. However, in the following we shall set aside the problem of capital utilization in conditions of effective demand failures (see, however, Kurz, 1990). We shall rather boldly assume that plant and equipment can be utilized at the normal desired degree.[1]

---

[*] Reprinted with permission from *Indian Economic Journal*, 2001.

1 Given the space limits to be respected, we can only offer an elementary discussion of a small subset of the problems arising in the present context. The reader interested in a more comprehensive and thorough treatment of the subject is asked to consult Kurz and Salvadori (1995).

All production, as we shall understand it in this chapter, involves some dealing of man with nature. As John Stuart Mill put it, 'man can only move matter, not create it'. The use of *natural resources* is indeed indispensable in production. When in certain theoretical conceptualizations this fact is not visible, then this does not mean that it is not there. It only means that the authors have for simplicity set aside the problem by assuming that natural resources are available in abundance. This amounts to assuming that their services are 'free goods'. This is a bold assumption, not least with regard to advanced economies which are typically characterized by the scarcity of some of their lands and the depletion of some of their stocks of raw materials etc. As is well known, the treatment of exhaustible resources poses formidable problems for economic theorizing. In this chapter we shall set aside the problem of scarce natural resources. (See, however, Kurz and Salvadori, 1995; chapters 10 and 12, for treatments of the problems of land and renewable and exhaustible resources, respectively, and chapters 13 and 14 in the present book.) Hence, in the models we shall be dealing with there will be no decreasing returns. Further, since we shall not be concerned with economic growth and the effects on labour productivity of the increase in the division of labour associated with the accumulation of capital, effects stressed by authors from Adam Smith to Allyn Young, Nicholas Kaldor and modern growth theorists, we shall also set aside increasing returns. The assumption underlying the following discussion is therefore that throughout the economy there are *constant returns to scale* and no external effects.

It is also an empirical fact that production generally involves *joint production*, that is, the generation of more than one physically discernible output. Cases in point are the production of coke and coal-gas and indeed many, if not all, chemical production processes. Often one or several of the joint products are 'bads' or 'discommodities' which nobody wants, but whose production is necessarily involved, given the technical options that are available, if the commodities that are wanted are to be produced. The emergence of a bad is a particularly obvious case in which the question of disposal cannot possibly be avoided. Much of economic literature assumes that disposal processes do not incur any costs whatsoever. However, from the point of view of the realism of the analysis the assumption of 'free disposal' is difficult to defend: most, if not all, disposal processes are in fact costly. The implication of this is that the product that is to be disposed of fetches a negative price, that is, the agent who is willing to take the product does not have to pay a price for it, but is paid a price for his willingness to take it. In this essay we shall set aside the intricacies of joint production proper and for the most part deal exclusively with economic systems characterized by single production. (For a treatment of joint production, see Kurz and Salvadori, 1995; chapter 8.)

Conceiving production as a circular flow does not mean that all commodities produced in an economy play essentially the same role in the system of production under consideration. In the classical economists, in particular Adam Smith and David Ricardo, we encounter the distinction between 'necessaries' and 'luxuries'. The former concept denotes essentially all commodities entering the wage basket in the support of workers. And since workers are taken to be paid at the beginning of the production period, wages form an integral part of the capital advanced in production. Moreover, since in the classical economists labour is taken to be an input needed directly or indirectly in the production of all commodities, necessaries and the means of production needed directly or indirectly in their production can be said to be indispensable in production in general and thus to 'enter' into all commodities, including themselves. Luxuries, like wage goods or necessaries, are pure consumption goods. However, in contradistinction to the latter the classical economists did not consider them as necessary in order to keep the process of production going. In the terminology of the classical authors, necessaries belong to 'productive consumption', whereas luxuries belong to 'unproductive consumption'. We encounter variants of the classical distinction in many later authors (see Kurz and Salvadori, 1995; chapter 13). The perhaps best known modern version of it is Piero Sraffa's distinction betweed 'basic' and 'non-basic' commodities. Basics are defined as commodities that enter directly or indirectly into the production of all commodities, whereas non-basics do not (Sraffa, 1960, pp. 7–8). Since Sraffa treats wages in most of his analysis as paid at the end of the production period, the wages of labour do not belong to the capital advanced, as in the classical authors. Therefore, his criterion of a commodity entering directly or indirectly into the production of all commodities is a purely technical one. In the following we shall set aside all difficulties concerning the existence of non-basic goods by assuming that only two commodities will be produced, both of which are basics. Hence all commodities are taken to rank equally, each of them being found both among the outputs and among the inputs, and each directly or indirectly entering the production of all commodities. (The reader interested in a discussion of cases with basic and non-basic products is referred to Kurz and Salvadori, 1995; chapters 3 and 4.)

Production requires *time*. The assumption of 'instantaneous' production entertained in conventional microeconomic textbooks can only be defended as a first heuristic step in the analysis of a complex phenomenon. The different activities involved in the generation of a product typically exhibit different lengths of time. Here we shall assume for simplicity that what will be called the 'periods of production' are of *uniform* length througout the economy. As James Mill stressed with regard to the approach chosen by the classical economists: 'A year is assumed in political economy as the period which includes a revolving cycle of production.' Using a uniform period of production (of a possibly much shorter length) involves, of course, the introduction of some fictitious products, occasionally referred to as 'semi-finished products' or 'work in progress'.

With fixed capital there is always a problem of the choice of technique to be solved. This concerns both the choice of the *pattern of utilization* of a durable capital good and the choice of the *economic lifetime* of such a good. The utilization aspect in turn exhibits both an *extensive* and an *intensive* dimension. The former relates to the number of time units within a given time period (day, week) during which a durable capital good is actually operated, for example, whether a single-, a double-, or a treble-shift scheme is adopted; the latter relates to the intensity of operation per unit of active time (hour) of the item, for example, the speed at which a machine is run. The economic lifetime of a fixed capital good and the pattern of its operation are, of course, closely connected. Yet things are more complex because modern production processes are increasingly characterized by the *joint utilization* of durable means of production, a fact emphasized in contributions to the genre of industrial-technological literature, which was an offspring of the Industrial Revolution. According to Marx modern industry was characterized by a 'system of machinery', an 'organised system of machines'. A proper discussion of fixed capital, including the empirically important case of the joint utilization of durable capital goods, however, is beyond the scope of this essay. The interested reader is once more referred to Kurz and Salvadori (1995; chapters 7 and 9). Here we shall restrict ourselves to the analysis of an exceedingly simple case with only a single type of fixed capital good, which is designed to illustrate some of the issues raised by the presence of durable instruments of production.

We now have to specify the institutional setting to which the following analysis is taken to apply. The specification of the institutional setting has important implications for the method of analysis adopted. We shall assume that there is *free competition*, that is, there are no significant barriers to entry in or exit from an industry. In these conditions producers will be concerned with minimizing costs of production. The result of this concern will be a tendency towards a *uniform rate of profits* on capital throughout the economy. The following analysis will indeed focus attention on what may be called *cost-minimizing systems of production*. The prices analysed are taken to express the persistent, non-accidental and non-temporary forces governing the economy. They correspond to what the classical economists called 'normal' or 'natural' prices or 'prices of production'. The method of analysis congenial to this setting is known as the *long-period method*. It is indeed the application of this method that characterizes the propositions derived in this essay. As we shall see, in the context of the simplified analysis presented here normal prices depend only on two factors:

(i) the real wage rate, or, alternatively, the rate of profits; and
(ii) the set of technical alternatives from which cost-minimizing producers can choose.

In the following we shall treat the level of the rate of profits as an independent variable. That is, we shall refrain from entering into a discussion of the factors affecting that level, or, in other words, from elaborating a theory of income distribution. However, it should be pointed out that proceeding in that way is compatible with the Post-Keynesian theory of income distribution as it was developed by Nicholas Kaldor, Joan Robinson, and Luigi Pasinetti. In that theory the rate of profits is considered as being determined by a given rate of growth of investment demand, reflecting 'animal spirits' (Keynes) of entrepreneurs, and given saving behaviour. (See the papers collected by Panico and Salvadori, 1993.) It should also be emphasized that the kind of approach developed in this essay is incompatible with a determination of the rate of profits in terms of the supply of and the demand for a factor called 'capital', the quantity of which could be ascertained prior to and independently of the determination of the rate of profits and relative prices. (On this see Kurz and Salvadori, 1995; chapter 14.)

There are a number of additional simplifying premises underlying the following analysis which should be mentioned. In parentheses we shall in some cases refer to contributions that transcend the limitations of this essay. The reader interested in getting a richer picture of the kind of analysis provided below is asked to consult the works cited. We shall deal with a closed economy without government (see, however, Steedman, 1979). There is no technical or organizational progress, that is, the set of technical alternatives mentioned in (ii) is given and constant (see, however, Schefold, 1976). Labour is assumed to be homogeneous, or, what amounts to the same thing, differences in quality are reduced to equivalent differences in quantity in terms of a given and constant structure of relative wage rates, the problem of the creation of skilled labour powers is set aside, and the work effort per hour is given and constant (see, however, Kurz and Salvadori, 1995; chapter 11). Wages are paid at the end of the production period.

The composition of the chapter is the following. Section 2 presents the single-products model with two commodities, both of which are basic. We shall first assume that there is no choice of technique, that is, there is only a single method of production available for each commodity. In a first step we shall define the concept of viability of the economy under consideration. Next we shall determine the maximum rate of profits and then analyse the dependence of prices on the level of the rate of profits, given the technical conditions of production. Section 3 allows for a choice of technique. We shall assume that there are several methods of production available to produce each of the two commodities by means of themselves. Given the rate of profits, the question is which of the different methods will be chosen by producers. More precisely, we are interested in determining the cost-minimizing *technique*(s) *of production*. It will be shown that cost minimization involves the maximization of the dependent distributive variable, that is, the wage rate. Section 4 provides a simple model with fixed capital. It will be assumed that a 'tractor' can be produced by means of labour and 'corn' and can then be used in the production of corn. To keep things as simple as possible, the tractor is taken to last at most for two periods and that old tractors can be disposed of at zero cost. It will be shown that there is a choice of technique problem involved concerning the length of time for which the tractor will be used (that is, one or two periods). Section 5 allows for different modes of operation of a fixed capital good; the case contemplated is single- and double-shift work. Section 6 contains some concluding considerations.

2. Two basic commodities

The two commodities will be called 'corn' (c) and 'iron' (i). Corn and iron are produced either directly or indirectly by means of corn and iron. Table 12.1 summarizes the technical features of the two production processes. Accordingly, a_{kh} ($h, k = c, i$) units of commodity h and l_k units of labour are needed to produce one unit of commodity k.

A commodity h will be said to enter directly into the production of commodity k, if

$$a_{kh} > 0$$

where $h, k = c, i$. A commodity h will be said to enter directly or indirectly into the production of commodity k, if

$$a_{kh} + a_{kc}a_{ch} + a_{ki}a_{ih} > 0$$

As mentioned, a commodity which enters directly or indirectly into the production of all commodities is a *basic* commodity; otherwise it is a *non-basic* commodity. Appendix A shows that both corn and iron are basic if and only if

$$a_{ci}a_{ic} > 0 \tag{12.1}$$

An economy is said to be *viable* if it is able to reproduce itself. In the present context this means that there are feasible activity intensities of the two processes, Y_c and Y_i, such that

$$Y_c \geqslant Y_c a_{cc} + Y_i a_{ic} \tag{12.2a}$$

$$Y_i \geqslant Y_c a_{ci} + Y_i a_{ii} \tag{12.2b}$$

$$Y_c \geqslant 0, \quad Y_i \geqslant 0, \quad Y_c + Y_i > 0 \tag{12.2c}$$

More precisely, we say that the economy is *just viable* if both weak inequalities (12.2a) and (12.2b) are satisfied as equations; and we say the economy is *able to produce a surplus* if at least one of them is satisfied as a strong inequality.

Let p_i be the price of one unit of iron in terms of corn (obviously the price of corn in terms of corn equals 1). Then, if a uniform rate of profits is assumed, and

Table 12.1 Technical features of production processes of corn and iron

	Material inputs		Labour		Outputs	
	Corn	*Iron*			*Corn*	*Iron*
Corn process	a_{cc}	a_{ci}	l_c	$\rightarrow$	1	—
Iron process	a_{ic}	a_{ii}	l_i	$\rightarrow$	—	1

if the wage rate is set equal to zero, the following equations hold:

$$(1 + R)a_{cc} + (1 + R)a_{ci} p_i = 1 \qquad (12.3a)$$

$$(1 + R)a_{ic} + (1 + R)a_{ii} p_i = p_i \qquad (12.3b)$$

where R is the *maximum rate of profits*. Further on, in order to be sensible from an economic point of view, it is required that

$$p_i > 0, \quad R \geqslant 0 \qquad (12.3c)$$

Appendix B shows that

(i) system (12.3) has one and only one solution if and only if the economy is viable. Otherwise there is no solution.
(ii) $R > 0$ if and only if the economy is able to produce a surplus, $R = 0$ if and only if the economy is just viable.

The two propositions are important because an economy that is not viable is of limited interest to economists. Equations (12.3) determine the wage rate and the price of iron when the rate of profits, r, equals R. With $r < R$, the following equations hold:

$$(1 + r)a_{cc} + (1 + r)a_{ci} p_i + w l_c = 1 \qquad (12.4a)$$

$$(1 + r)a_{ic} + (1 + r)a_{ii} p_i + w l_i = p_i \qquad (12.4b)$$

where the wage rate, w, and the price of iron, p_i, are measured in terms of corn. For each given r such that $0 \leqslant r \leqslant R$, equations (12.4) constitute a linear system in p_i and w whose solution is

$$w = \frac{1 - (a_{cc} + a_{ii})(1 + r) + (a_{cc} a_{ii} - a_{ci} a_{ic})(1 + r)^2}{(1 + r)a_{ci} l_i + [1 - (1 + r)a_{ii}] l_c} \qquad (12.5a)$$

$$p_i = \frac{[1 - (1 + r)a_{cc}] l_i + (1 + r)a_{ic} l_c}{(1 + r)a_{ci} l_i + [1 - (1 + r)a_{ii}] l_c} \qquad (12.5b)$$

Equation (12.5a) is known as the *w–r relationship*. Appendix C shows that

(iii) if $-1 \leqslant r < R$, w and p_i as defined by equations (12.5) are positive,
(iv) if $r = R$, p_i as defined by equation (12.5b) is positive (as we have seen above, $w = 0$ in this case),
(v) if $-1 \leqslant r \leqslant R$, the *w–r* relationship is a decreasing function.

Propositions (i)–(v) imply that viable economies exhibit properties that can easily be related to real world phenomena.

3. Choice of technique

Up till now it has been boldly assumed that there is only one way to produce each of the two commodities. In this section this very restrictive premise will be removed. In order to do so the following concepts are defined.

A *method* or *process of production*, or, for short, a *process*, to produce commodity $h(h = c, i)$ is defined as the triplet (a_{hc}, a_{hi}, l_h). The set of all available processes is called a *technology*.

Assume that there exist u processes to produce corn and v processes to produce iron. These processes are referred to as

$$(a_{cc}^{(h)}, a_{ci}^{(h)}, l_c^{(h)}) \quad h = 1, 2, \ldots, u$$

$$(a_{ic}^{(k)}, a_{ii}^{(k)}, l_i^{(k)}) \quad k = 1, 2, \ldots, v$$

In addition, assume that

$$a_{ci}^{(h)} > 0, \quad a_{ic}^{(k)} > 0 \quad \text{each } h, \text{ each } k$$

Let w, r, and p_i denote the ruling wage rate, rate of profits, and iron price, respectively. Then, processes $(a_{cc}^{(h)}, a_{ci}^{(h)}, l_c^{(h)})$ and $(a_{ic}^{(k)}, a_{ii}^{(k)}, l_i^{(k)})$ *are (are not) able to pay extra profits* if

$$(1 + r)a_{cc}^{(h)} + (1 + r)a_{ci}^{(h)} p_i + w l_c^{(h)} < 1 \quad (\geqslant 1)$$

$$(1 + r)a_{ic}^{(k)} + (1 + r)a_{ii}^{(k)} p_i + w l_i^{(k)} < p_i \quad (\geqslant p_i)$$

and they *do (do not) incur extra costs* if

$$(1 + r)a_{cc}^{(h)} + (1 + r)a_{ci}^{(h)} p_i + w l_c^{(h)} > 1 \quad (\leqslant 1)$$

$$(1 + r)a_{ic}^{(k)} + (1 + r)a_{ii}^{(k)} p_i + w l_i^{(k)} > p_i \quad (\leqslant p_i)$$

respectively. If a process is able to pay extra profits, producers would seek to adopt it in order to obtain the extra profits, and if they succeeded in doing so, the resulting rate of profit in the particular industry would be larger than r.

In a *long-period position at rate of profits r* no producer can obtain a higher rate of profit by operating another process because it is a position of rest (given the data of the problem, including the level of the general rate of profits). It should also be noticed that because none of the two commodities can be produced without the other also being produced, in a long-period position at least one process to produce each of the two commodities has to be operated. Hence, the pair (w, p_i) is a *long-period position at rate of profits r*, if the rate of profits r, the wage rate w, and the price of iron p_i are such that (a) no process is able to pay extra profits and (b) there is at least one process producing corn and at least one process producing iron that do not require extra costs. Accordingly, (w, p_i) represents a long-period position at the rate of profits r if

$$(1+r)a_{cc}^{(s)} + (1+r)a_{ci}^{(s)}p_i + wl_c^{(s)} = 1 \qquad \text{some } s$$

$$(1+r)a_{ic}^{(t)} + (1+r)a_{ii}^{(t)}p_i + wl_i^{(t)} = p_i \qquad \text{some } t$$

$$(1+r)a_{cc}^{(h)} + (1+r)a_{ci}^{(h)}p_i + wl_c^{(h)} \geqslant 1 \qquad \text{each } h$$

$$(1+r)a_{ic}^{(k)} + (1+r)a_{ii}^{(k)}p_i + wl_i^{(k)} \geqslant p_i \qquad \text{each } k$$

Processes $(a_{cc}^{(s)}, a_{ci}^{(s)}, l_c^{(s)})$ and $(a_{ic}^{(t)}, a_{ii}^{(t)}, l_i^{(t)})$, are operated, while processes which incur extra costs are not.

Let us now check whether the above system allows for solutions. In order to do this, define a *technique* as a set of two processes consisting of one process producing corn and the other iron. A technique is said to be *cost-minimizing* at a rate of profits $\hat{r}$ if at the corresponding wage rate and iron price no known process is able to pay extra profits. Appendix D proves the following.

Theorem 1

(a) *If there is a technique which has a positive p_i and a positive wage rate w for $r = \hat{r}$, then there is a cost-minimizing technique at the rate of profits $\hat{r}$.*

(b) *A technique which yields a positive price $\hat{p}_i$ and a nonnegative wage rate $\hat{w}$ for $r = \hat{r}$ minimizes costs at the rate of profits $\hat{r}$ if and only if no other technique allows a wage rate higher than $\hat{w}$ for $r = \hat{r}$.*

(c) *If there is more than one technique which minimizes costs at a rate of profits $\hat{r}$, then these techniques yield the same wage rate and the same $\hat{p}_i$ at $r = \hat{r}$.*

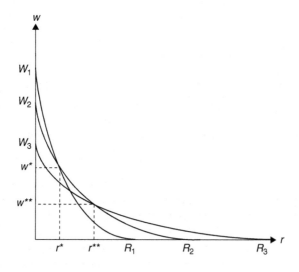

Figure 12.1 The w–r relationships and the wage-profit frontier.

Thus, if the w–r relationships relative to all techniques available are drawn in the same diagram (see Figure 12.1), the outer envelope represents the *wage–profit frontier* for the whole technology. The points on the wage–profit frontier at which two techniques are cost-minimizing are called *switch points*. If a technique is cost-minimizing at two disconnected ranges of the rate of profits and not so in between these ranges, we say that there is a *reswitching* of technique.

4. Fixed capital

Up till now it has been assumed that each process produces one and only one commodity. Let us now introduce a model that allows for joint production, but only in a special way. We shall assume that a fixed capital good, say a tractor, can be produced by means of another commodity, say corn. Corn can in turn be produced by means of itself and the tractor. The crucial idea now is that when a new tractor is used to produce corn, it produces at the same time a one year old tractor as a joint product. For simplicity we shall assume that the maximum *technical* lifetime of the tractor is two years. The equivalent of Table 12.1 for the new model is Table 12.2.

There are now three processes to produce corn instead of just one. Process (1) uses the new tractor as an input and produces an old tractor as a by-product. Process (2) uses an old tractor and produces no joint product, given our assumptions about the technical lifetime of the tractor. (The word 'tractor' must not lead the reader to think that at the end of the tractor's lifetime there is some scrap to be disposed of; yet, in the case in which there happens to be some scrap to be disposed of, an appropriate additional assumption would have to be introduced.) Process (4) is a consequence of the fact that we assume free disposal with regard to the one year old tractor. The fact that a one year old tractor can be disposed of is important because it allows us to determine the *economic* lifetime of the tractor as opposed to its technical lifetime. (The assumption that this disposal is free rather than costly is entertained only for the sake of simplicity.) If, in fact, it were

Table 12.2 Production with fixed capital

		Material inputs			Labour		Outputs		
		Corn	New tractor	Old tractor			Corn	New tractor	Old tractor
(1)	Corn process (new tractor)	a_1	1	—	l_1	→	b_1	—	1
(2)	Corn process (old tractor)	a_2	—	1	l_2	→	b_2	—	—
(3)	New tractor process	a_3	—	—	l_3	→	—	1	—
(4)	Corn process (truncated)	a_1	1	—	l_1	→	b_1	—	—

not economically convenient to employ the tractor for a second year, it would be jettisoned. This means that instead of process (1) process (4) will be used. (In this case we are effectively back in a model with only circulating capital goods – just as the one analysed in the preceding two sections.) Which of the two alternatives will be adopted is, of course, a choice of technique problem, analogous at the one already investigated.

We shall assume that old tractors are not consumables. If they were, then, in fact, process (1) should be operated, even if cost minimization would neccessitate producers to select process (4) instead of (1), in order to produce old tractors for the consumers. Finally, it will not have escaped the reader's attention that in this simple model we have set aside the possibilty of the joint utilization of tractors, that is, no process is using both old and new tractors.

When we dealt with single production we distinguished between two different problems. However, towards the end of Section 3, the results of the analyses of the two problems were put together in terms of the outer envelope of the different $w-r$ relationships, or wage frontier. The first problem studied was the dependence of the price of iron in terms of corn and the real wage rate (also in terms of corn) with regard to a single technique for all feasible levels of the rate of profits (see Section 2). The second problem concerned the choice of technique for a given rate of profits $r = \hat{r}$ (see Section 3). Having understood the basic logic underlying this procedure, the reader will not mind, not least in the interest of brevity, if with respect to fixed capital we shall skip the first step and immediately turn to the second one. Hence it will be assumed that there are altogether u processes of the kind of process (1) and the same number of processes of the kind of process (4), and there are v and z processes of the kind of processes (2) and (3), respectively. Appendix E shows that Theorem 1 of previous section can be generalized to the framework provided in this section and that in a cost-minimizing technique no produced commodity has a negative price.

5. Capital utilization

In the preceding section we have assumed that the pattern of utilization of fixed capital is given. This concerns both an extensive and an intensive dimension: the number of hours during which the durable instrument of production is operated per period, say per day, and the speed at which it is operated. In this section we shall allow for different modes of utilization, which poses just another kind of choice of technique problem. The example discussed will be *shift work*. More precisely, we shall assume that a machine can be operated in a single- and in a double-shift system.

Suppose that a pin manufacturer has the choice of operating a machine under a single (day) shift or under a double (day and night) shift. Suppose for simplicity that under the night shift the amount of direct labour and the quantities of the means of production used up per unit of output are the same as under the day shift. Hence, under the double-shift system the same yearly output could be produced by working half of the machinery twice as long each day as under the single-shift

Table 12.3 Shift work

Processes		Material inputs			Day labour	Night labour		Outputs	
		Pins	New machine	Old machine				Pins	Old machine
(1)	Single shift (first year)	a	1	—	l	—	→	b	1
(2)	Single shift (second year)	a	—	1	l	—	→	b	—
(3)	Double shift	a	$\frac{1}{2}$	—	$\frac{1}{2}l$	$\frac{1}{2}l$	→	b	—
(4)	Truncated process	a	1	—	l	—	→	b	—

system. Assume in addition that the machine's lifetime lasts two years under the single- and one year under the double-shift system, respectively. The technical alternatives from which the producer can choose are summarized in Table 12.3. Process (1) relates to the single-shift system when the new machine is utilized, whereas process (2) relates to the single-shift system when the one year old machine is utilized. Process (3) refers to the double-shift system. Process (4) relates to the single shift when the economic life of the machine is truncated. (The process to produce the new machine is not in the table.)

Assume that for the work performed at night not only the basic hourly wage rate w but also a premium $\alpha w > 0$ will have to be paid, so that the wage rate during the night shift amounts to $w(1 + \alpha)$. Obviously, the producer can compare the cheapness of the three alternatives for each rate of profits and the corresponding prices and basic wage rate. Under the conditions specified, the question of whether it would be profitable to schedule work regularly both at day and night instead of only at day is easily decided. By adopting the double-shift system the producer could economize on his machinery by one half per unit of output. On the other hand he would incur a larger wages bill. Hence, whether the double-shift system proves superior depends on the wage premium and the rate of profits, and can be decided in a way that is analogous to the problem of the choice of technique investigated in the previous section.

6. Concluding remarks

The chapter has analyzed in a general framework of the analysis, using, however, only simple models, some of the outstanding features of modern industrial economies, that is, commodities are produced by means of commodities and fixed capital goods play an important part in the production process. It has been shown that the framework elaborated allows a discussion of the intricate problem of the choice of technique and a consistent determination of the dependent variables under consideration: one of the distributive variables (the rate of profits or, alternatively, the real wage rate) and relative prices. It has also been shown that problems such as different patterns of utilization of plant and equipment can easily be analysed in the present framework. The chapter is designed to provide the basis for an analysis that takes production seriously.

Appendix A

If both corn and iron enter directly or indirectly into the production of both commodities, then by definition

$$a_{cc} + a_{cc}^2 + a_{ci}a_{ic} > 0 \tag{12.A1a}$$

$$a_{ic} + a_{ic}a_{cc} + a_{ii}a_{ic} > 0 \tag{12.A1b}$$

$$a_{ci} + a_{cc}a_{ci} + a_{ci}a_{ii} > 0 \tag{12.A1b}$$

$$a_{ii} + a_{ic}a_{ci} + a_{ii}^2 > 0 \tag{12.A1c}$$

Since none of the a's is negative, it is easily checked that if inequality (12.1) holds, then all inequalities (12.A1) hold. On the contrary, if inequalities (12.A1b) and (12.A1c) hold, then inequality (12.1) also holds. This is more easily seen by writing inequalities (12.A1b) and (12.A1c) as

$$a_{ic}(1 + a_{cc} + a_{ii}) > 0$$

$$a_{ci}(1 + a_{cc} + a_{ii}) > 0$$

Appendix B

Since inequality (12.1) holds, inequalities (12.2a) and (12.2b) imply that if at least one of the Y's is positive, then both are. Hence, inequalities (12.2) imply

$$Y_c > 0, \quad Y_i > 0. \tag{12.B1}$$

From inequality (12.2a), taking account of inequalities (12.B1) and (12.1), one obtains that

$$1 - a_{cc} > 0 \tag{12.B2a}$$

$$\frac{Y_c}{Y_i} \geqslant \frac{a_{ic}}{1 - a_{cc}} \tag{12.B2b}$$

Similarly, from (12.2b),

$$1 - a_{ii} > 0 \tag{12.B2c}$$

$$\frac{1 - a_{ii}}{a_{ci}} \geqslant \frac{Y_c}{Y_i} \tag{12.B2d}$$

Therefore inequalities (12.2) are consistent if and only if (12.B2a) and (12.B2c) hold and there is a real number Y_c/Y_i such that

$$\frac{1 - a_{ii}}{a_{ci}} \geqslant \frac{Y_c}{Y_i} \geqslant \frac{a_{ic}}{1 - a_{cc}}$$

Hence the economy is viable if and only if

$$1 - a_{cc} > 0 \tag{12.B3a}$$

$$(1 - a_{cc})(1 - a_{ii}) - a_{ci}a_{ic} \geqslant 0 \tag{12.B3b}$$

Inequality (12.B2c) is not mentioned since it is a consequence of inequalities (12.B3). The reader will easily recognize that if the economy is just viable, then the weak inequality (12.B3b) is satisfied as an equation, whereas if the economy is able to produce a surplus, then the weak inequality (12.B3b) is satisfied as a strong inequality.

To simplify the analysis of system (12.3), let us set

$$\lambda = \frac{1}{1 + R} \tag{12.B4}$$

Because of (12.B4) system (12.3) can be rewritten as

$$a_{cc} + a_{ci}p_i = \lambda \tag{12.B5a}$$

$$a_{ic} + a_{ii}p_i = \lambda p_i \tag{12.B5b}$$

$$p_i > 0, \quad 0 < \lambda \leqslant 1 \tag{12.B6}$$

System (12.B5) is equivalent to the following system:

$$z(\lambda) := \lambda^2 - (a_{cc} + a_{ii})\lambda + (a_{cc}a_{ii} - a_{ci}a_{ic}) = 0 \tag{12.B7a}$$

$$p_i = \frac{\lambda - a_{cc}}{a_{ci}} \tag{12.B7b}$$

It is easily checked that

$$z(a_{cc}) = z(a_{ii}) = -a_{ci}a_{ic} < 0$$

$$z(1) = (1 - a_{cc})(1 - a_{ii}) - a_{ci}a_{ic}$$

Hence, if the economy is viable, then $z(1) \geqslant 0$ or, more precisely, if the economy is able to produce a surplus, $z(1) > 0$, whereas if it is just viable, $z(1) = 0$. Thus one of the two solutions to equation (12.B7a), λ^*, is larger than $\max(a_{cc}, a_{ii})$ and smaller than 1 (if the economy is able to produce a surplus) or equal to 1 (if the economy is just viable). The other solution, on the other hand, is smaller than $\min(a_{cc}, a_{ii})$ but not smaller than $-\lambda^*$ since

$$z(-\lambda^*) = 2(a_{cc} + a_{ii})\lambda^* \geqslant 0$$

Finally, if we take account of equation (12.B7b), only the solution to equation (12.B7a) larger than a_{cc} can be associated with a positive p_i. Figure 12.B1 gives an example in which the economy is able to produce a surplus, $0 < a_{ii} < a_{cc}$ and $a_{cc}a_{ii} < a_{ci}a_{ic}$ (if $a_{cc}a_{ii} > a_{ci}a_{ic}$, the solution to equation (12.B7a) associated with a negative p_i is positive).

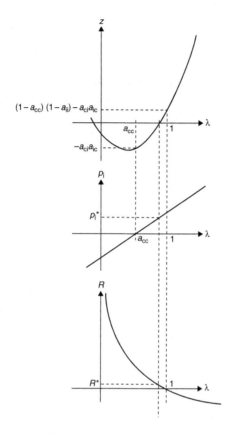

Figure 12.B1 Uniqueness of R.

Appendix C

From equations (12.3a) and (12.3b), and taking into account inequalities (12.1) and (12.3c), we obtain

$$1 - (1 + R)a_{cc} > 0$$
$$1 - (1 + R)a_{ii} > 0$$

This is enough to prove that if $-1 \leqslant r \leqslant R$, p_i as defined by equation (12.5b) and the denominator of the fraction in equation (12.5a) are positive. Moreover, since the equation (12.B7a) has no solution greater than $1/(1 + R)$, then

$$\left(\frac{1}{1+r}\right)^2 - (a_{cc} + a_{ii})\left(\frac{1}{1+r}\right) + (a_{cc}a_{ii} - a_{ci}a_{ic}) > 0$$

for $-1 < r < R$. Thus, $w > 0$ if $0 \leqslant r < R$ and $w = 0$ if $r = R$.

When there is a variation in the rate of profits r, the wage rate w also varies. Let us assume that r and w move in the same direction, for example, they increase simultaneously. Then equation (12.4a) requires that p_i falls, but equation (12.4b) rewritten as

$$\frac{1}{p_i}[(1+r)a_{ic} + wl_i] = 1 - (1+r)a_{ii}$$

requires that p_i rises. Hence we have a contradiction. Thus r and w cannot move in the same direction, that is, w is a decreasing function of the rate of profits.

Appendix D

Figure 12.D1 is useful to prove that for a given rate of profits $r = \hat{r}$ the propositions stated below hold. A corn process can be plotted in the (p_i, w) plane as a straight line such as FA in Figure 12.D1 (since $r = \hat{r}$). (Processes for which $1 < (1+\hat{r})a_{cc}$ can be left out of consideration.) Similarly, each iron process can be plotted as a straight line such as EA in Figure 12.D1. Notice that the decreasing straight line cuts the vertical axis at a positive value, whereas the increasing straight line cuts the vertical axis at a negative value.

Proposition D1. *If a process α is able to pay extra profits at the prices of technique β, then there exists a technique γ which can pay a wage rate larger than that paid by technique β.*

Proof The wage rate and the price of iron associated with technique β are represented in Figure 12.D1 by point A. Hence the relation between w and p_i relative to process α at $r = \hat{r}$ intersects the half-line AD by hypothesis. If this relation is a decreasing line (i.e. process α produces corn), it will intersect line AE at a point above and to the right of A. If, on the contrary, this relation is an increasing line (i.e. process α produces iron), it will intersect line AF at a point above and to the left of A. (Q.E.D.)

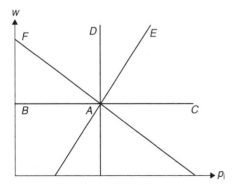

Figure 12.D1 Choice of technique.

Proposition D1 is sufficient to sustain that each technique which at the given rate of profits $\hat{r}$ is able to pay the highest possible wage rate is cost-minimizing at that rate of profits. The following Proposition D2 precludes the case in which a technique which is not able to pay the highest possible wage rate can be a technique which minimizes costs.

Proposition D2. *If technique α is able to pay a larger wage rate than technique β, then there is a process in technique α which is able to pay extra profits at the wage rate and iron price of technique β.*

Proof The wage rate and the iron price of technique β are represented in Figure 12.D1 by point A. Hence, the wage rate and the iron price of technique α are represented by a point which is either located in quadrant CAD or in quadrant BAD. In the first case, the process which produces corn if technique α is used will pay extra profits at prices relative to technique β. In the second case, the process which produces iron if technique α is used will pay extra profits at prices relative to technique β. (Q.E.D.)

Proposition D3. *If both technique α and technique β are cost-minimizing at the rate of profits $\hat{r}$, then the iron price corresponding to $r = \hat{r}$ is the same for both techniques.*

Proof The wage rate and the iron price of technique β are represented in Figure 12.D1 by point A. Since both techniques α and β pay the same wage rate, the wage rate and the iron price of technique α are given either by point A, or by a point located on AC (excluding point A), or by a point located on AB (excluding point A). In the second case, the process which produces corn if technique α is used will pay extra profits at prices of technique β. In the third case, the process which produces iron if technique α is used will pay extra profits at prices of technique β. It follows that the wage rate and the iron price of technique α are of necessity given by point A. (Q.E.D.)

Proof of Theorem 1 The 'only if' part of statement (b) is a direct consequence of Proposition D2. The 'if' part is a consequence of Proposition D1. Statement (c) is equivalent to Proposition D3. Statement (a) is a direct consequence of statement (b) since the number of processes is finite. (Q.E.D.)

Appendix E

In order to show that the same argument developed in Appendix D applies in the case of fixed capital, we first need to show that for $r = \hat{r}$ (p_{nt} is the price of a new tractor in terms of corn)

(i) each of the z processes producing new tractors can be represented as an increasing straight line in the (p_{nt}, w) plane;

(ii) each of the u processes producing corn with new tractors without producing old tractors can be represented as a decreasing straight line in the (p_{nt}, w) plane;

(iii) each of the $u \times v$ pair of processes of the kind of processes (1) and (2) can be represented as a decreasing straight line in the (p_{nt}, w) plane.

Statements (i) and (ii) are obvious, because the reference is to single-products processes like those we encountered in Section 3 and Appendix D. As regards statement (iii), the two processes mentioned determine the following equations, given the condition that each of them pays the rate of profits $\hat{r}$:

$$(1 + \hat{r})a_1 + (1 + \hat{r})p_{nt} + wl_1 = b_1 + p_{ot} \tag{12.E1a}$$

$$(1 + \hat{r})a_2 + (1 + \hat{r})p_{ot} + wl_2 = b_2 \tag{12.E1b}$$

where p_{ot} is the price of an old tractor in terms of corn. By multiplying both sides of equation (12.E1a) by $(1 + \hat{r})$ and adding the resulting equation and equation (12.E1b), the following equation is obtained:

$$(1+\hat{r})^2 a_1 + (1+\hat{r})^2 p_{nt} + (1+\hat{r})wl_1 + (1+\hat{r})a_2 + wl_2 = (1+\hat{r})b_1 + b_2 \tag{12.E2}$$

that is

$$w = \frac{(1 + \hat{r})[b_1 - (1 + \hat{r})a_1] + [b_2 - (1 + \hat{r})a_2] - (1 + \hat{r})^2 p_{nt}}{(1 + \hat{r})l_1 + l_2}$$

and since we are interested only in the cases in which

$$(1 + \hat{r})[b_1 - (1 + \hat{r})a_1] + [b_2 - (1 + \hat{r})a_2] > 0$$

statement (iii) is proved. But there is something more. If we look at equation (12.E2), it resembles the equation of a single-product process producing corn, where $(1 + \hat{r})b_1 + b_2$ is the output of corn, $(1 + \hat{r})a_1 + a_2$ is the input of corn, $(1 + \hat{r})$ is the input of a new tractor, and $(1 + \hat{r})l_1 + l_2$ is the labour input.[2]

---

2 It will not escape the reader's attention that if the tractor exibits the same efficiency throughout its life, that is, $a_1 = a_2 := a$, $l_1 = l_2 := l$, and $b_1 = b_2 := b$, then equation (12.E2) can be written as

$$(1 + \hat{r})a + \frac{\hat{r}(1 + \hat{r})^2}{(1 + \hat{r})^2 - 1} p_{nt} + wl = b$$

The reader will also notice that the second term on the LHS involves nothing but the well-known annuity formula giving the annual charge of a fixed capital good lasting n years,

$$\frac{r(1 + r)^n}{(1 + r)^n - 1}$$

in the special case in which $n = 2$.

In the following we shall refer to this fictitious process as a 'core process' to produce corn; of course, there are $u \times v$ of them. Similarly to the definitions given in Section 3 we say that a core process *is (is not) able to pay extra profits* at the rate of profits $\hat{r}$ if

$$(1+\hat{r})^2 a_1 + (1+\hat{r})^2 p_{\text{nt}} + (1+\hat{r})wl_1 + (1+\hat{r})a_2 + wl_2$$
$$< (1+\hat{r})b_1 + b_2 \qquad (\geqslant (1+\hat{r})b_1 + b_2)$$

and it *does (does not) incur extra costs* at the rate of profits $\hat{r}$ if

$$(1+\hat{r})^2 a_1 + (1+\hat{r})^2 p_{\text{nt}} + (1+\hat{r})wl_1 + (1+\hat{r})a_2 + wl_2$$
$$> (1+\hat{r})b_1 + b_2 \qquad (\leqslant (1+\hat{r})b_1 + b_2)$$

It is easily checked that if a process of type (1) or (2) (see Table 12.2) is able to pay extra profits, then there is a core process which is paying extra profits, and vice versa. This is enough to recognize that Propositions D1–D3 of Appendix D hold also in the present context. Only two remarks about the proofs are needed: first, anytime the word 'process' occurs the reader has to read 'process or core process'; second, with respect to Proposition D3 the proof refers to the price of new tractors only. If at least one of α and β is a technique which does not include a core process, then no change is required. If both techniques include a core process, then the proof provided in Appendix D is incomplete since we need to prove that also the price of old tractors is uniquely determined. But this is certainly the case: if the price of old tractors related to technique α were to be smaller than the one related to technique β, then the process of kind (2) in technique α would be able to pay extra profits at the prices of technique β, and the process of kind (1) in technique β would be able to pay extra profits at the prices of technique α. This is so because both the wage rate and the price of new tractors are the same in the two techniques. Hence a contradiction. Once Propositions D1–D3 are proved, Theorem 1 of Section 3 is also proved.

References

Kurz, H. D. (1990), 'Effective Demand, Employment and Capital Utilization in the Short Run', *Cambridge Journal of Economics*, **14**, pp. 205–217.

Kurz, H. D. and Salvadori, N. (1995), *Theory of Production. A Long-period Analysis*, Cambridge, New York and Melbourne: Cambridge University Press.

Panico, C. and Salvadori, N. (eds) (1993), *Post Keynesian Theory of Growth and Distribution*, Aldershot (UK): Edward Elgar.

Schefold, B. (1976), 'Different Forms of Technical Progress', *Economic Journal*, **86**, pp. 806–19.

Sraffa, P. (1960), *Production of Commodities by Means of Commodities*, Cambridge: Cambridge University Press.

Steedman, I. (1979), *Trade Amongst Growing Economies*, Cambridge: Cambridge University Press.

Part IV

Exhaustible resources and the long-period method

13 Classical economics and the problem of exhaustible resources*

Heinz D. Kurz and Neri Salvadori

In Section 1 we shall discuss the mathematical properties of the simple model proposed by Bidard and Erreygers (2001). We shall solve the model for a given real wage rate paid at the beginning of the uniform production period. In Section 2 we shall question the usefulness of the concept of a 'real profit rate' suggested by Bidard and Erreygers and their view that the choice of numéraire can have an impact on the mathematical properties of the system under consideration. In Sections 3 and 4 we assess some of the propositions put forward by Bidard and Erreygers. Section 3 deals with the fact that any economic model is bound to distort reality in some way and therefore can never be more than an attempt to 'approximate' important features of the latter. This is exemplified by means of the labour theory of value in classical economics, on the one hand, and by Ricardo's assimilation of the case of exhaustible resources to that of scarce land and thus its subsumption under the theory of differential rent, on the other. In certain well-specified circumstances royalties are replaced by rents, while in other circumstances neither rents nor royalties play any role. In Section 4 we turn to the so-called Hotelling rule. It is stressed that in order for this rule to apply there must be no obstacles whatsoever to the uniformity of the rate of profit across conservation and production processes, and the available amounts of the resources must be bounded and known with certainty. Therefore Hotelling's rule cannot be considered so generally applicable as Bidard and Erreygers seem to suggest.

1. The corn–guano model with a given real wage rate

Bidard and Erreygers propose a simple model to investigate the elementary properties of an economy employing exhaustible resources, a model, they maintain, which 'constitutes an adaptation and the theoretical equivalent of the standard corn model for the classical theory of long-term prices' (p. 244). We find their concern with simplicity laudable. However, with Albert Einstein we insist that while a model should be as simple as possible, it must not be simpler than that. Indeed in our view the model suggested by Bidard and Erreygers, or rather their interpretation

---

* Reprinted with permission from *Metroeconomica*, 2001.

of it, neglects aspects of the problem under consideration that are important and can already be seen at the suggested low level of model complexity.

The two authors point out that the argument in their 'corn–guano model' could be formulated either in terms of a given real wage rate or in terms of what they call a given 'real rate of profit'. They then decide to develop fully only the second variant but stress that in the alternative case the 'dynamic behaviour of the system is completely similar'. In both models wages are paid at the beginning of the production period. Since, as will be made clear below, we doubt that the concept of 'real rate of profit' can be given a clear meaning and useful analytical role in the investigation under discussion, we shall start from a given real (i.e. corn) wage rate paid *ante factum*.

In accordance with the two authors we assume that there are two commodities, corn and guano, which can be produced or conserved by the processes depicted in Table 13.1, where a_1 and a_2 are corn inputs per unit of corn output inclusive of the corn wages paid to labourers ($0 < a_1 < a_2 < 1$). The quantity side of the model is not made explicit by Bidard and Erreygers; it is just assumed that from time 1 to T processes (1) and (3) are operated, from time T to infinity process (2) is operated, and at time $T+1$ guano is exhausted and therefore processes (1) and (3) cannot be operated anymore. This assumption involves some sort of implicit theorizing and is invoked by us only in order to keep close to the procedure followed by Bidard and Erreygers. However, on the assumptions stated no difficulty appears to arise.[1]

The model has the following equations:

$$p_{t+1} = (1+r_t)(a_1 p_t + z_t) \quad 1 \leqslant t \leqslant T \tag{13.1.1}$$

$$p_{t+1} = (1+r_t)a_2 p_t \quad t \geqslant T \tag{13.1.2}$$

$$z_{t+1} = (1+r_t)z_t \quad 1 \leqslant t \leqslant T \tag{13.1.3}$$

where p is the price of corn, r the nominal rate of profit and z the price of guano at the time indicated by the corresponding subscript. The sequence of nominal rates

Table 13.1 The available processes of production and conservation

	Inputs			Outputs	
	Corn	Guano		Corn	Guano
(1)	a_1	1	→	1	—
(2)	a_2	0	→	1	—
(3)	—	1	→	—	1

1 Things would be different in the case in which wages are paid *post factum*. In this case, in fact, if the process producing corn without guano is more expensive in terms of labour input but less expensive in terms of corn input than the process producing corn with guano, we cannot exclude that corn is produced first without guano, then with guano until guano is exhausted, then without guano once again. For an example of this type, see Kurz and Salvadori (1997, pp. 248–9).

of profit $\{r_t\}$ is assumed to be given. However, it is easily checked that the given sequence plays no role in determining the relative present value prices in the sense that, if the sequences $\{p_t\}$ and $\{z_t\}$ are a solution to system (13.1) for the given sequence $\{r_t\}$, then the sequences $\{q_t\}$ and $\{u_t\}$ such that:

$$q_t = \prod_{\tau=0}^{t-1} \frac{1 + \sigma_\tau}{1 + r_\tau} p_t$$

$$u_t = \prod_{\tau=0}^{t-1} \frac{1 + \sigma_\tau}{1 + r_\tau} z_t$$

are also a solution to system (13.1) for a given sequence $\{\sigma_\tau\}$. This is so because r_t is the *nominal* rate of profit.

It is also easily checked that the above model can determine only the relative prices in the sense that, if the sequences $\{p_t\}$ and $\{z_t\}$ are a solution to system (13.1), then the sequences $\{\eta p_t\}$ and $\{\eta z_t\}$ are also a solution, where η is a positive scalar. This means that there is room for a further equation fixing the numéraire. The numéraire is chosen by the observer and is not related to an objective property of the economic system, apart from the obvious fact that the numéraire must be specified in terms of valuable things (e.g. commodities, labour) that are a part of the economy that is being studied. As Sraffa emphasized in the context of a discussion of the particular numéraire suggested by him: 'Particular proportions, such as the Standard ones, may give transparency to a system and render visible what was hidden, *but they cannot alter its mathematical properties*' (Sraffa, 1960, p. 23, emphasis added). We maintain that, whenever the choice of the numéraire seems to affect the objective properties of the economic system under consideration, then there is something wrong with the theory or model: the objective properties of the economic system must be totally independent of the numéraire adopted by the theorist. Hence the choice of a particular numéraire may be useful or not, but it cannot be right or wrong.

In order to fix the numéraire and to preserve the property that a change in the nominal rates of profit does not affect relative prices, the numéraire is to be set in terms of present value prices (at time θ); that is, we could add, for example, the equation:

$$\left[\sum_{t=0}^{\infty} (h_t p_t + k_t z_t) \prod_{\tau=0}^{t-1} (1 + r_\tau)^{-1} \right] \prod_{u=0}^{\theta-1} (1 + r_u) \tag{13.2}$$

where $\{h_t\}$ and $\{k_t\}$ are sequences of known non-negative magnitudes such that for some t either h_t or k_t, or both, are positive and $k_t = 0$ for all $t > T$.

In the following we will assume that $r_t = 0$, for each t. A change to another sequence of nominal rates of profit can be made at will, as indicated above. We shall also assume that $h_t = 0$ for each $t \neq T$, $h_T = 1$, $k_t = 0$ for each t, and

$\theta = T$ in equation (13.2). Then system (13.1)–(13.2) is more simply stated as

$$p_{t+1} = a_1 p_t + z_t \quad 1 \leqslant t \leqslant T \tag{13.3.1}$$

$$p_{t+1} = a_2 p_t \qquad t \geqslant T \tag{13.3.2}$$

$$z_{t+1} = z_t \qquad 1 \leqslant t \leqslant T \tag{13.3.3}$$

$$p_T = 1 \tag{13.3.4}$$

From equation (13.3.3) we see that:

$$z_t = z_0 \quad 1 \leqslant t \leqslant T \tag{13.4}$$

and then from difference equation (13.3.1), taking account of equation (13.3.4), we get:

$$p_t = \frac{z_0}{1-a_1} + \frac{1-a_1-z_0}{1-a_1} a_1^{t-T} \quad 0 \leqslant t \leqslant T+1 \tag{13.5}$$

Then from difference equation (13.3.2), taking account of equation (13.3.4), we obtain:

$$p_t = a_2^{t-T} \quad t \geqslant T \tag{13.6.1}$$

Finally, taking account of the fact that equations (13.3.1) and (13.3.2) are both satisfied for $t = T$, we obtain:

$$\frac{z_0}{1-a_1} + \frac{1-a_1-z_0}{1-a_1} a_1 = p_{T+1} = a_2$$

Hence

$$z_0 = a_2 - a_1$$

which, substituted in equations (13.4) and (13.5), completes the solution:

$$z_t = a_2 - a_1 \qquad\qquad 1 \leqslant t \leqslant T \tag{13.6.2}$$

$$p_t = \frac{a_2-a_1}{1-a_1} + \frac{1-a_2}{1-a_1} a_1^{t-T} \quad 0 \leqslant t \leqslant T+1 \tag{13.6.3}$$

What happens if there is a change of numéraire? Clearly, *relative* prices are unchanged. In fact, if $\{h_t\}$ and $\{k_t\}$ are sequences of known non-negative magnitudes (at least one of which is positive) such that the series $\sum_{t=T+1}^{\infty} h_t a_2^{t-T}$ is convergent, and if equation (13.3.4) is substituted by the equation:

$$\sum_{t=0}^{T}(h_t p_t + k_t z_t) + \sum_{t=T+1}^{\infty} h_t p_t = 1$$

then the solution becomes

$$z_t = H(a_2 - a_1) \qquad\qquad\qquad 1 \leqslant t \leqslant T$$

$$p_t = H\left(\frac{a_2 - a_1}{1 - a_1} + \frac{1 - a_2}{1 - a_1}a_1^{t-T}\right) \quad 0 \leqslant t \leqslant T+1$$

$$p_t = Ha_2^{t-T} \qquad\qquad\qquad t \geqslant T$$

where

$$H^{-1} = \frac{a_2 - a_1}{1 - a_1}\sum_{t=0}^{T} h_t + \frac{1 - a_2}{1 - a_1}\sum_{t=0}^{T} h_t a_1^{t-T}$$

$$+ \sum_{t=T+1}^{\infty} h_t a_2^{t-T} + (a_2 - a_1)\sum_{t=0}^{T} k_t$$

The reader might also be interested in what happens if we use a sequence of $\{r_t\}$ different from $r_t = 0$, for each t. As an example, let us consider the case of a constant positive sequence:

$$r_t = r > 0 \quad \text{for each } t$$

If, once again, $p_T = 1$, we get

$$z_t = (a_2 - a_1)(1 + r)^{t-T} \qquad\qquad 1 \leqslant t \leqslant T$$

$$p_t = \frac{(a_2 - a_1) + (1 - a_2)a_1^{t-T}}{1 - a_1}(1 + r)^{t-T} \quad 0 \leqslant t \leqslant T+1$$

$$p_t = [(1 + r)a_2]^{t-T} \qquad\qquad\qquad t \geqslant T$$

Obviously, in the special case in which

$$r = \frac{1 - a_2}{a_2}$$

the price of corn is constant from $t = T$ onward.

2. The question of the 'real rate of profit'

We have seen that, if the nominal rate of profit is zero at each t, then the price of guano is constant over time. We may now ask: is there also a sequence of nominal profit rates such that the price of corn is constant over time? Certainly there is.[2] One might also give a special name to this sequence, as is done by Bidard and Erreygers, and call it the sequence of 'real rates of profit'. But this is merely a name: the particular case referred to by it is neither more nor less important than any of the infinitely many possible representations of the genuine properties of the model under consideration. These properties concern in particular the following facts: (i) relative prices are independent of the numéraire and (ii) relative prices corresponding to the same t are also independent of the sequence of nominal rates of profit. As a consequence, at any given point in time the amount of corn the proprietor of guano can obtain by selling one unit of guano (or the amount of corn a worker can obtain for a unit of labour; or the amount of corn the owner of one unit of corn can obtain by investing it either in corn production or in guano conservation; or the amount of guano the owner of one unit of guano can obtain by investing it either in corn production or in guano conservation) is independent of the numéraire and of the sequence of nominal rates of profit.

Starting from the two amounts just mentioned we can obtain what in the literature is known as the *own rate of return* of corn and guano, respectively. Consider an investor who possesses one unit of commodity j (corn or guano) and divides the investment at time t in two parts: d_1 in the production of corn and d_2 in the conservation of guano ($d_1 + d_2 = 1$ and $d_2 = 0$ if $t > T$). Hence, if $t \leqslant T$, at time t inputs are bought which at time $t + 1$ yield $d_1 \pi_{jt}/(a_1 p_t + z_t)$ units of corn and $d_2 \pi_{jt}/z_t$ units of guano, where π_{jt} is the price of commodity j at time t. However, if $t > T$, then at time t an input of corn is obtained which at time $t + 1$ yields $\pi_{jt}/a_2 p_t$ units of corn. If at time $t + 1$ the investor wants to assess the yield of the investment in terms of commodity j, the answer is given by

$$\frac{d_1 \pi_{jt}}{a_1 p_t + z_t} \frac{p_{t+1}}{\pi_{jt+1}} + \frac{d_2 \pi_{jt}}{z_t} \frac{z_{t+1}}{\pi_{jt+1}} = (1 + r_t) \frac{\pi_{jt}}{\pi_{jt+1}} \qquad (t \leqslant T)$$

$$\frac{\pi_{jt}}{a_2 p_t} \frac{p_{t+1}}{\pi_{jt+1}} = (1 + r_t) \frac{\pi_{jt}}{\pi_{jt+1}} \qquad (t > T)$$

Thus the own rate of return on an investment of commodity j is

$$\rho_{jt} = (1 + r_t) \frac{\pi_{jt}}{\pi_{jt+1}} - 1 = r_t \left(1 - \frac{\pi_{jt+1} - \pi_{jt}}{\pi_{jt+1}} \right) - \frac{\pi_{jt+1} - \pi_{jt}}{\pi_{jt+1}}$$

2 The reader can easily check that the required sequence is

$$r_1 = \frac{(1 - a_1)(1 - a_2)a_1^t}{(a_2 - a_1)a_1^T + (1 - a_2)a_1^{t+1}} \qquad 0 \leqslant t \leqslant T$$

$$r_t = \frac{1 - a_2}{a_2} \qquad t \geqslant T$$

This rate is independent of the sequence of nominal rates of profit and of the numéraire adopted, as simple calculations show.[3] It is a *real* rate in the sense of Wicksell who defined interest in terms of parting with present goods 'in order in some way or other to obtain future goods *of the same kind*' ([1893] 1954, p. 107, emphasis added). The concept of a real or commodity rate of interest was also referred to by Sraffa in his criticism of Hayek's monetary overinvestment theory of the business cycle. Sraffa stressed that outside a long-period position of the economy (or, in Hayek's terminology, outside an 'equilibrium') 'there might be at any one moment as many "natural" rates of interest as there are commodities' (Sraffa, 1932, p. 49). He added with regard to an investor taking a loan:

> Loans are currently made in the present world in terms of every commodity for which there is a forward market. When a cotton spinner borrows a sum of money for three months and uses the proceeds to purchase spot, a quantity of raw cotton which he simultaneously sells three months forward, he is actually 'borrowing cotton' for that period. The rate of interest which he pays, per hundred bales of cotton, is the number of bales that can be purchased with the following sum of money: the interest on the money required to buy spot 100 bales, plus the excess (or minus the deficiency) of the spot over the forward prices of the 100 bales. – In [a long-period] equilibrium the spot and forward price coincide, for cotton as for any other commodity; and all the 'natural' or commodity rates are equal to one another, and to the money rate.
>
> (Sraffa, 1932, p. 50)

It could be argued that for $t \geqslant T$ the price of corn is constant over time if the nominal rate of profit is $(1 - a_2)/a_2$, which is the rate of profit that holds in the long period in an economy in which only the backstop technique is employed, and in this respect it can be considered the *long-period real* rate of profit (a well-defined concept). Hence one might be inclined to see whether the concept carries over to intertemporal analysis. However, any such inclination would immediately be frustrated: the fact that the price of corn is constant over time from time T onward if the nominal rate of profit coincides with the long-period *real* rate of profit, is a consequence of the fact that there is only one reproducible commodity contemplated by the model. Suppose instead that there are two commodities, corn and iron. Then at time T the relative price of the two does not need to be the one

---

3 Let $\{r_t\}$, $\{\sigma_t\}$, $\{\pi_t\}$ and $\{s_t\}$ be sequences such that $\{r_t\}$ and $\{\sigma_t\}$ are non-negative, $\{\pi_t\}$ and $\{s_t\}$ are positive and

$$s_t = h \prod_{\tau=0}^{t-1} \frac{1 + \sigma_\tau}{1 + r_\tau} \pi_t$$

Then

$$(1 + r_t) \frac{\pi_t}{\pi_{t+1}} = (1 + \sigma_t) \frac{s_t}{s_{t+1}}$$

prevailing in the long run even if they are produced from time T onward with the backstop processes. As a consequence, even if we take the long-period rate of profit as the nominal rate of profit from time T onward, prices will tend to the long-period prices only at infinity and will oscillate from time T onward. Using a modelling similar to that discussed in Kurz and Salvadori (2000), the following can be proved: to assume that the prices at time T are proportional to the long-period prices is equivalent to a very special assumption regarding the amounts of commodities and resources available at time 0. For lack of space we have to refrain from developing the argument in detail.

To conclude on the question of the *price* which Bidard and Erreygers take to be constant over time, we have to say that we were puzzled by sentences like:

> The *real profit* of an activity can be defined only by means of a standard. A measure of the real profitability of an activity is obtained when the value of the inputs at time t and the value of the outputs at time $t + 1$ are translated into comparable units of 'what really counts'.
>
> (pp. 246–7)

Unfortunately, the authors do not tell us 'what really counts', and why. Their references to Torrens and Fisher are not able to enlighten us. Until they can show conclusively that the concept of the 'real rate of profit' can be properly defined *and* can be put to productive analytical use, we see no reason to employ it.

3. On theoretical 'approximations'

Bidard and Erreygers maintain: 'A post-Sraffian economist who feels disquiet about the labour theory of value and has imposed upon himself the intellectual requirement of working with a consistent theory of prices cannot be satisfied with the "approximation" of royalty by rent. A consistent theory of exhaustible resources is needed just as much as a consistent theory of prices' (p. 245). Economic theorists cannot do without bold assumptions whose role is to allow for approximations of the properties of the economic system under consideration. The labour theory of value was such an approximation or theoretical device to render transparent what otherwise would have remained impenetrable, given the analytical tools available at the time. It was a useful tool at a certain stage of the development of the analysis. As Ludwig Wittgenstein remarked, a particular theory may be compared to a ladder that is useful to reach a higher standpoint. However, once this standpoint is reached and a fuller view of the landscape is possible, the ladder may turn out to be an instrument that is inferior to some other device to reach the higher standpoint, and possibly beyond, and it will therefore be abandoned. This applies also to the labour theory of value: it was an instrument that provided useful services to the classical economists by introducing a constraint binding changes in the distributive variables, but once the problem of the relationship between income distribution and relative prices, given the system of production in use, had been fully solved, the labour theory of value had to be dispensed with because it did not provide a correct and fully satisfactory picture of that relationship.

Any economic model is bound to distort reality in some way. Otherwise it would be identical to the 'seamless whole' and thus useless in interpreting aspects of the latter. Sraffa was prepared to allow such 'distortions' in his own conceptualization of the production process. He was clear at an early stage of his work, which was to lead to his 1960 book, that the assumption of self-replacement of an economic system does not mimic reality. In the following note dated 25 March 1946, from his hitherto unpublished papers, he first points out a difference between a *physical real cost* approach to the problem of value and distribution, which he endorsed, and the labour theory of value:[4]

> The difference between the 'Physical real costs' and the Ricardo–Marxian theory of 'labour costs' is that the first does, and the latter does not, include in them the natural resources that are used up in the course of production (such as coal, iron, exhaustion of land) – [Air, water etc. are not used up: as there is an unlimited supply, no subtraction can be made from ∞]. This is fundamental because it does away with 'human energy' and such metaphysical things.

He added:

> But how are we going to replace these natural things? There are 3 cases: a) they can be reproduced by labour (land properties, with manures etc.); b) they can be substituted by labour (coal by hydroelectric plant: or by spending in research and discovery of new sources and new methods of economising); c) they cannot be either reproduced nor substituted[5] – and in this case they cannot find a place in a theory of *continuous* production and consumption: they are dynamical facts, i.e. a stock that is being gradually exhausted and cannot be renewed, and must ultimately lead to destruction of the society. But this case does not satisfy our conditions of a society that just manages to keep continuously alive.
>
> (Sraffa's papers, D3/12/42: 33)

While a 'dynamic theory' would be needed to deal properly with exhaustible resources, Sraffa also reminded us of the intrinsic difficulties of elaborating such a theory. One of his notes reads:

> It is 'a fatal mistake' of some economists that they believe that, by introducing complicated dynamic assumptions, they get nearer to the true reality; in fact

---

4 The papers are kept at Trinity College Library, Cambridge. The references follow the catalogue prepared by Jonathan Smith, archivist. We are grateful to Pierangelo Garegnani, Sraffa's literary executor, for permission to quote from the hitherto unpublished material.
5 This is Sraffa's formulation, which we left as it is.

they get further removed for two reasons: a) that the system is much more statical than we believe, and its 'short periods' are very long, b) that the assumptions being too complicated it becomes impossible for the mind to grasp and dominate them – and thus it fails to realise the absurdity of the conclusions.

(Sraffa, D3/12/11: 33)

In his book Sraffa mentioned exhaustible resources only in passing and on a par with land: 'Natural resources which are used in production, such as land and mineral deposits . . . ' (Sraffa, 1960, p. 74). This is not the place for a full analysis of his view on the issue at hand. It must suffice to mention that he considered exhaustible resourses to be 'dynamical facts' which might be difficult to take account of in a 'theory of *continuous* production and consumption'. However, this did not make him abandon long-period analysis.

4. On Hotelling's rule[6]

Bidard and Erreygers write: 'Hotelling's rule is neither neoclassical nor classical; it is a necessary consequence of the notion of competitive solution: it is economic theory full stop' (p. 246). To be clear, Hotelling's rule (see Hotelling, 1931) is nothing but the application of the concept of a uniform rate of profit to all processes in the economy, whether these are conservation or production processes. But precisely because this is so, it applies only in certain circumstances and not in others. In particular, it presupposes that the following assumptions hold.

(i) The resource is available in homogeneous quality and in a quantity which at any moment of time is known with certainty.
(ii) The amount of the resource that can be extracted in a given period is only constrained by the amount of it left over from the preceding period.

If one of these assumptions is not met, then Hotelling's rule needs to be modified. The following case exemplifies this. It hardly needs to be stressed that assumption (i) is very bold indeed. In everyday experience new deposits of exhaustible resources are repeatedly discovered. The opposite extreme would consist in assuming the following.

(i*) For each exhausted deposit of the resource another one with the same characteristics is discovered and the cost of the search (in terms of labour and commodities) is always the same.

---

6 In this section we shall only touch upon some aspects of the problem under consideration, a full treatment of which is beyond the scope of this short note. Such a treatment will be the object of a forthcoming paper.

In this case, while each deposit would be exhaustible, the resource as such would not; and each deposit could in fact be treated as if it were a (reproducible) machine: the price of the new machine equals the cost of the search and the price of an old machine of age t equals the value of the deposit after t periods of utilization (see Kurz and Salvadori, 1995, pp. 359–60). The price of the resource would be constant over time, as is commonly assumed in long-period analysis.[7]

Assumption (i*) may be compared to the assumption employed in much of the literature on exhaustible resources and also in the paper by Bidard and Erreygers: the assumption that there is a productive backstop technique, which is known from the beginning. Both assumptions have the effect, in Sraffa's words, of satisfying the conditions of a society that manages 'to keep continuously alive'. These assumptions are indeed devices to avoid the 'end of the world' scenario, on which there is nothing to be said.

The classical economists and especially Ricardo were concerned with a world in which none of the above assumptions (i), (i*) and (ii) was taken to apply. Smith and Ricardo typically saw mines of different 'fertility' being wrought simultaneously as the normal state of affairs. By fertility they meant the amount of the resource, that can be extracted from the mine in a given period of time, for example, year, given the technique of extraction. This concept is analogous to their concept of fertility of land which refers to the amount of agricultural product that can be grown on a given plot of land of a given quality, using a given method of production. Hence, to extract a resource from a mine takes time, and a *capacity constraint* giving the upper limit of the resource that can be extracted per unit of time is the obvious assumption to make. The amount of a resource 'which can be removed' (Ricardo, 1951, p. 68) will generally fall short of the amount of the resource *in situ* at the beginning of an extraction period.[8] It is against this background that Ricardo maintained: 'If there were abundance of equally fertile mines, which any one might appropriate, they could yield no rent; the value of their produce would depend on the quantity of labour necessary to extract the metal from the mine and bring it to market' (Ricardo, 1951, p. 85). The absence of an abundance of equally fertile mines and the capacity constraint limiting the yearly output of any single mine in general necessitate the utilization of mines of different fertility in order to meet the effectual demand for the resource. In such circumstances, Ricardo emphasized, it is the 'relative fertility

---

7 Adam Smith ([1776] 1976) wrote about the discovery of new mines: 'In this search [for new mines] there seem to be no certain limits either to the possible success, or to the possible disappointment of human industry. In the course of a century or two, it is possible that new mines may be discovered more fertile than any that have ever yet been known; and it is just equally possible that the most fertile mine then known may be more barren than any that was wrought before the discovery of the mines of America' (*WN* I.xi.m.21). Hence, the option the theorist has is either to model the uncertainty referred to by Smith or to make a simplifying assumption such as, for instance, assumption (i*) above.

8 The assumption of a capacity constraint becomes clear, for example, when Ricardo (1951, p. 331) refers to the case of innovations in extracting coal: 'by new processes the quantity should be increased, the price would fall, and some mines would be abandoned'.

of mines [which] determines the portion of their produce, which shall be paid for rent of mines' (1951, p. 330). Smith and Ricardo were clear that the exhaustion of resources may constrain human productive activity. Thus Smith pointed out that 'useful fossils and minerals of the earth, & c. naturally grow dearer as the society advances in wealth and improvements' (*WN* I.xi.i.3; see also I.xi.d).

We may now ask: in which conditions is the classical approach to the problem of exhaustible resources in terms of the principle of differential rent *strictly* correct? From what has already been said it follows that this is a situation in which there are capacity constraints with regard to mines, and effectual demand is always such that it can never be met without operating also the backstop technology.[9] In this case prices are constant over time and the owners of mines receive a rent precisely as Ricardo maintained.

It need hardly be stressed that this observation does not imply a refutation of Hotelling's rule. The latter applies in certain conditions (possibly with some modifications), but not in all, and we employ it when appropriate (see, e.g. Kurz and Salvadori (2000), and Sections 1 and 2). However, the reader will by now, at the latest, be aware of the fact that that rule follows from a set of specific assumptions which define a particular theoretical 'world'. The analysis of such a theoretical world allows one to grasp some (but not all) aspects of the actual world exhibiting actual mines and oil or gas deposits. Obviously, to study different theoretical objects which allow one to grasp different aspects of actual processes of the exhaustion of resources is a perfectly sensible thing to do in order to increase one's understanding of the problem at hand. One might even consider the possibility of incorporating all these aspects in a single and more general model.

References

Bidard Ch. and Erreygers G. (2001) 'The corn–guano model', *Metroeconomica*, 53, pp. 243–53.

Hotelling H. (1931) 'The economics of exhaustible resources', *Journal of Political Economy*, 39, pp. 137–75.

Kurz H. D. and Salvadori N. (1995) *Theory of Production. A Long-period Analysis*, Cambridge University Press, Cambridge.

---

9 Obviously no assumption of this type is found in Smith or Ricardo, but an institutional aspect referred to by Smith has the same implication: 'There are some [coal-mines], of which the produce is barely sufficient to pay the labour, and replace, together with its ordinary profits, the stock employed in working them. They afford some profit to the undertaker of the work, but no rent to the landlord. They can be wrought advantageously by nobody but the landlord, who being himself undertaker of the work, gets the ordinary profit of the capital which he employs in it. Many coal-mines in Scotland are wrought in this manner, and can be wrought in no other. The landlord will allow nobody else to work them without paying some rent, and nobody can afford to pay any' (*WN* I.xi.c.13; quoted by Ricardo, 1951, pp. 329–30). Obviously, when these mines are exhausted they can no longer perform the same role as the backstop technology.

Kurz H. D. and Salvadori N. (1997) 'Exhaustible resources in a dynamic input–output model with "classical" features', *Economic Systems Research*, 9(3), pp. 235–51. Here reprinted as Chapter 14.

Kurz H. D. and Salvadori N. (2000) 'Economic dynamics in a simple model with exhaustible resources and a given real wage rate', *Structural Change and Economic Dynamics*, 11, pp. 167–79.

Ricardo D. (1951) *On the Principles of Political Economy and Taxation*, 1st edn 1817; in *The Works and Correspondence of David Ricardo*, edited by Piero Sraffa with the collaboration of Maurice H. Dobb, Vol. 1, Cambridge University Press, Cambridge.

Smith A. (1976) *An Inquiry into the Nature and Causes of the Wealth of Nations*, 1st edn 1776; in *The Glasgow Edition of the Works and Correspondence of Adam Smith*, R. H. Campbell, A. S. Skinner and W. B. Todd (eds), Vol. II, Oxford University Press, Oxford. In the text quoted as *WN*, book number, chapter number, section number, paragraph number.

Sraffa P. (1932) 'Dr. Hayek on money and capital', *Economic Journal*, 42, pp. 42–53.

Sraffa P. (1960) *Production of Commodities by Means of Commodities*, Cambridge University Press, Cambridge.

Wicksell K. (1954) *Value, Capital and Rent* (first published in German in 1893), George, Allen & Unwin, London.

14 Economic dynamics in a simple model with exhaustible resources and a given real wage rate*

Heinz D. Kurz and Neri Salvadori

1. Introduction

For well-known reasons, an economic system using exhaustible resources, such as ores of coal, oil or metal, constitutes one of the most difficult objects of investigation in the theory of production (see, e.g. Kurz and Salvadori, 1995, chapter 12; Kurz and Salvadori, 1997). In order to render the problem manageable, theorists frequently have recourse to strong simplifying assumptions. In much of the literature the problem is studied in a partial framework with a single kind of exhaustible resource: the prices of all commodities except the price of the resource are assumed to be given and constant over time. With natural resources that are used to produce energy, for example, this is clearly unsatisfactory, because it can safely be assumed that energy enters as an input in the production of most, if not all, commodities, which implies that a change in the price of energy has an impact on the prices of many, if not all, commodities. Hence, a general framework of the analysis is needed. Moreover, since with exhaustible resources both relative prices, income distribution and the quantities produced will generally change over time, in principle a dynamic analysis is required tracing the time paths of prices, quantities and the distributive variables.

Piero Sraffa, a pioneer of the modern 'classical' theory of production, distribution and value (see Sraffa, 1960; Unpublished Papers and Correspondence, Trinity College Library, Cambridge, UK, as catalogued by Jonathan Smith), was perfectly aware of these difficulties already at an early stage of his work. As is well known, he adopted the concept of production as a *circular flow*, which he had encountered in the writings of the physiocrats and the classical economists, and also in Marx. However, he was clear that the assumption of self-replacement of an economic system, which is to be found in these authors and on which he based some of his analysis, was a bold one. In the following note dated 25 March 1946 from his hitherto unpublished papers[1] he first points out a difference between

* Reprinted with permission from *Structural Change and Economic Dynamics*, 2000.

1 The reference to the papers follows the catalogue prepared by Jonathan Smith, archivist. We should like to thank Pierangelo Garegnani, literary executor of Sraffa's papers and correspondence, for granting us permission to quote from them.

a *physical real cost* approach to the problem of value and distribution, which he endorsed, and the labour theory of value:

> The difference between the 'Physical real costs' and the Ricardo–Marxian theory of 'labour costs' is that the first does, and the latter does not, include in them the natural resources that are used up in the course of production (such as coal, iron, exhaustion of land) [Air, water, etc. are not used up: as there is an unlimited supply, no subtraction can be made from ∞]. This is fundamental because it does away with 'human energy' and such metaphysical things.

He added:

> But how are we going to replace these natural things? There are three cases: a) they can be reproduced by labour (land properties, with manures etc.); b) they can be substituted by labour (coal by hydroelectric plant: or by spending in research and discovery of new sources and new methods of economising); c) they cannot be either reproduced nor substituted[2] – and in this case they cannot find a place in a theory of *continuous* production and consumption: they are dynamical facts, i.e. a stock that is being gradually exhausted and cannot be renewed, and must ultimately lead to destruction of the society. But this case does not satisfy our conditions of a society that just manages to keep continuously alive.
>
> (Sraffa's papers, D3/12/42: 33, Sraffa's emphasis)

Obviously, any economic model is bound to distort reality in some way. Otherwise it would be identical with the 'seamless whole' and thus useless in interpreting aspects of the latter. In no way do we want to dispute the usefulness of Sraffa's approach in his 1960 book, which hardly needs to be justified, given the rich harvest of important findings it yielded. At the same time the 'dynamical facts' Sraffa speaks of cannot be ignored and ought to be studied.

In this chapter we shall make a further probing step in this direction. Our aim is very modest, though. In two previous contributions we studied the problem of exhaustible resources in a multisectoral framework, using a dynamic input–output model. In this chapter we shall propose a significant modification of our previous formalizations, which, it is to be hoped, sheds some of their weaknesses. Compared with the earlier conceptualization, the new one exhibits the following features. While previously we started from a given nominal wage rate and a constant nominal rate of interest, we shall now assume a given and constant *real* wage rate, specified in terms of some given bundle of wage goods. Treating one of the distributive variables as given from outside the system of

---

2 This is Sraffa's formulation, which we left as it is.

production (or treating it as independently variable) and taking the other variables (rate of profits and royalties) as endogenously determined is much more 'classical' in spirit than the previous premises. In particular, the classical concept of the 'surplus' product, and its sharing out between capitalists and resource owners as profits and royalties, is given a clear physical meaning. Further, we shall assume that all realized nonwage incomes, profits and royalties, will be spent on consumption; for simplicity it is assumed that this part of consumption will be proportional to a given vector of consumption goods, which does not change over time. We shall set aside technical progress both in the methods of production extracting and in those using resources. Discoveries of new deposits (or resources) are excluded; existing stocks of resources are taken to be known with certainty at any given moment of time. To avoid the implication mentioned by Sraffa – the 'destruction of society' – we shall assume that there is a 'backstop technology', which allows one to produce the given vector of consumption goods without using any of the exhaustible resources. The example given in our previous contributions was solar or geothermal energy which could replace other forms of energy.

The composition of the chapter is as follows. Section 2 states the main assumptions that underlie the argument and presents the dynamic input–output model. Section 3 contains some preliminary result. Section 4 presents the complete analysis and the main results. Section 5 contains some concluding remarks.

2. The model and its assumptions

The formalization of the problem suggested in this chapter is based on the following simplifying assumptions. A finite number n of different commodities, which are fully divisible, are produced in the economy and a finite number m ($> n$) of constant returns to scale processes are known to produce them. Let $\mathbf{p}_t$ be the vector of prices of commodities available at time $t \in \mathbb{N}_0$ and let $\mathbf{x}_t$ be the vector of the intensities of operation of processes at time $t \in \mathbb{N}$. A process or method of production is defined by a quadruplet $(\mathbf{a}, \mathbf{b}, \mathbf{c}, l)$, where $\mathbf{a} \in \mathbb{R}^n$ is the commodity input vector, $\mathbf{b} \in \mathbb{R}^n$ is the output vector, $\mathbf{c} \in \mathbb{R}^s$ is the exhaustible resources input vector, and l is the labour input, a scalar; of course $\mathbf{a} \geqslant \mathbf{0}, \mathbf{b} \geqslant \mathbf{0}, \mathbf{c} \geq \mathbf{0}, l \geqslant 0$. The production period is uniform across all processes. It is important to remark that the inputs referred to in vector $\mathbf{c}$ are inputs of the resources *as they are provided by nature*; for example, extracted oil is *not* contained in $\mathbf{c}$, but in $\mathbf{b}$, if $(\mathbf{a}, \mathbf{b}, \mathbf{c}, l)$ is an extraction process, or in $\mathbf{a}$, if $(\mathbf{a}, \mathbf{b}, \mathbf{c}, l)$ is a process that uses it, unless the extraction costs are nil. The m existing processes are defined by quadruplets:

$$(\mathbf{a}_j, \mathbf{b}_j, \mathbf{c}_j, l_j) \quad j = 1, 2, \ldots, m$$

Then define matrices $\mathbf{A}$, $\mathbf{B}$, $\mathbf{C}$ and (now) vector $\mathbf{l}$ as follows:[3]

$$\mathbf{A} = \begin{bmatrix} \mathbf{a}_1^T \\ \mathbf{a}_2^T \\ \vdots \\ \mathbf{a}_m^T \end{bmatrix} \quad \mathbf{B} = \begin{bmatrix} \mathbf{b}_1^T \\ \mathbf{b}_2^T \\ \vdots \\ \mathbf{b}_m^T \end{bmatrix} \quad \mathbf{C} = \begin{bmatrix} \mathbf{c}_1^T \\ \mathbf{c}_2^T \\ \vdots \\ \mathbf{c}_m^T \end{bmatrix} \quad \mathbf{l} = \begin{bmatrix} l_1 \\ l_2 \\ \vdots \\ l_m \end{bmatrix}$$

Assume that the annual consumption of commodities by profit and royalty recipients is proportional to a vector $\mathbf{d}$, which, for simplicity, is assumed to be given and constant over time, that is, independent of prices and quantities, including the quantities of the exhaustible resources left over at the end of each production period. More specifically, assume that the total amounts actually consumed by capitalists and the proprietors of deposits of exhaustible resources are constant over time and equal to γ units of vector $\mathbf{d}$, $\gamma \geq 0$, where γ depends on the resources available at time zero. In addition, the real wage rate, defined by a commodity vector $\mathbf{w}$, is taken to be given and constant over time. Technical innovations of any kind are set aside. All exhaustible resources are private property. In conditions of free competition there will be a (tendency towards a) uniform nominal rate of profits r_t, across all production activities in the economy. This implies that, for each time $t \in \mathbb{N}_0$, the following inequalities and equations are to be satisfied:

$$\mathbf{Bp}_{t+1} \leqq (1 + r_t)(\mathbf{Ap}_t + \mathbf{Cy}_t) + \mathbf{lw}^T\mathbf{p}_{t+1} \tag{14.1a}$$

$$\mathbf{x}_{t+1}^T\mathbf{Bp}_{t+1} = \mathbf{x}_{t+1}^T[(1 + r_t)(\mathbf{Ap}_t + \mathbf{Cy}_t) + \mathbf{lw}^T\mathbf{p}_{t+1}] \tag{14.1b}$$

$$\mathbf{y}_{t+1} \leqq (1 + r_t)\mathbf{y}_t \tag{14.1c}$$

$$\mathbf{z}_{t+1}^T\mathbf{y}_{t+1} = (1 + r_t)\mathbf{z}_{t+1}^T\mathbf{y}_t \tag{14.1d}$$

$$\mathbf{x}_{t+1}^T(\mathbf{B} - \mathbf{lw}^T) \geqq \mathbf{x}_{t+2}^T\mathbf{A} + \gamma\mathbf{d}^T \tag{14.1e}$$

$$\mathbf{x}_{t+1}^T(\mathbf{B} - \mathbf{lw}^T)\mathbf{p}_{t+1} = (\mathbf{x}_{t+2}^T\mathbf{A} + \gamma\mathbf{d}^T)\mathbf{p}_{t+1} \tag{14.1f}$$

$$\mathbf{z}_t^T \geqq \mathbf{x}_{t+1}^T\mathbf{C} + \mathbf{z}_{t+1}^T \tag{14.1g}$$

$$\mathbf{z}_t^T\mathbf{y}_t = (\mathbf{x}_{t+1}^T\mathbf{C} + \mathbf{z}_{t+1}^T)\mathbf{y}_t \tag{14.1h}$$

$$\gamma > 0, \mathbf{p}_t \geqq \mathbf{0}, \mathbf{y}_t \geqq \mathbf{0}, \mathbf{z}_t \geqq \mathbf{0}, \mathbf{x}_{t+1} \geqq \mathbf{0} \tag{14.1i}$$

Inequality (14.1a) means that nobody can get extra profits by producing commodities available at time $t + 1$. Equation (14.1b) implies, because of inequalities (14.1a) and (14.1i), that commodities available at time $t + 1$ will only be produced if the ruling nominal rate of interest is obtained. Inequality (14.1c) means that nobody can get extra profits by storing exhaustible resources from time t

---

3 Transposition of a vector or a matrix is denoted by superscript T.

to time $t + 1$. Equation (14.1d) implies, because of inequalities (14.1c) and (14.1i), that exhaustible resources will be stored from time t to time $t + 1$ only if the ruling nominal rate of interest will be obtained by this storage activity. Inequality (14.1e) implies that the amounts of commodities produced are not smaller than the amounts of commodities required, and equation (14.1f) implies that if an amount is larger, then the price of that commodity is zero. Inequality (14.1g) implies that the amounts of exhaustible resources available at time t are not smaller than the amounts of exhaustible resources available at time $t + 1$ plus the amounts of exhaustible resources utilized to produce commodities available at time $t + 1$, and equation (14.1h) implies that if an amount is larger, then the price of that exhaustible resource is zero. The meaning of inequalities (14.1i) is obvious.

Model (14.1) is not yet complete, because some initial conditions are needed. A first obvious initial condition is that the amounts of exhaustible resources available at time 0 are given, that is:

$$\mathbf{z}_0 = \bar{\mathbf{z}} \tag{14.1j}$$

A second initial condition, which is perhaps less obvious, is that the amounts of commodities available at time 0 are given. This can be stated as

$$\mathbf{v}^\mathrm{T} \geq \mathbf{x}_1^\mathrm{T}\mathbf{A} + \gamma\mathbf{d}^\mathrm{T} \tag{14.1k}$$

$$\mathbf{v}^\mathrm{T}\mathbf{p}_0 = \left(\mathbf{x}_1^\mathrm{T}\mathbf{A} + \gamma\mathbf{d}^\mathrm{T}\right)\mathbf{p}_0 \tag{14.1l}$$

where $\mathbf{v}$ is a given positive vector.

It is easily checked that the given sequence $\{r_t\}$ plays no role in determining the relative actualized prices in the sense that if the sequences $\{\mathbf{p}_t\}$, $\{\mathbf{y}_t\}$, $\{\mathbf{z}_t\}$, $\{\mathbf{x}_{t+1}\}$ are a solution to system (14.1a)–(14.1l) for the given sequence $\{r_t\}$, then the sequences $\{\mathbf{q}_t\}$, $\{\mathbf{u}_t\}$, $\{\mathbf{z}_t\}$, $\{\mathbf{x}_{t+1}\}$ are a solution to the same system for the given sequence $\{\rho_t\}$ provided that:

$$\mathbf{q}_t = \prod_{\tau=0}^{t-1} \frac{1 + \rho_\tau}{1 + r_\tau}\mathbf{p}_t$$

$$\mathbf{u}_t = \prod_{\tau=0}^{t-1} \frac{1 + \rho_\tau}{1 + r_\tau}\mathbf{y}_t$$

This is so because r_t is the *nominal* rate of interest and thus incorporates also the rates of inflation, so that a change in r_t leaves unchanged the *real* rates of profit and involves only a change in the rates of inflation.

It is also easily checked that the above model can determine only the relative actualized prices in the sense that if the sequences $\{\mathbf{p}_t\}$, $\{\mathbf{y}_t\}$, $\{\mathbf{z}_t\}$, $\{\mathbf{x}_{t+1}\}$ are a solution to system (14.1a)–(14.1l); then the sequences $\{\eta\mathbf{p}_t\}$, $\{\eta\mathbf{y}_t\}$, $\{\mathbf{z}_t\}$, $\{\mathbf{x}_{t+1}\}$ are also a solution, where η is a positive scalar. In order to fix the numéraire and to preserve the property that a change in the nominal rates of profit does not affect relative prices, the numéraire is set in terms of actualized prices, that is, we add the following equation:

$$\sum_{t=0}^{\infty} \frac{\mathbf{u}_t^T \mathbf{p}_t}{\prod_{\tau=0}^{t-1}(1 + r_\tau)} = 1 \tag{14.1m}$$

where $\{\mathbf{u}_t\}$ is a sequence of known nonnegative vectors (at least one of which is semipositive).

In the following we will assume that $\{r_t\}$ is a constant sequence and that $r_t = 0$. A change to a more appropriate sequence of nominal rates of profit can be effected at any time, as indicated above. In the following it will also be assumed that $\mathbf{u}_t = \mathbf{d}$ in equation (14.1m). Then system (14.1) is more simply stated as

$$(\mathbf{B} - \mathbf{lw}^T)\mathbf{p}_{t+1} \leqq (\mathbf{Ap}_t + \mathbf{Cy}_t) \tag{14.2a}$$

$$\mathbf{x}_{t+1}^T(\mathbf{B} - \mathbf{lw}^T)\mathbf{p}_{t+1} = \mathbf{x}_{t+1}^T(\mathbf{Ap}_t + \mathbf{Cy}_t) \tag{14.2b}$$

$$\mathbf{y}_{t+1} \leqq \mathbf{y}_t \tag{14.2c}$$

$$\mathbf{z}_{t+1}^T\mathbf{y}_{t+1} = \mathbf{z}_{t+1}^T\mathbf{y}_t \tag{14.2d}$$

$$\mathbf{v}^T \geqq \mathbf{x}_1^T\mathbf{A} + \gamma\mathbf{d}^T \tag{14.2e}$$

$$\mathbf{v}^T\mathbf{p}_0 = (\mathbf{x}_1^T\mathbf{A} + \gamma\mathbf{d}^T)\mathbf{p}_0 \tag{14.2f}$$

$$\mathbf{x}_{t+1}^T(\mathbf{B} - \mathbf{lw}^T) \geqq \mathbf{x}_{t+2}^T\mathbf{A} + \gamma\mathbf{d}^T \tag{14.2g}$$

$$\mathbf{x}_{t+1}^T(\mathbf{B} - \mathbf{lw}^T)\mathbf{p}_{t+1} = (\mathbf{x}_{t+2}^T\mathbf{A} + \gamma\mathbf{d}^T)\mathbf{p}_{t+1} \tag{14.2h}$$

$$\mathbf{z}_t^T \geqq \mathbf{x}_{t+1}^T\mathbf{C} + \mathbf{z}_{t+1}^T \tag{14.2i}$$

$$\mathbf{z}_t^T\mathbf{y}_t = (\mathbf{x}_{t+1}^T\mathbf{C} + \mathbf{z}_{t+1}^T)\mathbf{y}_t \tag{14.2j}$$

$$\mathbf{z}_0 = \bar{\mathbf{z}} \tag{14.2k}$$

$$\sum_{t=0}^{\infty} \mathbf{d}^T\mathbf{p}_t = 1 \tag{14.2l}$$

$$\gamma > 0, \mathbf{p}_t \geqq \mathbf{0}, \mathbf{y}_t \geqq \mathbf{0}, \mathbf{z}_t \geqq \mathbf{0}, \mathbf{x}_{t+1} \geqq \mathbf{0} \tag{14.2m}$$

Each of the exhaustible resources is assumed to provide directly or indirectly[4] services that are useful in production. However, it is assumed that the same kind of services can also be produced by solar energy, the source of which does not risk exhaustion in any relevant time-frame. More specifically, we shall assume that the commodities annually required for consumption, defined in terms of vector $\mathbf{d}$,

---

4 Assume, for instance, that electric energy can be produced from oil which is extracted from the ground. The unextracted oil is the resource, whereas the extracted oil is a commodity produced by means of that resource. Then we say that the resource produces electric energy *indirectly*.

can be produced without using exhaustible resources. Hence, there is a 'backstop technology'. The processes defining that backstop technology $(\bar{\mathbf{A}}, \bar{\mathbf{B}}, \mathbf{0}, \bar{\mathbf{l}})$ are obtained from $(\mathbf{A}, \mathbf{B}, \mathbf{C}, \mathbf{l})$ by deleting all the processes using directly some natural resource (i.e. process $(\mathbf{e}_i^T\mathbf{A}, \mathbf{e}_i^T\mathbf{B}, \mathbf{e}_i^T\mathbf{C}, \mathbf{e}_i^T\mathbf{l})$ is in the set of processes $(\bar{\mathbf{A}}, \bar{\mathbf{B}}, \mathbf{0}, \bar{\mathbf{l}})$ if and only if $\mathbf{e}_i^T\mathbf{C} = \mathbf{0}^T$). We may conveniently summarize what has just been said in the following:

Assumption 1. *There is a scalar r^* and there are vectors $\mathbf{x}^*$ and $\mathbf{p}^*$ which solve the system*

$$\mathbf{x}^T(\bar{\mathbf{B}} - \bar{\mathbf{A}} - \bar{\mathbf{l}}\mathbf{w}^T) \geqq \mathbf{d}^T \tag{14.3a}$$

$$\mathbf{x}^T(\bar{\mathbf{B}} - \bar{\mathbf{A}} - \bar{\mathbf{l}}\mathbf{w}^T)\mathbf{p} = \mathbf{d}^T\mathbf{p} \tag{14.3b}$$

$$\bar{\mathbf{B}}\mathbf{p} \leqq \left[(1+r)\bar{\mathbf{A}} + \bar{\mathbf{l}}\mathbf{w}^T\right]\mathbf{p} \tag{14.3c}$$

$$\mathbf{x}^T\bar{\mathbf{B}}\mathbf{p} = \mathbf{x}^T\left[(1+r)\bar{\mathbf{A}} + \bar{\mathbf{l}}\mathbf{w}^T\right]\mathbf{p} \tag{14.3d}$$

$$\mathbf{x} \geqq \mathbf{0}, \ \mathbf{p} \geqq \mathbf{0}, \ \mathbf{d}^T\mathbf{p} = 1 \tag{14.3e}$$

In the following discussion we will refer to the processes operated at the intensity vector $\bar{\mathbf{x}}$, obtained by augmenting vector $\mathbf{x}^*$ with zeros, as the 'cost-minimizing backstop processes', and we will denote these processes by the quadruplet $(\hat{\mathbf{A}}, \hat{\mathbf{B}}, \mathbf{0}, \hat{\mathbf{l}})$.

The assumption that there is a backstop technology (i.e. Assumption 1) is necessary in order to avoid the 'end of the world' scenario, on which there is nothing to be said. This is the case because we excluded discoveries of new deposits (or resources) and innovations. Seen from this perspective, Assumption 1 may be considered as a sort of simple corrective device to counterbalance the bold premises that underlie our analysis. The following assumptions characterize the backstop technology and the cost-minimizing backstop processes.

Assumption 2. *The backstop technology is such that it converges to the processes $(\hat{\mathbf{A}}, \hat{\mathbf{B}}, \mathbf{0}, \hat{\mathbf{l}})$. In other words, the backstop processes $(\bar{\mathbf{A}}, \bar{\mathbf{B}}, \mathbf{0}, \bar{\mathbf{l}})$ are such that the system made up by equations and inequalities (14.2a), (14.2b), (14.2e), (14.2f), (14.2g), (14.2h) and (14.2l) and the first two and the fifth of inequalities (14.2m), with $\mathbf{A} = \bar{\mathbf{A}}, \mathbf{B} = \bar{\mathbf{B}}, \mathbf{C} = \mathbf{0}, \mathbf{l} = \bar{\mathbf{l}}$, is such that, for each of its solutions (if there is one), there is a natural number θ^* such that, for each $t \geqslant \theta^*$, only the processes $(\hat{\mathbf{A}}, \hat{\mathbf{B}}, \mathbf{0}, \hat{\mathbf{l}})$ are operated.*

Assumption 3. *The number of cost-minimizing backstop processes is exactly n (the number of commodities); the matrix $[\hat{\mathbf{B}} - \hat{\mathbf{l}}\mathbf{w}^T]$ is invertible; the matrix $[\hat{\mathbf{B}} - \hat{\mathbf{l}}\mathbf{w}^T]^{-1}\hat{\mathbf{A}}$ is nonnegative; and the eigenvalue of maximum modulus of matrix $[\hat{\mathbf{B}} - \hat{\mathbf{l}}\mathbf{w}^T]^{-1}\hat{\mathbf{A}}$ is smaller than unity.*

Assumption 3 certainly holds if there is no joint production and if the real wage rate is such that, for each commodity, no more than one process producing it can be operated in the long run. In fact, in this case, we can order processes $(\hat{\mathbf{A}}, \hat{\mathbf{B}}, \mathbf{0}, \hat{\mathbf{I}})$ in such a way that $\hat{\mathbf{B}}$ is diagonal, with the elements on the main diagonal all positive; finally, the other properties mean just that the backstop technology can support the given real wage rate $\mathbf{w}$. This assumption implies also that r^* as determined in system (14.3) is positive, since the eigenvalue of maximum modulus of the matrix $[\hat{\mathbf{B}} - \hat{\mathbf{I}}\mathbf{w}^\mathrm{T}]^{-1}\hat{\mathbf{A}}$ equals $(1 + r^*)^{-1}$, which has been assumed to be smaller than 1.

3. A preliminary result

Assume that system (14.2) has a solution. Call the set of processes operated at time t in such a solution the *position at time t*. Because the number of processes is finite, the number of possible positions is also finite. Hence, at least one position is replicated for an infinite number of times. Because the amounts of exhaustible resources available at time 0 are finite, and because the vector of the amounts of resources utilized in a position employing exhaustible resources is bounded from below (recall that vector $\gamma\mathbf{d}$ is constant over time), with regard to any position which is replicated an infinite number of times we have: either it does not use exhaustible resources at all; or, if it uses them, it includes processes which can be operated in order to produce the consumption vector $\gamma\mathbf{d}$ without using exhaustible resources, which means that the intensities of operation of the processes in the position under consideration can be changed from time t to time $t + 1$ in order to reduce the amounts of natural resources utilized continuously. Hence, we can divide the period from time 0 to infinity into two subperiods: a finite subperiod from time 0 to time τ' and an infinite subperiod from time $\tau' + 1$ to infinity, on the condition that, in the second subperiod, only the backstop processes $(\bar{\mathbf{A}}, \bar{\mathbf{B}}, \mathbf{0}, \bar{\mathbf{I}})$ concur in determining the dynamics of the prices of producible commodities. Moreover, if Assumptions 2 and 3 hold, we can divide the period from time $\tau' + 1$ to infinity into two subperiods: a finite subperiod from time $\tau' + 1$ to time τ'' and an infinite subperiod from time $\tau'' + 1$ to infinity, on the condition that, in the second subperiod:

$$\mathbf{p}_t = \mathbf{A}^{*t-\tau''}\mathbf{p}_{\tau''}$$

$$\mathbf{y}_t = \mathbf{y}_{\tau''}$$

where $\mathbf{A}^* = [\hat{\mathbf{B}} - \hat{\mathbf{I}}\mathbf{w}^\mathrm{T}]^{-1}\hat{\mathbf{A}}$. If process $(\mathbf{a}_j, \mathbf{b}_j, \mathbf{c}_j, l_j)$ is a process in a position replicated for an infinite number of times, such that $\mathbf{c}_j \geqslant \mathbf{0}$, then

$$(\mathbf{b}_j - l_j\mathbf{w})^\mathrm{T}\mathbf{A}^{*t+1-\tau''}\mathbf{p}_{\tau''} - \mathbf{a}_j^\mathrm{T}\mathbf{A}^{*t-\tau''}\mathbf{p}_{\tau''} = \mathbf{c}_j^\mathrm{T}\mathbf{y}_{\tau''} \quad \text{each } t \geqslant \tau''$$

that is,

$$[(\mathbf{b}_j - l_j\mathbf{w})^\mathrm{T}\mathbf{A}^* - \mathbf{a}_j^\mathrm{T}]\mathbf{A}^{*t-\tau''}\mathbf{p}_{\tau''} = \mathbf{c}_j^\mathrm{T}\mathbf{y}_{\tau''} \quad \text{each } t \geqslant \tau''$$

Hence, Assumption 3 implies that

$$\mathbf{c}_j^\mathrm{T}\mathbf{y}_{\tau''} = 0$$

$$(\mathbf{b}_j - l_j\mathbf{w})^\mathrm{T}\mathbf{A}^* = \mathbf{a}_j^\mathrm{T} \tag{14.4}$$

In other words, the exhaustible resources eventually used in the position replicated for an infinite number of times have a zero price and the input–output conditions relative to producible commodities of any process using exhaustible resources in the position replicated for an infinite number of times satisfy the proportionality condition (14.4). A process $(\mathbf{a}_j, \mathbf{b}_j, \mathbf{c}_j, l_j)$ such that $\mathbf{c}_j \geqslant \mathbf{0}$ and equation (14.4) holds is certainly a dominated process, because there is a combination of some other processes which require exactly the same inputs except the exhaustible resources $\mathbf{c}_j$, which are not needed, and produce the same outputs. Hence, there appears to be no harm in adopting the following

Assumption 4. *There is no process* $(\mathbf{a}_j, \mathbf{b}_j, \mathbf{c}_j, l_j)$ *such that* $\mathbf{c}_j \geqslant \mathbf{0}$ *and equation (14.4) holds.*

Assumptions 1–4 ensure that processes $(\hat{\mathbf{A}}, \hat{\mathbf{B}}, \mathbf{0}, \hat{\mathbf{I}})$ constitute the unique position which can be replicated for an infinite number of times. This fact suggests the following problem, the study of which is a preliminary step to an analysis of system (14.2). Let θ be a positive natural number and let us investigate the following system (14.5).

$$(\mathbf{B} - \mathbf{lw}^T)\mathbf{p}_{t+1} \leqq (\mathbf{Ap}_t + \mathbf{Cy}_t) \quad 0 \leqslant t \leqslant \theta - 1 \tag{14.5a}$$

$$\mathbf{x}_{t+1}^T(\mathbf{B} - \mathbf{lw}^T)\mathbf{p}_{t+1} = \mathbf{x}_{t+1}^T(\mathbf{Ap}_t + \mathbf{Cy}_t) \quad 0 \leqslant t \leqslant \theta - 1 \tag{14.5b}$$

$$\mathbf{y}_{t+1} \leqq \mathbf{y}_t \quad 0 \leqslant t \leqslant \theta - 1 \tag{14.5c}$$

$$\mathbf{z}_{t+1}^T\mathbf{y}_{t+1} = \mathbf{z}_{t+1}^T\mathbf{y}_t \quad 0 \leqslant t \leqslant \theta \tag{14.5d}$$

$$\mathbf{v}^T \geqq \mathbf{x}_1^T\mathbf{A} + \gamma\mathbf{d}^T \tag{14.5e}$$

$$\mathbf{v}^T\mathbf{p}_0 = (\mathbf{x}_1^T\mathbf{A} + \gamma\mathbf{d}^T)\mathbf{p}_0 \tag{14.5f}$$

$$\mathbf{x}_t^T(\mathbf{B} - \mathbf{lw}^T) \geqq \mathbf{x}_{t+1}^T\mathbf{A} + \gamma\mathbf{d}^T \quad 1 \leqslant t \leqslant \theta - 1 \tag{14.5g}$$

$$\mathbf{x}_t^T(\mathbf{B} - \mathbf{lw}^T)\mathbf{p}_t = (\mathbf{x}_{t+1}^T\mathbf{A} + \gamma\mathbf{d}^T)\mathbf{p}_t \quad 1 \leqslant t \leqslant \theta - 1 \tag{14.5h}$$

$$\mathbf{x}_\theta^T(\mathbf{B} - \mathbf{lw}^T) \geqq \gamma\mathbf{d}^T + \gamma\mathbf{d}^T(\mathbf{I} - \mathbf{A}^*)^{-1}\mathbf{A}^* \tag{14.5i}$$

$$\mathbf{x}_\theta^T(\mathbf{B} - \mathbf{lw}^T)\mathbf{p}_\theta = [\gamma\mathbf{d}^T + \gamma\mathbf{d}^T(\mathbf{I} - \mathbf{A}^*)^{-1}\mathbf{A}^*]\mathbf{p}_\theta \tag{14.5j}$$

$$\bar{\mathbf{z}}^T \geqq \mathbf{x}_1^T\mathbf{C} + \mathbf{z}_1^T \tag{14.5k}$$

$$\bar{\mathbf{z}}^T\mathbf{y}_0 = (\mathbf{x}_1^T\mathbf{C} + \mathbf{z}_1^T)\mathbf{y}_0 \tag{14.5l}$$

$$\mathbf{z}_t^T \geqq \mathbf{x}_{t+1}^T\mathbf{C} + \mathbf{z}_{t+1}^T \quad 1 \leqslant t \leqslant \theta - 1 \tag{14.5m}$$

$$\mathbf{z}_t^T\mathbf{y}_t = (\mathbf{x}_{t+1}^T\mathbf{C} + \mathbf{z}_{t+1}^T)\mathbf{y}_t \quad 1 \leqslant t \leqslant \theta - 1 \tag{14.5n}$$

$$\sum_{t=0}^{\theta-1}\mathbf{d}^T\mathbf{p}_t + \sum_{t=\theta}^{\infty}\mathbf{d}^T\mathbf{A}^{*t-\theta}\mathbf{p}_\theta = 1 \tag{14.5o}$$

$\mathbf{p}_t \geqq \mathbf{0}, \mathbf{y}_t \geqq \mathbf{0}, \quad 0 \leqslant t \leqslant \theta$ (14.5p)

$\mathbf{z}_t \geqq \mathbf{0}, \mathbf{x}_t \geqq \mathbf{0}, \quad 1 \leqslant t \leqslant \theta$ (14.5q)

$\gamma > 0$ (14.5r)

System (14.5) can be considered as consisting of the first θ steps of system (14.2), on the assumption that $\mathbf{x}_{\theta+1} = \gamma \bar{\mathbf{x}}$, and therefore

$$\mathbf{x}_{\theta+1}^T \mathbf{A} = \gamma \mathbf{d}^T (\mathbf{I} - \mathbf{A}^*)^{-1} \mathbf{A}^*,$$

that is, on the assumption that, at time $\theta + 1$, the cost-minimizing backstop processes are operated and are operated at the cost-minimizing backstop intensities to produce γ times the consumption vector, and, as a consequence, the price vectors for $t > \theta$ mentioned in the equation fixing the numéraire are

$$\mathbf{p}_t = \mathbf{A}^{*t-\theta} \mathbf{p}_\theta$$

Because of the equilibrium theorem of linear programming, system (14.5a)–(14.5q) is equivalent to each of the following two linear programming problems, which are dual to each other:

(Primal):

Min $\mathbf{v}^T \mathbf{p}_0 + \bar{\mathbf{z}}^T \mathbf{y}_0$

s.t. $\mathbf{A}\mathbf{p}_t - (\mathbf{B} - \mathbf{l}\mathbf{w}^T)\mathbf{p}_{t+1} + \mathbf{C}\mathbf{y}_t \geqq \mathbf{0} \quad 0 \leqslant t \leqslant \theta - 1$

$\mathbf{y}_t - \mathbf{y}_{t+1} \geqq \mathbf{0} \quad 0 \leqslant t \leqslant \theta - 1$

$\sum_{t=o}^{\theta-1} \mathbf{d}^T \mathbf{p}_t + \mathbf{d}^T (\mathbf{I} - \mathbf{A}^*)^{-1} \mathbf{p}_\theta = 1$

$\mathbf{p}_t \geqq \mathbf{0}, \mathbf{y}_t \geqq \mathbf{0} \quad 0 \leqslant t \leqslant \theta$

(Dual):

Max γ

s.t. $\mathbf{x}_1^T \mathbf{A} + \gamma \mathbf{d}^T \leqq \mathbf{v}^T \quad 0 \leqslant t \leqslant \theta - 1$ (14.6a)

$-\mathbf{x}_t^T (\mathbf{B} - \mathbf{l}\mathbf{w}^T) + \mathbf{x}_{t+1}^T \mathbf{A} + \gamma \mathbf{d}^T \leqq \mathbf{0}^T \quad 1 \leqslant t \leqslant \theta - 1$ (14.6b)

$-\mathbf{x}_\theta^T (\mathbf{B} - \mathbf{l}\mathbf{w}^T) + \gamma \mathbf{d}^T (\mathbf{I} - \mathbf{A}^*)^{-1} \leqq \mathbf{0}^T$ (14.6c)

$\mathbf{x}_1^T \mathbf{C} + \mathbf{z}_1^T \leqq \bar{\mathbf{z}}^T$ (14.6d)

$\mathbf{x}_{t+1}^T \mathbf{C} - \mathbf{z}_t^T + \mathbf{z}_{t+1}^T \leqq \mathbf{0}^T \quad 1 \leqslant t \leqslant \theta - 1$ (14.6e)

$\mathbf{z}_t \geqq \mathbf{0}, \mathbf{x}_t \geqq \mathbf{0} \quad 1 \leqslant t \leqslant \theta$ (14.6f) where γ does not need to be nonnegative. The following proposition gives an if and only if condition of the existence of a solution to system (14.5).

Proposition 1. *If there is a backstop technology, system (14.5) has a solution for* $\theta = \theta'$, *if and only if the following Assumption 5 holds.*

Assumption 5. *There are two finite sequences* $\mathbf{x}_t$, *and* $\mathbf{z}_t$ $(t = 1, 2, \ldots, \theta')$ *and a positive real number* γ *such that system (14.6) holds for* $\theta = \theta'$.

Proof   It is easily checked that there is a real number $\sigma > 0$ so large and a real number β such that the two finite sequences:

$$\mathbf{p}_t = \frac{\beta}{(1 + r^*)^{t+1}} \mathbf{p}^* \quad (t = 0, 1, \ldots, \theta')$$

$$\mathbf{y}_t = \sigma \mathbf{e} \quad (t = 0, 1 \ldots, \theta')$$

are feasible solutions to the primal; then both the primal and the dual have optimal solutions with a positive optimal value of γ if and only if Assumption 5 holds, because of the duality theorem of linear programming.   (Q.E.D.)

4. The complete analysis and the main results

The following proposition provides an information about the solutions to system (5) *for different* θ's.

Proposition 2. *If system (14.5) has a solution for* $\theta = \theta'$, *then it has a solution for* $\theta = \theta''$, *each* $\theta'' \geqslant \theta'$.

Proof   If the two finite sequences $\mathbf{x}'_t, \mathbf{z}'_t$ $(t = 1, 2, \ldots, \theta')$ and the real number γ' satisfy system (14.6) for $\theta = \theta'$, then the two finite sequences $\mathbf{x}''_t, \mathbf{z}''_t (t = 1, 2, \ldots, \theta'')$ with $\mathbf{x}''_t = \mathbf{x}'_t$, and $\mathbf{z}''_t = \mathbf{z}'_t$ for $t = 1, 2, \ldots, \theta'$, and $\mathbf{x}''_t = \gamma' \bar{\mathbf{x}}$ and $\mathbf{z}''_t = \mathbf{z}'_\theta$ for $t = \theta' + 1, \theta' + 2, \ldots, \theta''$, and the real number γ' satisfy system (14.5) for $\theta = \theta''$.   (Q.E.D.)

Assume now that there is a natural number θ' such that Assumption 5 holds. Then, because of Proposition 2, for each $\theta \geqslant \theta'$, the maximum value of the dual (exists and) is positive; we will call it γ_θ. Moreover, for each $\theta \geqslant \theta'$, four infinite sequences $\{\mathbf{x}_{t\theta}\}$, $\{\mathbf{z}_{t\theta}\}$, $\{\mathbf{p}_{t\theta}\}$ and $\{\mathbf{y}_{t\theta}\}$ are defined, where, for $t \leqslant \theta$, $\mathbf{p}_{t\theta}$ and $\mathbf{y}_{t\theta}$ equal the corresponding elements of the optimal solution of the primal, and $\mathbf{x}_{t\theta}$ and $\mathbf{z}_{t\theta}$ equal the corresponding elements of the optimal solution of the dual and, for $t \geqslant \theta$, we have:

$$\mathbf{p}_{t\theta} = (\mathbf{A}^*)^{t-\theta} \mathbf{p}_{\theta\theta}$$

$$\mathbf{y}_{t\theta} = \mathbf{y}_{\theta\theta}$$

$$\mathbf{x}_{t\theta} = \gamma_\theta \bar{\mathbf{x}}$$

$$\mathbf{z}_{t\theta} = \mathbf{z}_{\theta\theta}$$

where matrix $\mathbf{A}^* = [\hat{\mathbf{B}} - \hat{\mathbf{I}}\mathbf{w}^T]^{-1}\hat{\mathbf{A}}$ has the properties mentioned in Assumption 3. The following remarks are immediately checked:

Remark 1. *For each $t \geqslant 0$ and for each $\theta \geqslant \max(t + 1, \theta')$, $\mathbf{p}_{t\theta}$, $\mathbf{p}_{t+1,\theta}$, and $\mathbf{y}_{t\theta}$ satisfy inequality (14.2a).*

Remark 2. *For each $t \geqslant 0$ and for each $\theta \geqslant \theta' + 1$, $\mathbf{p}_{t\theta}$, $\mathbf{p}_{t+1,\theta}$, $\mathbf{y}_{t\theta}$, $\mathbf{y}_{t+1,\theta}$, $\mathbf{x}_{t+1,\theta}$, $\mathbf{x}_{t+2,\theta}$, $\mathbf{z}_{t\theta}$, $\mathbf{z}_{t+1,\theta}$, and γ_θ satisfy inequalities and equations (14.2b)–(14.2m).*

As a consequence,

Proposition 3. *The sequences $\{\mathbf{p}_t^*\}$, $\{\mathbf{y}_t^*\}$, $\{\mathbf{x}_t^*\}$, $\{\mathbf{z}_t^*\}$ and the real number γ^* defined as*

$$\mathbf{p}_t^* = \lim_{\theta \to \infty} \mathbf{p}_{t\theta} \tag{14.7a}$$

$$\mathbf{y}_t^* = \lim_{\theta \to \infty} \mathbf{y}_{t\theta} \tag{14.7b}$$

$$\mathbf{x}_t^* = \lim_{\theta \to \infty} \mathbf{x}_{t\theta} \tag{14.7c}$$

$$\mathbf{z}_t^* = \lim_{\theta \to \infty} \mathbf{z}_{t\theta} \tag{14.7d}$$

$$\gamma^* = \lim_{\theta \to \infty} \gamma_\theta \tag{14.7e}$$

constitute a solution to system (14.2).

Proof It is easily checked that if there are the limits (14.7), and if they are finite, then the sequences $\{\mathbf{p}_t^*\}$, $\{\mathbf{y}_t^*\}$, $\{\mathbf{x}_t^*\}$, $\{\mathbf{z}_t^*\}$, and the real number γ^* constitute a solution to system (14.2). In fact, if $\mathbf{p}_t^*$, $\mathbf{p}_{t+1}^*$, $\mathbf{y}_t^*$ do not satisfy inequality (14.2a) for some t, then there is a $\tau \geqslant \max(t+1, \theta')$ such that for that τ and for each $\theta \geqslant \tau$ Remark 1 is contradicted. Similarly, if $\mathbf{p}_t^*$, $\mathbf{p}_{t+1}^*$, $\mathbf{y}_t^*$, $\mathbf{y}_{t+1}^*$, $\mathbf{x}_{t+1}^*$, $\mathbf{x}_{t+2}^*$, $\mathbf{z}_t^*$, $\mathbf{z}_{t+1}^*$, γ^* do not satisfy any of inequalities or equations (14.2b)–(14.2m) for some t, then there is a $\tau \geqslant \max \theta' + 1$ such that for that τ and for each $\theta \geqslant \tau$ Remark 2 is contradicted. In order to show that limits (14.7) do exist, it is enough to check that, because of Remark 2, $\gamma_{\theta+1} \geqslant \gamma_\theta$. Hence, the sequence $\{\gamma_\theta\}$ is increasing and, because it is bounded (it must satisfy inequality (14.5e)), it is convergent. Since γ_θ is the maximum value of the dual linear programme above, this is enough to assert that all the mentioned limits exist. This proves also that the limit (14.7e) is finite. To show that limits (14.7a) and (14.7b) are finite, it is enough to remark that

$$0 \leqslant \mathbf{p}_{t+1}^* \leqslant \mathbf{A}^* \mathbf{p}_t^*, \quad 0 \leqslant \mathbf{y}_{t+1}^* \leqslant \mathbf{y}_t^*, \quad \text{and} \quad \bar{\mathbf{z}}^T \mathbf{y}_0^* + \mathbf{v}^T \mathbf{p}_0^* = \gamma^*$$

The fact that limits (14.7c) and (14.7d) are finite is an obvious consequence of inequalities (14.2e), (14.2g), (14.2i) and equation (14.2k). (Q.E.D.)

5. Concluding remarks

In this chapter a dynamic input–output model has been developed which is able to deal with exhaustible resources based on a number of simplifying assumptions. In particular, each resource is taken to be available in a quantity which, at time 0, is known with certainty. Discoveries of new resources (or deposits of known resources) are excluded. Technical progress in the industries extracting or utilizing the resources is set aside. It is assumed that there is a 'backstop technology', which implies that exhaustible resources are useful but not indispensable in the production and reproduction of commodities. The real wage rate is given and constant. The annual consumption of commodities by profit and royalty recipients is assumed to be proportional to a given vector of commodities which is constant over time. On the basis of these assumptions the paths followed by the endogenous variables – especially the royalties paid to the owners of the exhaustible resources, the quantities produced of the different commodities and their prices – are determined once a sequence of nominal profit rates is given. A change in such a sequence does not affect the quantities produced or the relative royalties and prices actualized at any time. One aspect of the solution of the model is the structural change of the economy over time, that is, the change in the methods of production adopted to satisfy effectual demand and the intensities with which the processes are operated, the overall level and composition of employment, etc.

Acknowledgements

We wish to thank Christian Bidard for his valuable comments on our earlier work on the problem of exhaustible resources (see Kurz and Salvadori, 1995, chapter 12, 1997), which have been partly responsible for the elaboration of the model discussed. We also wish to thank Giuseppe Freni and Christian Lager for useful discussions.

References

Kurz, H. D., Salvadori, N., 1995. Theory of Production. A Long-period Analysis. Cambridge University Press, Cambridge.

Kurz, H. D., Salvadori, N., 1997. Exhaustible resources in a dynamic input-output model with 'classical' features. Econ. Syst. Res. 9, 235–51.

Sraffa, P., 1960. Production of Commodities by Means of Commodities. Cambridge University Press, Cambridge.

Part V
Criticism of neoclassical theory

15 Reverse capital deepening and the numéraire[*]

A note

Heinz D. Kurz and Neri Salvadori

1. Introduction

The critique of the neoclassical theory of income distribution started by Joan Robinson in the early 1950s (cf. Robinson, 1953) was given new momentum with the publication of Piero Sraffa's *Production of Commodities by Means of Commodities* (Sraffa, 1960).[1] However, for quite some time the main issue of the critique appears to have been somewhat uncertain to many participants in the capital controversies, both advocates and adversaries of marginalism. A clear expression of the main issue was given by Garegnani ten years after the publication of Sraffa's book:

> [A]fter following in the footsteps of traditional theory and attempting an analysis of distribution in terms of 'demand' and 'supply', we are forced to the conclusion that a change, however small, in the 'supply' or 'demand' conditions of labour or capital (saving) may result in drastic changes of [the rate of profit] and [the wage rate]. That analysis would even force us to admit that [the rate of profit] may fall to zero or rise to its maximum, and hence [the wage rate] rise to its maximum or to fall to zero, without bringing to equality the quantities supplied and demanded of the two factors.
>
> (Garegnani, 1970, p. 426)

This problem arises as a consequence of 'reverse capital deepening', that is, the possibility that in a multisectoral economy the relationship between capital per unit of labour and the rate of profit (rate of interest) may be increasing. (In a one-commodity economy the relationship is necessarily decreasing.)

It is also known that in a multisectoral economy the shape of the relationship between capital per unit of labour and the rate of profit depends on the numéraire. Therefore, someone might be inclined to think that the main criticism put forward

* Reprinted with permission from *Review of Polical Economy*, 1998.
1 It should be pointed out that Joan Robinson left no doubt that her attack on marginal theory was largely inspired by ideas she learned in conversation with Piero Sraffa.

against neoclassical theory in the capital controversies is simply a question of the choice of numéraire.

If this view were to be correct it would have important implications. This may be exemplified with regard to the problem of the stability of equilibrium. Clearly, the question of whether an equilibrium is stable or not must be totally independent of the numéraire adopted, since stability or instability is an objective property of the economic system under consideration. On the contrary, the numéraire is chosen by the observer at his or her will and is not related to an objective property of the economic system, apart from the obvious fact that the numéraire must be specified in terms of valuable things (e.g. commodities, labour) that are a part of the economy that is being studied. As Sraffa emphasized with respect to another question concerning a particular numéraire: 'Particular proportions, such as the Standard ones, may give transparency to a system and render visible what was hidden, *but they cannot alter its mathematical properties*' (Sraffa, 1960, p. 23, emphasis added).

In this chapter we will show that what is relevant is whether the relationship between the capital per unit of labour and the rate of profit is increasing or not *when* the chosen numéraire is the *consumption unit*. Only with this choice of numéraire can we, in fact, assume that 'a given amount of capital in value terms' can be drawn as a vertical straight line in the plane which has the 'quantity of capital' on its horizontal axis and the level of the rate of profit on its vertical axis. A change in the numéraire changes both the supply curve and the demand curve but leaves unaltered whether the supply curve cuts the demand curve from above or from below, that is, it does not change the stability property of the system.

2. Preliminaries

While the surplus approach of the classical economists conceived of the real wage as determined *prior* to profits and rent, the neoclassical approach aimed to explain all kinds of income *symmetrically* in terms of supply and demand in regard to the services of the respective factors of production: labour, land and 'capital'.[2] Historically, neoclassical theory can be shown to derive from a generalisation, to all factors of production, including capital, of the theory of rent in terms of land of uniform quality and intensive margins (see, in particular, Bharadwaj, 1978). Assume that 'corn' can be produced with unassisted labour and land. Variable proportions of the two factors can then be shown to imply equality between the marginal products and the rates of remuneration of the factor services, that is, the wage rate and the rent rate in terms of the product. A decreasing relationship between the wage rate and the quantity of labour employed is built up. This relationship is commonly called the demand function for labour. The downward sloping demand function for labour is confronted with a supply function, derived

---

2 We beg the reader's pardon that in sketching the problem under discussion we shall follow closely the exposition developed in Kurz and Salvadori (1995, chapter 14).

from the optimal choices of utility maximizing individuals regarding the desired consumption of corn and leisure time, and, consequently, the desired labour time. The two functions are presumed to intersect at some point; let us call this point E. It gives the equilibrium values of total employment and the real wage rate in the economy as a whole. With flexible wages, point E is assumed to be an attractor, or centre of gravitation. Starting from a level of the wage rate higher than the market clearing level, the number of labourers employed would be smaller than the number of those seeking employment. Unemployed labourers would then start bidding down the real wage until it reaches the level compatible with full employment. Similarly, with an initial wage rate smaller than the market clearing level and hence the demand for labour larger than the supply, landowners, unable to find additional workers at the going wage rate, would start bidding up wages. Assuming other things to be equal, including the amount of land available for the production of corn, in both cases the system would tend towards the equilibrium position E.

A similar picture can be obtained if corn is produced by labour and by capital consisting exclusively of corn (seed corn), on homogeneous land that is available in unlimited quantities, that is, a free good. With continuously variable proportions between labour and (corn) capital, K, the argument developed for the labour–land case carries over to the present case. Hence a similar equality would hold between the rate of profit (interest), r, and that of wages on the one hand and the marginal products of (corn) capital and labour on the other. Figure 15.1 illustrates the argument in terms of the capital market. With (corn) capital in given supply, $K = K^*$, the equilibrium rate of profit would occur at the point where the demand function for capital, KK', derived on the assumption that there is full employment of labour, intersects the vertical supply function $K^*K^{*'}$, that is, at E' with r^* as the equilibrium rate of profit.

This is the analogy between capital or land and labour drawn by the early marginalist authors. The question is whether this analogy holds good in cases that are less special than the one in which capital consists exclusively of corn, that is, a commodity homogeneous with the product, and land is not scarce: or the case in which produced means of production do not exist. The answer given by the early

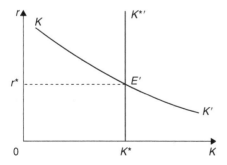

Figure 15.1 Demand and supply determination of the rate of profits.

marginalist economists was in the affirmative. It was contended that the simple case essentially carries over to the general case in which heterogeneous capital goods are used in production and in which land can be in short supply.

Expressing the 'quantity of capital' in given supply in *value* terms is necessitated by the following consideration. Careful scrutiny shows that the advocates of the traditional neoclassical theory of distribution, with the notable exception of Walras (at least until the fourth edition of the *Eléments*), were well aware of the fact that in order to be consistent with the concept of a long-run equilibrium the capital endowment of the economy could not be conceived of as a set of given physical amounts of produced means of production. For, if the capital endowment is given in kind, only a short-run equilibrium, characterized by differential rates of return on the supply prices of the various capital goods, could be established by the forces constituting supply and demand. However, under conditions of free competition, which would enforce a tendency towards a uniform rate of profit, such an equilibrium could not be considered – in the words of Hicks (1932, p. 20) – a 'full equilibrium'. Hence the 'quantity of capital' available for productive purposes had to be expressed as a value magnitude, allowing it to assume the physical 'form' suited to the other data of the theory: the endowment of the economy with factors of production other than 'capital'; the technical alternatives of production; and the preferences of agents.

Thus, the formidable problem for the neoclassical approach in attempting the determination of the general rate of profit consisted of the necessity of establishing the notion of a market for 'capital', the quantity of which could be expressed independently of the price of its service, that is, the rate of profit. Moreover, the plausibility of the supply and demand approach to the theory of distribution was felt to hinge upon the demonstration of the existence of a unique and stable equilibrium in that market (see, e.g. Marshall, 1920, p. 655n). With the 'quantity of capital' in given supply, this, in turn, implied that a monotonically decreasing demand function for 'capital' in terms of the rate of profit had to be established.

This inverse relationship was arrived at by the neoclassical theorists through the introduction of two kinds of substitutability between 'capital' and labour (and other factors of production): substitutability in consumption and in production. According to the former concept a rise in the rate of profit relative to the real wage rate would increase the price of those commodities, whose production exhibits a relatively high ratio of 'capital' to labour, compared to those in which little 'capital' per worker is employed. This would generally prompt consumers to shift their demand in favour of a higher proportion of the relatively cheapened commodities, that is, the 'labour-intensive' ones. Hence, in the economy as a whole the 'capital'– labour ratio, or 'capital intensity', and the rate of profit are inversely related. The second concept, substitutability in production, we have already encountered in the discussion of the model with corn capital. A rise in the rate of profit relative to the wage rate would make cost-minimizing entrepreneurs in the different industries of the economy employ more of the relatively cheapened factor of production, that is, labour. Hence, through both routes 'capital' would become substitutable for labour, and for any given quantity of labour employed a decreasing demand schedule for 'capital' would be obtained. Figure 15.1 was thus held to illustrate not only the hypothetical world with corn capital alone, but also the 'real world' with heterogeneous capital goods. The conclusion was close at hand that the division of the product between wages and profits can be explained in terms of the relative scarcity of the respective factors of production, labour and 'capital', where the latter is conceived of as a value magnitude that is considered independent of the rate of profit.

We may distinguish between several versions of traditional (i.e. long-period) neoclassical theory. First, there is the macroeconomic version which claims that there exists an aggregate production function with total labour employed together with the 'capital' stock in existence, explaining both total output and its distribution as wages and profits, thanks to the principle of marginal productivity. Second, there is the microeconomic version which claims that production functions with 'capital' as an input can be formulated for each single commodity. Finally, since *all* versions of neoclassical theory start from the premise that the economy as a whole is endowed with a given capital, we may distinguish between different versions according to which concept of the 'capital' endowment is advocated. There are essentially three alternatives, two of which are based on notions of 'real' capital, while the third is based on the notion of 'value' capital. The three are: (i) capital conceived of as a subsistence fund, that is, the version developed by Jevons and Böhm-Bawerk; (ii) capital conceived of as a set of quantities of heterogeneous capital goods, that is, the version elaborated by Walras and (iii) capital conceived of as a value magnitude, that is, the version put forward by Wicksell, J. B. Clark and Marshall. (For a more detailed discussion of these alternatives, see Kurz and Salvadori, 1995, pp. 433–43.)

The use of the value of capital as a factor of production alongside the factors of labour and land, which are measured in terms of their own technical units in the production function of single commodities, was already rejected by Knut Wicksell. This implied 'arguing in a circle' (Wicksell, 1934, p. 149), since capital and the rate of interest enter as a cost in the production of capital goods themselves. Hence, the value of the capital goods inserted in the production function depends on the rate of interest and will generally change with it. The problem here is that relative prices, and thus also the prices of capital goods, generally depend on income distribution. Even though the phenomenon under consideration has been well known since the classical economists and was referred to also by several neoclassical authors, especially Wicksell (e.g. Wicksell, 1934, pp. 147–51), the earlier authors were not fully aware of the complications involved. In particular, they were of the opinion that with a rise in the rate of profit r, given the system of production, the ratio of prices of any two commodities would either stay constant or rise or fall, throughout the range of variation of r. This opinion was closely related to the hypothesis that the capital–labour or capital–output ratios of the different industries could be brought into a ranking that is independent of distribution. Yet, as Sraffa has shown, this is generally not possible; that is, 'the price of a product . . . may rise or it may fall, or it may even alternate in rising and falling, relative to its means of production' (Sraffa, 1960, p. 15). Therefore, to characterise

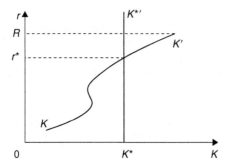

Figure 15.2 Reverse capital deepening.

an industry as 'capital intensive' or 'labour intensive' in general makes no sense unless the level of the rate of profit is specified at which this characterization is supposed to apply.

We talk of *reverse capital deepening* when the relationship between the value of capital (per capita) and the rate of profit is increasing. The negative implication of reverse capital deepening for traditional theory can be illustrated by means of the example of Figure 15.2, in which the value of capital corresponding to the full employment level of labour is plotted against the rate of profit. Obviously, if with traditional analysis we conceived of the curve KK' as the 'demand curve' for capital, which, together with the corresponding 'supply curve' $K^*K^{*\prime}$ is taken to determine the equilibrium value of r, we would have to conclude that this equilibrium, although unique, is unstable. With free competition, conceived of (as it is in neoclassical theory) as including the perfect flexibility of the distributive variables, a deviation of r from r^* would lead to the absurd conclusion that one of the two income categories, wages and profits, would disappear. According to the critics of traditional neoclassical theory, this result demonstrates all the more impressively the failure of the supply and demand approach to the theory of normal distribution, prices and quantities.

We may ask now: What does it mean to say that the 'supply curve of capital' is a vertical straight line? Are there implicit assumptions which allow one to do this? What would happen if we were to adopt another numéraire? In the following these questions will be answered together with the main one: since, as we know, a change in numéraire affects the 'demand curve' of capital, may this also affect the stability property of equilibrium?

3. The meaning of taking the 'quantity of capital' as given in *value* terms

Figure 15.2 is used by us for the sole purpose of illustrating the difficulty a traditional neoclassical economist would have to face when confronted with the problem of reverse capital deepening. Translating that phenomenon into the usual supply-and-demand framework would lead to a constellation like the one depicted. Therefore, our argument should be read as follows: even if there were *no* conceptual problems of conceiving the two curves as the demand and the supply curve, respectively, the neoclassical economist would be confronted with a serious problem: the instability of the resulting equilibrium.

But is it true that there are no conceptual problems with regard to the demand and the supply curve? The 'demand' curve has been built up by starting from a (finite or infinite) number of processes available to produce the n commodities (where each process produces only a single commodity and uses as inputs only labour and produced commodities); the assumptions underlying its construction are:

(i) consumption goods are consumed in given proportions (that is, substitution in consumption is set aside), or, which amounts formally to the same thing, there is only one consumption good;
(ii) the growth rate is uniform and given (possibly zero);
(iii) the numéraire consists of the consumption bundle.

Let us briefly show how the 'demand curve' is built up. A collection of n processes, each producing a different commodity, is called a *technique* and is described by the triplet $(\mathbf{A}, \mathbf{I}, \mathbf{l})$, where $\mathbf{A}$ is the material input matrix, the identity matrix $\mathbf{I}$ is the output matrix, and $\mathbf{l}$ is the (direct) labour input vector. If technique $(\mathbf{A}, \mathbf{I}, \mathbf{l})$ is used, commodities are consumed in proportion to vector $\mathbf{d} \geqslant \mathbf{0}$, the growth rate equals $g \geqslant 0$, and the system is normalized in such a way that one unit of labour is employed, then the intensity vector $\mathbf{x}$ and consumption per unit of labour c must be such that:

$$\mathbf{x}^{\mathrm{T}} = c\mathbf{d}^{\mathrm{T}} + (1 + g)\mathbf{x}^{\mathrm{T}}\mathbf{A}$$

$$\mathbf{x}^{\mathrm{T}}\mathbf{l} = 1$$

Furthermore, if technique $(\mathbf{A}, \mathbf{I}, \mathbf{l})$ holds, the rate of profit equals $r \geqslant 0$, and the numéraire consists of the consumption basket $\mathbf{d}$, then the price vector $\mathbf{p}$ and the wage rate w must be such that:

$$\mathbf{p} = (1 + r)\mathbf{A}\mathbf{p} + w\mathbf{l}$$

$$\mathbf{d}^{\mathrm{T}}\mathbf{p} = 1 \tag{15.1}$$

Hence, at the (given) growth rate g and at the rate of profit r the capital–labour ratio relative to technique $(\mathbf{A}, \mathbf{I}, \mathbf{l})$ is

$$k_{\mathrm{D}} = \mathbf{x}^{\mathrm{T}}\mathbf{A}\mathbf{p}$$

It is known (see e.g. Kurz and Salvadori, 1995, chapter 5) that there is a real number R such that for each rate of profit r such that $0 \leqslant r \leqslant R$ there is a cost-minimizing technique and, as a consequence, for each r there is a capital–labour ratio k_D. If there is more than one cost-minimizing technique for a given r, then they share the same price vector, but in this case we have a range of k_D's because cost-minimizing techniques may be combined: this means that the 'demand curve' is a function in the whole range $0 \leqslant r \leqslant R$ except for a number of levels of r, for each of which it consists of vertical segments.[3]

Then, if the above assumptions (i)–(iii) hold, a 'demand curve' can be built up even though it does not need to be a function, and, in general, will be a correspondence. A brief discussion of assumptions (i)–(iii) is appropriate. Assumption (i) is justified only on the grounds that the construction serves a purely critical purpose: it implies special preferences (all consumers have the same utility function and all consumption goods are perfect complements to one another). Similarly for assumption (ii). On the contrary, assumption (iii) is meaningful only if statement (i) holds. These assumptions can be considered concessions to the theory which is criticised. Indeed, in this case the supply function of capital is independent of the demand function for capital, because the consumption basket does not depend on relative prices and income distribution and thus on the equilibrium solution of the economic system under consideration. It would not otherwise be possible to fix the supply of capital independently of the equilibrium values of the rate of profit and relative prices, which in turn would depend on the demand function for capital.

Now let us turn to the supply curve. Since statement (iii) above holds, the fact that the supply curve is a vertical line has a clear meaning: what is given as 'capital' in value terms is expressed as equivalent to a given amount of the consumption unit. In fact, the given value of capital is to be specified in a way that is congenial to the concept of 'capital' entertained in the neoclassical theory. As is well known, this concept conceives of capital as forgone consumption: as we have seen, if capital goods are heterogeneous, the 'given capital' must be expressed as a value magnitude; but in this conceptualization 'capital' is considered the result of saving; saving is in turn envisaged as abstention from consumption. Therefore, it was close at hand to conceive of the 'quantity of capital' available in a given economy, that is, the 'supply of capital', $k_S(r)$ in units of some consumption bundle **d**.

This approach to the problem of 'capital' has a long tradition in the marginal theory of value and distribution. We encounter it, for example, in William Stanley Jevons with his concept of 'free capital'. As the following passage shows, there the consumption bundle was identified with the basket of wage goods: 'By free capital I mean the wages of labour . . . [in its] real form of food and other necessaries of life. The ordinary sustenance requisite to support labourers of all ranks when engaged upon their work is really the true form of capital' (Jevons, 1871, pp. 242–3).

---

3 If the number of available processes is finite or countable, the values of r for which there is more than one cost-minimizing technique may be finite (in both cases) or countable (in the latter case only), but if the number of available processes is infinite but not countable, each single value of r may have this property, or none, or a finite or infinite number of values; see Bellino (1993).

A similar view was advocated by Eugen von Böhm-Bawerk (1891) with his concept of the 'subsistence fund'. Böhm-Bawerk was of course not of the opinion that the entire social capital available to an economy at a given moment of time is exclusively made up of means of subsistence. As a matter of fact, only a small part of it consists of the latter, whilst a large part is embodied in plant and equipment. However, the entire capital may be *measured* in terms of those goods, from whose consumption one must abstain in order to get the different kinds of capital goods, or, what is the same thing, in terms of those consumption goods that can be produced by means of the capital goods. This is so, Böhm-Bawerk expounded, because 'all goods which appear today as the stock or parent wealth of society... will, in the more or less distant future... ripen into consumption goods, and will consequently cover, for a more or less lengthy time to come, the people's demand for consumption' (Böhm-Bawerk, 1891, p. 322). Therefore, in Böhm-Bawerk, the social subsistence fund expresses the entire social capital and not just the wage capital.

Knut Wicksell, who developed his own theory from a critical examination of Böhm-Bawerk's, stressed that because of the heterogeneity of capital goods 'It may be difficult – if not impossible – to define this concept of social capital with absolute precision as a definite quantity. In reality it rather is a complex of quantities' (Wicksell, 1934, p. 165). With the concept of real capital being impossible to define 'with absolute precision', the capital endowment of the economy can be conceived of only as a fluid that can assume any form without changing its size, the latter being expressed in terms of the consumption unit. This is indeed what Wicksell does in the *Lectures on Political Economy*. (For a detailed discussion of Wicksell's approach to the problem of capital and distribution, see Kurz, 1998.)

Hence, the 'quantity of capital' in a given supply is to be expressed in terms of the consumption basket. Yet, in order for the supply curve to be *independent* from the demand curve in Figure 15.2, the argument must be based on assumption (i). Therefore, while for the conceptual difficulties mentioned it is not possible, in general, to interpret the two curves in Figure 15.2 as the demand and the supply curve, these difficulties are set aside by means of the given assumptions. Therefore the equilibrium rate of profit is determined by the equation:

$$k_{\mathrm{D}}(r) = k_{\mathrm{S}}(r) \tag{15.2}$$

where $k_{\mathrm{S}}(r)$ is a constant if the consumption good is used as numéraire.

4. Stability of equilibrium and numéraire

The argument in this section is based on assumptions (i)–(iii) of the previous section (for a similar argument, see Potestio, 1996). In addition we shall postulate that in the relevant range k_{D} is a continuous and differentiable (not necessarily monotonic) function of $r: k_{\mathrm{D}} = k_{\mathrm{D}}(r)$. Let us now define a bundle of commodities **b** that differs from bundle **d** (**b** ≠ **d**). (It goes without saying that all bundles referred to in this note are assumed to be semipositive.) We define:

$$m_D(r) = \frac{k_D(r)}{n(r)}$$

where $n(r) = \mathbf{b}^T\mathbf{p}(r)$, and $\mathbf{p}(r)$ is the price vector when the numéraire is set as in equation (15.1) above. That is, $m_D(r)$ is the 'demand' for capital when the numéraire is specified as

$$\mathbf{b}^T\mathbf{p} = 1$$

rather than by equation (15.1). Obviously

$$m_D'(r) = \frac{k_D'(r)n(r) - n'(r)k_D(r)}{[n(r)]^2}$$

and therefore there is no reason to assume that the sign of $k_D'(r)$ equals the sign of $m_D'(r)$. This simple fact might mislead the reader into thinking that a change in the numéraire could change the stability property of the system. The (inattentive) reader might even be of the opinion that in order to establish this point it is enough to show that a change in numéraire could affect the sign of the slope of the demand curve. An upward sloping demand curve – the case of reverse capital deepening, which according to the critics of neoclassical theory demonstrates the failure of that theory – may by a judicious change in numéraire be rendered downward sloping. However, it is easily shown that what matters is *not* whether the demand curve is increasing or not, but whether it is increasing or not *when the consumption unit is used as the numéraire*. Indeed, irrespective of the numéraire that is used, what is relevant is whether or not the supply curve cuts the demand curve from above. It is only when the consumption unit is used as numéraire that the supply curve is a vertical line and, as a consequence, the question can be reduced to whether or not the demand curve is increasing. In fact, if equation (15.2) is replaced by

$$m_D(r) = m_S(r) \tag{15.3}$$

where

$$m_S(r) = \frac{k_S(r)}{n(r)}$$

not only is the equilibrium rate of profit unchanged, but so is the stability property. This is clear from the fact that:

$$\text{sign}\,[k_D'(r) - k_S'(r)] = \text{sign}\,[m_D'(r) - m_S'(r)]$$

whenever equations (15.2) and (15.3) are satisfied, since $n(r)$ is positive and whenever equations (15.2) and (15.3) are satisfied:

$$m_D'(r) - m_S'(r) = \frac{k_D'(r) - k_S'(r)}{n(r)}$$

Figure 15.3 illustrates the demand and the supply curves when two different numéraires are adopted. In Figure 15.3(a) the consumption unit is the numéraire

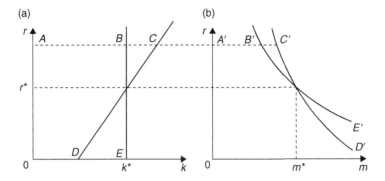

Figure 15.3 Demand and supply curves for two numéraires.

and the supply curve is the vertical straight line BE; for simplicity, the demand curve has also been drawn as a straight line, CD. In Figure 15.3(b) the numéraire is not the consumption unit: the new numéraire is assumed to involve a downward sloping demand function for capital, $C'D'$. However, as the figure shows, a change in numéraire affects also the shape and location of the supply function, $B'E'$, but does not affect the stability property of the equilibrium. The two curves are built up in such a way that for each rate of profit the ratio between the segments AB and $A'B'$ equals the ratio between the segments AC and $A'C'$ (and equals the price of the bundle of commodities used as numéraire in Figure 15.3(b) in terms of the consumption good).[4]

5. Conclusions

In this note it has been shown that under the specified assumptions the economic properties of the economic system, especially the stability property of neoclassical long-period equilibrium, do not depend on the numéraire adopted by the theorist. The importance of reverse capital deepening, as discussed subsequent to the publication of Piero Sraffa's *Production of Commodities by Means of Commodities* in the so-called Cambridge controversies in the theory of capital, is to be seen in the fact that if it is obtained in the neighbourhood of equilibrium, then the latter is unstable. The instability of equilibrium throws into doubt, however, the applicability of the demand and supply approach to the theory of income distribution, because a deviation from equilibrium would lead to the absurd conclusion that one of the two income categories contemplated, wages and profits, could disappear.

---

4 The functions used to draw the pictures are $k_\mathrm{D} = 1 + r(CD)$, $k_\mathrm{S} = 2(BE)$, $m_\mathrm{D} = (1+r)^{-1}$ $(C'D')$, $m_\mathrm{S} = 2(1+r)^{-2}(B'E')$.

Acknowledgements

This note was inspired by a discussion paper by Paola Potestio (1996). We would like to thank Gary Mongiovi and an anonymous referee of this journal for useful suggestions. Neri Salvadori also thanks the CNR (the Italian Research Council) and the MURST (the Italian Ministry of University and Technological and Scientific Research) for financial support. The usual caveats apply.

References

Bellino, E. (1993) Continuous switching of techniques in linear production models, *Manchester School*, 61, pp. 185–201.

Bharadwaj, K. (1978) *Classical Political Economy and Rise to Dominance of Supply and Demand Theories* (New Delhi, Orient Longman).

Böhm-Bawerk, E. von (1891) *The Positive Theory of Capital* (London, Macmillan).

Garegnani, P. (1970) Heterogeneous capital, the production function and the theory of distribution, *Review of Economic Studies*, 37, pp. 407–36.

Hicks, J. R. (1932) *The Theory of Wages* (London, Macmillan).

Jevons, W. S. (1871) *The Theory of Political Economy* (London, Macmillan); reprint of the 4th edition (1965) (New York, Kelley).

Kurz, H. D. (1998) Über das 'Perpetuum mobile des Volkswirtschaftsmechanismus' und eine 'theoretische Verkehrtheit' – Knut Wicksell und die Einheit von Produktions- und Distributionstheorie, in E. Streissler (ed.), *Knut Wicksell als Wirtschaftstheoretiker* (Berlin, Duncker & Humblot), pp. 131–86.

Kurz, H. D. and Salvadori, N. (1995) *Theory of Production. A Long-period Analysis* (Cambridge, Cambridge University Press).

Marshall, A. (1920) *Principles of Economics*, 8th edn (London and Basingstoke, Macmillan, 1977); 1st edn 1890.

Potestio, P. (1996) On certain aspects of neo-Ricardian critique of neoclassical distribution theory, Discussion Paper No. 30, Dipartimento di Scienze Economiche, Università di Roma 'La Sapienza'. A revised version was published as 'The aggregate neoclassical theory of distribution and the concept of a given value of capital: towards a more general critique', *Structural Change and Economic Dynamics*, 10 (1999), pp. 381–94.

Robinson, J. V. (1953) The production function and the theory of capital, *Review of Economic Studies*, 21, pp. 81–106.

Sraffa, P. (1960) *Production of Commodities by Means of Commodities. Prelude to a Critique of Economic Theory* (Cambridge, Cambridge University Press).

Wicksell, K. (1934) *Lectures on Political Economy*, vol. I (London, George Routledge & Sons).

16 Reswitching – simplifying a famous example[*]

Heinz D. Kurz and Neri Salvadori

1. Introduction

In his rightly famous paper on 'Heterogeneous capital, the production function and the theory of distribution' Piero Garegnani (1970) presented a numerical example which was referred to many times in the literature on reswitching (see, e.g. Howard, 1979, pp. 123–5). Although there is a continuum of techniques in the example, there is reswitching. (As a matter of fact all techniques but one reswitch.) The example uses the well-known workhorse of much of steady-state capital theory, the Hicks–Samuelson–Spaventa model, in which there is a capital good sector (producing a durable instrument of production) and a consumption good sector (producing corn). It is assumed that for each value of a parameter there is a process producing corn and a process producing a capital good, which is different for each value of the parameter, such that the former process uses the product of the latter process and labour to produce corn, whereas the latter process uses its own product and labour to produce the capital good. Sato (1974) has proved that if there are two parameters rather than one, and if in addition some continuity and differentiability conditions are introduced just 'for mathematical convenience', then reswitching does not occur anymore. However, Salvadori (1979) has shown that those continuity and differentiability conditions are actually equivalent to the assumption that in one of the two sectors there is a neoclassical production function exhibiting the usual properties and therefore the capital goods are all the same one and capital heterogeneity is effectively ruled out.

Despite the great attention Garegnani's numerical example has attracted in the literature, there has been no attempt to provide a simpler version of it. The example uses in fact equations in which exponential functions and roots of degree 10 of powers of degree 11 appear. This might give rise to the impression that highly complex conditions are to be met in order to obtain reswitching with a continuum of techniques. But this is not so. In this chapter we shall present an example with exactly the same properties as Garegnani's, but using just algebraic equations.

---

[*] Reprinted with permission from *Economics, Welfare Policy and the History of Economic Thought. Essays in honour of Arnold Heertje*, Edward Elgar, 1999.

2. Preliminaries

It is convenient to present Garegnani's example in a way which clarifies what are the ingredients that are necessary to obtain reswitching.

Let $U = \{u \in \mathbb{R} | 0 \le u < 2\}$ be a set of indices. Let us assume that for each $u \in U$ there is a commodity, called u-commodity, which can both be utilized to produce itself and to produce another commodity, called corn. Corn is the only commodity required for consumption. Finally, for each u there are the processes defined by Table 16.1, where $x = 27 e^{-2u}$, $y = 5 + \sqrt[10]{u^{11}}$, and e is the base of natural logarithms.

For each u, which defines a *technique*, we may calculate the w–r *relationship* corresponding to that technique. We get:

$$w = \frac{1 - yr}{y + (x - y^2)r} \tag{16.1}$$

As is well known, the *wage frontier* is the outer envelope of the w–r relationships relative to the different techniques. In the present case we find it by setting the derivative with respect to u of the RHS of equation (16.1) equal to zero. That is:

$$(xy' + 2xy + y^2 y')r^2 - 2(x + yy')r + y' = 0 \tag{16.2}$$

where $y' := 1.1 \sqrt[10]{u}$ is the derivative of y with respect to u (the derivative of x with respect to u, x', equals $-2x$). Equation (16.2) is a second degree equation in r. To show that there is reswitching of all relevant techniques it is enough to show that for each relevant u equation (16.2) has two solutions in the relevant range.

From the elementary theory of second degree equations we have that equation (16.2) has two real solutions if and only if

$$(x + yy')^2 - (xy' + 2xy + y^2 y')y' \ge 0$$

Table 16.1 Garegnani's numerical example

	Material inputs		Labour		Outputs	
	Corn	u-commodity			Corn	u-commodity
(u)	0	$\dfrac{x}{1+y}$	$y - \dfrac{x}{1+y}$	$\rightarrow$	1	0
$(2+u)$	0	$\dfrac{y}{1+y}$	$\dfrac{1}{1+y}$	$\rightarrow$	0	1

that is, if and only if

$$x - y'^2 \geq 0$$

or, in terms of u:

$$27 \, e^{-2u} \geq 1.21 \sqrt[5]{u} \qquad (16.3)$$

The same theory ensures that for $u = u^*$, where u^* is the (real) value of u for which the weak inequality (16.3) is actually satisfied as an equality, the two real solutions to equation (16.2) coincide.[1] By calculation $u^* \approx 1.505$ and the two solutions to equation (16.2) for $u = u^*$ are both:

$$r^* = \frac{x + yy'}{xy' + 2xy + y^2 y'} = \frac{1}{5 + \sqrt[10]{u^*}(1.1 + u^*)} \approx 0.13$$

where the functions of u, x, y, and y' in the first fraction are calculated at $u = u^*$.[2] Hence, if and only if $0 \leq u \leq u^*$ equation (16.2) has two real solutions, which both equal r^* for $u = u^*$.

For each u the maximum rate of profit, R_u, is obtained from equation (16.1) for $w = 0$:

$$R_u = \frac{1}{y} = \frac{1}{5 + \sqrt[10]{u^{11}}}$$

As a consequence:

$$\max_u R_u = \frac{1}{5}$$

and the maximum rate of profit for the whole economy is 1/5. Then we have to show that the two real solutions to equation (16.2) for u such that $0 \leq u \leq u^*$ are

---

1 We cannot, of course, know a priori that there is a unique u^*, since the equation which determines it is transcendent. The calculation can, however, show that there is a unique real solution for u^* since function

$$v(u): = 27 \, e^{-2u} - 1.21 \sqrt[5]{u}$$

is defined for $u \geq 0$ only, it is decreasing in the entire range of definition, $v(0) = 27 > 0$, and

$$\lim_{u \to \infty} v(u) = -\infty$$

2 Since $x(u^*) = [y'(u^*)]^2$, the first fraction can be stated as

$$\frac{y'^2 + yy'}{y'^3 + 2yy'^2 + y^2 y'} = \frac{1}{y' + y}$$

both not smaller than 0 and not greater than 1/5 in order to have reswitching. The former condition can be proved by using Descartes' rule[3] since:

$$(xy' + 2xy + y^2 y') > 0$$

$$-2(x + yy') < 0$$

$$y' \geq 0$$

in the relevant range. In order to apply Descartes' rule also to obtain the latter condition we substitute $(\theta + 1/5)$ for r in equation (16.2) and get the equation in θ:

$$(xy' + 2xy + y^2 y')\theta^2 + \left[\frac{2(xy' + 2xy + y^2 y') - 10(x + yy')}{5} \right] \theta$$

$$+ \frac{xy' + 2xy + y^2 y'}{25} - \frac{2(x + yy')}{5} + y' = 0$$

Then, by showing – using Descartes' rule – that both solutions to the equation in θ are smaller than 0, we actually show that both solutions to equation (16.2) are smaller than 1/5, because:

$$r = \theta + \frac{1}{5}$$

Since

$$(xy' + 2xy + y^2 y') > 0$$

---

3 Descartes' rule connects the variations or permanences of the signs of the coefficients of algebraic equations to the signs of the solutions of the same equations. In the present context we are only interested in Descartes' rule concerning equations of the second degree. Let a second degree equation be expressed in its canonical form:

$$ax^2 + bx + c = 0$$

With regard to coefficients a and b (b and c) call it a 'variation' if $ab < 0$ ($bc < 0$) and a 'permanence' if $ab > 0$ ($bc > 0$). Descartes' rule maintains that to each variation there corresponds a positive solution and to each permanence a negative solution. Moreover, if a variation precedes a permanence (a permanence precedes a variation), then the solution with the largest absolute value is positive (negative). As is well known, the solutions to an equation of second degree expressed in its canonical form are given by

$$x_1 = \frac{-b - \sqrt{b^2 - 4ac}}{2a} \qquad x_2 = \frac{-b + \sqrt{b^2 - 4ac}}{2a}$$

and thus

$$x_1 + x_2 = -\frac{b}{a} \qquad x_1 x_2 = \frac{c}{a}$$

If $ab < 0$ (a variation), then the sum of the solutions is positive, that is, the solution with the largest absolute value is positive. The reverse is true if $ab > 0$ (a permanence). In the case of two variations or two permanences $ac > 0$, which implies that $x_1 x_2 > 0$. Therefore, the solutions of the equation have the same sign. In the case of a variation and a permanence (independently of the order) $ac < 0$, $x_1 x_2 < 0$, and the solutions of the equation have opposite signs.

in the relevant range, we just need to show that:

$$2(xy' + 2xy + y^2y') - 10(x + yy') > 0$$

$$(xy' + 2xy + y^2y') - 10(x + yy') + 25y' > 0$$

that is

$$2xy' + x(4y - 10) + (2y - 10)yy' > 0$$

$$xy' + 2x(y - 5) + y'(y - 5)^2 > 0$$

which is certainly the case since $x > 0$, $y' \geq 0$, $y \geq 5$ in the relevant range. It is also checked that for $u = 0$, the two solutions to equation (16.2) are $r = 0$ and $r = 1/5$.

To sum up, for u increasing from 0 to u^*, the smaller solution to equation (16.2) increases from 0 to r^* and the larger solution decreases from 1/5 to r^*. If we look at the other side, for r increasing from 0 to r^*, u increases from 0 to u^* and there is no reswitching in this segment; but for r increasing from r^* to 1/5, u decreases from u^* to 0 and each technique met in this segment has been met in the previous segment.

3. Simplifying the example

Let U be a set of indices to be defined. Let us assume that for each $u \in U$ there is a commodity, called u-commodity, which can both be utilized to produce itself and to produce another commodity, called corn. Corn is the only commodity required for consumption. Finally, for each u there are the processes defined by Table 16.1, where x and y are functions of u to be defined.

For each u the w–r relationship is again given by equation (16.1), but now we cannot take advantage of the fact that $x' = -2x$. Instead of equation (16.2) we now have:

$$(xy' - yx' + y^2y')r^2 - (2yy' - x')r + y' = 0 \tag{16.2*}$$

which is also a second degree equation in r. To show that there is reswitching of all relevant techniques, it is enough to show that for each relevant u equation (16.2*) has two solutions in the relevant range. Equation (16.2*) has two real solutions if and only if

$$(2yy' - x')^2 - 4(xy' - yx' + y^2y')y' \geq 0$$

that is, if and only if

$$x'^2 - 4xy'^2 \geq 0 \tag{16.3*}$$

We want to fix x and y in such a way that in the set U there is a unique u^* which satisfies the weak inequality (16.3*) as an equality. Moreover, we want there to be a subset of U such that for each u in this subset equation (16.2*) has two real solutions (i.e. inequality (16.3*) is satisfied) and these two real solutions are between 0 and

$$\max_{u \in U} R_u = \max_{u \in U} \frac{1}{y(u)}$$

That is all. But if we want equation (16.2*) to be an algebraic equation in u, then $x(u)$ and $y(u)$ must be either polynomials or ratios of polynomials. We need the degrees of the involved polynomials to be large enough to have enough coefficients to fix in order to satisfy the equations and the inequalities required. (These coefficients will eventually be the data of the example, but now they are the unknowns since we want to construct the example.)

From equation (16.2*) we obtain that if 0 must be a solution for r for some u, then for that u we must have that $y' = 0$. Moreover, if u is such that $y' = 0$, then there are two solutions for r, one is $r = 0$, the other is $r = 1/y$ (provided that $x' \neq 0$). This implies that y' cannot be a constant. It could be a polynomial of degree 1, then y is a polynomial of degree 2 and, as a consequence, $y^2 y'$ is a polynomial of degree 5. If we want equation (16.2*) to be an equation in u of degree 2, then x must be a polynomial of degree 4 such that all the monomials of a degree larger than 2 of the polynomials $xy' - yx' + y^2 y'$ and $2yy' - x'$ equal zero. Hence, if $x: = au^4 + bu^3 + cu^2 + du + e$ and $y: = fu^2 + gu + h$ where a, b, c, d, e, f, g, h are coefficients to be determined, then equation (16.2*) is of degree 2 in u if and only if

$$2af - 4af + 2f^3 = 0$$

$$ag + 2bf - (4ag + 3bf) + f^2 g + 4f^2 g = 0$$

$$bg + 2cf - (4ah + 3bg + 2cf) + 2fg^2 + 4f^2 h + 2fg^2 = 0$$

$$4f^2 - 4a = 0$$

which are certainly satisfied if $a = f^2$ and $b = 2g$. To make things as simple as possible, we can set $a = f = 1$ and $b = c = g = 0$. Then $x: = u^4 + du + e$ and $y: = u^2 + h$ and equation (16.2*) becomes

$$[du^2 + 2(e + h^2)u - dh]r^2 - (4hu - d)r + 2u = 0 \qquad (16.2^{**})$$

The discriminant of the equation of second degree in r (16.2**) is

$$\Delta(u) = (4hu - d)^2 - 8u[du^2 + 2(e + h^2)u - dh]$$

It is easily checked that

$$\Delta(0) = d^2$$

is positive if $d \neq 0$. Let us impose that $\Delta(1) = 0$. This implies that the set U can be set as $\{u \in \mathbb{R} | 0 \leq u < \bar{u}\}$, where $\bar{u} > 1$ is close enough to 1, provided that $\Delta(u) > 0$ for $0 \leq u < 1$. Since

$$\Delta(1) = (4h - d)^2 - 8[2(e + h^2) + d - dh] = d^2 - 16e - 8d$$

$\Delta(1) = 0$, if and only if

$$16e = d^2 - 8d \tag{16.4}$$

If equation (16.4) holds, equation (16.2**) becomes

$$[8du^2 + (d^2 - 8d + 16h^2)u - 8dh]r^2 - 8(4hu - d)r + 16u = 0 \tag{16.2***}$$

and its discriminant is

$$\Delta(u) = -64[8du^3 + (d^2 - 8d)u^2 - d^2] = 64d(8u^2 + du + d)(1 - u)$$

If $u = 1$, equation (16.2***) has two coincident solutions:

$$r^* = \frac{4(4h - d)}{d^2 + 16h^2 - 8dh} = \frac{4}{4h - d}$$

Note that

$$0 < r^* < R$$

if and only if

$$d < 0$$

since

$$R = \max_{u \in U} R_u = \max_{u \in U} \frac{1}{u^2 + h} = \frac{1}{h} > 0$$

Finally we have to check whether the technical coefficients of the techniques defined by Table 16.1 are nonnegative, that is, for $u \in U: x > 0$, $y > 0$, $y(1+y) > x$.

Since $d < 0$, the function $x(u)$ is certainly positive for $0 \leq u < \bar{u}$ if[4]

$$e = \frac{d^2 - 8d}{16} \geq -d \tag{16.5}$$

the function $y(u)$ is certainly positive since $h > 0$, whereas the function $y(u)$ $[1 + y(u)] - x(u)$ is certainly positive for $0 \leq u < \bar{u}$ if

$$h(1 + h) > \frac{d^2 - 8d}{16} \tag{16.6}$$

Since $d < 0$ inequality (16.5) is satisfied if and only if $d \leq -8$. For $d < 0$ and $h > 0$, inequality (16.6) is certainly satisfied for:

$$h > -\frac{1}{2} + \frac{\sqrt{4 - 8d + d^2}}{4}$$

Hence a simple solution is $d = -16$, $e = 24$, $h = 5$. Then $x: = u^4 - 16u + 24$ and $y: = u^2 + 5$ and equation (16.2*) becomes:

$$(-8u^2 + 49u + 40)r^2 - 2(5u + 4)r + u = 0 \tag{16.2****}$$

It is easily checked that the discriminant of the equation in r (16.2****) is a polynomial of degree 3 which is zero, if and only if either

$$u = 1$$

or

$$u = 1 \pm \sqrt{3}$$

---

4 Actually x is positive for each $d < 0$. In fact, if we consider the inequality $x > 0$ as an inequality in d we have

$$d^2 + (16u - 8)d + 16u^4 > 0$$

which is satisfied for each d if $u \geq \sqrt{2} - 1$. If $0 \leq u < \sqrt{2} - 1$, then such an inequality is satisfied if either:

$$d > 4 - 8u + 4\sqrt{(1 - u)^2(1 - 2u - u^2)}$$

or

$$d < 4 - 8u - 4\sqrt{(1 - u)^2(1 - 2u - u^2)}$$

The former inequality contradicts $d < 0$; then we must just show that for $0 \leq u < \sqrt{2} - 1$ the latter inequality is satisfied when $d < 0$. That is, for $0 \leq u < \sqrt{2} - 1$

$$1 - 2u - (1 - u)\sqrt{1 - 2u - u^2} \leq 0$$

Since $1 - 2u > 0$ in the relevant range, it is enough to prove that in this range

$$(1 - 2u)^2 - (1 - u)^2(1 - 2u - u^2) \geq 0$$

which is certainly the case.

and since it is continuous everywhere and it is positive for $u = 0$, it is positive in the range:

$$1 - \sqrt{3} < u < 1$$

and, as a consequence, it is certainly positive for

$$0 \leq u < 1$$

For each u such that $0 \leq u \leq 1$, equation (16.2****) has two solutions, which coincide for $u = 1$. These solutions are:

$$r = \frac{5u + 4 \pm 2\sqrt{2u^3 - 6u^2 + 4}}{40 + 49u - 8u^2}$$

In particular, if $u = 0$

$$r = \frac{4 \pm 4}{40} = \begin{cases} 0 \\ \dfrac{1}{5} \end{cases}$$

When u increases from 0 to 1, the smaller solution increases continuously, whereas the larger one decreases continuously until both equal 1/9 for $u = 1$.

4. The new example

Let us summarize the example we have found. Let $U = \{u \in \mathbb{R} \mid 0 \leq u < 1.01\}$ be a set of indices. Assume that for each $u \in U$ there is a commodity, called u-commodity, which can both be utilized to produce itself and to produce a further commodity, called corn. Corn is the only commodity required for consumption. For each u there exist the processes defined by Table 16.2.

For each u the w–r relationship is

$$w = \frac{1 - (u^2 + 5)r}{u^2 + 5 - (1 + 16u + 10u^2)r}$$

the outer envelope is found by setting the derivative with respect to u equal to zero. The second degree equation in r (9.2****) is obtained in this way. If $0 \leq u \leq 1$, equation (16.2****) has two real solutions, which both equal 1/9 for $u = 1$. Both solutions are positive and smaller than 1/5 for $0 < u \leq 1$, and for $u = 0$ the two solutions are $r = 0$ and $r = 1/5$. Hence for u increasing from 0 to 1, the smaller solution to equation (16.2****) increases from 0 to 1/9 and the larger solution decreases from 1/5 to 1/9. If we look at the other side, for r increasing from 0 to 1/9, u increases from 0 to 1 and there is no reswitching in this segment; but for r increasing from 1/9 to 1/5, u decreases from 1/9 to 1 and each technique met in this segment has been met in the previous segment.

Table 16.2 The new numerical example

	Material inputs		Labour		Outputs	
	Corn	u-commodity			Corn	u-commodity
u	0	$\dfrac{u^4 - 16u + 24}{u^2 + 6}$	$\dfrac{11u^2 + 16u + 6}{u^2 + 6}$	$\rightarrow$	1	0
$1.01 + u$	0	$\dfrac{u^2 + 5}{u^2 + 6}$	$\dfrac{1}{u^2 + 6}$	$\rightarrow$	0	1

The simplicity of the example proposed has also another advantage. equation (16.2****) can be read as an equation in u. In this case it is better written as:

$$8r^2u^2 - (49r^2 - 10r + 1)u - (40r^2 - 8r) = 0 \tag{16.7}$$

This allows one in a very simple way to determine u as a function of r:

$$u = u(r): = \frac{49r^2 - 10r + 1 - \sqrt{\Delta(r)}}{16r^2} \tag{16.8}$$

where

$$\Delta(r) = 3681r^4 - 1236r^3 + 198r^2 - 20r + 1$$

Obviously, equation (16.7) has also another solution, but it is not the function we are interested in, since the values of u so determined are not in $U = \{u \in \mathbb{R} | 0 \le u < 1.01\}$. This is simply seen by considering the case in which $r = 1/9$. The solution (16.8) to equation (16.7) is $u = 1$, as expected. The other one is $u = 4 > 1.01$.[5]

Once we have the function $u = u(r)$, we can substitute it for u in the formula giving the single w–r relationship. In this way we find the wage frontier:

$$w = \frac{1 - [u(r)^2 + 5]r}{u(r)^2 + 5 - [1 + 16u(r) + 10u(r)^2]r}$$

that is

$$w = \frac{1 - 20r + 51r^2 + \sqrt{\Delta(r)}}{2(5 - 51r - 54r^2)}$$

5 Similarly, for $r = 1/5$, the solution (16.8) to equation (16.7) is $u = 0$, as expected, whereas the other one is $3 > 1.01$. And the limit for $r \to 0$ of the solution (16.8) to equation (16.7) is 0, as expected, whereas the limit of the other one is infinite.

5. Conclusion

The starting point of this chapter is the famous numerical example provided by Garegnani (1970), demonstrating the reswitching of techniques in the case in which there is a continuum of techniques. It is shown that a considerably simplified example can be given, preserving all the important properties of the original example. This should suffice to dispel the idea that excessively complex conditions are to be met in order to have reswitching under the specified circumstances. The new example put forward has also the advantage of allowing a much simpler determination of the cost-minimizing technique for alternative values of the rate of profit.

References

Garegnani, P. (1970), 'Heterogeneous capital, the production function and the theory of distribution', *Review of Economic Studies*, 37, 407–36.

Howard, M. C. (1979), *Modern Theories of Income Distribution*, London and Basingstoke: Macmillan.

Salvadori, N. (1979), 'The technology frontier in capital theory. A comment [to K. Sato]', *Economic Notes*, 117–24.

Sato, R. (1974), 'The neo-classical postulate and the technology frontier in capital theory', *Quarterly Journal of Economics*, 88, 353–84.

17 Franklin Fisher on aggregation[*]

Marco Lippi and Neri Salvadori

1.

The core of the book by Franklin Fisher (1993) on aggregation is a collection of articles on the conditions under which it is possible to aggregate heterogeneous capital goods into a single magnitude which can be used as a variable in an (aggregate) production function. Except for three chapters (7, 10, 11) that for brevity will not be considered here, we may divide its content into two distinct parts. In the first (chapters 1–6) the author looks for restrictions on the (microeconomic) production functions, and finds very stringent conditions. In the second (chapters 8 and 9) the author looks for restrictions on macroeconomic variables (the labor's share in output, in particular) such that Cobb–Douglas production functions fit well the macro data, in spite of the lack of microfoundation.

The discussion of two elementary cases will be sufficient to give the flavor of the first part. Consider first the three-factor production function:

$$F(k_1, k_2, m)$$

where k_1 and k_2 are capital inputs and m is labor. The problem is whether there exists an "index" of capital, that is a function $G(k_1, k_2)$, and a two-factor production function H, depending only on "capital" and labor, such that:

$$F(k_1, k_2, m) = H(G(k_1, k_2), m)$$

Now suppose that G and H exist and consider in the plane (k_1, k_2), for a given $\overline{m}$, the family of isoquants:

$$F(k_1, k_2, \overline{m}) = H(G(k_1, k_2), \overline{m}) = y$$

Let $P^* = (k_1^*, k_2^*)$ be a point in the plane (k_1, k_2), the slope in P^* of the isoquant through P^* is

$$-\frac{\partial G(k_1^*, k_2^*)/\partial k_2}{\partial G(k_1^*, k_2^*)/\partial k_1}$$

* Reprinted with permission from *Journal of Economic Behaviour and Organization*, 1994.

and is therefore independent of $\bar{m}$ (this is nothing but a geometric illustration of Leontief's theorem, see p. xvi). On the other hand, an example as simple as:

$$F(k_1, k_2, m) = k_1 + k_2 m$$

in which the restriction above is violated, illustrates how stringent the condition for the existence of G and H are.

The author, of course, studies models which are much more complicated than the one just considered. Nonetheless, we think that a fair assessment of his results is that they show that capital stock can be aggregated consistently only under extremely strong conditions. See, for example, chapter 2, corollary 2.3 (p. 47). This is a necessary and sufficient condition for the existence of aggregate capital stock in a vintage two-factor model. Under the assumption that "all change is capital altering" (change is the technical change as new vintages come into being), the condition is that a very complicated identity (p. 46), involving the second derivatives of the production function holds for some vintage. (The reader will notice that the condition stated above for our simple model can be expressed by saying that the derivative of the slope with respect to m, which is an expression involving second derivatives of the production function, vanishes identically.) We do not report the identity here. We only note that from an economic point of view there is no argument in its favor. Therefore, it represents an arbitrary reduction of the dimension of the space of all possible production functions. Loosely speaking, the condition defines a zero-probability subset of the total space.

Let us assume, now, that there are two firms and that the production functions of these firms are:

$$F_i(k_{1i}, k_{2i}, m_i) = H_i(G_i(k_{1i}, k_{2i}), m_i) \quad (i = 1, 2)$$

The problem is whether there exists an "index" of capital, that is, a function $L(k_{11} + k_{12}, k_{21} + k_{22})$, and a two-factor production function M, depending only on "capital" and labor, such that:

$$F_1(k_{11}, k_{21}, m_1) + F_2(k_{12}, k_{22}, m_2) = M(L(k_{11} + k_{12}, k_{21} + k_{22}), m_1 + m_2)$$

The author analyzes this model in some detail. The simplest version is perhaps that of chapter 5, in which all capital goods are mobile and there is no technical change. The result obtained is that aggregation is possible if and only if either $H_1(.,.) = H_2(.,.)$ or $F_1(.,.) = F_2(.,.)$. The F_i's do not need to be scalars; they can be vectors. In the special case in which firm 1 produces only commodity 1 and firm 2 produces only commodity 2 "the production possibility frontier for the entire system will consist only of flats; relative outut prices will be fixed . . . and it is hardly surprising that output aggregation is possible" (p. 135). If, moreover, labor is the only primary factor, for example, if all commodities but labor are produced, the aggregate production function exists if and only if the labor theory of value holds! This is a result which played some role in the reswitching debate.

2.

However, the fact that the search for an aggregate capital stock leads to strong and unwarranted conditions becomes clear when the author motivates the switch between the first and the second part of the book: "...the question...arises of whether there are any other circumstances under which an aggregate production function appears to do well despite a lack of foundation for it at the micro level" (p. xix). In other words, once it is clear that aggregation theory does not yield the expected results, one can ask: so, why do Cobb–Douglas functions fit "fairly well"? A contribution of the author to solve this puzzle is contained in chapters 8 and 9, which are based on simulation experiments. The result is that, even when aggregation is not theoretically possible, a Cobb–Douglas function can work well provided the wage share is held approximately constant in the experiment; otherwise it does not work. A full understanding of the result would imply getting into simulation and estimation details. Here we limit ourselves to the observation that aggregation problems *in general* can be solved either by restricting the agents' functions (production functions in our case), or by restricting the behavior of the independent variables. Trivially, if the ratio between the two capital goods in our example above were approximately fixed, an aggregate production function would exist. In a more indirect and sophisticated way, chapters 8 and 9 explore restrictions put on the independent variables. However, it is worth noticing that the admitted lack of microfoundation causes a substantial shift of approach in chapters 8 and 9. Here the authors' attitude is more that of a dispassionate scholar studying the reasons why ancient people used to believe in many gods than that of the believer himself.

3.

We would like to make two comments. First, these papers belong to an epoch in which, irrespective of the position held on fundamental issues, many scholars were engaged in trying to find a solid microfoundation for macroeconomics. By this we mean a theory of the behavior of micro entities *and* a theory of aggregation dealing with individual differences between such microentities. The concept of microfoundation which has instead been prevailing in the last fifteen years has simply dropped the second requirement by flatly assuming a single representative consumer, producer, capital good. Fisher's book belongs to an intellectual environment and period in which a dramatic difference between micro and macro was perceived. Thus this reprint of his old papers should not only be welcome for its intrinsic value; it is also to be hoped that it may stimulate the readers to reconsider how fascinating and theoretically challenging is the reality behind the representative things.

Our second comment refers more to the historical outline contained in the "Introduction" than to the book itself. In particular, many a reader may find it hard to understand why Joan Robinson was wrong, or, at least, so wrong. This is not the place to discuss in detail Joan Robinson's view of the subject. Nonetheless, we think that her insistence on the fact that capital aggregation is possible only under very special conditions cannot be challenged. Moreover, it is also indisputable that this fact undermines the standard presentation of macroeconomics at her time. She would, probably, consider microeconomics not as an end in itself but as a necessary step toward macroeconomics. This may explain why the fall of the aggregate production function meant to her the fall, or the necessity of a radical re-foundation, of the whole field of economics. All in all, Franklin Fisher, still a protagonist of neoclassical economics, does not seem to be ready to forgive the UK Cambridge heretics. Interestingly, no other author contributing to the debate from the English side is even quoted in this book. Moreover, there appears to exist an unsolved tension in the book which is well illustrated in terms of the following two propositions: "Aggregate production functions practically never exist. . . . The implications for the intellectual history of the 'Cambridge versus Cambridge' debate are left to the reader" (p. 136).

Reference

Fisher, Franklin M. (1993) *Aggregation: Aggregate Production Functions and Related Topics*. Collected *papers by Franklin M. Fisher*, edited by John Monz, The MIT Press, Cambridge, MA.

18 Wicksell and the problem of the 'missing' equation*

Heinz D. Kurz

Triggered by a stimulating paper by Bo Sandelin (1980), there has been a debate about Knut Wicksell's theory of capital and distribution that is known as "Wicksell's missing equation." To this debate have contributed, among others, Sandelin (1980, 1982), Takashi Negishi (1982a,b, 1985 (chapter 9)), Larry Samuelson (1982), and Tom Kompas (1992, chapter 4). The issue under consideration is whether or not Knut Wicksell had put forward a theory of capital and interest that is closed in the sense that the data, or independent variables, from which he started suffice to determine the unknowns, or dependent variables, especially the "natural" rates of wages, rents, and interest. The mentioned authors claim that there is one equation "missing" in Wicksell's theory and that his formal system of equations is underdetermined. The question then is how to close the system in a way that is faithful to Wicksell. The authors under consideration differ in terms of the closures they suggest.

In this chapter I will argue that while the contributions under discussion are valuable because they help to clarify some of Wicksell's arguments and illustrations, their common premise is dubious: there is no equation missing in Wicksell's theory. The problem is rather that in the course of his endeavor to develop a coherent long-period supply-and-demand analysis of income distribution, Wicksell became increasingly aware of the fact that his attempt to establish the rate of interest as the "reward for waiting" was confronted with a serious, indeed insurmountable, problem: that of defining the "quantity of capital" independently of the rate of interest. He understood that with heterogeneous capital goods and deprived of Eugen von Böhm-Bawerk's device of the "average period of production" to aggregate them, the initial endowment of the economy of capital could only be given in *value* terms. Wicksell saw that this undermined the basic idea underlying neoclassical theory: that there is an analogy between the different factors of production – labor, land, and capital – and their rates of remuneration. Originally put forward by Johann Heinrich von Thünen, that idea had inspired several authors, including Léon Walras, Böhm-Bawerk, and Wicksell himself, to elaborate a theoretical

* Reprinted with permission from *History of Political Economy*, 2000.

edifice explaining the distribution of income in terms of a single principle: that of the (relative) scarcity of the factors of production. In the course of his work Wicksell became increasingly aware that the idea met with considerable difficulties. In particular, whereas the original factors of production – labor and land – can be measured in their own technical units, the capital endowment of the economy had to be given in terms of a sum of value. His lack of enthusiasm for this option – the only one at his disposal, if the supply-and-demand approach to the long-period theory of income distribution was to be adhered to – therefore reflects a fundamental difficulty of the theory. While this is explicitly or implicitly confirmed by those authors who suggest some alternative closures of the system, the inattentive reader might (wrongly) get the impression that these closures allow one to overcome that theoretical difficulty. In this chapter I will attempt to draw the attention back to the central problem of Wicksell's theory and to put the discussion about the missing equation in the perspective of his overall intellectual program.

I will show that Wicksell approached the two problems of capital theory, the remuneration of capital on the one hand and its accumulation on the other, in separate logical stages. In a first stage he took the capital endowment of the economy as given; that is, he treated it as a datum or an independent variable, and determined the natural rate of interest in terms of the relative scarcity of capital. It is in this part of the analysis that he deemed it possible to postulate functional relations of known properties. In the corresponding system of equations the "quantity of capital" is treated as an *exogenous* magnitude. In a second stage he dealt with the formation of capital, focusing attention on the factors affecting its accumulation over time. In this part of the analysis the capital stock at any moment of time is taken to be a dependent or *endogenous* variable. However, because of the complexity and variability of the factors affecting saving and investment behavior, Wicksell was convinced that this part of the analysis was not amenable to a treatment in terms of functional relations, at least not for the time being. He therefore confined himself to what are essentially qualitative considerations. For obvious reasons, if one were to stick closely to Wicksell's own approach, then the debate about his missing equation ought to relate only to the first stage, that is, that part of the analysis which in his view allows for a mathematical treatment.

The composition of this chapter is as follows. Section 1 provides a brief summary account of the alternative closures suggested by some of the authors who maintain that there is an equation missing in Wicksell's formal analysis. Section 2 argues that a common element of these contributions is that they interpret Wicksell's argument and his "static" method of analysis as referring to a stationary economy *strictu sensu*. Section 3 then documents that Wicksell showed little interest in strictly stationary conditions, because the principal object of his inquiry was a growing economy in which capital accumulates. The static method he adopted was explicitly designed to study, however imperfectly, the distribution of income in such a growing economy. Yet, since neither Wicksell nor his contemporaries distinguished carefully between "static method" and "stationary state," the two were often confounded and Wicksell's analysis was misunderstood as referring to strictly stationary conditions. Section 4 discusses briefly Wicksell's consecutive attempts to develop a theory of income distribution by generalizing the principle of supply and demand from the singularly special case of a "non-capitalistic" production with homogeneous labor and homogeneous land to the general case of a "capitalistic" production with heterogeneous capital goods. Section 5 contains some concluding remarks.

1. Alternative closures

Bo Sandelin (1980, p. 29) introduces the discussion of Wicksell's theory of capital and interest as follows:

> It is a well-known fact that one equation is "missing" in Wicksell's various formalizations of his capital theory; this implies that one central magnitude has to be determined exogenously. After some vacillation *Wicksell chooses the value of capital as an exogenous variable of his system.*
>
> (Bo Sandelin, 1980, p. 29, emphasis added)

Hence, strictly speaking there is *no* equation missing in Wicksell's theory of capital and interest.[1] Wicksell attempted to determine the amounts of the different commodities produced, the distribution of income, and relative prices in terms of the following sets of data: (1) the preferences of consumers and (2) the technical alternatives from which cost-minimizing producers can choose. To these he added (3) the given endowments of the economy of the original factors of production – labor and land – and, as Sandelin rightly points out, the economy's endowment of capital, conceived as a given value of capital.

More precisely, Wicksell took the quantity of capital as given in terms of a unit of consumption that also serves as the *numéraire* to express wages and prices. This value magnitude is given from outside the system: it is an *exogenous* variable designed to represent the amount of social capital in existence in the economy at a given moment in time. The productive powers of the economy under consideration are taken to be defined in terms of data (2) and (3). In Wicksell's theory of the rate of interest the size of (the value of) capital is thus *not* determined endogenously. It is not reckoned among the unknowns of the problem under consideration, but among its data.[2]

---

1 This is confirmed by Larry Samuelson (1982, p. 301), who begins his comment on Sandelin as follows: "It is well known that Wicksell's capital theory is one equation short of being determinate ... and that Wicksell addresses this problem by assuming the value of capital to be given exogenously."
2 From a logical point of view there appears to be no principal difference within the framework of Wicksell's supply-and-demand approach to the theory of income distribution between giving the amount of capital and giving the amounts of labor and land. Hence, with the same right with which the closing of his system in terms of a given capital endowment is questioned, one might question taking the supplies of labor and land as given. However, as we shall see, whereas giving the amounts of labor and land (in their own technical units) has a clear meaning, this is not so with regard to value capital.

Sandelin is very clear about this fact. Yet Wicksell's "vacillation" prompts Sandelin to contemplate alternative ways of closing the system. Rather than assuming an exogenously given value of social capital, one might, he suggests, follow Friedrich August von Hayek and start with "a given structure of real capital";[3] or Luigi Pasinetti and treat the rate of interest as an independent variable.[4] Yet there is still another alternative to "close" the system:

> In this article we shall consider a third possibility: basing the discussion on the wine-storage problem, we shall derive one additional equation which describes the condition for an optimal amount of labor, as seen from the entrepreneur's point of view; in other words, we shall introduce the "missing equation."
>
> (Bo Sandelin, 1980, p. 29)

In substance, Sandelin's proposal amounts to replacing constant returns to scale by variable returns in Wicksell's wine-storage problem. In this case, and assuming a *partial* framework, characterized by a given world market price of wine as a known function of its age, the profit-maximizing (representative) firm chooses its optimum size and thus the optimum amount of labor to be employed. The *value of capital* is then *endogenously* determined by appropriately discounting forward the wage payments invested in the storage of wine. Sandelin stresses that this "closure" of the system involves a significant departure from Wicksell's original approach. He writes that "the marginal productivity of social capital in the Wicksellian sense now becomes a somewhat obscure concept" and that "one cannot follow Wicksell in deriving the marginal productivity of social capital.... This means that the Wicksellian marginal productivity of social capital becomes a doubtful notion" (1980, pp. 29–30).

---

3 It is not clear how a "given structure of real capital" should be compatible with a long-period equilibrium of the economy, characterized by a uniform rate of interest – Wicksell's "natural" rate. As is well known, Walras in the *Elements* ([1874] 1954) assumed that the economy's endowment of capital is given in terms of quantities of physically specified capital goods, that is, a given structure of physical capital. However, in the fourth edition of his magnum opus Walras had to admit that, contrary to his previous view, with an arbitrarily given vector of capital goods proper there is no reason to presume that the requirement of a uniform "rate of net income" – Walras's expression for the rate of interest – is met; see, for example, Kurz and Salvadori, 1995, p. 439–41. Hayek, in *The Pure Theory of Capital*, to which Sandelin refers, effected a break with long-period marginalist theory and claimed to be no longer concerned with the determination of *the* rate of interest (see Hayek, 1941, p. 41). Otherwise he would have had to allow, as Wicksell knew very well (see Section 4), that the "structure of real capital" cannot be taken as given, but rather had to be treated as an endogenous variable.

4 Taking with Pasinetti the rate of interest as given involves, of course, a fundamental change in the theory. In fact, Pasinetti, a critic of neoclassical theory, advocates the "classical" approach to the problem of value and distribution as it was revived by Piero Sraffa (1960). It should be stressed already at this point that in a classical framework taking the rate of interest as given does not imply stationary or steady-state conditions.

To avoid a possible misunderstanding, it should be noted that it was Wicksell himself who, upon his discovery of the famous so-called Wicksell effect (see, e.g. Wicksell [1893] 1954, pp. 137–8), drew the conclusion that the theory of interest, as it had been put forward by Thünen, could not be sustained (other than in a partial context). In fact, Wicksell was no follower of that theory, but rather advocated what he considered to be the more general and, as he hoped, logically coherent supply-and-demand theory of income distribution. One could, however, say, as I have done already in the above, that the alternative closures suggested draw attention to a fundamental difficulty of Wicksell's own construction.

In a comment on Sandelin's paper, Negishi (1982b, p. 310) confirms that there is an equation missing in Wicksell's theory of capital; in a related paper dealing with Böhm-Bawerk's famous "Three Grounds" he rightly stresses that closing the system via a given amount of capital in value terms deprives the analysis of much of its explanatory power (1982a, p. 164; see also Negishi, 1985, chapter 9). In addition, he argues that the three closures mentioned by Sandelin do not exhaust the set of alternatives and suggests himself two further variants. Instead of changing the production function in the case of the example of the wine-storage problem, Negishi (1982b) introduces explicitly the saving behavior of the capitalist, which derives from intertemporal utility maximization. This involves considering "the value of capital as an endogenous variable" (1982b, p. 310). In his other contribution (Negishi, 1982a) he develops an overlapping generations model with a stationary population, where each agent lives for two periods, the first being the working period, the second the retirement period. In the former the income of the agent exceeds his consumption, that is, he saves, whereas in the latter things are the other way round, that is, he dissaves all the capital previously built up. Negishi demonstrates that even assuming away time preference, the rate of interest may be positive due to the individual agent's concern with better provision for wants in the second than in the first period and the superiority of more roundabout processes of production. Hence, Wicksell is said to have been right in his criticism of Böhm-Bawerk that time preference was not all that important in the theory of interest.[5]

Thus it seems that there are a number of ways to interpret and eventually solve the problem of the missing equation. Depending on the alternative adopted one arrives at a different system. This in turn seems to imply that Wicksell's analysis is characterized by a certain openness and arbitrariness which contradicts the otherwise praised clarity and definiteness of his reasoning. We may then ask: why did Wicksell close the system as he did? However, before we turn to that question we shall first ask whether the alternative closures suggested share a common element and whether that common element reveals why Wicksell, given his intellectual program, did not adopt any of the solutions proposed.

---

5 The two causes given relate, of course, to the first and the third of Böhm-Bawerk's three grounds. We shall come back to them in Section 4, where we will deal with Wicksell's interpretation of their interplay.

2. The common element in the suggested interpretations

A closer look at the proposed alternative closures of Wicksell's capital theory shows that they all presuppose *stationary* economic conditions in the strict sense of the concept of stationarity, that is, time invariant data (1)–(3), listed above. This involves, in particular, a constant working population, a constant technical knowledge, and, most important in the present context, an unchanging endowment of capital. That is, in the conceptualizations suggested there is neither capital accumulation nor capital decumulation over time: gross savings (which are taken to equal gross investments) are just sufficient to replace periodically the produced means of production used up in the production process. In these interpretations Wicksell's "static" point of view is taken to imply a concern with economic systems characterized by a capital stock that does not change over time. Starting from such a presupposition involves, of course, looking for a state of the economic system such that the forces working in the direction of a growing capital stock are exactly balanced by the forces working in the opposite direction. To determine such a state then amounts to determining *endogenously* the capital equipment of the economy, both as regards its overall *size* (in terms of the *numéraire*) and its *composition*, that is, that capital stock which, together with the other data (preferences, technical alternatives, and endowments of the primary factors of production, labor, and land), accounts for strictly stationary conditions.

The treatment of the capital endowment (of the *stationary* economy) as a dependent rather than an independent variable is indeed the common characteristic feature of the interpretations under consideration.[6] Interestingly, prior to the debate about Wicksell's missing equation, Guy Arvidsson (1956) had maintained that strictly stationary conditions and thus the constancy of social capital are perfectly compatible with a positive level of the rate of interest, provided each individual at the end of his life is inclined to bequeath the same amount of wealth or capital that he inherited. And Jack Hirshleifer (1967) had argued that with intertemporal utility maximization stationary conditions obtain if the rate of interest equals the rate of time preference. With the corresponding quantity of capital in an otherwise Wicksellian framework there are no motives to any further accumulation (or decumulation) of capital. Yet, did Wick-sell's "static" method involve strictly stationary conditions, which is the explicit or implicit view held in much of the interpretative literature on Wicksell's theory of capital and interest?

This is answered in the positive by Tom Kompas (1992) in an interesting attempt to come to grips with the complexities of Wicksell's approach to the problem

---

6 As has been indicated in footnote 4, while stationary (or steady-state) conditions imply the endogenous determination of the value of capital, the contrary is not true. Thus, with given levels of gross output, given technical alternatives of production, and a given real wage rate (or, alternatively, a given rate of profits), as in Sraffa, 1960, the value(s) of social capital compatible with one (or several equiprofitable) cost-minimizing system(s) of production is (are) determined, but the system(s) under consideration need not be in a stationary or a steady state; see, for example, Kurz and Salvadori, 1995.

of capital and interest and to that of capital accumulation.[7] In Kompas's view, "Wicksell, except in *provisional* terms, with substantial qualification, does not take the value of aggregate capital as given to solve for a stationary equilibrium" (p. 132). By "stationary equilibrium" Kompas means a situation in which net savings are nil, which in turn is taken to imply the equality between the rate of interest and the (collective) rate of time preference (p. 114). According to Kompas, Wicksell intended to close the system in terms of a savings function and intertemporal preferences, but essentially "for analytical simplicity" (p. 11) took the value of capital as a datum. Wicksell and Walras are said to have "set out clear and consistent theories of long-run equilibrium for a stationary economy" (p. vii).

3. Wicksell's "static" method vs the stationary state

As is well known, notwithstanding important differences between different authors, the marginalist economists from William Stanley Jevons to Alfred Marshall, from Léon Walras to Gustav Cassel, and from Eugen von Böhm-Bawerk to Knut Wicksell all attempted to explain the shares of wages, profits, and rent in terms of a single principle: that of the relative scarcities of the respective factors of production, labor, capital, and land. Whereas the classical authors, especially David Ricardo, applied that principle only in order to explain the rent of land, the marginalist authors were convinced of the universal applicability of that principle to all factors and their remunerations alike.

Wicksell was deeply impressed by the Böhm-Bawerkian version of neoclassical theory, that is, what Paul A. Samuelson (1987, p. 908) called the "marginal-productivity-of-time paradigm." In *Value, Capital, and Rent*, originally published in German in 1893, Wicksell ([1893] 1954, p. 20) defined his own contribution essentially as an attempt to provide an "exact, mathematical treatment of the theory of capital interest" in a general equilibrium framework based on Böhm-Bawerk's temporal approach. In Wicksell's view the theory of capital and interest had to tackle two main problems: (1) it had to explain the *origin and level of interest*, that is, identify the factors that give rise to a positive rate of interest; and (2) it had to explain the *origin and formation of capital* (cf. pp. 21–2). The former problem belonged to the theory of interest proper, whereas the latter belonged to the theory of capital accumulation and economic growth. The former problem, Wicksell surmised, may be dealt with using the "static" method, whereas a satisfactory treatment of the latter necessitated a "dynamical" analysis.

According to Lionel Robbins (1930, p. 195), the ambiguity of the concept of "static" method was responsible "for some of the most important doctrinal confusions of the past." Indeed, as Robbins emphasized, that method of analysis was not distinguished with sufficient clarity from the concept of "stationary equilibrium," so that people were easily misguided to confound the two. While Robbins did not

---

7 I am grateful to one of the referees for referring me to Kompas's book, which had escaped my attention.

explicitly deal with Wicksell's contributions, his general assessment applies also to them. In fact, following Böhm-Bawerk's lead, both in *Value, Capital, and Rent* and in the *Lectures on Political Economy* Wicksell ([1901] 1934, p. 7) approached the first of the two problems mentioned "mainly from the static point of view, i.e. we shall assume, in principle, a society which retains unchanged from year to year the same population, the same area of territory and the same amount of capital, and remains on the same level of technical achievement." In another place he stated that, "for the moment, . . . we shall content ourselves with what has been called the *static* aspect of the problem of equilibrium, i.e. the conditions necessary for the maintenance, or the periodic renewal, of a *stationary state of economic relations*" ([1901] 1934, p. 105). These and similar specifications of the data and thus the framework in terms of which he sought to determine the rate of interest look indeed as if stationary conditions *strictu sensu* are implied. However, this impression is quickly dispelled by numerous other passages. Thus, in his early contribution to capital theory he referred to the "fundamental – and simplest – hypothesis" of a "*stationary* economy in which capital and the other economic factors *can be thought of* as an approximately unalterable sum" ([1893] 1954, p. 22, second emphasis added), a formulation that is echoed in his mature work (cf. Wicksell [1901] 1934, pp. 184, 193). He left no doubt, however, that this is a simplifying device in order to come to grips, as a first approximation, with the problem of distribution. The real economy of his time, Wicksell kept stressing (cf. in particular part 3 of volume 1 of the *Lectures*), was an economy in motion in which capital accumulated. The static method is therefore not meant to do away with this fact: "*the accumulation of capital* is itself, even under stationary conditions, a necessary element in the problem of production and exchange" ([1901] 1934, p. 203). The clearest expression of Wicksell's method of analysis, and of the problematic character of the terminology used, is perhaps the following:

> We shall assume *stationary conditions* as the foundations of our observations. This will not prevent us from considering changes in the quantities concerned, provided that we do not take into account the actual transition stage, which is a much more complicated problem, but assume that these changes have already become final, so that "static equilibrium" (a stationary state) is again restored.
>
> (Wicksell ([1901] 1934, p. 152)

To study the problem of income distribution in a "dynamic" framework, Wicksell surmised, was not yet possible: "the laws of capital formation have been too little studied for a treatment of the subject in its entirety to be of much real use" (p. 203).

To summarize, Wicksell opted for a treatment of the two main problems of the theory of capital and interest in two consecutive steps. First, the determination of the rate of interest, the wage rate, and the rent rate should be approached in a static framework, in which the amounts of the respective factors of production – capital, labor, and land – are taken to be in given supply; he in fact even assumed vertical supply functions (cf. [1901] 1934, p. 105). The rates of remuneration determined in this way would reflect the relative scarcities of the factors of production. In a second step he would then proceed to the discussion of the impact of changes in one or several of the data, in particular the amounts of the productive factors, on the distribution of income. Part 3 of volume 1 of the *Lectures*, "Capital Accumulation," documents well his comparative static analysis of the problem of income distribution when capital accumulates. This approach in two steps is clearly expressed in the following passage:

> Both logically and for purposes of exposition it would seem right to begin by examining the effects of *a given supply of capital already accumulated*, and *then* to inquire the causes which influence, and eventually alter, this supply.
>
> (Wicksell, p. 155, first emphasis added)

Therefore, it would be wrong to think that in dealing with the problem of income distribution Wicksell assumed stationary conditions *strictu sensu*. He did not.[8]

8 Larry Samuelson maintained that Wicksell intended "to close the model via a theory of savings behavior" (1982, p. 301; see also pp. 302–3 and 306). It can hardly be doubted that Wicksell would have liked to be possessed of a theory of savings of sufficient generality that could also be formalized. This would have allowed him to tackle both the problem of the remuneration of capital and that of its accumulation in terms of a single mathematical theory of the production and distribution of wealth. Alas, in his view such a theory of savings was not available. This is why he felt obliged to adopt his two-stage procedure. This was clearly a second-best solution, but the only one at his disposal. Kompas (1992) has put forward a careful study of Wicksell's analysis that contains several interesting observations. However, in a fundamental respect I think his interpretation is wrong. He is well aware of Wicksell's agnosticism as regards the theory of savings. Nevertheless he feels entitled to do what Wicksell thought could not be done: "To close the system, add an expression representing savings behaviour," and, in addition, impose a "zero net savings" condition (1992, p. 94) in order to obtain strictly stationary conditions. Kompas follows his own suggestion and introduces savings functions as they are to be found in the more recent neoclassical literature (see, e.g. pp. 110, 117, 131). In this way, the capital endowment of the economy becomes an endogenous variable. This interpretation is difficult to sustain. First, Kompas takes Wicksell's "static" method to involve a concern with a "stationary equilibrium," which it does not (see, again, Robbins's clarification). Second, had Wicksell seen the possibility of closing the system in terms of a general savings function, he could be expected to have done so. Therefore, in this regard Kompas is forced to read into Wicksell what he cannot find there verbatim. Yet, had Wicksell believed it possible to close the system in terms of a general savings function, then there would have been no need for him to tinker with a stationary equilibrium: he could have provided a theory cast from a single die, dealing both with the production, distribution, *and* accumulation of wealth. In short, he could have provided a full-fledged dynamic theory. It is not clear why he should not have done so in case he could. Third, Kompas stresses that determining endogenously the capital endowment by assuming a stationary state involves fixing the rate of interest at the *exogenously* given level of the (collective) rate of time preference. This amounts to treating the rate of interest, which Wicksell was keen to determine, as a datum or independent variable. Hence, what in Wicksell was an *unknown*, in the interpretation under consideration has become a known magnitude. (If the rate of time preference were itself to be considered an endogenous variable that tends to follow any upward or downward trend of the actual rate of interest, as Wicksell in places appears to assume, then Kompas's suggestion would involve closing the system by directly fixing the rate of interest instead of the value of capital.)

There is additional evidence that Wicksell did not intend to study the problem of distribution in terms of a strictly stationary state of the economy. To see this we have to turn to his criticism of Walras and his successors. These are said

> to hold a theory of interest which contains both formal and material defects and which is *seriously incomplete*. Walras' formula for interest, as may easily be seen . . . [,] reduces itself, on the assumption of *stationary* conditions, simply to the equation $F(i) = 0$, in which $F(i)$ is the amount of annual savings conceived as a function of the rate of interest i. In other words, it expresses the *truism* that, in the stationary state, the inducement to new savings must have ceased; *but it affords no answer to the question why a given amount of existing social capital gives rise to a certain rate of interest*, neither higher nor lower.
>
> (Wicksell [1901] 1934, p. 171, the second emphasis is Wicksell's)

Hence Walras's theory is accused of being "seriously incomplete" because it determines the rate of interest only for the strictly stationary state, in which there is no incentive to net savings or dissavings, and fails to determine it for an arbitrarily "given amount of existing social capital."[9] Böhm-Bawerk on the other hand is credited with having attempted to provide precisely the missing piece of analysis.[10]

We may conclude that Wicksell was not really interested in the stationary state of the economy *strictu sensu*. The actual trend of the economy he experienced exhibited capital accumulation and economic growth and there were no indications that the stationary state was around the corner. Economic theory had to study this state of affairs and not the purely hypothetical one in which net savings were nil. The static point of view adopted by him was designed to throw some light on the

---

9 Because Wicksell was not concerned with a stationary equilibrium but with an economy in which capital accumulates, there is nothing "perplexing" (cf. Kompas 1992, p. 102) about the fact that in the *Lectures* he would still treat fixed capital items as "rent goods." Since in a growing economy there is no presumption that long-lived fixed capital is ever fully adjusted to the other data of the system, which are themselves subject to permanent change, it should come as no surprise that "the adjustment to equilibrium is explicitly ignored" with regard to fixed capital (cf. Kompas, 1992, p. 102).

10 Böhm-Bawerk is criticized, however, for his attempt to solve the problem of the *existence* of interest independently of that of the *level* of the rate of interest (cf. Wicksell [1901] 1934, p. 171). In fact, Böhm-Bawerk thought that the former problem could be settled without any reference to the endowments of "capital," labor, and land of the economy, whereas the latter required taking these quantities as known. In this context it should be mentioned that by taking these endowments as given, Böhm-Bawerk did not imply strictly stationary conditions. In this regard his method of analysis does not differ from that employed by Wicksell. In the excursuses to his *Positive Theory of Capital* he vehemently denied Ladislaus von Bortkiewicz's accusation that his analysis was based on such an assumption: "Of course, the concept of 'static' or 'stationary' cannot be given such an unusual and contradictory meaning as Bortkiewicz once did in his polemic zeal. . . . Bortkiewicz recognizes a society only as 'stationary' when it neither makes actual progress, *nor has ever made it in the past*. But it is apparent that such a limitation of the concept of 'stationary' is not only arbitrary and very unusual, but it also lacks its right of existence" (Böhm-Bawerk [1889] 1959, p. 3:216, n. 39).

actual, growing economy in terms of a comparative static analysis of consecutive states of the economy characterized, *inter alia*, by different "quantities of capital" in existence. Wicksell was aware that this was not fully satisfactory, because defining any such state by a given and unchanging social capital implied that the net social product consisted only of consumption goods, whereas in an economy in which capital accumulates it consists also of investment goods. However, he was of the opinion that with a slowly growing economy the error involved was perhaps negligible. The static method, he concluded, was the best at hand and allowed one to investigate, albeit imperfectly, the implications of changes in factor endowments and technical knowledge on the distribution of the product. In particular, it was taken to allow one to determine, at least "approximatively," one of the key variables of the economy: the general rate of interest.

After having expounded the method of analysis employed by Wicksell we may now briefly summarize the content of his theory in his two main contributions to the theory of capital and interest. This then leads us back to the problem of the closure of his system and thus to the question of whether there is an equation missing.

4. Wicksell's supply-and-demand theory of distribution and the problem of "capital"

As is well known, Böhm-Bawerk ([1889] 1959) had put forward "Three Grounds" for interest: (1) "different circumstances of want and provision" in the present and in the future; (2) the "under-estimation of the future," that is, a positive time preference; and (3) the "technical superiority of present over future goods," that is, the superiority of more "roundabout" processes of production.

Wicksell shared Böhm-Bawerk's basic theoretical vision and was convinced that the latter's analysis contained the key to solving the two main problems of the theory of capital and interest. Yet, in Wicksell's view Böhm-Bawerk had not fully grasped the proper status of each of the three grounds and their interaction. Already in *Value, Capital, and Rent* Wicksell ([1893] 1954, pp. 21–2) set out his own understanding of the proper division of labor among the three grounds in tackling the two problems; essentially the same view is found in the *Lectures* ([1901] 1934, pp. 154–6).[11] For given endowments of the factors of production, including capital, the third ground is said to allow one to determine the rate of interest, i, as the "marginal product of waiting." This provides a preliminary answer to the first main problem of capital theory. In an economy that, according to Wicksell, was still far away from being saturated with capital, the resulting "natural" rate of interest may be expected to be larger than the (average) rate of time preference in society, ρ, contemplated by the second ground. With $i > \rho$, a sufficient condition for positive net capital formation is met. This leads immediately to the first ground, which supposes a growing income per capita and which now turns out to be merely

---

11 Similar views are in Wicksell, 1928. For the argument below that follows, see also Hansson, 1993; Boianovsky, 1998; Kurz, 1998.

a consequence of i exceeding ρ. Finally, the greater the difference between i and ρ, the greater, *ceteris paribus*, the pace at which capital accumulates and the economy grows. Setting aside technical progress and population growth, as capital accumulates, its relative scarcity decreases, which will be reflected in a falling rate of interest. Other things equal, this implies a gradual deceleration in the formation of new capital. As Wicksell ([1901] 1934, p. 209) stressed, "Under such conditions, we should therefore expect a continual accumulation of capital – though at a diminishing rate – and, at the same time, a continual fall in the rate of interest."[12] This is taken to provide some elements of a preliminary answer to the second main problem.

As regards the concept of the quantity of capital in given supply, Wicksell had been aware since the beginning of his investigation that this required him to define a measure of the capital endowment of the economy, which consists of heterogeneous capital goods, that is independent of the rate of interest and relative prices. The same problem had already bothered Böhm-Bawerk, who, as is well known, had attempted to replace a vector of physically heterogeneous capital goods with a scalar: the "average period of production." According to this concept, time could serve as the sought measure of capital.

4.1. Value, capital, and rent

When Wicksell came across that concept, or, as he preferred to call it, the "average period of investment,"[13] he was at first enthusiastic about its potentialities. In *Value, Capital, and Rent* he expressed the view that Böhm-Bawerk's concept "will presumably prove extremely fruitful" (Wicksell [1893] 1954, p. 22). His own formalization of the theory was indeed designed to demonstrate this:

> Since . . . the relatively definite and very simple concept of the lengthening of the process of production [i.e., of the "average period of production"] replaces the older, vague, and multiform idea of productivity of capital, the theory of capital-interest can be treated in as exact a fashion as the theory of ground-rent before.
>
> (Wicksell [1901] 1934, pp. 116–17)

---

12 The parallel to the simple neoclassical growth model of Robert Solow, with a given rate of population growth (λ), a given proportional savings function with s as the (marginal and average) propensity to save, a linear homogeneous Cobb-Douglas production function, and setting aside technical progress, is obvious. The rate of growth outside the steady state, g, is given by

$$g = sF_K + \alpha\lambda$$

where F_K is the marginal product of capital, which equals the rate of interest, and α is the partial elasticity of production with regard to labor. (There is no time preference in Solow's model.) As capital accumulates relative to labor, the marginal product of capital will fall and so will the rate of growth.

13 See the terminological discussion in Wicksell, 1896, pp. 30–1.

He stressed that a "definite" solution of the problem of distribution required taking the amount of capital as a given magnitude. "We can," he maintained, "determine without difficulty the position of equilibrium finally attained, with the help of our equations set forth above – but only if we assume that the present capital is a known magnitude" (p. 156).[14]

However, already in his early contribution there are passages indicating that the concept was perhaps not as powerful as Wicksell would have liked it to be. First, there is a remarkable contrast in the passage just quoted between "relatively definite" and "exact." Yet there is more direct evidence available. Abandoning Böhm-Bawerk's assumption of natural services as free goods, Wicksell got two "average periods of investment" – one related to labor, the other to land. There is only a singularly special case, which he qualified as "a first approximation" (p. 147), in which the two kinds of capital, or "average periods," can be aggregated independently of relative prices and income distribution: this is the case in which all commodities (final products) exhibit the same proportions of labor to land at every single stage of their production, that is, the dated quantities of labor and of land show the same profiles in the production of all commodities.[15] Wicksell also saw that Böhm-Bawerk's concept was unable to deal properly with fixed capital and decided to evade the problem by treating durable instruments of production as "rent-goods" (p. 99).[16] Yet, it is not clear whether or not by the time of the publication of *Value, Capital, and Rent* he had been fully aware of the fact that the concept of the "average period" breaks down even in the case with a single primary factor and circulating capital only, the workhorse of much of Böhm-Bawerk's argument, if *compound* instead of single interest is used in the calculations.[17] While he saw that compound interest was necessitated by the assumption of free competition, he seemed to think that using simple interest involved an admissible simplification and no "essential alteration" (p. 126). As we know, this presumption cannot be sustained (see, e.g. Kurz and Salvadori, 1995, pp. 436–7).[18]

Wicksell's original expectation as to the potentialities of the "average period of investment" was frustrated. The demand-and-supply theory of the rate of interest was confronted with the problem that the average period of investment did not

---

14 It deserves to be mentioned that not only in the *Lectures* but already in *Value, Capital, and Rent* Wicksell expressed the quantity of capital as a value sum. However, as Garegnani (1960, pp. 127–30) observed, on the assumption that the concept of the "average period" was valid, there was no need to do so in the earlier work.

15 The parallel of this case to the case of a uniform "organic composition of capital" across all industries in Marx is close at hand.

16 See, however, his discussion of Gustaf Åkerman's problem in Wicksell [1901] 1934, pp. 258–99.

17 In his paper "Kapitalzins und Arbeitslohn," published in 1892, Wicksell showed some awareness that the value of capital depends on the way of calculating interest (see Wicksell 1892, 846; also Wicksell [1893] 1954, 123 n, 143 n). I am grateful to one of the referees for having drawn my attention to these passages.

18 Apparently, by the time of the *Lectures* Wicksell was aware of the problem; see, for example, Wicksell [1901] 1934, p. 205.

provide a measure of the quantity of capital in given supply that was independent of the rate of interest. Was there a way out of the impasse?

4.2. Lectures on political economy

The idea that heterogeneous capital goods could be aggregated independently of (relative) prices and the rate of interest had turned out to be illusory. Wicksell ([1901] 1934, p. 145) drew the consequences and admitted that "all these requisites [i.e. produced means of production] have only one quality in common, namely that they represent certain quantities of exchange value, so that collectively they may be regarded as a single sum of value." Yet, the need to express the available quantity of capital in the economy as a sum of *value* in terms of some *numéraire* destroyed the alleged analogy between the three kinds of income – wages, rents, and profits – and the corresponding factors of production – labor, land, and capital:

> This analogy between interest, on the one hand, and wages and rent, on the other, is incomplete. . . . Whereas labour and land are measured each in terms of its own *technical* unit (e.g. working days or months, acre per annum)[,] capital, on the other hand, . . . is reckoned . . . as a sum of *exchange value*. . . . In other words, each particular capital-good is measured by a unit extraneous to itself. However good the practical reasons for this may be, *it is a theoretical anomaly which disturbs the correspondence which would otherwise exist between all the factors of production.*"
> (Wicksell [1901] 1934, pp. 148–9, last emphasis added)

One might contemplate, with Walras, the possibility of treating each kind of capital good as a separate factor, which would remedy the "defect," Wicksell surmised. He added: "But, in that case, productive capital would have to be distributed into as many categories as there are kinds of tools, machinery, and materials, etc., and a unified treatment of the rôle of capital in production would be impossible." However, in competitive equilibrium the rate of interest "is the same on all capital," that is, the interest obtained is proportional to the values of the different capital goods ([1901] 1934, p. 149). Concerned with a "unified treatment of the rôle of capital," Wicksell had no alternative but to assume the capital endowment of the economy as given in value terms. This involved a "theoretical anomaly" – but deprived of the "average period" there was no other way open to him, *if* the demand-and-supply approach to the theory of income distribution in a long-period framework was to be preserved.

It was also no longer possible to describe the production of single commodities in terms of the average period of investment. Wicksell therefore decided to consider "the total amount of a commodity produced as a function (homogeneous and linear) of all the quantities of labour and land employed (i.e. annually consumed) both *current* and *saved up*" (p. 203). He thus postulated a production function for commodity j, which in our notation can be written as

$$y_j = f_j(l_{1j}, l_{2j}, l_{3j}, \ldots; b_{1j}, b_{2j}, b_{3j}, \ldots) \quad (j = 1, 2, \ldots, n)$$

where l_{1j} and b_{1j} indicate current services of labor and land, l_{2j} and b_{2j} indicate services in the previous period, and so forth. He reiterated his earlier view that capital is not an original factor of production, but a derived one: it is nothing but "a single coherent mass of saved-up labour and saved-up land" ([1901] 1934, p. 150). Accumulated labor and land are taken to "have been able to assume forms denied to them in their crude state, by which they attain a much greater efficiency for a number of productive purposes." Capitalistic processes of production are roundabout, and it is the time element of production that is important: the increase in efficiency is a "necessary condition of interest" (p. 150). The upshot of Wicksell's mature theory of capital and interest is summarized in the following statement:

> *Capital is saved-up labour and saved-up land. Interest is the difference between the marginal productivity of saved-up labour and land and of current labour and land.*

> (Wicksell [1901] 1934, p. 154)

With the wage per unit of (homogeneous) labor and the rent per acre of (homogeneous) land paid at the end of the elementary production period (month or year), in static *equilibrium* the values of the marginal products of the dated quantities of labor and land are equal to the wage rate and rent rate, w and q, properly discounted forward (see pp. 156, 204); that is:

$$\frac{\partial y_j}{\partial l_{kj}} p_j = w(1+i)^{k-1} \quad (j = 1, 2, \ldots, n; k = 1, 2, \ldots)$$

$$\frac{\partial y_j}{\partial b_{kj}} p_j = q(1+i)^{k-1} \quad (j = 1, 2, \ldots, n; k = 1, 2, \ldots)$$

with p_j as the price of commodity j and i as the rate of interest. All value magnitudes are expressed in terms of a common *numéraire* consisting of one or several consumption goods.

In equilibrium the total quantity demanded of each factor equals the total quantity supplied of that factor.[19] The formulation of this condition causes no problem with regard to labor and land, which can be measured in terms of their own technical units. With given quantities of labor, L, and land, B, whose supplies are taken to

---

19 As Wicksell ([1919] 1934, p. 228) pointed out in his criticism of Cassel's theory of general equilibrium, there is no presumption that all factors in given supply can be fully employed and fetch a positive income. Wicksell was in fact one of the first authors to indicate that general equilibrium should be characterized in terms of *in*equalities rather than equations. However, in the bit of his own analysis we are concerned with here he proceeded as if all factors could be fully employed. With a sufficient degree of substitutability in production, which he assumed, this is indeed the case.

be given and independent of the respective rates of remuneration, in equilibrium we have (see p. 204):[20]

$$L = \sum_{j=1}^{n} \sum_{k=1}^{\infty} l_{kj}$$

$$B = \sum_{j=1}^{n} \sum_{k=1}^{\infty} b_{kj}$$

The supply-equals-demand condition is more difficult with regard to capital. This is due to the fact that

> it may be difficult – if not impossible – to define this concept of social capital with absolute precision, as a definite quantity. In reality, it is rather a *complex* of quantities.
>
> (Wicksell [1901] 1934, p. 165)

However, Wicksell insisted that both the question of the existence and that of the actual level of the rate of interest cannot be answered "without referring to the market for capital" (p. 171). Finally, in order to be consistent with the concept of a full competitive equilibrium, characterized by a uniform rate of interest, the "amount of *capital*" (p. 204) available in the economy at the beginning of the production period, K, can be given in value terms only, representing a certain quantity of the *numéraire*. In equilibrium that sum of value must be equal to the value of capital employed (p. 204), which consists of "labour power capital" and "land power capital":

$$K = w \sum_{j=1}^{n} \sum_{k=2}^{\infty} l_{kj}(1+i)^{k-1} + q \sum_{j=1}^{n} \sum_{k=2}^{\infty} b_{kj}(1+i)^{k-1}$$

It is this latter equation that caused Wicksell a lot of headaches.[21] In fact, it is not clear what sort of constraint is this that forces the right-hand side of the equation to be equal to a given amount of a consumption good, for example, corn. What does it mean here for $(w; r; l_{11}, l_{21}, \ldots; b_{11}, b_{21}, \ldots; \ldots; l_{1n}, l_{2n}, \ldots; b_{1n}, b_{2n}, \ldots)$ to be constrained in this way?

---

20 In Wicksell's formalization the time index (k in the formulas) does not go to infinity, but to a given finite period. Since that period cannot be known independently of the solution of the system of equations, the above formulation appears to be more correct.

21 Sandelin (1980, p. 38) rightly stresses that Wicksell "did not accept measuring the productive capital in value units without objections. But for practical reasons, and to study the rate of interest, he found no better solution."

Yet, the logic of his supply-and-demand approach to the theory of income distribution forced Wicksell to invoke such an equation.[22] He emphasized with reference to his model with two industries that

> if these values are summed and are put equal to a *certain given quantity* – the total exchange value of the capital employed in *the two industries together*, expressed in terms of the first commodity, we shall then obtain the *necessary* [additional] *relation, and the problem will at last be completely determinate.*
> (Wicksell [1901] 1934, pp. 204–5, first and third emphases added)

In this conceptualization the *physical composition* of social capital K in terms of the l_{kj} and b_{kj} is a part of the equilibrium solution to the problem of value and distribution rather than one of its data. "In equilibrium," Wicksell emphasized, "the composition of the sum total of capital is thus definitely fixed" (p. 204).

Hence, if there was a "vacillation" on Wicksell's part, it concerned not so much the type of closure of the system – it certainly had to be closed in terms of a given amount of capital – as the fact that he was forced to retreat to the concept of a value measurement of capital. The meaning of a constraint on production and distribution specified in these terms was unclear and deprived the theory of its definiteness. Indeed, it questioned the usefulness of the entire theory.[23]

Wicksell did not draw this radical conclusion, but contented himself with the supposition that giving the capital endowment in value terms provided a sufficiently good approximation of the amount of what he called "real capital" (p. 165). Apparently, he was inclined to interpret the difficulty under consideration broadly in the light of his earlier observation that "in such questions we can never achieve more than approximately valid conclusions" (p. 184). The weakness of this supposition

---

22 It should come as no surprise that the same theoretical necessity is felt in the wine-storage example. There Wicksell assumed that "the capital of the community is just sufficient for a storage period of t years – t being assumed to be known." He then calculated the demand for value capital and concluded "if the social capital is exactly equal to this there will be equilibrium" ([1901] 1934, p. 179).

23 Ian Steedman has pointed out to me that the "Wicksell closure problem" is just a variant of the problem of the wages fund. Consider a two-period Wicksell model, with wages paid *ex post*. If $Y = Y(L_0, L_1)$, then $\partial Y/\partial L_0 = w$ and $\partial Y/\partial L_1 = (1 + i)w$. With a linear homogeneous production function, we have

$$Y = wL_0 + (1 + i)wL_1$$

or

$$Y = wL + iK$$

with $L = L_0 + L_1$ and $K = wL_1$. Since in this model there are no advances on the first stage, wL_1 is the "wages fund" of the second stage. What is the *meaning* of taking K as given? What kind of constraint is this that requires wL_1 to be equal to a given amount of corn per period? As is well known, Wicksell was critical of the wages fund doctrine. His reluctance to accept the closure of his theory of distribution in terms of a given value of capital may have had as its deeper reason the fact that he saw that the critique leveled at the wages fund theory applied also to his closure.

is close at hand. As Pierangelo Garegnani (1990, p. 38) stressed, "What such a justification of a value measurement ignores is the fact that, in order to speak of one of the magnitudes as a workable approximation to another, we should first be able to define the second magnitude exactly: and the "real capital" magnitude is precisely what, in most relevant cases, cannot be defined" (see also, Sandelin, 1990). Today we know that Wicksell's hope was futile: modern capital theory has shown that the value magnitude of capital can vary in any direction and to almost any degree as distribution changes, even though "real capital," that is, the vector of capital goods, is unaltered (see, e.g. Mas-Colell, 1986; Garegnani, 1990).

5. Conclusion

In this chapter I have argued that there is no equation "missing" in Knut Wicksell's theory of capital and interest. The uneasiness with which Wicksell in the *Lectures* introduced the given amount of capital as a value sum, which, in equilibrium, is taken to be equal to the value of capital in demand by cost-minimizing producers, rather reflects his awareness of the difficulties of the theory of distribution he had elaborated, starting from Böhm-Bawerk's conceptualization. The promise that the "average period of production" would allow one to consistently aggregate heterogeneous capital goods had turned out to be illusory, because that concept could not be defined independently of the rate of interest, that is, the unknown of the problem under consideration. There was only the option of defining the capital endowment of the economy in value terms, the meaning of which, however, was dubious. Wicksell's belief, and it was just a belief, that value capital could be considered as approximating "real capital" is untenable in general.

In the contributions to the debate about Wicksell's missing equation the problem of defining the capital endowment of the economy independently of the rate of interest is avoided. The emphasis is on stationary (or steady) states *strictu sensu*, in which both the size and the composition of the social capital are determined endogenously. This involves a significant departure from Wicksell's analysis. As we have seen, Wicksell showed little interest for the singularly special case of the stationary (or steady) state. He was rather concerned with an economic system in motion in which capital accumulates and income per capita grows. He sought to approach the two main problems of capital theory, that is, the problem of the origin and level of interest and that of the origin and formation of capital, in separate logical stages. In a first stage, which according to Wicksell allowed postulating functional relations of known properties, the amount of capital was treated as an independent variable; its relative scarcity was taken to hold the key to the determination of the rate of interest. This was effected in terms of a system of simultaneous equations. In a second stage he then discussed the formation of new capital. In his view this problem had not yet been studied carefully enough to be put into mathematics. "Unfortunately, such a theory [of savings and investment] has not been worked out, and the phenomena which it should explain depend on a number of motives – partly selfish, partly altruistic, but in any case very complex" (Wicksell [1901] 1934, pp. 207–8).

Hence, while the alternative closures suggested provide useful insights into some of Wicksell's considerations, they are not able to remedy the deficiency of his supply-and-demand theory of distribution.

Acknowledgments

This chapter was first drafted while I was a visiting professor at the University of Stuttgart-Hohenheim in July 1998. I am grateful to Harald Hagemann and his colleagues for their hospitality and the discussions we had, and to Pierangelo Garegnani, Christian Gehrke, and Ian Steedman for their comments on an earlier draft of this chapter. I would also like to thank Bo Sandelin for his valuable suggestions on another chapter of mine which deals with some of the issues raised in this one; see Kurz 1998. The useful remarks of two anonymous referees are gratefully acknowledged. Unless otherwise stated, all emphases in quotations are in the original.

References

Arvidsson, G. 1956. On the Reasons for a Rate of Interest. *International Economic Papers* 6: 23–33.
Böhm-Bawerk, E. von. [1889] 1959. *Capital and Interest*. 3 vols. Translated by George D. Huncke and Hans F. Sennholz (vols 1–2) and Hans F. Sennholz (vol. 3). South Holland, Ill.: Libertarian Press.
Boianovsky, M. 1998. Wicksell, Ramsey, and the Theory of Interest. *European Journal of the History of Economic Thought* 5: 140–68.
Garegnani, P. 1960. *Il capitale nelle teorie della distribuzione*. Milan: Giuffrè.
Garegnani, P. 1990. Quantity of Capital. In *Capital Theory*, edited by J. Eatwell, M. Milgate, and P. Newman, 1–78. London and Basingstoke: Macmillan.
Hansson, B. 1993. The Existence of a Positive Rate of Interest in a Stationary State: A Wicksellian Enigma. In *Swedish Economic Thought: Explorations and Advances*, edited by Lars Jonung, 33–45. London: Routledge.
Hayek, F. A. 1941. *The Pure Theory of Capital*. Chicago: Routledge & Kegan Paul.
Hirshleifer, J. 1967. A Note on the Böhm-Bawerk/Wicksell Theory of Interest. *Review of Economic Studies* 34: 191–9.
Kompas, T. 1992. *Studies in the History of Long-Run Equilibrium Theory*. Manchester and New York: Manchester University Press.
Kurz, H. D. 1998. Über das "Perpetuum mobile des Volkswirtschaftsmechanismus" und eine "theoretische Verkehrtheit": Knut Wicksell und die Einheit von Produktions- und Distributionstheorie. In *Knut Wicksell als Ökonom*, edited by Erich Streissler. Berlin: Duncker & Humblot.
Kurz, H. D. and N. Salvadori. 1995. *Theory of Production: A Long-Period Analysis*. Cambridge: Cambridge University Press.
Mas-Colell, A. 1986. Capital Theory Paradoxes: Anything Goes. In *Joan Robinson and Modern Economic Theory*, edited by G. R. Feiwel, 505–20. London: Macmillan.
Negishi, T. 1982a. Wicksell's Missing Equation and Böhm-Bawerk's Three Causes of Interest in a Stationary State. *Zeitschrift für Nationalökonomie* 42: 161–74.
Negishi, T. 1982b. Wicksell's Missing Equation: A Comment. *HOPE* 14: 310–11.

Negishi, T. 1985. *Economic Theories in a Non-Walrasian Tradition.* Cambridge: Cambridge University Press.

Robbins, L. 1930. On a Certain Ambiguity in the Conception of Stationary Equilibrium. *Economic Journal* 40: 194–214.

Samuelson, L. 1982. On Wicksell's Missing Equation. *HOPE* 14: 301–7.

Samuelson, P. A. 1987. Wicksell and Neoclassical Economics. In vol. 4 of *The New Palgrave: A Dictionary of Economics*, edited by J. Eatwell, M. Milgate, and P. Newman, 908–10. London: Macmillan.

Sandelin, B. 1980. Wicksell's Missing Equation, the Production Function, and the Wicksell Effect. *HOPE* 12: 29–40.

Sandelin, B. 1982. On Wicksell's Missing Equation: A Comment. *HOPE* 14:308–9.

Sandelin, B. 1990. The Danger of Approximation: Wicksell's Mistake on the Average Period of Investment. *HOPE* 22: 551–5.

Sraffa, P. 1960. *Production of Commodities by Means of Commodities.* Cambridge: Cambridge University Press.

Walras, L. [1874] 1954. *Elements of Pure Economics.* Translated by W. Jaffé. London: Allen & Unwin.

Wicksell, K. 1892. Kapitalzins und Arbeitslohn. *Jahrbücher für Nationalökonomie und Statistik* 59: 552–74.

Wicksell, K. [1893] 1954. *Value, Capital, and Rent.* Translated by S. H. Frowein. London: Allen & Unwin.

Wicksell, K. 1896. *Finanztheoretische Untersuchungen nebst Darstellung und Kritik des Steuerwesens Schwedens.* Jena: Gustav Fischer.

Wicksell, K. [1901] 1934. *Lectures on Political Economy.* Vol. 1. Translated by E. Classen. London: George Routledge & Sons.

Wicksell, K. [1919] 1934. Review of *Theoretische Sozialökonomie*, by G. Cassel. Appears as "Professor Cassel's System of Economics," translated by E. Classen, Appendix 1 of Wicksell [1901] 1934, 219–57.

Wicksell, K. [1923] 1934. Realkapital und Kapitalzins. Review of *Realkapital und Kapitalzins*, by Gustaf Åkerman. English translation by E. Classen as Appendix 2 of Wicksell [1901] 1934, 258–99.

Wicksell, K. 1928. Zur Zinstheorie (Böhm-Bawerks Dritter Grund). In *Die Wirtschaftstheorie der Gegenwart, Dritter Band: Einkommensbildung*, edited by H. Mayer *et al.*, 199–209. Vienna: Julius Springer. English translation by Timothy Chamberlain in vol. 1 of *Selected Essays in Economics*, edited by Bo Sandelin. London: Routledge, 1997.

Name index

Subject index

Printed in the United States
by Baker & Taylor Publisher Services